Journey Continued

'The second part of my life I hope to write before I die.' With these words Alan Paton ended the first volume of his autobiography, *Towards the Mountain*. He had complelted the second part and corrected the proofs, and this book was at the printer ready for machining and binding, when on 12 April Alan Paton died peacefully at his home after a brief illness.

Author's works cited

Cry, the Beloved Country: A Story of Comfort in Desolation (Scribner, New York, 1948: Jonathan Cape, London)

Lost in the stars: The Dramatization by Maxwell Anderson of Cry, the Beloved Country (Sloane Associates, New York, 1950); Jonathan Cape and Bodley Head, London, 1951)

Too Late the Phalarope (Scribner, New York, 1953: Jonathan Cape, London; Frederick L. Cannon, Cape Town)

'Salute to My Greatgrandchildren' (St. Benedict's House, Johannesburg, 1954);

The People Wept (the author, Kloof, Natal, 1959)

'Meditation for a Young Boy Confirmed' (S.P.C.K., London, 1959)

The Charlestown Story (Liberal Party, Johannesburg, 1959)

Tales from a Troubled Land (Scribner, New York, 1961: published as *Debbie Go Home*, Jonathan Cape, London)

Hofmeyr (Oxford University Press, Cape Town, 1964: Oxford University Press, London, 1965; abridged by D. C. Lunt and published as *South African Tragedy: The Life and Times of Jan Hofmeyr*, Scribner, New York, 1965)

For You Departed (Scribner, New York, 1969: published as *Kontakion for You Departed*, Jonathan Cape, London)

The Long View (ed. Edward Callan, Praeger, New York, 1967: Pall Mall Press, London, 1969)

Instrument of Thy Peace: Meditations Promoted by the Prayer of St. Francis (Seabury Press, New York, 1968: Collins, London, 1970)

Hofmeyr (paperback of the Scribner abridgement, Oxford University Press, Cape Town, 1971)

Apartheid and the Archbishop: The Life and Times of Geoffrey Clayton, Archbishop of Cape Town (David Philip, Cape Town, 1973: Scribner, New York: Jonathan Cape, London)

Knocking on the Door: Shorter Writings (ed. Colin Gardner, David Philip, Cape Town, 1975: Scribner, New York; Rex Collings, London)

Towards the Mountain: An Autobiography (Scribner, New York, 1980: Oxford University Press, London; David Philip, Cape Town)

Ah, but Your Land Is Beautiful (David Philip, Cape Town, 1981: Scribner, New York; Jonathan Cape, London)

Alan Paton

Journey Continued

An Autobiography

OXFORD UNIVERSITY PRESS
1989

THE INDEX WAS COMPILED BY PETER ANDERSON

Oxford University Press, Walton Street, Oxford OX2 6DP

Oxford New York Toronto
Delhi Bombay Calcutta Madras Karachi
Petaling Jaya Singapore Hong Kong Tokyo
Nairobi Dar es Salaam Cape Town
Melbourne Auckland

and associated companies in
Berlin Ibadan

Oxford is a trade mark of Oxford University Press

First published in the UK 1988 by Oxford University Press
First issued as an Oxford University Press paperback 1989

British Library Cataloguing in Publication Data
Paton, Alan, 1903–88
Journey continued: an autobiography.
1. Fiction in English.   South African writers.   Paton, Alan 1903–.   Biographies.
I. Title
823
ISBN 0–19–282684–0

Printed in Great Britain by
Richard Clay Ltd.
Bungay, Suffolk

To members of the.

Liberal Party of South Africa

and in memory of

those who have died

Chapter 1

This is the second volume of my autobiography. The first part was called *Towards the Mountain* and the mountain was the holy mountain of Isaiah, where they do not hurt or destroy and towards which some of us spend our lives travelling. For some of us, it signifies a dream that will never be realised but the dreaming of which will determine our lives. Some believe that the dream will be realised at the time of what is called the Second Coming, though Isaiah seems to have thought that the heavenly Utopia would happen at the First Coming, when the wolf would dwell with the lamb, and the leopard would lie down with the kid, and the calf and the young lion would come together, and a little child would lead them. The phrase the Second Coming was given a new and despairing meaning by Yeats in his poem of the same name, when he asked

> *And what rough beast, its hour come round at last,*
> *Slouches towards Bethlehem to be born?*

Yet soon after he had written this poem he wrote another called 'A Prayer for My Daughter', a poem of humble hope and love. So one despairs today and hopes tomorrow.

There are also some who believe that this whole dream of the holy mountain, and of the leopard lying down with the kid, is not worthy of anything but the contempt of rational men and women. Such people believe indeed that such dreaming is an obstacle to the liberation of mankind from darkness and superstition. I do not belong to those who believe thus. I belong rather to those who move at times unwillingly, and at times unbelievingly, to the conclusion that we are the apex of the Creation. Einstein said, 'The most incomprehensible thing about the universe is that it is comprehensible at all.' Why is it comprehensible to us? Was it meant to be comprehensible to us? Is it the work of an Infinite Intelligence that has made it possible for us to comprehend it piece by piece as we and our knowledge evolve?

But this book is not concerned with the universe, about which I am not competent to write. It is concerned with that small part of the universe that we call the Earth, and it is even more immediately concerned with that small part of the Earth where I was born and have lived my life.

Like any other country it has ineffable dreams and slouching beasts on their way to Bethlehem. Good and evil struggle here day and night. Despair bows us down today and hope lifts us up tomorrow. We laugh and we cry. Yet we are not in all respects like any other country. In one way we differ from them all. This book will be largely about that.

My first book ended with the words, 'The second part of my life I hope to write before I die.' So I start today, hoping my hope will be fulfilled.

Is it a vanity to write the story of one's life? Partly, no doubt. But partly not. For it is also the story of millions of people, and they are my countrymen and women. And by virtue of their racial histories and origins, their customs and languages, they make up a country, or a nation if it may so be called, unlike any other upon the earth.

I was born on 11 January 1903. It was in the year 1948 that two of the decisive events of my life occurred (that is, if I exclude events of a more personal nature). At the end of January 1948, while I was still principal of Diepkloof Reformatory, *Cry, the Beloved Country* was published by Charles Scribner's Sons of New York. It became an instant best-seller and is still a best-seller today nearly forty years later. It was published in many other languages and is still republished in several of them. I should add that it never made the big league of Michener and *Gone with the Wind*.

On 2 March 1948 Sir Alexander Korda of London Films asked to make a film of it, and a few days later the distinguished American dramatist Maxwell Anderson asked to make a musical play of it. It won several literary prizes, and the business of being a well-known writer together with the business of running a reformatory, was becoming unmanageable. I decided, with my wife Dorrie's support, that I would resign from Diepkloof Reformatory and take a chance as a full-time writer. Charles Scribner (the third Charles of the great publishing line) urged me to go slowly. He wrote: 'The sales on your book are still relatively small to the furore that it has produced. Friends of mine who rarely read a book are enthralled by it. The Church (including R.C.s) are preaching about it, and capitalists and leftists embrace it equally.'

I did not take Charles Scribner's advice. I resigned my principalship, and I left the safe world of the civil service. I left its security and its responsibility and its anonymity, and its correct neutrality over what were often deeply moral issues, and above all, perhaps, its guarantee that a civil servant could not be dismissed except for 'grave moral turpitude', which meant money or sex.

I can be excused for feeling a bit muddled. Here suddenly I was, to use a word that always embarrasses me, 'famous'. Suddenly Dorrie and I had more money than we had ever had before. This first royalty cheque from Scribner was the biggest that I had ever received. People paid court to us, some because *Cry, the Beloved Country* had overwhelmed them, some just because I had become famous. Did we behave well? Let me say at once that Dorrie behaved *very* well, in a manner that was in those days called demure. As for myself, I appeared outwardly modest, and while this modesty concealed a great deal of pride, I don't think it concealed much arrogance.

In any event one cannot really forget the journey to the mountain, just because one has become famous and moderately rich. Of that time I wrote a few words in *Towards the Mountain* which I presume to repeat:

I entertained one foolish notion, and that is that I would never wear a formal suit of clothes again, but would lead the independent and unconventional life of a writer. It came to nothing. I did not have it in me to become a Bohemian.

Let us accept the supposition that I behaved reasonably well during this triumphal period. Did everyone accept the supposition? Certainly not. I did not much mind the allegations that the whole affair had gone to my head, provided they did not come from my friends. But one or two of these allegations *did* come from my friends. This was painful.

But it is quite understandable. You go ahead in your profession, and so do many of your old school and college friends, as teachers, lawyers, doctors, physicists, mathematicians. Some of you do well. Then suddenly one of you shoots into world view not in the accustomed pursuit, but in an entirely new field, in my case that of fiction, and is hailed a worthy successor to that legendary figure, Olive Schreiner, who achieved world fame in 1883 with her novel *The Story of an African Farm*.

For at least two of my old friends, my shooting into the world sky was painful. They continued to be on speaking terms with me, but the warmth was gone. One died many years ago and we can no longer be reconciled. The other died in 1985 and our friendship had been restored.

Some of my readers will remember the name of Neville Nuttall, with whom in my student days I entered the world of English literature. His admiration for *Cry, the Beloved Country* was unbounded. But more remarkable was his total lack of envy. After all, it was he who had been the student of English and French and Latin, whereas I had been the student of physics and mathematics. And still more remarkable, one of his dearest desires was to gain recognition as a writer. His first book, *The Trout Streams of Natal* was a well-written unpretentious book, revealing his deep love of the countryside and the sport of trout fishing. Having heard, probably more than once, that *Cry, the Beloved Country* had been started in Trondheim and finished in San Francisco, he inscribed his book 'Started in Newcastle and finished in Dundee', these being two northern Natal towns about twenty-five miles apart. His generosity towards me and my writing continued until his death in 1983.

I have said that the publication of *Cry, the Beloved Country* in 1948 was one of the two decisive events of my life. The second event came soon after on 26 May when the Afrikaner Nationalists came to power, with their policies of rigid racial separation, in fact the policies of apartheid. This was also a decisive event in the lives of millions of my fellow South Africans. It was also – though this was not seen at first – to become a decisive event in the lives of millions of other people in other countries of the world, who came to feel an intense hatred of the policies of apartheid, and an intense hatred of those who enforced them. This hatred – or at least dislike and contempt – came later to be extended to all white South Africans, and indeed to any South Africans at all, of whatever colour or race, who appeared to concur in and benefit from apartheid. Even those white South Africans who have always opposed apartheid are not immune to this dislike and contempt.

One cannot understand the immense significance of the Afrikaner Nationalist victory in 1948 unless one knows something about the history of the country in which it happened. This history I gave in the eighth chapter of *Towards the Mountain*, and I do not think that I should do it again. But I shall try in as few words as possible to explain why the Afrikaner Nationalist victory was so decisive an event in many lives. And this I must do, because the consequences of that victory constitute the main theme of this book. This account will be brief and oversimplified.

Before 1652 European contacts with southern Africa were limited to those made by shipwrecked sailors. But in that year the Dutch East

India Company established a refreshment station at the Cape for their ships on the way to and from Batavia. The early Dutch were in the course of time joined by Germans and by French Huguenot refugees, who with other European immigrants formed the people who were later to be called the Afrikaners. The other inhabitants of this relatively large country known today as South Africa (approximately the size of Texas, California and Utah combined, or of France, Germany and Great Britain combined, one-sixth the size of Australia) were the diminutive San (once called the Bushmen), the Khoikhoi (once called the Hottentots), and African immigrants from the north (Xhosa, Zulu, Sotho, Twsana, and others).

In the course of time the Europeans moved north and north-east from the Cape. They had many clashes with the Xhosa, who were nearest to them, but the San retreated into the interior, and the Khoikhoi either retreated or became subservient. During this period the Afrikaner people were being born, but so were another people, the Cape Coloured people, of Khoikhoi, Malay, African and European blood, the Malays having been brought as slaves from the East.

In the more remote parts of the Cape of Good Hope, the Afrikaner, called the Boer (that is, the farmer), ruled because he had the gun. His control as master and slave-owner was autocratic and no doubt varied from cruel to humane. But his isolation came to an end in 1806 when the British finally annexed the Cape of Good Hope, which now became the Cape Colony.

The Boers had disliked the rule of the Dutch East India Company, but they disliked British rule even more. The British by the Fiftieth Ordinance of 1828 gave rights to Khoikhoi labour, they anglicised the courts of justice, they broke all tradition by training and arming Khoikhoi soldiers, who could be used against white offenders. The wild freedom of the Boer was coming to an end. The final blow was the emancipation of the slaves, and the manner in which it was done.

Many of the Boers decided that they could no longer endure British rule, and so began, from 1835 onwards, the northward migration known as the Great Trek. There were many causes of the Trek, but the prime cause was the desire of the Boers to get away from these alien ideas of racial equality which to them were abhorrent. In the course of their trek to the north, the Boers conquered one black chiefdom after another, they set aside inadequate land for those they conquered, and they finally established their two republics, of the Transvaal and the Orange Free State. In the Transvaal it was categorically laid down in the constitution that there was to be 'no equality in Church or State'. It was hardly necessary to say what kind of equality was meant.

It was over sixty years later, in 1899, that the British, for the basest of motives, provoked the republics into declaring war. This was the Anglo–Boer war, which the British won in 1902. The Transvaal and the Orange Free State became British colonies. The legacy of hatred would have been much more bitter had it not been for three remarkable men, the Boer leaders General Louis Botha and General Jan Smuts and the new Liberal Prime Minister of Great Britain, Sir Henry Campbell-Bannerman. They produced a miracle. In 1910 the two old British colonies of Natal and the Cape of Good Hope and the two new British colonies of the Transvaal and the Orange River came together to form the Union of South Africa.

The British parliament made two tremendous concessions to the principle of 'no equality in Church or State'. It allowed the entrenchment of a colour bar in the constitution of the Union, and it provided the means whereby the Union parliament would be later enabled, first to amend and finally to abolish, the Cape franchise which allowed suitably qualified coloured and African males to exercise a parliamentary vote.

Yet these concessions did nothing to modify the resentment of the extreme Afrikaner Nationalists, who wanted to have nothing to do with the British Empire of which they were now a part, and who wanted nothing less than either the restoration of the two lost republics, or even more ambitiously the creation of a Republic of South Africa. Most ambitiously of all, they wanted a republic completely separated from the British Empire.

In 1910 General Botha became the first Prime Minister of the Union of South Africa, but his path was not to be easy. His extreme conciliatoriness towards the conqueror was distasteful to his powerful colleague General J.B.M. Hertzog, who insisted on the priority of South Africa's interests at all times. In January 1914 Hertzog became the leader of a new National Party, the party of the Afrikaner Nationalists, and his party was greatly strengthened when General Botha declared war on Germany in August, and ranged the Union on Britain's side. To the new Afrikaner Nationalists it was monstrous that they should, twelve years after their conquest, take up arms for the conqueror.

Although Hertzog could in white politics be called a moderate, many of his followers were not, and their aim was unequivocal, namely to take over the government of South Africa. This in fact was realisable because of what might be called an historical or statistical accident – Afrikaners constituted sixty per cent and English-speaking whites forty per cent of the white electorate. All that had to be done was to wean Afrikaners away from the 'conciliation' policies of Botha and Smuts. This Dr. D.F. Malan finally succeeded in doing, and on 26 May 1948 the National Party defeated Smuts's United Party and took over the government. The 'true Afrikaner' had at last come into his own.

The shock to the United Party, and to English-speaking people in general, and indeed to many people of other races, was made yet more painful by the exultation of the Nationalists, the roaring crowds on Pretoria's Church Square, the jubilations in Potchefstroom, Witbank, Standerton, Bloemfontein, Caledon, Stellenbosch, the blowing of motor horns, the singing of the songs and anthems, all the prayers and boasts and promises and new dedications of those for whom the dawn was breaking after a night of long despair.

The morning after the great victory had been won, Malan (now aged seventy-four) arrived in Pretoria, and was given a tumultuous reception. Men and women wept unashamedly in the streets. Before Malan entered the Prime Minister's office he prayed silently that he might prove worthy of this great office, and he no doubt gave thanks for the triumph of Afrikanerdom.

For Afrikanerdom was free again. And what was it going to do with its freedom? First of course, it would rejoice in it, as it was doing now. But what would it do next? It would do nothing less than restore again, in a modern form more suited to the times, the old and sacred doctrine of 'no equality in Church or State'. It would separate race from race, in every conceivable place and at every conceivable time, in hospitals, schools, universities, trains, buses, cinemas, theatres, and above all, in residential areas. Mixed racial marriages would be forbidden, and mixed racial sexual relationships also. However, for residential, economic, and political purposes, all white people would be considered as belonging to one race. But not in the schools, for Afrikaans-speaking children and English-speaking children would have their separate institutions.

Victorious Afrikanerdom would do at least one thing more. It would make life hard for those who opposed too vigorously the doctrine and practices of racial separation. It would give to its Minister of Justice the power to silence, detain, banish, any vehement opponent of these doctrines, and it would put these Ministerial actions beyond the power of any court of law or restrain or question. By law it would put the Minister of Justice above the law.

However, one new element would enter into these new politics and this new philosophy, an element hardly noticeable in the days of the old republics. These resurrected doctrines would be given a new moral justification, not merely that of self-preservation, but that of peace and security for all the peoples in South Africa. Each race would not be given an assurance of the maintenance of its racial identity, of its culture, of its language, of its God-given right to develop along its own lines. 'Apartheid' was the keyword of the new politics, but 'identity' was the keyword of the new philosophy. Learned men – who should have known better – talked about 'identity' endlessly. If the Afrikaner had found his identity, then surely he would help everyone else to find it too. And God help those who didn't want to be helped to find it.

In every solemn and portentous address by the architects and philosophers of the new Utopia, the keyword 'identity' would be sounded endlessly, until one wanted to stand up and cry out, 'I don't want an identity, and if I should want an identity, I don't want to take it from you.' But of course one would have to remember the new powers which would soon be given to the Minister of Justice.

Such were the two decisive events of my life. The first, the modest fame that came from the book, opened many new doors. The second, the coming to power of apartheid, was to close many others.

The first was to open the doors to the exciting life of a writer and a Bohemian. The second pointed towards the inexorable mountain.

But the conflict was not to come yet. First one must enter the world of fame and pleasure. With modesty of course.

Chapter 2

It was our good fortune that we were able to leave Diepkloof Reformatory on 30 June 1948. Soon all black reformatories would be placed under the new and inflexible Minister of Native Affairs, Dr. Hendrik Frensch Verwoerd, and he would have broken me and my heart. He had nothing but contempt for Diepkloof, nothing but contempt for the grand theories of freedom and responsibility, and nothing but contempt – or something very near it – for black people. One by one the directives would have come from Pretoria. The whole system of freedom within the reformatory would have come under the scrutiny of a new breed of inspectors, hard and authoritarian. The system of home leave would almost certainly have been abolished. Worst of all, it is possible that the system of apprenticeship to white farmers would have been restored, and that our slowly growing subdepartment of aftercare and job placement would have been abolished too.

Even if I had not written a best-seller, I would still have had one more route of escape. I could have gone back to the Natal Education Department, back to the job of schoolmastering. What is more, I would have been welcomed back. The Director of Education in Natal at that time was Ronald Banks. Soon after I resigned from Diepkloof, he urged me to return to the department. The reason for this was not my reputation as a teacher. It was because I was an English-speaking South African, and the Natal provincial executive did not want to appoint an Afrikaans-speaking director.

I think I made up my mind almost immediately. Was I going to sacrifice my future Bohemian career for the sake of sitting in a big office in Pietermaritzburg from the windows of which I could look down on the statue of Queen Victoria? Was I going to sacrifice the excitement of London and New York for the sober delights of Pietermaritzburg? I told Ronald Banks gently that I had embarked on a new life, and could not possibly return to schoolmastering. He accepted my decision regretfully.

I thus made way for an Afrikaner. His name was Lucien Biebuyck, and I wrote of him in my first volume. He had taught with me at Maritzburg College twenty years earlier, and he called my class the Tickey Bazaar, which was a kind of supermarket of those early days, full of noise and conversation. He was about two months junior to myself, so I would have been appointed on the grounds of seniority. However, I had declined, and he was to become Director of Education – one of the best that Natal had ever known.

So I turned away from my profession, yet even now, two or three times a year, I dream that I am back in the classroom or at Diepkloof Reformatory. If one is made for that sort of thing, the classroom is one of the happiest places where one can ever be.

Our entry into the Bohemian life was very decorous. We rented a cottage at Anerley, a little seaside village on the south coast of Natal, about seventy miles south of Durban. Our life can be described by one word and one only – it was idyllic. After an early-morning cup of tea we would walk to the Southport beach, where we could swim in the Indian Ocean or in the Southport pool. Back to Anerley through a field of flowers, to the local shop to buy the newspaper, and home to the cottage for breakfast. After breakfast we would go to the post office to collect the mail, the size of which brought me local fame. Then home to deal with the requests, the beggings, the invitations, the praises, the condemnations. Among the condemnations is a letter from an angry white farmer in Zululand who had just read *Cry, the Beloved Country* and who described it as a pack of lies, an act of treachery towards my country, and a lot of sentimental twaddle. There is also a letter from Earl Wavell, expressing quite different opinions.

After lunch we would have a siesta, enjoy afternoon tea at four o'clock, and then take the dogs for a walk through Anerley–Southport. After sundown, drinks and dinner with some wine, we would read, and go early to bed.

The climate was also idyllic, the summer several degrees cooler than Durban, the winter mild and frost-free. The vegetation was subtropical, green and luxuriant, with handsome trees, *Mimusops caffra*, the red milkwood, *Erythrina caffra* with its orange-scarlet flowers, and *Erythrina lysistemon* with its still more striking scarlet flowers, and many others. Growing under and amongst those trees were the wild bananas, *Strelitzia nicolai*, with most spectacular flowers, and occasional bunches of stunted fruit that came to nothing. The cultivated bananas of Natal are not indigenous but were imported from Asia. Great tracts of the Natal coast are given over to the cultivation of the giant perennial grass known as sugar cane, *Saccharum offici*. In order to achieve this, hundreds of thousands of acres of coastal forest were destroyed, with no apparent harm to the soil. The verdant coastal hills of Natal, planted to sugar cane, are a sight of considerable beauty.

Did this earthly paradise provide a climate suitable for the writing of literature? I did not ask myself this question. But my friend and mentor, the Right Honourable J.H. Hofmeyr asked it, or one like it. He noted in his diary his surprise that I had not yet decided what to do with my future. I did not know that he had written this until ten or more years later, when I was writing his life. He did not address the question to me, but to his diary. If he had addressed his question to me, what would I have answered to him? That I was trying the Bohemian life? I could not have done it. Duty was the keyword of his life, not pleasure.

I could have told him that in the following year Maxwell Anderson would be presenting a play on Broadway, and Korda of London Films would be preparing a film, and that I could not really do any worthwhile writing until these two things were over and done with. But he would not have understood it. Life wasn't like that. From the days of his early childhood he had lived by duty. At the age of six, on a Sunday morning when his mother was ill and could not go to church, he had set up a pulpit in her room and had preached to her from the text, 'Little children, keep yourselves from idols.' How could one mention the Bohemian life to a man who had once been a child like that?

For all my years until then I had lived a life, not so brilliant or eminent as his, but just as conscientious and industrious. He would have approved fully of that. But this retreat to Anerley with no announcement of work in view or work in progress, was something that did not accord with his principles. That was not his idea of duty. All his life he had done his duty, to his mother, his school, his university, and above all, to his God and his country. He fulfilled every duty except his duty to himself.

In a way the fall of General Smuts on 26 May 1948 and the coming to power of the new National Party under Dr. D.F. Malan, had brought him great relief. For the years of the Second World War, he as acting Prime Minister had practically administered the country owing to the frequent absences of General Smuts abroad.

He wrote in his diary on 11 July 1948:

I am enjoying my *seisachtheia** and generally feeling at peace with the world. The position is different from what it was when I was out of the government in 1938. Then I had a sense of grievance – I felt that I had personally been badly treated and that I could not rest until my position had been restored. . . . What I am concerned about now is not the personal aspect, but the danger to the country.

Four days later he wrote that he seemed 'at last to have reached the stage of being able to enjoy an unhurried unworried life – at least till Parliament starts'.

On 29 September he did something unprecedented. He left parliament in Cape Town to return to his home in Pretoria, three days before the end of the session. At long last he was beginning to do his duty to himself. But it was too late. On the night of Friday–Saturday 26–27 November he suffered a heart attack. But he had promised to open the new cricket ground of the Young Men's Christian Association at Bedfordview, Johannesburg, on the Saturday. Much against his mother's wish he decided to keep this engagement. Was it not a kind of duty? The gathered dignitaries were shocked by his appearance, but what could one say to such a man? It is the custom to open a new cricket ground by receiving the first ball, and he decided to do this. He began to walk to the cricket pitch, and the subdued players gathered round to shake his hand. Hofmeyr now realised that he could not continue, and agreed to be taken home. Six days later he died, after whispering to his brother, 'Tell my friends to carry on.'

The next morning, at our breakfast table in our cottage at Anerley, I read that he was dead. For days I could think of nothing else. I wrote the short poem, 'On the Death of J.H. Hofmeyr', with its bitter stanza:

> *Clap iron bell clap iron clapper*
> *Clap your iron hands together*
> *Clap the loud applause*
> *That life denied him*
> *Clap the dead man*
> *And if you can*
> *The dead man's cause*
> *Clap in beside him*

He has been one of the great influences in my life. He was not a great man in the category of Smuts, Churchill, Nehru, Gandhi. Roosevelt. Three things made it impossible. The first was the dominating possessiveness of his mother. The second was his extraordinary school career; he began when he was eight, and finished when he was twelve, and he went to university as a boy amongst men. The third

* Greek for 'a shaking off of burdens'.

insuperable obstacle was that he lived his whole life in the shadow of Smuts.

He died at the age of fifty-four, a white South African who had hardly begun the process of emancipation from the corruption of having lived his life in a white supremacy society. In any event his emancipation was idealist and theoretical rather than practical and personal. By many he was regarded as the champion of black people, but he hardly knew any of them.

I had a great love for him, difficult to express to such a shut-in man. When he died he was fifty-four and I was forty-five. When I finished the writing of his life I was sixty, and I want to record that it is a great advantage to a biographer to be writing the life of a man who is, in this strange sense, younger than himself. When I was younger, I would have accepted his moral example without question. When I was older I would not. There can be no doubt that he shortened his own life, not because of duty, but because of something which he would have called 'duty' but which was much more complicated and complex than that. I am often asked, 'Which do you regard as your best book?' To that I answer, 'I would not place *Hofmeyr* second to any of the others.'

I should like to write one more thing about my friend and mentor. Although I think that his concept of duty was excessive, I do not want to suggest that he had no pleasures. These were simple and unsophisticated. He had a passion for the game of cricket, though he was an indifferent performer. He liked the rough-and-tumble of a boys' camp. He liked food. He was not a dainty eater. He was almost a teetotaller, though in his later years he would take a glass of sherry.

He liked books and reading. He had no understanding of art or music. He liked poetry of the Newbolt kind, but I never heard him say a good word for the *Rubaiyat*. He had one supreme grace. He was saved from being a puritan or a prig by his sense of humour, and by his wit too. As a teller of jokes, especially those which illumined the subject on which he was talking, he had no superior. It was my privilege to write his life.

Why did I not write a sequel to *Cry, the Beloved Country* as indeed I was urged to do? Why did I not exploit this rich vein? Why did I not become the superior counterpart to Edgar Rice Burroughs, with his endless series of books about Tarzan? Something told me not to do it. Something told me that *Cry, the Beloved Country* was a book that should not be repeated or imitated. In any case I did not want to write a novel before setting out for London and New York.

But I did not stop writing. It must have been about the beginning of 1949 that I wrote 'To a Small Boy Who Died at Diepkloof Reformatory', which, whether it be good or bad, has an attraction for older boys and girls. It was followed by several poems, four of which I still think of with favour. They were 'Samuel', 'The Discardment', 'The Stock Exchange', and 'I Have Approached a Moment of Sterility'.*

But the idyllic peace of this first year of rest from labour was shattered on 13 January 1949. In Durban at an Indian-owned shop near the crowded Victoria Street bus rank, an African boy was assaulted by the shopkeeper and was taken to hospital, for a reason that was never made clear. Rumours spread like wildfire, one that the African boy was dead, another that an African boy had been knocked down and killed by an Indian-owned bus. Fighting between Africans and Indians broke out at the bus rank, and violence spread to other parts of Durban.

On Friday 14 January, the violence spread farther. The night of Friday was one of murder, looting, and arson. The Indians of Durban were in a state of fear, first because they were hopelessly outnumbered by the Zulus, second because they did not have a martial tradition, and third because they knew that many whites had no sympathy for them in their dangerous situation.

On Saturday 15 January it was reported that fifty people were dead and three hundred injured. Whole families of Indians were murdered in their homes, and many shops and houses set on fire. The violence was made worse by the fact that many Zulu men, some married, some not, lived unnatural lives in single barracks in the industrial areas, and the violence was for them an outlet for pent-up energies and emotions.

Some of the white people of Durban behaved in an unspeakable fashion. The Anglican vicar of St. Paul's in the centre of the city, the Rev. Vernon Inman, reported seeing Indians being pursued and struck down while white onlookers jeered at them. Inman visited the Cato Manor police station, and saw 'a dreadful scene of slaughter and horror'. St. Paul's Hall became a haven, and Inman defied any pursuer to cross the threshold. Another Anglican priest, the Rev. Alphaeus Zulu. told how one of his Zulu parishioners had saved his Indian landlord and family by 'putting them in a truck wearing doeks† like African women, with the man at the back shouting Zoo-lu! Zoo-loo!, which was the watchword'.

There was another side to the coin of which Inman wrote: 'Later that day . . . I was following a car with Indians in it. They were taking pot shots at any black they saw – I saw them doing it. I saw them drop two.'

The violence continued for at least a week longer, and spread to

---

* In *Knocking on the Door: Shorter Writings*.

† The Rev. Alphaeus Zulu was himself a Zulu. For this story and others I am indebted to the Rev. R. G. Clarke's unpublished thesis, *For God or Caesar?* A doek is a cloth worn as a head-covering.

Pietermaritzburg, and along the Natal coast north and south of Durban. Not far from Anerley–Southport, in the seaside town of Port Shepstone, the Indian population was filled with fear and anxiety because of the many hundreds of thousands of Africans who live in the black reserves that lie in the hinterland. Dorrie and I would have been ready to try to emulate the example set by people like Vernon Inman, but our neighbour, a very decent young white policeman, told us there would be no trouble, and luckily he was right. The violence died away, and the final estimate of casualties was one hundred and forty-two dead and one thousand and eighty-seven injured, of whom fifty-eight died of their injuries. Fifty Indians had died, all at the hands of the Africans. Eighty-seven Africans died, most at the hands of the police and military. Outwardly peace was restored, but the violence left the Indian people in a state of insecurity that persists until today, though people do not speak about it openly.

What were the causes of the violence? The official judicial commission appointed by the Prime Minister was one of the most inept bodies in our history. It dismissed the possibility that the speeches of leading white politicians demanding that Indians should be sent back to India, constituted one of the causes. According to the commission, this idea 'emanated from the intelligentsia. Nor was discriminating legislation a factor.' 'Natives in the mass' accepted discrimination as between themselves and whites; what they resented violently was discrimination that favoured Indians. According to the commission, the seduction of African women by Indian men was a powerful motive, as was also the exploitation of African customers by Indian shopkeepers. In conclusion, the commission condemned strongly those whites who encouraged Africans to attack Indians, and called them 'degraded specimens of their race'.

Vernon Inman had an understanding of the situation much deeper than that of the learned commission. The causes were for him not only racial, but social and economic. The violence was a direct consequence of the injustices and inequalities of a most complex racial society, dominated by a powerful white élite. Inman declared: 'We have to rebuild society. It will take a long, long time – if a long time is still allotted to us, which I doubt.'

That had been said many times before Inman said it, and it has been said many times since. And it is still being said today.

Inman likened our society to a volcano, and said that it was absurd to think, as the commission did, that 'vigilant police' could prevent another eruption.

One bizarre and terrible feature of the violence was that the 'degraded specimens' of the white race, while they with shouts and jeers were encouraging the Zulus to attack the Indian population, were themselves physically safe when present at these scenes of violence. Why should that have been so? More than one white observer commented that the violence offered a way of catharsis to the Zulus, who were able to vent their rage against the kind of society in which they lived, by attacking the weakest and most defenceless members of it. I have no doubt that there is truth in this.

So South Africa returned to that strange peace that it enjoys of living on the slopes of a volcano, and not knowing when it will erupt again. Not one of us knows whether we will be able to exercise some kind of divine wisdom that will help to damp down the fires of the sullen earth.

The violence left the whole question of apartheid and separate development unresolved. The Afrikaner Nationalists regarded the violence as an inevitable consequence of a chaotic and unplanned society, and they were therefore determined to press ahead with the making and carrying out of laws which separated the races in every possible place and on every possible occasion.

The violence had another quite different consequence. It brought about closer cooperation between the leaders of the Indian and African Congresses. The immediate cause may have been the assault on a Zulu boy by an Indian shopkeeper, but the 'fundamental and basic causes of the disturbances are traceable to the political, economic, and social structures of this country'.* This statement did not greatly worry the Afrikaner Nationalists. They saw the hand of communism at work!

* Statement issued by Joint Meeting of African and Indian leaders, 6 February 1949.

Chapter 3

Well, that's enough of sorrow. The volcano has gone back to slumber, and the bright lights of London and New York are waiting, the excitement of the world of the theatre and the film studios and the television and the book prizes. Zoltan Korda, younger brother of the urbane, polished, hard-as-steel Sir Alexander, wants me to go to London in August to work with him on the writing of the script for the film. The three Korda brothers, Alexander, Zoltan, and Vincent, are the sons of Hungarian peasants and, through the mystery of genes, with some good luck of course, Alexander has become a genius of films. He lives in the penthouse of Claridge's Hotel in the style of a great aristocrat. Zoltan and Vincent live in considerable style too, but neither has the grand air of their brother, of whom they stand in awe.

Dorrie and I decided that I must go to London on my own, because she felt that she should stay to be near our twelve-year-old son Jonathan. He had been greatly aggrieved when we decided to live in Natal, and to leave him at St. John's College in Johannesburg. He asked to finish his schooling in Port Shepstone, but we would not agree. He was deeply attached to his mother, and his school holidays in Anerley–Southport were the only bright spots in his dark and forsaken life. But one strict rule had to be observed. The words 'holiday' and 'school' were never to be used in his presence. It was a great offence to ask him if he were 'enjoying his holiday'. The greatest offence of all was to ask him if he had enjoyed his holiday. This otherwise gentle boy would fly into what appeared to be an ungovernable rage and would take much pacifying. It was sobering to realise that deep emotional hurts can be healed by money. All these rages and glooms aside, the fact was that he enjoyed both holiday and school.

I must close this domestic account by relating another strange matter. Our elder son David had also been at St. John's College, but before entering his final year he had asked to be allowed to leave school and to become a farmer. I told him, 'I try not to interfere in your life, but you must first take your matriculation. After that we can talk again.' He went on to pass his matriculation in the first-class, and decided to go to Rhodes University College in Grahamstown to study law. The following year he went to the University of Natal, where he studied psychology for five years. He finally graduated Master of Arts and became a university lecturer. He then decided he had made a mistake and should have studied medicine. By this time he was married, and his schoolteacher wife and I agreed to support him for six years, at the end of which he graduated M.B., B.Ch. But he was not finished yet. After three years of hospital work he decided to study radiology, but luckily he was awarded a scholarship, so that his wife and his father no longer needed to support him. At the age of thirty-seven he graduated M.Med. This was the career of the boy who wanted to leave school when he was fifteen. When I am in low spirits I always remember, and boast too sometimes, that I am the father of the most educated son in South Africa. This may not be true, but it must be pretty near it. After all, this would-be dropout spent twenty-seven years of his life at school.

Before I left for London, I decided to attend the July camp at the Students' Christian Association. We were now living at Southport, and our house was about a mile from the camp. I decided to leave Dorrie for ten days and to live under canvas. I suppose I did it out of duty, or in remembrance of J.H. Hofmeyr, whom I first met at a boys' camp at Umgaba in 1926. But in 1949 I had lost the zest for it. I did not go again.

In August I went to London and stayed in style, not at Claridge's but at the Piccadilly, as a guest of London Films. So began a long and close association with Zoltan Korda. Though he did not have the grand air of his brother Alexander, he had a kind of genius of his own. After a preliminary meeting with Alexander, during which the great man gave me extravagant praise for *Cry, the Beloved Country*, and at the same time gave me the powerful impression that it would be dangerous to offend him, Zoltan and I adjourned to the big room where we were to work together for some weeks.

He first told me that I was to get the credit for the script. I received this news with mixed feelings. It was another taste of fame, but I had no desire to become a script-writer, and I had no confidence that I would be any good at it. Zoltan brushed my objections aside. He would construct the script, I would just have to write it. So I yielded, and became a kind of superior amanuensis.

Zoltan had a vivid and fertile imagination. I would not hesitate to say that, while he was making the film, he thought of nothing else, except his wife, whom he had left in Hollywood, and of whom he talked a great deal. He knew every high-class restaurant in London, and he took me out almost every evening, but our conversation was almost always about the film. His favourite place was the Czarda, partly because it was Hungarian, partly because they treated him with inordinate respect. Sometimes he would invite Zuzhi, a beautiful young Hungarian girl who worked for London Films; alas I have not seen her since, but she made herself a name in something or other, something to do with design, I think.

When we met in the morning, I could see that Zoltan had been chewing the cud most of the night.

'Something about nature, Alan, I want something about nature.'

Then he would say apologetically, 'I know the first chapters are full of nature. But I want something – one line maybe – about small nature.'

'Something about a flower?'

His face lights up, as though I have said something extremely creative.

'That is it,' he says, 'a flower.'

I was later to learn that in the studio he could be moody and arrogant, but in our script room he was very humble.

'You are the writer,' he says. 'That is why we pay you. I am not a writer.'

On another morning he says to me, 'Death, there is much death in your book, but in a film it is good. One can always play with death.'

Then that evening at Prunier's or Quaglino's he would tell me about Hungary and his boyhood, a hard life without luxuries. One of his favourite stories of Hungary was of the time when the authorities in some city put a chemical in the swimming-baths so they could tell at once when any person was urinating in the water. Then an official would call out from some kind of watchtower, 'Mr. Smith, you are doing something in the water, report at once to the office of the Superintendent.' During the telling of these stories of his boyhood he would be caught up in an ecstasy of delight and nostalgia, but the last thing he would ever have wanted to do was to return to the country of his birth. He was not a man for hating, but his hatred of Stalin and the U.S.S.R. and the creed of communism was intense, and when he spoke about these things, his hatred would contort his face. Apart from films and his private world, his supreme passion was for human freedom. If this passion were thwarted, he would be seized by rage, and this humble and quiet man would be capable of creating most unedifying scenes. I shall later tell a story of this. We had one important thing in common, and that was a love of freedom and the rule of law, and a complementary hatred of authoritarianism.

In October I went to New York, where the final rehearsals of the musical by Maxwell Anderson and Kurt Weill were taking place. The musical was called 'Lost in the Stars', and one of the reasons for calling it by this title was that Anderson and his associates were not willing to call it *Cry, the Beloved Country*, unless London Films agreed to pay some kind of fee. This would have been on the grounds that their film would receive free publicity if the musical were a Broadway success. However, Alexander Korda refused to do anything of the kind, and so 'Lost in the Stars' it remained.

Anderson had another reason for giving the musical this name. Some years before, he and Weill had written a song called 'Lost in the Stars', but for some reason it had not been used. Now had come the chance to use it. It was to be given a prominent place in the musical, and what is more it was to give the musical its own name.

On my first night in New York, after I had met the Anderson family, Kurt Weill and his wife Lottie Lenya, the director Rouben Mamoulian, Todd Duncan and other members of the cast, I attended one of the closing rehearsals of 'Lost in the Stars'. It was an unnerving and at times painful experience. It was my story indeed, but the idiom was strange, except for those parts which reproduced the actual language of the book. I kept on telling myself that the making of a book and the making of a play were two separate creative acts. The drinking-dive in Shanty Town was like nothing to be seen in Johannesburg and the dialogue was like nothing to be heard there.

The song 'Lost in the Stars', sung by Todd Duncan playing the part of the humble and unsophisticated black priest Stephen Kumalo, was highly sophisticated, and it was extremely painful for me to hear my humble hero in a role that he could never have taken. It was made still more painful for me by the fact that the song belonged to the death-of-God genre, or to put it more accurately, to the desertion-of-God genre. God had created the universe, and more especially He had created the earth, but now He had gone away, 'forgetting the promise that we heard Him say'. So 'we are lost out here in the stars'.

I was to learn later that Anderson was in fact expressing his own loss of faith. He had come from an evangelical Baptist background, but had lost his early faith. Although my feelings at that rehearsal were confused in the extreme, a resentment was no doubt building up in me that he should give to his play, 'based on' my book, a title which to me was alien and unfitting. It is quite true that Stephen Kumalo, when he learned that his son had killed a man, suffered a sense of God's desolation, but this was not the theme of my book.

I may say that this terrible evening was made more endurable by the beauty of the singing and by Kurt Weill's music. The chorus 'Cry, the Beloved Country' was powerful and beautiful, and moved me deeply, but these were not the words of a stranger, they were my own.

So the rehearsal came to an end, but my ordeal was about to begin. They crowded round me, wanting to know how I felt. Alas, my eyes were not shining. If they had been, there would not have been much need for words. But because they were not I had to say some words. I said that the choruses moved me deeply, and that that was a triple compliment to the writer and the composer and the singers. I admitted that the whole experience was confusing and strange, but I implied that it would become less confusing and less strange. I thought of all the good things I could say, but there were not enough. If there had been any friendship developing between Anderson and myself, it had been nipped in the bud. He was – to me – a withdrawn and taciturn man, and he was to stay that way. Of the strength and beauty of his script, I had not said one word. I was a failure. Finally the ordeal was over, and I went home to the Hotel Dorset, where the Andersons were also staying. I crept to bed, wishing that I were back in Anerley–Southport.

While the rehearsals were proceeding, I received news from the *Sunday Times* of London that *Cry, the Beloved Country* was to be awarded its annual book prize of £1,000. My book was to share the honours with *The Jungle Is Neutral* by Frederick Spencer Chapman, but although Chapman and I were to be joint-winners, we were to be towered over by a super-winner, the great Winston Churchill, who in October 1948 had published *The Gathering Storm*, the first volume of his series *The Second World War*.

The *Sunday Times* wanted to know if I would receive my prize in person, and though I had planned to stay in the United States for some months, I decided in view of my great wealth to go to London for a few days. What is more, I asked Dorrie to meet me there, and then to fly with me to New York, where we could see 'Lost in the Stars'. After that we would fly to San Francisco to visit with Aubrey and Marigold Burns, who played such an important part in getting *Cry, the Beloved Country* published, and to whom I dedicated the Scribner edition of the novel. The full story of their remarkable help is told in *Towards the Mountain*.

I was to meet Dorrie in London on 5 November, but I still had many things to do in New York. I was given a grand luncheon by the *New*

York Herald Tribune Women's Book Club, the other guests being David Lilienthal, who had been director of the Tennessee Valley Authority, and was now chairman of the United States Atomic Energy Commission, and Alfred Bertram Guthrie, who was author of the best-selling novel *The Big Sky*, and in the following year the winner of the Pulitzer Prize for literature. Each of us had to say a few words, Lilienthal, tall and distinguished-looking, Paton neither tall nor distinguished-looking, and Guthrie, brash and self-confident. It was Guthrie who made the biggest impression. He told some extremely broad jokes, which did not amuse the audience of between one and two thousand women, all readers of books, and I should imagine highly respectable. Guthrie's first joke was coldly received, but he seemed quite insensitive to its reception. To my astonishment he went on to tell a second and a third, and these two were even more coldly received than the first. Our beautiful chairwoman, Irita van Doren of the *Herald Tribune*, did her hostly duty, and smiled wanly at the jokes. When the luncheon was over, several dignified women apologised to Lilienthal and myself for the embarrassment we had been caused, but in fact we were more embarrassed for them than for ourselves.

There were more of these occasions, though none so grand as the *Herald Tribune* luncheon. *Time* and *Life* gave me a luncheon in that stupendous place, the Rockefeller Centre, and at another luncheon I received the annual 'Page One' award from the Press Club. I met another tall and distinguished-looking man, Pandit Jawaharlal Nehru, who had invited me to the Hotel Gotham to tell him about the status and difficulties of the Indian people of South Africa. We discussed what has since become a constant topic, the question of the use of sanctions to bring about a change in the racial policies of the Nationalist government. One of the most crippling of these sanctions would have been the cutting off of oil supplies to South Africa, which had no oil of her own. I remember Mr. Nehru's comment to this day; he said to me, 'Mr. Paton, oil companies are more powerful than governments.'

What is it that makes one use the adjective 'great' to describe certain human beings? As I have written earlier, the five 'great' men of my time were Smuts, Churchill, Nehru, Gandhi, and Roosevelt. Reluctantly I would add Stalin to this list. I would find it impossible to add Hitler. The first quality such human beings must manifest is a superior intelligence. I am not quite sure how superior Gandhi was in this regard, but Nehru in the presence of Gandhi felt that he was in the presence of greatness. Therefore there must be a second quality, which may be called that of 'character', or more fancifully, of 'soul', and one supposes that courage and persistence must be two of its essential characteristics. All that I can say is that in the presence of Nehru I felt that I was also in the presence of greatness. I have not mentioned the names of Einstein and Lenin, though I have no doubt that in the world of the pure intellect Einstein was supreme, and I suppose that Lenin was the supreme world-shaker. I shall leave one thorny question alone – why are there no women in my lists? Is it because my life has been lived in a world of war? Did someone mention Joan of Arc? Or Mother Teresa?

Then of course there was one other very special occasion, to which I looked forward with some apprehension, and that was the opening night of 'Lost in the Stars'.

It was an outstanding success. People wept and shouted and clapped. At the end there were ovations, for the cast, the singers, the dramatist, the composer, the director, and for the author of *Cry, the Beloved Country*. After the theatre we all adjourned to Sardi's, where there were more celebrations and congratulations and laughter and tears. I can't remember that anyone made a speech, but after it was all over we returned to our hotels, to sleep and to dream and to wake the next morning to find out what the critics thought of it all.

When I arrived in the hotel breakfast room, the Anderson family was already there, surrounded by newspapers. Brooks Atkinson wrote, 'Out of a memorable novel has come a memorable musical drama.' Howard Barnes wrote that Anderson had 'captured the full essence of the original'. There could be no doubt that 'Lost in the Stars' had succeeded brilliantly.

I did my best to join in the rejoicing, but my heart wasn't in it. Maxwell Anderson knew it, and so did his wife. I am sure that *Cry, the Beloved Country* had moved him deeply, and that his musical play was 'based on' the book. But his view of life and the world was very different from mine. Barnes was wrong; Anderson did not capture 'the full essence of the original'. It is interesting to know that Anderson and Weill had at one time discussed the possibility of composing a service to use at the funerals of unbelievers. The service was never composed, but Maxwell Anderson, speaking at Weill's funeral in April 1950, recited eight lines that would have formed part of it. These lines were used in the musical 'Lost in the Stars':

> A bird of passage out of night
>   Flies in at a lighted door,
> Flies through and on in its darkened flight
> · And then is seen no more.
> This is the life of men on earth:
>   Out of darkness we come at birth
> Into a lamplit room, and then –
>   Go forward into dark again,
> Go forward into dark again.

I think Anderson described himself correctly as an unbeliever. He was not an atheist, and certainly not a militant one. In fact, if 'Lost in the Stars' is to be taken seriously, he believed that there had been a Creator, and that he had gone away, leaving us lost out here in the stars.

I flew to London on the day before Dorrie was due from Johannesburg, and for some reason was late at the airport to meet her. I was remorseful but she was radiant, and in her demure way dressed as smart as smart could be. We took a taxi back to the flat that Zoltan had got for us in St. James's Street, and made love to each other, wordlessly.

This was her first step into the new and exciting world that I had myself entered not so long before. She took it bravely and apprehensively, but did not speak much – if at all – of her apprehension. In the end we conquered it in the simplest way possible, by her warmth and integrity. She said to me – and indeed she did not often say such things – 'In my family I was the lucky one.'

The grand *Sunday Times* function was held at the Dorchester. The super-winner wasn't present, so Spencer Chapman and I shared the honours. We did not speak at the function, but both of us later talked to big audiences, Chapman about the jungle, and I about the craft of writing. He and I parted on the most friendly of terms, and we were to meet again in South Africa, for in 1956 he was appointed headmaster of the famous school of St. Andrew's in the city of Grahamstown.

On our first evening in New York we went to see 'Lost in the Stars'. Dorrie was not enthusiastic about it, but she might well have been influenced by my own disenchantment. We were not sorry after three days to fly to San Francisco to stay with Aubrey and Marigold Burns.

It would be foolish of me to disparage the world of the theatre, but I was not sorry to leave it. After all I was luckier than the novelist who sold his book to a dramatists' company and complained that all they used of it was the title. My publisher Charles Scribner, very wise in the ways of the world, told me that there was only one thing to do if you sold a book, and that was to go nowhere near the theatre or the studio.

Yet the world of the theatre, to which I had no desire to belong, gave me one experience that I shall always remember. The scene was the dining-room of the Hotel Algonquin, and I can see it as clearly as if it happened yesterday. We had all gone to the Algonquin one night after the theatre for some celebration or other. The large room was full of noise and laughter. Then for some reason it all began to die away. For the same reason one after another of us stood up. This was because a little white-haired man had entered the room, and it appeared that he was on his way to bed. I said to my neighbour, 'Who's that?' He said to me reverentially, 'It's Arthur Rubinstein.'

Chapter 4

After a few days in New York, we flew to San Francisco to stay with the Burnses in their house on Cypress Drive, Fairfax, through the centre of which rose up those four redwood trees through holes cut in the floors and ceilings. The children were nearly three years older than they had been when I first met them. Martha was now fifteen, still demure and beautiful. Hal was now ten, and Christopher six. I have described in some detail Christopher's manners and behaviour in *Towards the Mountain.*

It only remains to add that these characteristics were even more striking three years later. Dorrie was unpacking her suitcase, and Christopher insisted on helping her. He would break open packages to see what was inside them and throw down the most carefully folded items of clothing so that he could get at others. Not even the most private and delicate of garments were safe from his hands. At last Dorrie could stand it no longer, and did something out of the ordinary. She gave Christopher what is known as a sharp crack, and he ran off to his mother uttering loud cries of pain and humiliation. Soon after that he was removed to a friend's home out of consideration for his personal safety. (Twenty years later he had grown up to be very nice-looking and responsible, with a job in an international airline which enabled him to send his father round the world for almost nothing.)

We had only four days in San Francisco, seeing the unforgettable sights, Muir Woods, Mount Tamalpais, the city, the bay, and the great bridge of the Golden Gate. Then Dorrie flew back to New York, London, and Johannesburg, in order to be there for Jonathan's confirmation on 26 November. With the help of the Burnses I found a cabin at a place called Lane's Flat, between Leggett and Eureka. I was the only occupier of a cabin, for the Americans do not travel much in November, and the following few months, even in the mild Californian winter. I was lucky too, because Lane's Flat Cabins kept their cafeteria open all the year round to cater for the crews of the trucks that thundered past, night and day, south to San Francisco, and north to Portland, Seattle, and Vancouver. I decided to stay there for some weeks to write.

My cabin was some thirty or so feet from the Eel River, and some ten to twenty feet higher. At night I would hear the salmon jumping, ascending rapids and falls, and sometimes leaping vertically several times their own lengths. They were making for the headwaters of the Eel River and this would be the last journey of their lives. Having reached their destination, the female would spawn in a nest of gravel, and the male would fertilise her eggs. Then, having fulfilled the main purpose of life, they lose all further interest in it, and drift downriver to die.

All this takes place in the great redwood forest. The older trees at Lane's Flat were all more than three hundred feet tall, with diameters of up to twenty feet, and girths up to sixty feet and more. To live under such giants was an extraordinary experience. It was a fair walk from my cabin to the cafeteria, and at first the immensity of the trees was overwhelming. It was easy to walk at Lane's Flat, because, as the name implies, it was a level piece of ground, one of the few level places in this region of great hills and valleys. I once tried to walk in the forest itself, but I had to give it up because the forest floor is covered with lopped and fallen branches. My daily exercise was to walk along the San Francisco–Vancouver road, but this was not pleasant because of the incessant roar of the trucks along what was in 1949 a very narrow road.

When the salmon spawning was over, Lane's Flat experienced another phenomenon of nature. Snow began to fall in the interior, and the Eel River began to rise steadily. When I arrived it had been a vigorous stream running over rocky rapids, but now it became a river, and then began to climb the thirty feet that separated it from my cabin. There were a few steps leading to the cabin, and when the water had reached the lowest step, I though I should mention the fact to the proprietor of Lane's Flats. He told me not to worry, because the water would rise no further. And he was right. In my diary for 17 January there is the laconic entry: 'Eel River at my door.'

And what about the writing? What did I go there for? To write a novel? I must confess that I cannot remember. My diaries – which were the most uninformative of documents – say that on 23 November

I 'commenced my novel'. There are subsequent references to later chapters. All I know is that the Burnses visited me at Lane's Flat and read what I had written. I am sure they said it was good, but at some later date I must have consigned the book to the flames (or perhaps even to the Eel River, I cannot remember). The Burnses were very good and took me to Mount Shasta and Mount Lasser. They brought Martha and Hal, but decided to leave Christopher in Fairfax with their helpful friend. Martha sat in front with her parents, and I sat at the back with Hal. Hal was not in the least interested in Mount Shasta; his sole interest was to pinch my thigh. I pushed his hand away on several occasions, but he was unrepulsable. Then, like Dorrie, I abandoned my pacifist philosophy, and gave him a good pinch in return. Hal, like Christopher, burst into loud cries of outrage, pain, and humiliation. Aubrey stopped the car immediately and hauled Hal out by the scruff of his neck. Hal's parents did not ask for explanations, they knew the truth already. Martha came to sit with me, and our journey continued peacefully. The next time Aubrey and Marigold visited me, they left all three children with helpful friends. Thus the noble experiment of acquainting their offspring with the deep thoughts of a great writer was finally abandoned.

But what was I doing there? I started going without breakfast and rising at eleven a.m. Then I decided that this was immoral and gave it up. I did physical exercises regularly, and read a great deal, daily portions of St. Mark's gospel, Robert Frost, Thoreau's *Walden*, Dos Passos. I recorded that I read Ruggiero on Existentialism – 'didn't understand it but it was magnificent'. I wrote a number of modern psalms, and two or three more chapters of the novel that has vanished completely from my consciousness. On 17 December I recorded that at supper in the cafeteria I was 'much elevated by reading Thoreau on Spring'. On most evenings I would have three whiskies and play Patience. In case my readers are now disgusted by this account of my useless life, I record that on 14 December I wrote, 'Bed 2.0 a.m. Too much writing.' I wrote an article on penal reform, and recorded 'Read script – very good', but what script it was I do not know. I read Faulkner's *Sanctuary* and a good deal of Walt Whitman.

On 21 December I went to Cummings and sent a Christmas cable to 'Three Favourites' and to Zoltan Korda. On 23 December Aubrey and Marigold arrived to take me to Fairfax for Christmas, and on that same day I received my own Christmas cable from 'Three Favourites'. I was as homesick as I had been three years before in Trondheim, when I wrote the first chapter of *Cry, the Beloved Country*. The present homesickness was to have a consquence similar to that of three years before – not quite so spectacular, but just as real.

On 24 November I had sent Jonathan a cable on the occasion of his confirmation, which took place two days later. On the fourth day of the year 1950 I wrote in the small hours, and did exactly what is described in the following lines:*

I rise from my dream, and take suddenly this pen and this paper
For I have seen with my eyes a certain beloved person, who lives in a distant
*   country.*
I have seen hands laid upon him, I have heard the Lord asked to defend him,
I have seen him kneel with trust and reverence, and the innocence of him
*   smote me in the inward parts.*
I remembered him with most deep affection, I regarded him with fear and
*   with trembling,*
For life is waiting for him, to wrest the innocence from his young boy's eyes,
So I write urgently for this beloved person, and indeed for all beloved persons,
I write indeed for any person, whoever may find something in these words.

I finished 'Meditation for a Young Boy Confirmed' before the dawn. It will be clear to the reader that it was written under the influence of strong emotion. I should like to quote a few more lines from it, because they will give confirmation of Jonathan's 'ungovernable rages' when either of us dared to mention, or even to hint at, the fact that the school holidays were coming to an end.

Listen to one more word from me, now that I begin to take my hands from
*   you.*
Now God be thanked for this so brief possession, so full of joy,
This zest for life, this keen anticipation of some quite trivial thing.
This ingenuity for making occupations, these programmes strictly adhered to,
This typewriter sadly out of gear, on which were thundered out messages,
*   poems, plays, and proclamations,*
These rages, these lunatic stampings, these threats of leaving home,
For these withdrawals of affection, when you sat pouting like a pigeon,
For these restorations, at all costs to be accepted gravely, even with penitence,
For this reverence, this eagerness, this confidence in many persons,
For all these gifts we give our thanks.

Then I put my pen down and went to sleep, amid the sounds of the rising Eel River, one of these sounds being the hurling of rock against rock by the angry water.

So much for my idle life at Lane's Flat. If I had done nothing more than write 'Meditation for a Young Boy Confirmed', I should have felt that it had been worth it. But I wrote something else that also satisfied me deeply, and because it is reasonably short, I am going to reproduce it here. It is called 'A Psalm of the Forest',* the forest being that of

* From *Knocking on the Door*.

Lane's Flat, but the actual trees of the poem, and the monkeys that played in them, being imported from Africa.

I have seen my Lord in the forest, He goes from tree to tree laying His hands
    upon them.
The yellowwoods stand upright and proud that He comes amongst them, the
    chestnut throws down blooms at His feet.
The thorns withdraw their branches before Him, they will not again be used
    shamefully against Him.
The wild fig makes a shade for Him, and no more denies Him.
The monkeys chatter and skip about in the branches, they peer at Him from
    behind their fingers,
They shower Him with berries and fruits, they shake the owls from their
    hiding places,
They stir the whole forest, they screw up their faces,
They say to each other unceasingly, It is the Lord.
The mothers cuff their children, and elder brothers the younger,
But they jump from tree to tree before Him, they bring down the leaves like
    rain,
Nothing can bring them to order, they are excited to see the Lord.
And the winds move in the upper branches, they dash them like cymbals
    together,
They gather from all the four corners, and the waterfalls shout and thunder,
The whole forest is filled with roaring, with an acknowledgement, an
    exaltation.

After I had finished these two poems, and had spent some days in reading and re-reading 'Meditation', I decided that it was time to move on. I always advise aspiring poets to read and re-read their poems before they give a thought to having them published. One hopes that as a result of such reading and re-reading, all cleverness, all infelicities, all falsenesses, will be thrown away. If I were to republish 'Meditation' today, I should make a limited number of small changes. If I were to republish 'Psalm' I should make no changes. But of course 'Meditation' is a much more complex poem, and needs much greater attention. I also advise aspiring poets that should this reading and re-reading begin to dull their critical powers, then they should put the poems away for a time.

When I left Lane's Flat I was given a small party by the staff of the cafeteria. I had not come close to any of them, and they kept a friendly distance from me, being more used to truck drivers than to writers. However, we parted on good terms, and I took a bus to Fairfax and the Burnses. On my way back to New York I planned to stay with the famous American actress Judith Anderson and her husband Luther

Greene at Santa Barbara, and then to move on to Los Angeles to see Aldous Huxley. I parted from the Burnses with many thanks for their kindnesses and some tears. I parted affectionately from Martha, and in a reasonably friendly way from Christopher. Hal showed no feelings of regret over my departure. He had not forgotten the big pinch.

Judith and Luther lived in a big stone house set in the stone hills behind Santa Barbara. I had seen her act only once, and that was not in the flesh, but in the film 'Rebecca' based on Daphne du Maurier's novel of that name. She was an actress of tremendous and sombre power, and one of her great triumphs had been the 'Medea' of Robinson Jeffers. Luther and she took me to the Big Sur to meet the dramatist-poet and his wife. The conversation had to be carried on by the three of us and Mrs. Jeffers; the poet did not say a word. While we were talking, a bird came and perched on the windowsill, and I said to Jeffers, 'What's that bird?' Without a word he went to the bookshelves, pulled out a book, opened it at a certain page, and handed it to me, still without a word. That was the sum total of our communication. Jeffers, Judith Anderson, and 'Medea' – a formidable trio.

After a few very peaceful days with Judith and Luther Greene, I left Santa Barbara for Los Angeles, to meet one of the most extraordinary Englishmen of the century, and one of the most gifted and prolific of writers. He and Zoltan Korda had worked with each other on the film script of Huxley's story *The Gioconda Smile*. However, the film was called 'A Woman's Vengeance' on the grounds that no one would have heard of the Gioconda. So a striking title was lost. It was Zoltan who insisted that I must see Huxley when I visited California, and I wrote to tell him that I was coming. I needed little persuasion. I had read most of Huxley's books, but above all I wanted to meet the writer of *The Perennial Philosophy*. Cyril Connolly, who had known Huxley well in England, and who had been alternatively captivated and repelled by his books, went to California to visit him, and said, 'I loved him again.' He wrote that Huxley radiated 'both intelligence and serene goodness', and he was struck by 'the strange new quality of sublimated sensuality, intellectual pity, spiritual grace'. Such an appraisal coming from a tough nut like Connolly is indeed remarkable, yet I did not find any difficulty in believing it to be true. Huxley was undoubtedly a man of spiritual grace. He was not a Christian, but if he had chosen to be one, he would have become a Quaker. That is not surprising, because he held most dogmas to be ridiculous. One could never imagine Huxley becoming what is known as a 'devout churchman'.

Huxley held one supreme dogma, and that was the existence of what he called 'the divine Ground'. In *The Perennial Philosophy* in the chapter titled 'Self-knowledge', he wrote the following words, which express for me one of the deepest of all truths, the same indeed that is expressed by John in his first epistle:

Fear cannot be got rid of by personal effort, but only by the ego's absorption in a cause greater than its own interests. Absorption in any cause will rid the mind of some of its fears but only absorption in the loving and knowing of the divine Ground can rid it of *all* fear. For when the cause is less than the highest, the sense of fear and anxiety is transferred from the self to the cause – as when heroic self-sacrifice for a loved individual or institution is accompanied by anxiety in regard to that for which the sacrifice is made.

I had been born in a country of fear, and I had feared many things in the course of my life. I had even at one time entertained what might well be the greatest fear of all, that in the perennial struggle between good and evil, good would be defeated. In that case I must have championed some cause that was less than the highest. Huxley went on to write:

Whereas if the sacrifice is made for God, and for others for God's sake, there can be no fear or abiding anxiety, since nothing can be a menace to the divine Ground and even failure and disaster are to be accepted as being in accord with the divine will.

A year or two before he died, he was interviewed by John Chandos, who asked the man who had written about a 'sacrifice . . . made for God' whether he 'had any direct line . . . to an individual upstairs'. Huxley was faintly amused, and said, 'I certainly don't. I mean, what Blake calls "Nobodaddy Aloft", I have no feelings about.' But he went on to say in a rising voice, 'I am entirely on the side of the mystery. I mean, any attempt to explain any of the mystery is ridiculous . . . I believe in the *profound and unfathomable mystery of life* . . . which has a sort of divine quality about it.'

Sybille Bedford, Huxley's biographer, wrote that his philosophy was governed by the equation: Man cannot be happy unless he is virtuous, he cannot be virtuous without God, he cannot realise God if he is without virtue.

It should be clear by this time that Huxley's 'religion' was not an easy thing to be understood by a person like myself, who am not much inclined towards mysticism, and not totally without dogmas. But my few hours with him were too short. One would not have thought that he was talking to a novice entering a world in which he was a master. Connolly was right about the spiritual grace. Huxley said kind words to me about *Cry, the Beloved Country*. He also said that he, like many others, had learned a good deal about a distant country of which he had known almost nothing at all.

I left Los Angeles on 27 January for New York, where I had to fulfil some speaking appointments. I must record that Maxwell Anderson would not let me come to say goodbye. His wife told me over the telephone that he was working on a new play, and that he never saw anybody when he was writing. I had to be content with sending him good wishes.

Then I flew to London, where on 5 March I was to speak in St. Paul's Cathedral – in fact I was to 'preach' but I am always a bit chary of writing or speaking about it. I was to be the second layman to 'preach' there in some two hundred and fifty years, the first having been Sir Stafford Cripps.

This extraordinary honour, which was given me by the Dean and Chapter, was really the work of Canon John Collins. It was the beginning of a friendship with John Collins, which lasted until his death in 1982, and with his wife Diana, which has lasted until today. Of the important part they were both to play in my life, and of the hatred he was to arouse in white South Africa, especially among Afrikaner Nationalists, I shall have later to tell.

To use the words of my son Jonathan concerning his confirmation, 'Everything went off satisfactorily.' It was time for me to return to the country from which I had been absent for nearly seven months.

At intervals in the period when I was writing and thinking about Aldous Huxley, I was reading C.S. Lewis's *Surprised by Joy*. Huxley, according to Sybille Bedford, believed that Man could not be virtuous without God, but he had no feelings about any 'individual upstairs'. Lewis on the contrary moved from the 'Absolute' to 'spirit' to 'God', then to a final acceptance of Jesus Christ as Lord. Lewis very reluctantly gave up the 'Absolute', because in the Absolute 'there was nothing to fear; better still, nothing to obey'. A brief study of these two men reveals to one anew the miracle of diversity of individuality and personality.

I can add myself as a further humble example of this diversity. I have written that to me religion is in large measure a dedication of the will, in other words, an obedience to what I believe to be the will of God. C.S. Lewis wrote in *Surprised by Joy*, 'As for what we commonly call Will, and what we commonly call Emotion, I fancy these usually talk too loud, protest too much, to be quite believed, and we have a secret suspicion that the great passion or the iron resolution is partly a put-up job.'

Well, there it is. I have been devoting my life to a magnificent deception. If C.S. Lewis had still been alive, I would have written to ask him who were 'we' who had the secret suspicion.

Chapter 5

When I got back to South Africa at the end of March 1950, I found my friends in low spirits. The National Party government had now been ruling for nearly two years, and had taken the first steps in the creation of a society where inter-racial contact would be reduced to a minimum on every conceivable occasion and in every conceivable place. Many of us comforted ourselves with the thought that the Nationalist bark would be proved to be much worse than the bite. Now we were about to find that the bite would be just as savage as the bark.

How does a determined government set about separating the races of a country that has for centuries been the meeting-place of the peoples of three continents, that has created a new indigenous people called originally the Cape Coloured people, a country with great mineral riches, as a consequence of which it has entered the industrial age and has drawn many of these diverse peoples into one single indivisible economy? How does one do it? Obviously one must have full control of the machinery of government. On 26 May 1948 the white National Party achieved this full control. What did it do?

The first and obvious thing to do is to stop all these different people from loving one another; in other words, you must make this loving of one another a criminal offence. Perhaps I should be more exact and say that you must make the *making of love* to one another a criminal offence. A Christian country cannot really go so far as to make it an offence for a white man to love a black woman (because after all the second great Christian commandment is that we should love one another), but a Christian government can presumably make it an offence for a white man and a black woman to *make love* to one another. This step was first taken in 1927 by the South African parliament, which made it a criminal offence for a white person to *make love* to an African person. It was not however a criminal offence for a white person to make love to an Indian or a coloured person. But now in 1949 the Afrikaner Nationalist parliament made it an offence for any white person to have any sexual relationship with any person who was not white. There were purists who wanted it to be made an offence for *any* person to make love to *any* person of another racial group, but the white parliament never got as far as that. After all – one might as well face the truth – the parliament was really concerned only with white purity.

The second obvious thing to do is to stop all these people from marrying one another. In the 1930s Dr. D.F. Malan, the leader of the Nationalist opposition, had tried to force the Hertzog government into passing a Mixed Marriages Act, but he was always foiled by my friend and mentor J.H. Hofmeyr, then Minister of the Interior. Dr. D.F. Malan exploited very skilfully the fact that there were members of the Hertzog government who were much closer to Malan than to Hofmeyr on the question of mixed marriages. Hofmeyr's colleague, J.H. Grobler of Brits, wanted to make marriages between whites and Indians illegal. Major Roberts, independent M.P. for Vrededorp, wanted to make all mixed marriages illegal. It is instructive to study Hofmeyr's arguments against mixed marriages. They were not based on moral grounds. Hofmeyr argued that in nine years there had been only thirty-nine marriages between white persons and Indians. He argued that if mixed marriages were prohibited, the number of extra-marital relationships would increase. The followers of Malan were outraged that an Afrikaner would argue in such a fashion. When Malan came to power in 1948, all these difficulties about mixed marriages disappeared, and in 1950 the Mixed Marriages Act was passed.

Parliament had now decreed that any inter-racial marriage or any inter-racial sexual relationship was illegal. But how was one to know to what race a person belonged? In many parts of the country it would have been impossible, especially in the Cape, where many coloured people passed as white, and where indeed many white people were in fact coloured. Some sadistic white clerk had instituted the infamous comb test. A person whose racial identity was uncertain was required to put a comb into his or her hair, and then required to bend the head. If the comb stayed in, the person was coloured; if the comb fell out, the person was white. Some coloured people were deeply affronted by these tests; others were not – they were used to insult. So was passed in 1950 the Population Registration Act, which was designed to fix the 'race' of every person in the Union of South Africa. The Act itself had painful consequences for those families, part of whom lived as white, and part as coloured, but who nevertheless maintained their family bonds, and indeed lived in the same streets and suburbs.

But this indiscriminate living was to come to an end too. In 1950 Dr. Eben Dönges, Minister of the Interior, introduced the Group Areas Bill, which was regarded by him as the 'cornerstone of apartheid'. Under this law separate residential areas for the different racial groups were to be established in every city, town, and village. This law was to cause the uprooting of hundreds of thousands of Indian and coloured people, and a much smaller number of whites. The law affected very few Africans because their residential rights were already controlled under the Urban Areas Act, and they lived in areas adjacent to the white cities, called variously 'locations' and 'townships'. Many Indian and coloured people had lived for a century and more in the areas from which they were now expelled, and had built substantial houses and had established gardens. Much of this property was now of tremendous value, but the owners seldom received anything like this value. These expropriations led to the enrichment of many white speculators, but often broke the hearts of the Indian and coloured owners, especially those who were old.

I am sure that many of my readers will find it difficult to believe that such things could have happened. We had no difficulty about believing it, because it was happening all around us. But there was something else that people like myself found difficult to understand, and that was how a Christian government (for the Afrikaner is more churchly religious than the English-speaking people, and much more inclined to invoke the name of the Almighty) could do such things to people.

Many years later I wrote these lines about Trevor Huddleston and an old black woman who is about to be moved by this Christian government from her home in Sophiatown.*

– I do not want them to touch me, Father. But if you help me into the truck I shall go.

– I will help you, mother, and as soon as I can I shall come to your new house in Meadowlands.

– Give me a minute, Father. I must say goodbye to my house. My husband built that house many years ago when we were both young. I am glad he is not here today.

– The old woman stands for a moment at the gate of her house. She shuts her eyes, she is praying. What is she praying for? That some angel with a sword will come down to defend it? Or does she give thanks for the life that she lived there? Or does she ask forgiveness for those who have taken her house

* From the novel *Ah, but Your Land Is Beautiful.*

from her?
— I am ready, Father.
Meadowlands. The name is beautiful.

How can a government do such things? How can anyone, Christian or not, do such things? There are several answers to this question. The first is that the goal of racial separation is so ineffable, so clearly desired by God when He created the separate races, that any means of reaching it is justifiable. In such circumstances the end justifies the means. There may be a bit of suffering of course. But surely suffering and the reaching of noble goals are inseparable? Furthermore, one must never forget that all races are going to benefit from this separation.

There is a second reason for doing such things, and that is white fear. The white man is heavily outnumbered in South Africa, and he must do these things to protect his identity. He is the bearer of Christianity to a pagan continent, and therefore he is also the bearer of what is called 'civilisation'. Therefore it is important that he maintain his identity. But of course he will also preserve the identity of others.

The third reason is not so respectable as the first two, and most white people would not like to admit it in public. The reason is racial abhorrence, the horror of touching a black skin, the horror of eating with black people. Although it is not respectable to admit to this in public, it has been done, and by no less a person that Mrs. Betsy Verwoerd, the widow of the Prime Minister from 1958 to 1966.

The fourth reason is also not respectable, and it is racial arrogance. There can be no doubt that this arrogance dates back to the arrival of the Dutch at the Cape of Good Hope in 1652, when the first Europeans developed a contempt for the Khoikhoi and the San. This arrogance was often displayed by a Minister of Dr. Malan's government of 1948, the Honourable Eric Louw, who referred to the coloured people as 'Hotnots', to the African people as 'Kaffirs', and to the Indian people as 'Koelies'. There is no evidence to show that his Prime Minister thought that such language was distasteful.[*]

The fifth and last reason would never be ·acknowledged in any circumstances whatsoever. It is plain and simple greed. Sophiatown in Johannesburg, District Six in Cape Town, Cato Manor in Durban, were settled by various people not white, in times when white people did not wish to live there, because they were relatively remote. But as the white cities grew, and encircled these several areas, their land value became enormous. They could therefore be expropriated, and

[*] This is no longer done by Cabinet Ministers, nor indeed by any responsible Afrikaner. People are fined by the courts for using the word 'Kaffir'.

'reasonable' compensation given, but now their value as land for white occupation would be trebled, quadrupled, quintupled. Many white people became rich on the Group Areas Act.

It is time for me to close this account, but in fact I have said enough. I could mention other laws, but these are enough, the Immorality and Mixed Marriages Acts, the Population Registration Act and the Group Areas Act. These four offer sufficient proof of the implacable determination of the Nationalist government to enforce apartheid in every possible sphere of life. But of course everything would be done with justice.

How was it possible for the majority of the Afrikaner people to believe that these things could be done with justice? I think the answer was that *they had to believe it*. If they had not been able to believe it, their whole world of morality and safety and security would have collapsed. Their revered leader Dr. D.F. Malan had actually said of the Group Areas Act that it would enable the coloured people to live with 'proper pride', because they would be given a place of their own where they would not be subject to being pushed around. Now Dr. Malan was a man of considerable intelligence. How could he believe such a thing? It was because he too *had to believe it*. One should also note that he was a man with strong religious convictions. How can one unravel such enigmas? There is only one explanation, and that is that when one's ruling motive is fear, one is capable of doing and believing anything. Aldous Huxley undoubtedly knew something there.

Let me record that there were some Afrikaners who regarded this new turn in Afrikaner history with the deepest concern. One of their writers, Jan Rabie, wrote a book called *Ons, die Afgod* ('We, the Idol'). He meant that Afrikanerdom was making an idol of itself, to which it would bow down and worship. Afrikanerdom was committing the sin of the Israelites who worshipped the Golden Calf, made for them by their own High Priest. But there were too few of such men and women to turn the irresistible tide of Afrikaner power.

I must mention one law more. It was not itself a racial law, but it was a law to protect all racial laws. It was the Suppression of Communism Act of 1950.

The Afrikaner Nationalists' fear and hatred of communism was pathological. Communism was the anti-Christ, Godlessness incarnate. Of some Afrikaner Christians it would have been permissible to say that their religion was not primarily Christian but was primarily anti-communist. It was possible for a young Afrikaner Christian to say publicly of communists, that he would kill them for Christ.

But this fear and hatred of communism existed not only because of its danger to Christianity. It existed also because coommunism was a threat to the survival of the Afrikaner and his racial identity. Communists did not believe in apartheid or in the colour bar. The South African Communist Party of 1950 not only courted black opponents of apartheid but exerted over some of them a considerable political and ideological influence. In fact some of the leading black politicians were members of the Communist Party. It was not the totalitarian nature of communism that was abhorrent to the Afrikaner Nationalist; he was to become a pretty good totalitarian himself. What he abhorred was the supposedly egalitarian nature of the communist State. Had he not embarked on the Great Trek in order to get away from the threat of egalitarianism? And had he not founded republics where there was to be 'no equality in Church or State'?

Lastly, communism was a threat to the growing material affluence of the Afrikaner people. They had picked themselves up from the dust after their defeat in the Anglo–Boer War, and had entered in increasing numbers the world of commerce and industry, which had been the preserve of the English-speaking people. Communism threatened this new affluence, and it threatened also the land monopoly enjoyed by white South Africans, land which had been acquired by the wars of conquest.

The Suppression of Communism Act made the Communist Party of South Africa an unlawful organisation. It gave extraordinary powers to the Minister of Justice. It empowered him to ban any person from public life if he 'deemed' such a person to be furthering the 'aims of communism'. It was not necessary for such a person to have belonged to the Communist Party or even to have expressed approval of the tenets of communism. Many of my friends were banned from public life under this Act, although they were in fact opposed to communism. They were banned for one reason and one only, and that was because they were opposed to apartheid, a considerable number of them on moral and religious grounds. Although I have written that they were banned from 'public life' they were to a large extent banned from private life also. When my friend Peter Brown was banned, he was not allowed to attend the birthday parties of his own children, because one of the terms of his banning order was that he might not attend any gathering. Even more ridiculous was the case of another friend of mine, Jean Hill, a woman of strong religious convictions. One of the terms of her banning order (and indeed of all banning orders) was that she might not speak to any other banned person. After she had been banned, her husband Ken Hill was also banned, but the Minister decreed that he would be allowed to speak to his wife. However, the Minister forgot to decree that Jean Hill would be allowed to speak to her husband. Therefore she continued to break the terms of her banning order for seven months, at the end of which time the University of Natal prevailed on the Minister to lift the ban on her husband. The government was totally untroubled by these absurdities, nor did it concern itself with the even greater absurdity that no people could have been more opposed to the doctrines of communism than these.

I shall conclude this sorry tale by relating the story of the grotesque banning of Robert Sobukwe, a university teacher who spent nine years in the notorious prison on Robben Island. When he was released from prison he was exiled to Kimberley under a severe banning order, but his spirit was indestructible. He qualified as a lawyer and, because he wanted to travel overseas, he was granted a passport by the Minister of the Interior. However, his passport was useless to him, because the Minister of Justice would not allow him to travel to the airport.

I shall answer one last question. Why was I never banned? The answer is quite simple. It was not because the Minister of Justice was satisfied that I was not a communist. It was because I had written *Cry, the Beloved Country*.

The Suppression of Communism Act was our first deliberate step away from the rule of law. The powers given to the Minister and the actions taken by him under the Act were not subject to the review of any court of law. If he 'deemed' a person to be furthering the aims of communism, then he could ban such a person from public life. The most extreme step allowed by the Act was house arrest, and the most extreme form of house arrest was to be confined to one's home for twenty-four hours of every day. It was one of the provisions of the Act that a banned person could not meet with more than one person at a time, because the courts eventually ruled that three people constituted a 'gathering'. Most banned persons found this the most grievous restriction of all.

We were not only taking our first deliberate step away from the rule of law. We were also stepping away from what is called 'the West', from the countries of which the forebears of all white South Africans had come. We were stepping away from the political and legal and spiritual traditions of the West. The Afrikaner Nationalist scorned any criticism from the West. Our very intelligent Prime Minister Dr. D.F. Malan actually claimed that one day the nations of the West would come to South Africa to learn how to deal with the problems caused by the presence of different races in the same society. It was also his opinion that the West was decadent, while South Africa was spiritually stead-fast and strong. In 1950, and for a good many years thereafter, the Afrikaner Nationalist government was at the height of its moral and spiritual arrogance.

One of the Afrikaners who had tried to stem this moral slide was my friend J.H. Hofmeyr, who died in December 1948. On 11 September 1950 General Smuts died. The once-great United Party went into a long and irreversible decline, and during these discreditable years did not produce another Smuts or Hofmeyr. Parliamentary opposition to the Afrikaner Nationalist Party began to die away.

Well, again that's enough of sorrow. Let us get back to the gay and glittering world of films.

Chapter 6

In April of 1950 I met Zoltan Korda in Johannesburg. His advance party had been in South Africa for some weeks, spying out the land, and planning ways and means of coping with the difficulties that would confront black actors from overseas, used to the freedom of Britain and the United States, and now working for some weeks in a fierce colour-bar country.

The old black priest of *Cry, the Beloved Country*, Stephen Kumalo, was to be played by Canada Lee, who had been a boxer but had suffered a serious injury to his eye and had retired to the safer world of acting, for which he luckily had gifts.

The young black priest, Theophilus Msimangu, was to be played by Sidney Poitier, a most handsome young man of twenty-six, born in Nassau, but now a citizen of the United States, and an up-and-coming actor. He was not required in Ixopo, and we were to meet him later in Johannesburg.

There were two other black actors from overseas. One was Charles McRae from the States, who was to play the part of the old priest's friend, and the other was a young black girl, Vivien Clinton, whose parents had come from the West Indies and now lived in Exeter, England. She was to play the part of the girl friend, later the wife, of Absalom, son of the old priest.

The accommodation of the white actors from overseas presented no problems. But where were the black actors to stay? In 1950 no hotel would have taken them, and it was unthinkable that they should be accommodated in some black lodging house, whose facilities in those days were certainly not of the standard to which they were accustomed. Zoltan's advance party solved all these problems with considerable skill.

Kumalo's church at Ndotsheni was very near the narrow-gauge railway station of Carisbrooke, where the early parts of the film would be made. Now it so happened that Dorrie's brother Garry Francis (the Huckleberry Finn of my first volume) lived on the farm 'Rayfield', also near the station of Carisbrooke. London Films asked him to accommodate Lee and McRae, and offered to build a very substantial extension to his house, where the actors could live and eat. In addition to paying Garry Francis a generous fee for looking after them, London Films would give him the substantial extension as a gift.

My brother-in-law agreed to the arrangement and I have never ceased to admire him and his wife Doreen for doing so. They had never had a black person to the house except as a servant. It is almost one hundred per cent certain that no white farmer in the whole Ixopo countryside had ever had a black guest, nor any white resident in the village of Ixopo. It is almost certain that the only black guests that the white countryside had ever known would have been at the Catholic mission station at Mariathal or the Catholic hospital of Christ the King.

London Films also made arrangements for the accommodation of the young girl Vivien Clinton. The Plough Hotel, which had also never had a black guest, agreed to accommodate her in a caravan in the hotel grounds, and to feed her 'from the table'. This also worked out well; Vivien was shy and undemanding, and in the morning she would emerge from her caravan and join the carefree company at Carisbrooke for the filming. Zoltan was extremely solicitous for her, and indeed for the two black male actors as well, and ensured that they would not be neglected during the weekends. They were taken to Pietermaritzburg and Durban, and were made a great fuss of in both cities.

Visitors streamed to the scene of the filming. Ixopo, and most other places in South Africa, had never been host to a film company before. It was like a great picnic with a serious end in view. The month of May is one of the most beautiful of the year in Natal; the sun shines all day and the air is crisp and clear. Zoltan presided over this fascinating and in some ways unreal world like some kind of impish god. He had his own chair and no one else dared sit in it. I had my own chair too, and so did the leading actors. Zoltan had brought his two leading white actors from England, Charles Carson as Jarvis senior, and Joyce Carey as Mrs. Jarvis. Berdine Grunewald, a South African actress, was also there, playing the part of the young widow of Arthur Jarvis. She later married Robert Ardrey, the well-known American author, who wrote several controversial books about man and society, including *The*

Territorial Imperative and *The Hunting Hypothesis*. He was a kind of anthropological and psychological and sociological Arthur Koestler and, like Koestler, he was looked at askance by the professionals, or some of them. He died in 1980, leaving Berdine and three children.

The impish god Zoltan had the proverbial iron hand in the velvet glove, but sometimes he would take the glove off and exhibit the ferocity of his brother Alexander. However, I soon learned that he was not omnipotent. His technical crew were members of a trade union and were led by a difficult and not impressive man who knew the rights of workers and who felt, even in this remote part of the South African countryside, the might of the unions behind him. Zoltan was torn in two between his perfectionist ideals as a film director and his democratic respect for the rights of labour. I have seen him more than once denied the privilege of the five-minutes' overtime that would have enabled a particular sequence to be completed. In such cases the impishness disappeared and he would listen with inscrutable countenance to the *fiat* of the union leader of the crew.

In my opinion he had one fault as a director. There were times when he, in the hearing of all, belittled the work of one or other of his actors. He began to develop a dislike for Canada Lee, and unfortunately the dislike was tinged at times with contempt. Canada was not the brightest of men, and it was said that the batterings he had suffered as a boxer were the cause of this. Zoltan would not have spoken to Poitier as he spoke to Canada, but life had knocked the fight out of the ex-boxer, and he received Zoltan's criticisms with pained smiles.

The inhabitants of Nokweja (the Ndotsheni of the novel), the small black 'location' adjoining my brother-in-law's farm, watched the comings and goings of the film company with wonder. Most of them knew what a film was, and many had been to see one or more of them, but in 1950 they were among the few black people in South Africa who had ever seen a film being made. Zoltan, with that sense of propriety which was one of his most attractive characteristics, made it his business to invite the local chief, the minister of the church, and the headmaster of the school, to see how a film was made. When the filming at Ixopo was done, it was announced that London Films would build a new church to replace the one in which much of the action took place. Gifts of blankets and clothes and food and children's sweets were given most generously, and Zoltan left Ixopo in a blaze of glory.

London Films had had to make somewhat different arrangements for the black actors in Johannesburg. They had rented a kind of country mansion some miles from the city, where the actors, now joined by Sidney Poitier and Edric Connor, lived in solitary splendour. We were also joined by Geoffrey Keen, who was to play the part of

Father Vincent of Sophiatown, and Michael Goodliffe, who was to be the young Afrikaner welfare officer of Diepkloof Reformatory, one of the white men who 'hid their kindness, or brought it out with fierceness and anger, and hid it behind fierce and frowning eyes'.* Another newcomer was Lionel Ngakane, a young black man from Johannesburg who was to play the part of Kumalo's wayward son Absalom. This was the first time he had acted in a film, and it started him off on a film career. It was also a 'first' for Reggie Ngcobo, who took the part of a taxi-driver. At that time he was a clerk in a magistrate's office, but went on to become a successful lawyer, and later still a wealthy real-estate dealer. The part of Stephen Kumalo's worldly-wise brother John, the rabble-rousing politician, was taken by Edric Connor of London, who was not only an actor, but a notable singer. Zoltan did his screen tests well, and not one of his choices was a failure. He did something more than that – he opened for some black people a door into a new and exciting world, a world unimaginably different from one in which they had lived, which was often one of drudgery and struggle or, if they gave up, of drink and purposelessness.

That was thirty-five years ago, but it still happens that I meet a black man or woman in the street, whose face lights up to see me. 'Do you remember me?' When I am asked that question, I am almost invariably being addressed by a man who was once a boy at Diepkloof Reformatory or by a man or woman who had had the great fortune to be given a small part in the film. If I do not remember the person, I temporise and say, 'I know your face, but I do not remember your name.' And then the answer, 'My name is Phineas (or Joyce), and I played the part of the policeman (or nurse) in *Cry, the Beloved Country*. Oh, I am glad to see you. I remember well that time. But it is now many years.' So we part and go our several ways, but I have seen a black face light up with the memory of a magic time in what may have been a hard and bitter life.

Zoltan now decided to take six days off to go to the Kruger National Park. Its area is eight thousand square miles (thirteen thousand square kilometres), about the same size as Wales or the state of Massachusetts. It is one of the great national parks of the world and is the home of elephants, lions, leopards, cheetahs, giraffes, hippopotami, crocodiles, warthogs, baboons, jackals, hyenas, zebra, wildebeest, and of many kinds of antelopes, ranging from the lordly eland and kudu to the small and delicate steenbok and blue duiker, both of these perfect creatures standing less than twenty inches (65 centimetres) in height. Another beautiful antelope, the impala, is intermediate in size and is found throughout the length and breadth of the park. Impalas are extremely graceful in motion and can leap eight or ten times their fully

* Quoted from *Cry, the Beloved Country*.

extended length.

Let me give a clearer idea of the vastness and grandeur of the park: it was estimated (in 1980) that there were approximately 150,000 impala, 1,500 lions, 600 to 900 leopards, 250 to 300 cheetah, 7,500 elephants, over 4,000 giraffe, 400 eland, more than 500 rhino (white and black), and more than 2,000 hippopotami. There are also more than 450 species of birds.

There are ten or more rest camps along the road from Pafuri in the extreme north to the two southern gates of Malelane and Crocodile Bridge. These camps provide simple and adequate accommodation and are kept spotlessly clean. The restaurants also are clean and efficient, and the service, provided largely by black Shangaans, is friendly and cheerful, in fact almost avuncular, even paternal. One leaves the park with a sense of having been in one of the most peaceful and well-ordered parts of our often troubled country.*

Zoltan was fascinated by the park. His knowledge of the names and habits of its animals, most of which he had never seen before, was extensive. His enjoyment was increased by the fact that the park officials, instructed by Pretoria, paid special attention to us, and took us to places the ordinary tourist is not allowed to enter. It was a memorable visit, and was made still more memorable for me by an incident on our journey back to Johannesburg. It showed something about which I wrote earlier, Zoltan's intense hatred of anything that smacked of authoritarianism.

We took the road back that runs through Belfast, Middelburg and Witbank. Somewhere along the way the whole highway was being torn up and rebuilt, by an army of workers and tremendous yellow machines, in those days driven by white men only. Zoltan and I, driven by a black driver engaged by London Films, had to fall behind one of these towering machines. Controlling it was a white operator, and we must have done something to anger him, because he shouted and screamed at us, making signals that we were to slow up or stop or do something different from what we were doing. These instructions were shouted at our black driver, but unfortunately the noise of the towering yellow machine was so deafening that we could not hear what the operator

* I must add to this account that in 1949 there was a rigid colour bar in Kruger Park. In fact the whole park was closed to black visitors. A separate rest camp called Balule was opened some twenty years ago for black visitors. It was decidedly inferior to the other camps, and it was patronised so little that eventually it was closed down. At the time of writing, the National Parks Board has set aside certain areas which have no colour bar. It is in fact a kind of modified Group Areas Act that is in operation. When will the plunge be taken into the deep end? I don't know. Many of the white tourists to the park are the most bigoted and conservative whites in South Africa.

was saying. At last it dawned on the operator that we could not hear him. He stopped his engine and shouted abuse at the driver, the kind of abuse that semi-literate whites are likely to shout at black men who have the impertinence to drive motorcars.

By this time Zoltan was in an uncontrollable rage. He leapt out of the car and directed a stream of incoherent invective at the man on the yellow machine. It was difficult to hear everything he was saying, but it certainly had something to do with Hitler and the Nazis. I would have guessed that the man on the machine had heard about the Nazis, and I would also have guessed that he would not have thought it a great insult to be called one. Zoltan brought out the book in which he kept a list of the birds of the Kruger Park, and was taking down the number of the yellow machine. The white driver had calmed down a good deal, for how was he to know what dreadful power might be in the hands of this white person? He waved us on, and Zoltan climbed back into the car, wearing his look of impenetrable inscrutability.

We travelled on in complete silence, and as fas as I can remember, neither of us alluded to the incident. Was it Zoltan the artist rebelling against the yellow machine? Or was it Zoltan the Hungarian Jew remembering the suffering of both Hungary and Jewry under Hitler and Stalin? In any event it was something to remember.

Zoltan now flew back to London, where I was to join him later in the year, for the shooting of the interior scenes of the film. I was beginning to wish that the whole business would come to an end, and to realise that it was time for me to get back to writing. This was made very clear to me by Vincent, the third Korda brother. 'You shouldn't be doing this,' he said bluntly. 'You were meant to be a writer of books, not film scripts.' I knew that he was right and, what was more, the idea of a new novel was beginning to take shape in my mind.

Somewhere in some country town in the province of the Transvaal, a white policeman was being charged under the Immorality Act. In those days the Act was fierce and pitiless.* The white police were subjected to many temptations. If a white man were found at night in a black area, the suspicion would be at once that he was looking for a woman, but if he were a policeman the presumption would be that he was looking for a criminal. The white police in their cruising vans would often pick up black men and women, and the temptation to seduce or coerce the women would always be there. A white policeman could be on solitary night-duty in a police station, and an attractive black woman could be in custody in one of the cells.

There were always some white policemen liable to yield to such

* In 1985 the racial clause of the Act was repealed.

temptations, and there were others who led sexually conventional lives. But there were still others who were fanatical believers in white supremacy, white purity, white identity, and who would relentlessly have exposed any of their colleagues who had fallen prey to temptation.

The court case in the Transvaal was like many others. The policeman had been faced with temptation and he had yielded to it. If he had stopped there, his delinquency might never have been discovered. But he repeated his offence, and was eventually caught and charged.

The story in itself was not unusual. What moved me deeply was that the policeman's wife sat in court throughout the trial, and by her demeanour showed that she had forgiven him. There was also the implication that when he was discovered, he had confessed to her. Acts of infidelity are as common in South Africa as in any country in the world, and such acts of forgiveness are also not unknown. But the forgiving of a white man – and especially an Afrikaner – by his wife when the act of infidelity had been committed with a black woman has an emotional and moral quality that is unknown in any other country in the world. And I might as well face the fact that I am incapable of writing a story that does not have an emotional and moral quality. Therefore I decided to write a story about an Afrikaner who offended against the Immorality Act. In the event, my story was to differ greatly from the original, but that of course is a prerogative of creative fiction.

Cry, the Beloved Country was written in a dozen different places, among them the Hotel Bristol in Trondheim, the great liner *Queen Elizabeth*, a hotel on the rim of the Grand Canyon in Colorado, and finally the Hotel Somerton in San Francisco. The second novel *Too Late the Phalarope* was written in two places only, the Green Bank Hotel in Falmouth, Cornwall, and 2 Park Street, London, a most exclusive establishment for the use of visiting diplomats, a privilege obtained for me by Jonathan Cape. It was at 2 Park Street that the book was finished.

After its publication in 1953 by Cape I did not read *Too Late the Phalarope* again until 1978, twenty-five years later. I retired to bed with a cold and decided to read it again. Away with mock modesty! I was not ashamed of the book. Away with all modesty! I was proud of the book. It is a better-constructed book than *Cry, the Beloved Country*, but how I constructed it I do not know. I am asked why I chose to tell it in the first person, and why I chose a woman, Tante Sophie, as my narrator. I have no idea. All I know is that during my temporary retirement to bed I formed the opinion that *Too Late the Phalarope* was the kind of book that, once you put it down, you could pick up again.

The experience of writing a novel is quite unlike that of writing a biography or an autobiography or a memoir. It is more exciting. All of these can be and should be creative forms, but the biography, and the history also, are bound to relate actual happenings and indeed are condemned if they relate imaginary ones, whereas the novel is a relation of imaginary events and the doings of imaginary people, though both of course may be based on actual events and people. The writing of biography and history is much harder work than the writing of a novel, unless of course the novel isn't working, and then the writing of it becomes the hardest work of all. The satisfaction of completing a biography or a history is very considerable, but does not approach the satisfaction of completing a novel, or indeed whatever the creator finds to be good – a play or a poem or, I would assume, a painting or a sonata or a work of sculpture.

It has been claimed that in the writing of a story the characters take over, and write the story for the story-teller. This is a pleasant fancy. What is true, however, is that the development of character and story often takes place (except in blatantly manufactured novels) in the subconscious mind. When I am in the grip of the 'creative urge' I often wake from sleep because some exciting idea has broken through the barrier of consciousness, like those salmon in the Eel River breaking the silence of the night with their leaps up the stream, on their way to create also.

I finished *Too Late the Phalarope* with satisfaction. It was not only because I thought it was a good story; it was because it was about my country, and about my strange countryman the Afrikaner. Anthony Delius, an English-speaking South African novelist with a good understanding of the Afrikaner, said that I had not captured him. Braam de Vries, one of our leading Afrikaner writers, said that I had. I agreed with Braam de Vries. Jonathan Cape said to me, 'You've written two novels. They are quite different and shouldn't be compared. They are equally good.'

There were two things I had to do before I returned home. The one was to go to Scotland for a purpose I shall explain in the next chapter. The other was to see the completed film of *Cry, the Beloved Country*.

The film was shown in the small theatre at 146 Piccadilly, the headquarters of London Films. There were perhaps a dozen of us there, maybe more. But I can name only four of them with certainty, the three Korda brothers and myself. The theatre was darkened and the film began. The little girl is running to the church with a letter for the priest, the *umfundisi*. He is not used to letters and hardly dares to open it, 'for once such a thing is opened, it cannot be shut again'. The letter is from a priest in Sophiatown, Theophilus Msimangu, who writes to Kumalo to tell him he must come to Johannesburg because his sister Gertrude is 'very sick'. Kumalo is terrified at the idea of going to Johannesburg. It is not only terror of the big city, but where is the money to come from?

The only money they have is what he and his wife have saved to send their son Absalom to St. Chad's, but Absalom too has gone to Johannesburg, and has never come back. Kumalo compensates for his fear by speaking harshly to his wife, but she has now taken the matter into her own hands. He must go to Johannesburg tomorrow. So one of his faithful friends carries his bag to Carisbrooke, a small wayside halt where, by courtesy of the South African Railways, a small narrow-gauge train is waiting. It is all very beautiful, very humble, and a little bit sad.

Suddenly the lights of the theatre at 146 Piccadilly are turned on. Sir Alexander is on his feet. He turns to his brother and speaks to him in tones of barely controlled ferocity. 'When does your film start?' he says. 'When does your film start?'

Chapter 7

There was another book that I wanted to write, and that was the life of J.H. Hofmeyr. It was necessary to see all those men and women in England and Scotland who had known him well.

There was three men in Scotland whom I particularly wanted to see. One was John Macmurray, Professor of Philosophy at the University of Edinburgh. The second was William Macmillan, Director of Colonial Studies at St. Andrew's University. The third was retired Professor Herbert Le May, who had the grand address of Sorn Castle. These three men had been professors at the Johannesburg University College, under their youthful principal J.H. Hofmeyr, who had been appointed to his post at the age of twenty-four, to the delight of some and the anger of others. All three had been at the college during the most painful year of Hofmeyr's life, and had lived through the stormy events of what came to be known as the Stibbe affair.

Professor E.P. Stibbe was head of the department of Anatomy at the college, and was a good and popular teacher, and an amiable man. Sometime in 1921 Stibbe's wife and children went away to the coast for a holiday, and Mrs. Stibbe arranged that her husband should stay in the boarding house run by the mother of the head college typist, Miss Frances Roy. Stibbe would walk with Miss Roy to the college and would often, or sometimes, wait in the afternoon to walk back with her to the boarding house. Stibbe was also seen with Miss Roy at the cinema, and tongues began to wag. Hofmeyr, encouraged by his mother, whose sexual code was of the strictest kind, and whose interest in real or rumoured sexual misdemeanours was of the most avid, decided to speak to Stibbe about the matter, and was told that it was none of his business. Hofmeyr then took the matter to the Council, who, acting on the principal's advice, informed Stibbe that his connection with the college 'should be severed'. Later the Council, unhappy about its decision on more grounds than one, adopted an ancient stratagem, and offered Stibbe the chance to resign, which he did. Council did something worse; it decided to destroy the minutes of the meeting at which Stibbe had been dismissed.

These events occurred while the college was in recess, but as members of the Senate learned one by one that Stibbe had resigned after pressure from the Council, many of them were outraged by the Council's failure to consult the Senate. But they were outraged further when they learned from Stibbe that he had first been dismissed. They were also outraged by what they construed as Hofmeyr's manoeuvres and vindictiveness, and by their own conviction that Mrs. Hofmeyr was behind it all. Hofmeyr had by his action alienated almost the entire Senate, and Council and Senate had also become alienated from each other.

This battle lasted throughout the year of 1922, and was ended only by the decision of a highly respected arbitrator that, because Stibbe had resigned, there was nothing further to be done. Hofmeyr and his mother had won, but at great cost to the college and to the principal himself. He had lost many of his friends, and had suffered mentally and physically throughout the long and bitter struggle. One of the reasons why he did not break was that behind him was the indomitable figure of his mother.

It was my hope that these three men would help me to unravel the complications of the Stibbe affair, and my hope was realised except for one thing: at that time not one of them, or I myself, had any knowledge that the minutes of a certain Council meeting had been destroyed. It was to be many years before I found that out.

There is a conclusion to this story. When I got back home, I went to see Mrs. Hofmeyr. She was always very direct in her conversation. She asked me, 'Where have you been?' I told her that amongst my activities had been visits to Macmurray at Edinburgh, Macmillan at St. Andrew's, and Le May at Sorn Castle. She asked why I had been to see them, and I told her that I had gone to ask them about the Stibbe affair.

She drew herself up to her full height, which was not very great, but the action itself would have terrified braver men than I. She said, 'But I told you all about the Stibbe affair.'

I said to her, 'Mrs. Hofmeyr, when one is writing a man's life, one must go to everyone who knew something about him.'

She looked at me out of hard and hostile eyes. At last she knew that the book would be mine, not hers. She said, with that slight stammer that always gave added significance to what she was saying, 'I don't think we'll m-m-meet again.'

And she was right. We did not. I went on with the research for the book, and indeed wrote several chapters, but was forced to conclude that it could not be published while she was alive, and it looked as though she would live for ever. In fact she lived for more than ten years after her son's death in 1948. She was resentful that, although her son had been dead for nearly two years, his life had not yet been written. She expressed her dissatisfaction to Dorrie with something of a sneer. She said to Dorrie, 'My son wrote the life of Onze Jan in one year. My son was only eighteen.' Dorrie said to her – quite correctly but very unwisely – 'Mrs. Hofmeyr, this won't be that kind of book.' They did not meet again either.

J.H. Hofmeyr's life of his senior cousin, another Jan Hendrik Hofmeyr, affectionately called Onze Jan, was a boy's book. It was factually sound, as was to be expected from so serious a young man. It had no drama, but Hofmeyr did not go in for drama, though at least twice in his life he had taken part in political drama, on moral, not political grounds. Deneys Reitz, Hofmeyr's fellow Minister in Smuts's Cabinet, a dashing soldier and hunter, called his colleague's book 'A dull book about a dull man', and in fact that is what it was, especially when compared with Reitz's own exciting books *Commando* and *Trekking On.*

So Mrs. Hofmeyr and I parted. Of all the women I have known, she had the fiercest will. Sometimes one sees in large advertisements of coming films pictures of men, women, and children fleeing from some sacked and burning city. On their faces are expressions of panic and terror. It was quite impossible to imagine such a look on Mrs. Hofmeyr's face. Anger, contempt, yes. Terror, never. She was often likened to a gorgon, those mythical women whose looks could turn men into stone. Some other name would have had to be found for her. Her looks turned men into jelly.

When J.H Hofmeyr died, his mother held Smuts in large degree responsible, in that he had placed heavy burdens upon her son. Smuts knew that he must go to the house in William Street, Pretoria, to pay his respects to her. He, who was afraid of so little, dreaded the encounter. On the day after Hofmeyr's funeral, Smuts told his wife that she must accompany him. He did not wish her to come in, but to wait in the car for him, so that he would have a reason for making his visit short; he told her that he did not expect to be away for more than ten minutes. When he returned he said little, but told her that the visit was as painful as he had expected and that Mrs. Hofmeyr had accused him of a great share of the responsibility for her son's death. Smuts seldom replied under attack, and on this occasion a reply would have seemed to him unseemly.

What Zoltan and Sir Alexander said to each other after I left London, I do not know. But I do know that Zoltan spent endless hours cutting, splicing, pondering, viewing and reviewing. He was one of the most industrious persons I ever encountered. He speeded up the opening scenes, but not by much. For him the film of *Cry, the Beloved Country* was to be some kind of tragic and poetic idyll, whereas Sir Alexander wanted more action. Whether Sir Alexander saw it again, I do not know, but eventually it was finished.

London Films were as generous as ever (except for the miserable thousand pounds they paid for the filming rights). They decided – Zoltan of course – that the world première would be held in Durban, and that the takings for a grand opening night should go to any good cause that I chose. It so happened that Toc H Southern Africa was planning to establish a much-needed settlement for the treatment of tuberculosis among African people, in the Valley of a Thousand Hills, near Botha's Hill in Natal. I decided that the proceeds from the première would go to the new settlement.

One of the moving spirits in this new venture was the Rev. Bill Evans, the full-time Toc H staff man for Natal. Bill and his wife Anne lived at the Toc H House in Durban, and their aim was to make of the House a serving community. The plan to establish a settlement was given a tremendous boost when Don McKenzie, one of the men living in the House, decided that he would give up his personnel job with the Metal Box Company and take over the management of the venture. Don was then in his late forties, and he was what it called a 'confirmed bachelor'. He stipulated that he was to be paid five pounds per month. He had what is known as charisma, and his smile could melt a heart of stone. The gentlemen of the press, a tough lot, decided that he was a modern saint. The première was attended by the cream of Natal – the white cream I mean – and it gave a good start to the new settlement.

The second world première – if there can be such a thing – was held of course in Johannesburg. The guests of honour were to be the Prime Minister and Mrs. Malan. After all, had I not brought honour to South Africa? I sat next to Mrs. Malan, and we had to look at some fairly harrowing pictures of the black slums. At the interval she said to me, 'Do you really think that Johannesburg looks like that?' I said to her, '*Mevrou*, I lived thirteen years of my life among scenes like that.'

– And this is Shanty Town, my friend.

Even here the children laugh in the narrow lanes that run between these tragic habitations. A street of iron, a few planks, hessian and grass, an old door from some forgotten house. Smoke curls from vents cunningly contrived, there is a smell of food, there is a sound of voices, not raised in anger or pain, but talking of ordinary things, of this one that is born and that one that has died, of this one that does so well at school, and that one who is now in prison. There is drought over the land, and the sun shines warmly down from the cloudless sky. But what will they do when it rains, what will they do when it is winter?*

Zoltan had made no attempt to make the slums of Johannesburg look worse than they were. No special sets were built to show these desolate places. The black people of places like Pimville and Sophiatown were only too glad to give London Films the freedom of their streets and houses. They were in fact proud to do so. They were much more worldly-wise than the people of Ndotsheni, and much more accustomed to the world of the cinema. Who knows – perhaps their houses, even their faces, might be seen by people in faraway places like London and New York?

I do not suppose for one moment that Mrs. Malan was a heartless or indifferent woman. She just did not want to believe that any place in the country of which her husband was the Prime Minister could look as these places looked. She was like so many white South Africans – they are not as much shocked by such places as by the fact that people write about them, especially in books that are read all over the world. If this is done by a white South African it is the worst form of disloyalty. It shows a hatred of one's country. It is called – in the miracle of language – 'fouling one's own nest'.

It is time to bring the story of my gay life to an end. I did one more thing of which Vincent Korda would have disapproved; I went again to London in April 1953 for the third world première. I close with one piece of information which may surprise some. The film of *Cry, the Beloved Country* was not a financial success. Beyond the thousand pounds that my agent Annie Laurie Williams got for the rights, I received very little money. Perhaps Sir Alexander was right after all. It was an idyll that didn't come off.

Should I have taken a high moral stand and refused to attend a première to which the Prime Minister and his wife had been invited as guests of honour? After all he was engaged in a struggle to remove the coloured voters of the Cape to a separate roll. It never occurred to me to

* From *Cry, the Beloved Country*.

refuse to attend. It would have been a terrible shock to Zoltan Korda if I had done so. After all, the production of *Cry, the Beloved Country* was a great event in South African film history and, I am sure, a great event in Zoltan's life. I could not have done it, even had I thought of it.

Dr. Malan was determined to amend the Cape franchise, and to move coloured voters to a separate roll. He was told by the government legal advisers that he no longer required a two-thirds majority because the Union of South Africa had become a sovereign state by the Statute of Westminster in 1931. Therefore in June 1951 parliament, by a simple majority, placed coloured voters on a separate roll. However, in March 1952 the Appellate Division of the Supreme Court in Bloemfontein, South Africa's highest court of appeal, declared the Act invalid. Dr. Malan was outraged that a court of law could set aside a decision by a sovereign parliament. Nothing could show more clearly how far the Afrikaner Nationalist Party was from accepting the American concept that every legislative act should conform to the requirements of a sovereign constitution.

But Malan had some very clever Ministers. One of them was Dr. Eben Dönges, who devised an ingenious plan, and that was for parliament to constitute itself the highest court of all. In fact this new court was to be alled the High Court of Parliament, and it would have power to reverse any decision by the Appellate Court to invalidate an Act of Parliament.

This august High Court sat in Pretoria in August of 1952, and declared the Appellate decision to be invalid. But, alas, a few days later the Cape Supreme Court declared the High Court of Parliament Act to be invalid, and this was later confirmed by the Appellate Division. Malan was outraged again, but he was also baffled. There was sufficient of the democrat left in him to make him shrink from tampering with the judiciary itself. He now staked his hopes on winning a two-thirds majority in the imminent 1953 election.

White opposition was at a low ebb. Many white people of my acquaintance fell into the habit of saying primly, 'We never discuss politics.' I approached one of our leading white sportsmen, and asked him if he would join in a protest against the proposed ejection of all Indian residents and owners from Cato Manor in Durban, a proposal which had filled many Indian people with intense anxiety about the future. To my delight he agreed, but the next morning he telephoned me to say that he had slept over the matter, and had decided against it. He was very apologetic, and told me that he had never had anything to do with politics and could not begin now. 'Bill,' I said, 'this is not a question of politics, it's a question of justice.' I produced an even stronger card, which I thought would appeal to him as a sportsman.

'Bill,' I said, 'it's a question of fair play.' But it didn't work. He was one of the most popular men in all South Africa, and he kept his popularity because he had never stood for anything higher than fair play on the sports field. It is ironic to remember that at one time the outside world demanded the removal of the colour bar in sport. Today it demands that removal of the colour bar from every department of the South African society.

White opposition to the Afrikaner Nationalist government flared up for the last time in 1951. Veterans of the Second World War came together in great numbers to defend the coloured vote. The movement came to be called the Torch Commando, and was led by one of the most distinguished pilots of the war, Group Captain 'Sailor' Malan. Tremendous meetings were held in Johannesburg, Cape Town, Pretoria, Pietermaritzburg, Durban. Within a few months the membership of the commando had climbed to one hundred thousand, and a few months after that it reached two hundred thousand. I joined it myself, though I was no military figure. There was a feeling of hope in the air.

At the same time something else was happening. There were other people in Johannesburg, Cape Town, Pretoria, Pietermaritzburg, Durban who were asking themselves: 'Isn't it time we nailed some kind of colours to our mast? Isn't it time to found a new political party that would be open to any person whatsoever? Isn't it time to reject altogether any kind of racial discrimination, any kind of racial legislation?'

Doom was approaching me, and the end of the glorious freedom of the writer's life.

Chapter 8

I must not give the impression that I thought we could live at Anerley–Southport for ever, or that I thought I would ever enjoy the 'glorious freedom of the writer's life'. I had once entertained the foolish notion that I would never wear a formal suit of clothes again. That would have meant a break, not with a manner of dressing but with a whole manner of life. It would have meant, in fact, a turning away from duty. It was indeed a foolish notion.

There were two things that made such a break impossible. One was my religion. The other was the strange and beautiful country into which I had been born. At some time in 1952 Trevor Huddleston asked me to speak at St. Benedict's House, the Priory, Rosettenville. All the addresses were published in what were known as St. Benedict's Booklets and mine was called 'Salute to My Greatgrandchildren'.

I read 'Salute' this morning before I began to write. All this happened thirty-five years ago, before my own two sons were married but now I have grandchildren who are in their twenties. It is possible that I may have greatgrandchildren after all.

My greatgrandchildren will live their lives in the 21st Century and I send them a salute from the middle of the 20th. Their future, the future of our country, and of the great continent of Africa, are always in my thoughts. For my own future I am not much concerned; but I am concerned for the future of my children, and yours and their children's children, and for the future of all children, whosoever they may be. To my own children's children I send this salute.

Who knows what kind of country they will be living in? Will they be living peacefully in the Union of South Africa? Or in some larger Union, even the United States of Africa? Or will they have returned from fear or grim necessity, to that other continent from which their forefathers came? Or will they be dead, having lost their lives in some violence or terror?

As I read these words now I am moved by them, even though I myself wrote them. Although it all happened thirty-two years ago, I remember the occasion as though it were yesterday.

How are you all? I wish I could come there for a minute. I would stand for one minute in your streets, and would read there the history of fifty years. I would look into your faces, and I would know if you were still looking for a magic, and not for the truth.

What did I mean when I said I would know whether they were still looking for a magic? I meant a magic solution, where you don't have to give anything, you don't have to yield anything, you don't have to suffer anything, yet everyone would be happy. It was the magic of Racial Separation. In the year 1952 when I gave the 'Salute', that was the magic that was being offered to the white people of South Africa.

My dear children,
    Have you ever read Leo Marquard's *Peoples and Policies of South Africa*? That will tell you the truth about our age, without exaggeration or cleverness. I was proud of the book and the writer.
    Tell me, did they listen to his calm quiet voice? Did they listen when he told them that if you start building a fortress you will have to guard it with your life, all your life? That you will have to make fortress-love, eat fortress-food, have fortress-pleasure and worship a fortress-God?
    A lost Afrikaner they called him. Then may they all be lost, so that we may all be saved.
    Your loving Greatgrandfather.

In 1952 the Afrikaners were undoubtedly building for themselves a fortress. Today in 1987 some of them are beginning to understand what it means to live a fortress-life. It means that you are, day in, day out, year in, year out, on guard. It means that if you don't go out in peace, others will come in, in war. One thing is certain, the day of the fortress is done.

Tell me, was there violence? Or do you live in the midst of violence? Or do you yet fear a violence to come? Do you oppress? Or are you oppressed? Or has oppression gone? I wish I could come there for a moment. I wish I could stand for a minute in your streets. Then I should know the answer for myself. But my wish and hope and prayer for you is the same as it was, that you live in a land without fear.

'Salute' tells one thing clearly. It tells what thoughts were then occupying my mind and the minds of many of my friends.

My dearest Greatgrandchildren,

Tell me, is there any Liberal Party there? Or is it in hiding? Or is the need for it perhaps gone, and does the wolf dwell with the lamb, and the leopard lie down with the kid, and the child put its hand on the cockatrice's den? I find it hard to write anything to you but questions. That is because I do not know in what kind of world you live. I do not know whether you are living in the last days of our present society, or whether you are living in a new society, or whether you are living in a time of travail.

Your loving Greatgrandfather.

Have you ever seen the Victoria Falls? Then you have seen one of the great wonders of our earth. I wrote to my greatgrandchildren about them.

One holiday we all went to the Victoria Falls and we sailed on the great river in a boat. There are islands there and quiet waters, and trees hang down into them, and coloured birds are calling and crying in the peace. Then the great river quickens and shudders, and goes streaming away before you, green and foaming, and the boat quickens and shudders too, for you are drawing near to the great fall of smoke and thunder. And the captain turns the boat, so that it draws back from the brink, and you return to the islands and the safety and the peace.

You know my prayer for you, that you live in a land of peace. I pray that the captain turned.

Your loving Greatgrandfather.

I close this part of my story with the closing line of 'Salute'.

And you know my wish for you, and for all people's children's children, that they may live in a land without fear, where there is an assurance for all of 'fair and equal justice, of impartial administration, and reasonable opportunities for material and spiritual progress'.

Your loving Greatgrandfather.

The words quoted in that last 'Salute' came from the published policy statement of the United Party, which had been the party of J.H. Hofmeyr. They are quoted with irony. Like all statements of intent, they must not be interpreted too freely. Indeed it is safer not to interpret them at all. Hofmeyr was accused of having caused his party's defeat just because he interpreted its policy statement too freely! Today his interpretations of 1948 would be regarded as ultra-conservative.

There is a second and greater irony. Though those words did not appear in the policy statement of Dr. Malan's National Party, the party would have declared that it stood for the same things. But it would have declared that it had an allegiance even deeper, and that was to the policy of separate development, for it was only through separate development that these ideals would ever be realised. Separate development was the fortress in which the Afrikaner was going to live. No one would be able to get in, and no one would be able to get out.

As for myself, I was beginning to realise that, deep though my love of literature was and deep as was my love of writing, my love of country was unfortunately greater.

> *The time is out of joint; O cursed spite*
> *That ever I was born to set it right.*

There were quite a number of us who thought that the time was out of joint, but I do not think that we thought we were born to set it right, except one perhaps, of whom I shall write later. We certainly thought we had some kind of duty to *attempt* to set it right. We were, on the whole, a moral set of creatures. We had decided that nothing could be expected from the United Party. It had a noble statement of intent, but it did not seem to do anything about it. So we – to put it quite bluntly – were going to do better. We came from every part of South Africa, even from the deep caves of the Orange Free State and the northern Transvaal. At least two of us came from Shangri La, in other words, Anerley–Southport. But these two decided to halt at a halfway-house before they rejoined the wicked world. Dorrie and I offered ourselves to Don McKenzie, to work for him for a year at the Toc H T.B. Settlement at a wage, each of us, of five pounds a month.

By this time, Don's reputation as a saint was well established. His charisma was undiminished and his smile could still melt the heart of a stone. He was liable to fits of impatience and bad temper, especially when he had to work with books, official books I mean, ledgers, records, correspondence. So Dorrie was a boon and a blessing, she being a very capable secretary and treasurer. This enabled Don to get out of the office and go round the settlement, tweaking the children's ears and smiling at the nurses. I place it on record that the Toc H T.B. Settlement was one of the happiest places in South Africa, especially for black children. Whenever Don appeared outside the office, the children would greet him with cries of 'Oo, la-la'. Such things don't happen every day in this country.

When Don was in his office wrestling with some great problem, it was dangerous to go near him. If you knocked, he would say in a voice of extreme resignation and with no trace of a smile on his face, 'Come in.' Mind you, if some wealthy benefactor had knocked, Don would have been up in a second and out of his chair with a smile and would have had another thousand pounds out of him or her in the twinkling of an eye.* He loved to make speeches, but he hated preparing them.

* This of course is a gross exaggeration.

He was genuinely filled with apprehension while he was preparing his speech, but when he delivered it, he would have his audience prostrate in the aisles, in prayers or laughter. He had nothing short of genius for making funny, sad, simple, sincere, heart-warming speeches. People found themselves reaching for their handkerchiefs and pocket-books. Over women he threw a spell, Jewish women, Hindu women, Muslim women, Christian women. Money poured into the settlement for new wards to commemorate this or that. Far from having financial problems, the settlement grew rich. Our builder was Denis Dold, a decent, efficient, unsentimental man. He taught me a new English phrase. When he encountered difficult building problems he would throw up his shoulders and say, 'This is the final end.'

Don derived a certain sardonic amusement from having a famous writer on his staff. He described my post as that of Compost Manager. Indeed I made a lot of compost; on the sixty acres of the settlement there were grass and leaves in great abundance. This compost was spread thickly over the estate and we grew vegetables, flowers, grass and trees. In this I enjoyed the help of Anne Evans, while Bill Evans carried out his work as full-time Toc H staffman for Natal. In addition to my post as Compost Manager, I was also manager of the workshop, where our men patients made sandals for a factory in nearby Pinetown. I had never made a sandal in my life, but an instructor came up from the factory and showed the men how to do it. After a few days they were very proficient and what is more, some of them became excellent instructors themselves. Therefore, there was no need for me to do anything but supervise, that is, when I was not composing on the compost heap. There was no need to inspire the men with a love of labour, for they received a percentage on each pair of sandals. One of our men became so adept that he could make a sandal in seven minutes – or was it seven seconds? – no, it must have been seven minutes, because otherwise he would have become a millionaire.

I must give an example of Don's sardonic turn of humour. The buildings of the settlement were on high flat ground which sloped away sharply to a narrow valley below. There we decided to build a dam so that we could have cheap water for our gardens. A hardy Afrikaner came to build the dam and in my capacity as Compost and Factory Manager, I visited him daily. One day Don wanted my help for something or other and not being able to find me up above, went down to the dam and asked our builder if he had seen Alan Paton. The builder looked blankly at Don and asked, 'Who is Alan Paton?' Don liked to tell this story in company and in part it was a dig at the builder and in part a dig at me.

I had an exciting experience at the dam. I visited it one day when it had filled, and there swimming and diving on the dam were a pair of Cape dabchicks, the smallest of the grebes. How had they got there? There was no other sheet of water within many miles of us. How had they discovered that there was a new sheet of water awaiting occupation? So far as I know, they are not in the habit of flying over the countryside looking for water. Do they smell water from afar off? I have to admit that I do not know. All I know is that I sat and watched them with a kind of rapture. Why should that be so? Throughout the ages, writers and philosphers have tried to explain the great attraction that birds exercise over human beings. As I sat there watching the dabchicks swimming and diving, I had my own explanation. I was under the spell of the Creation. I was in a way engaged in an act of worship, of the Maker of the galaxies and the Black Holes and the great blazing suns and of two little waterbirds on the new dam of the Toc H T.B. Settlement. What is more, he had made food for them too, for they were diving incessantly beneath the water. I thought of those words in the Book of Common Prayer: Holy, holy, holy, Lord God of hosts, heaven and earth are full of thy glory: Glory be to thee, O Lord most High. I picked myself up reluctantly and went back to the work of Compost Management.

It was in this year 1953 that *Too Late the Phalarope* was published. It never attained the fame of *Cry, the Beloved Country*, but it achieved something which its predecessor had not; it was chosen in the United States as the Book of the Month. I was told, confidentially of course, that this was partly – or perhaps wholly – because the Book of the Month Club wanted to make amends for having rejected *Cry, the Beloved Country* five years before. This may or may not be true, but the award is of inestimable value to a writer, especially one who is not securely established. It helped me to write several books which were important to me, but which were not money-spinners at all. Yet my main support throughout my writing life has always been and still is, *Cry, the Beloved Country*.

There was for me another important event in 1953. Some time in the previous year I had met a young Pietermaritzburg man with the name of Peter Brown, whose most important achievement to date had been to drive from Algiers to Kano across the Sahara Desert in 1947. His other claim to fame was that he could drink enormous quantities of beer, up to thirty and more pints in the course of a day. He was a young man of considerable means, but was now developing what is known as a 'social conscience' about things like justice, equality and the rule of law, a conscience which was to cost him dear. This conscience was outraged by the racial laws that were pouring out of parliament and was deeply troubled by the increasing racial alienation in South Africa.

It was in this same year 1952 that various groups in the country, and in particular the African National Congress and the South African Indian Congress, decided to launch a civil-disobedience campaign along Gandhian lines. Many Indian and coloured and African people offered to defy such laws and customs. One of the offences which they committed was to sit in railway waiting-rooms and other places reserved for 'whites only'. By the end of the year, more than eight thousand people had been arrested and charged for such offences and sentenced to short terms of imprisonment, for the law did not regard their crimes in a very serious light. By now the startling news was received that a white man, Patrick Duncan, son of a former Governor-General of the Union of South Africa, was to challenge the law by going into a place reserved for 'blacks only', namely the black municipal location administered by the town of Germiston, near Johannesburg. Patrick was hoping that amongst others, Manilal Gandhi, of the Phoenix Settlement near Durban, son of the great Mahatma, would go with him into the location. It is another proof of the complexity and incomprehensibility of our country that Manilal hesitated to join Patrick because the civil-disobedience campaign had come to be known as the 'Defiance Campaign' and Manilal didn't mind disobeying authority, but he didn't like the idea of defying it.

Julius Lewin, Professor of Law at the University of the Witwatersrand and highly regarded in African National Congress circles, invited Patrick and Manilal to lunch on the day of the disobedience or defiance. Now it so happened that Dorrie and I were in Johannesburg on this historic day, though for quite a different reason, and Julius asked us to lunch as well. It was my first meeting with Patrick, who had resigned from his post as a judicial commissioner with the British administration in Basutoland in order to join the Defiance Campaign. He was on crutches, having broken his leg in a collision with another car, an accident caused by his carelessness.

So I met one of the most extraordinary of human beings.

Out of his bluest of blue eyes shot flames that consumed any cruelty or cant within burning distance, and he had the ruddiest cheeks in the world, giving him the appearance of abounding health. He was a man of passionate beliefs, and had a veneration for Mahatma Gandhi. He believed with all his heart that *satyagraha*, the soul-force, the power of truth, was able to topple empires.*

I shall have more to tell of Patrick Duncan, for he was important in my life. He and I became more and more closely associated in the next eight years. My opinion of him oscillated between total admiration for his uprightness and courage, and total exasperation with the irration-

* From the novel *Ah, but Your Land Is Beautiful.*

ality and unpredictablity of his enthusiasms. He also knew that the time was out of joint, but he did not curse his fate that he was born to set it right. That is why he had been born and he did not rebel against it. Set afire by the flames that shot from those blue eyes, Manilal realised that it was foolish to distinguish between disobedience and defiance. He told Patrick that he would go with him into Germiston location.

When the lunch was over and Dorrie and I were alone together, she said to me, 'You would have liked to, too, wouldn't you?' I admitted it, but I was not ready yet.

It was thoughts like these that were troubling many minds, including Peter Brown's and mine, and a number of other people throughout South Africa were thinking it was time to stand up and be counted. Some of us did this reluctantly, for we too did not like the idea of defying the civil authority.

However, I felt that my immediate duty was to complete my year of Compost Management.

Chapter 9

On the afternoon of the Lewin lunch, Patrick Duncan and Manilal Gandhi met more than thirty other defiers outside the gate of the Germiston location. About one half of the defiers were Indians, about one third were Africans, and the remainder white. Patrick was asked to lead, which he did at a great pace on his crutches. They marched round and round the location, singing defiance songs, and followed by an excited crowd. After all, who had ever seen anything like this before?

Patrick called for a chair and stood on it, the picture of health and confidence, to say some words in English and Sotho.

Today South African people of all kinds have come among you. They have come with love for you and with peace. We have not come to make trouble. I ask you on the long road that lies ahead not to make trouble but to do what you have to do with love.

He then gave the cry of freedom 'Mayibuye! Afrika! Afrika! Afrika! Afrika!', which are Zulu words meaning 'Come back, Africa!' or 'May Africa return!' Then for good measure he said some words in Afrikaans, 'Julle vryheid kom! Julle vryheid kom deur die Kongres,' which means 'Your freedom is coming! Your freedom is coming through the Congress.'* So far no one had been arrested, and Bettie du Toit, a white trade-union worker, said to a policeman, 'Aren't you going to arrest us?' So they were all arrested, and taken off to the Germiston police station,

* The Congress was the African National Congress, the A.N.C.

where they were held for the statutory forty-eight hours before they were charged with several offences, one of them being that they had entered a location without a permit.

The government's response to Patrick Duncan and all other defiers was resolute and powerful. In the language Afrikaans such action is called *kragdadig*, and the quality of character required to perform such actions is called *kragdadigheid*.* It is a quality that the Afrikaner Nationalists like to show the world. But their opponents have given it a further meaning, and *kragdadigheid* has come also to mean the quality of being 'stupidly powerful'.

There can be no doubt that while in public the government declared the Defiance Campaign to be subversive, in private they found it humiliating. The campaigners were serious enough about their defiance, but they also took it as a joke. The penalties for entering the wrong waiting-room were light, and offenders, after spending a week in prison, would relax for a day or two and then go back to the waiting-room. So parliament passed the very *kragdadig* Criminal Law Amendment Act of 1953, and made it a very serious offence to break any law, however trivial, 'by way of protest'. For such an offence a person could now be sent to jail for three years, or could be fined three hundred pounds, or could be given ten lashes, or could be given any two of these punishments. The punishment for inciting a person to break a law by way of protest was even heavier. The inciter could be sent to jail for five years, or fined five hundred pounds, or given ten lashes, or any two of these. But the government, though *kragdadig*, was also humane, as indeed befits a Christian government, and it decided not to lash any person over fifty.

That was the end of the Defiance Campaign. A week in jail may be a joke, but three years is not. The organisers of the campaign called it off.

In April 1953 the government gave another, and very convincing, proof of its strength. In the general election it increased its strength from seventy-nine to ninety-four.† The United Party dropped from sixty-five to fifty-seven. There could be no doubt that Afrikaner Nationalism was going from strength to strength.

The Torch Commando, after its brave displays of strength and its tremendous rallies in big, largely English-speaking, cities, began to fade away. Why did this movement, so full of hope, come to nothing? There was one big reason: the Afrikaans universities and high schools

* *Krag* is 'power'. *Daad* is a 'deed' or 'action'. *-heid* is a suffix denoting quality, such as '-ness'.

† I should note that six of these seats were allotted by the government to South West Africa (Namibia), which was not part of the Union. Dr. Malan did this to increase his small majority. But the 1953 results showed that he need not have done it.

were no longer turning out United Party members, they were turning out Nationalists. Many Afrikaans-speaking United Party parents watched with sorrow the slow dying of the great conciliation tradition of Botha and Smuts. Their children weren't interested in conciliation, they were interested only in being Afrikaners. They certainly were not interested in the maintenance of the Cape coloured franchise.

There was another reason for the collapse of the Torch Commando. It also had the 'worm i' the bud'. It had come into being to protest against any interference with the Cape coloured vote. But the number of its coloured members was negligible. In the Free State, Transvaal, and Natal, it had no coloured members at all, on the specious grounds that in those three provinces they had no vote to lose. This must be regarded as the fatal weakness in all white opposition movements at that time. They could offer no real opposition to the colour bar, nor to the policies of apartheid and racial separation, because they were themselves infected. The Torch Commando virtually destroyed itself on Alamein Day, 1953, when it excluded coloured ex-servicemen from the celebrations.

Meanwhile other groups of people had been meeting in Cape Town, Johannesburg, Pietermaritzburg, Durban and other places, to consider how they could nail their colours to the mast, and what sort of colours they should be. The Cape Town liberal group grew from seven to one hundred members in a short time, and among these were a number of African and coloured people. Johannesburg had two liberal groups, one more conservative than the other. The Rev. Bill Evans, full-time staff man for Toc H Natal, and now living at the Tuberculosis Settlement, joined me in sending out invitations for a meeting at Botha's Hill of people who we felt would be interested in forming some kind of opposition movement. Bill's actions were regarded coldly by the board of management of the Tuberculosis Settlement, and by his employers, the Natal area of Toc H. My own actions were not less coldly received, but I was less vulnerable. I was a well-known writer, I held the highest position in Toc H Southern Africa, that of Honorary Commissioner, appointed directly from London, and I had been elected unopposed as President of the Convocation of the University of Natal. Things in Toc H were moving towards some kind of climax, and I shall tell this dismal tale later in this chapter.

Earlier in the year of 1953, the various liberal groups that had sprung up in the main centres of population came together to form the South African Liberal Association. It was decided to invite ex-Chief Justice N.J. de Wet to become our president, an invitation that he did not accept. Meanwhile four vice-presidents were elected, Margaret Ballinger, Edgar Brookes, Leo Marquard and myself. But on 16 April, the National Party scored its tremendous victory. Therefore on 9 May, the Liberal Association formed itself into the Liberal Party of South Africa, with Margaret Ballinger as president, Leo Marquard and myself as vice-presidents, and Oscar Wollheim and Leslie Rubin as chairman and vice-chairman respectively.

Our emergence as a political party was not universally well received. The strongest attacks came from J.G.N. Strauss, leader of the United Party, and Yusuf Dadoo, the leader of the Transvaal Indian Congress, who declared that we were 'half-baked'. The strong Congress movement, composed of the South African Indian Congress, the African National Congress, the South African Coloured Peoples Organisation, and the white Congress of Democrats, accused us of weakening the only true opposition in the country. In Durban Margaret Ballinger and I had a hot reception from the Natal Indian Congress, and two of their redoubtable speakers, J.N. Singh and I.C. Meer, accused us of 'dividing the people'. They, and others, were understandably angry that the white members of the new Liberal Party had not joined the white Congress of Democrats. The African National Congress was also displeased with us for recruiting African members.

Why had we not joined the Congress of Democrats, the C.O.D? The answer was very simple. Although the C.O.D. was not a communist organisation – legally it was now impossible to have any such organisation – it was the heir to the banned Communist Party of South Africa. Not all of its members were believing communists, but many had been members of the banned Communist Party. Between communists and liberals – even if they cooperated on certain well-defined projects – there is a fundamental incompatibility. I assume that this is in part a matter of temperament, but it is also a matter of belief, and no doubt the nature of one's beliefs is in some degree determined by one's temperament. However, there are some matters of belief in which the incompatibility is insoluble. A liberal cannot accept that the use of any means is justifiable if the end is good; a communist can. A liberal shrinks from the idea of a centrally controlled society, and a centrally controlled economy; a communist does not. The liberal belief in the separation of powers is not acceptable to communists. A liberal believes that a centrally controlled economy kills private initiative and drive, and leads to a drab and dreary existence. A liberal believes in the rule of law, the communist believes in the rule of the party. The communist believes that the party should control almost every human activity, including literature, music, art, religion – the list is endless. One has only to read that magnificent journal *Index on Censorship* to realise that this is so. I should say at once that if one reads *Index on Censorship* one learns that the yearning of governments to control private lives is not limited to the communist countries.

I was in the course of the next few years to speak on the same platform with members of the C.O.D. Almost invariably we kept our distances. However, I became very close to one of them, and this was extraordinary because he was the Big Chief of them all. He was an Afrikaner, and his name was Abram Louis (Bram) Fischer. At the time of his birth in 1908 his grandfather Abraham Fischer was the Prime Minister of the Orange River Colony, and his father later became Judge-President of the Orange Free State.* Bram was a brilliant student, and went to Oxford as a Rhodes Scholar from 1931 to 1934. Sometime after his return he took what was for an Afrikaner a most extraordinary step; he joined the Communist Party of South Africa. It is impossible to exaggerate the courage required for an Afrikaner to take such a step. But even more extraordinary was the fact that he visited the small country towns of the Transvaal and the Orange Free State to organise black workers and to recruit them for the Communist Party. His actions outraged the Afrikaner farmers of the *platteland*,† and the fact that his father and grandfather had been Afrikaner heroes made his actions still more outrageous.

After the Communist Party had been outlawed by parliament, the Congress of Democrats was established, and Bram, though not its titular head, was its most influential and respected member. In spite of his political views, he was greatly respected in his profession. When I write that I became 'close' to him, I mean that we had a deep affection for each other. When I praised him in my own circles, one of my liberal friends said to me, 'Paton, don't bluff yourself. When Bram comes to power, you'll be the first one to have your throat cut.' I didn't believe that, but I was ready to believe that if Bram came to power, an emissary would be sent to me with a one-way air-ticket, and with a message, 'Get out of here as fast as possible.'

What would Bram have done if he had come to power? He would of course have changed the whole structure of South African society. He would have broken the hearts and spirits of a million Afrikaners because he would have taken away from them their most precious possession, their land. He would, I think – although he was a white man – have enjoyed the trust and confidence of a very great many of his black fellow South Africans. But this is not the real question that I

* When the Republic of the Orange Free State was defeated in the Anglo–Boer War of 1899–1902, it became the Orange River Colony. When it entered the Union of South Africa in 1910, it again became the Orange Free State.

† *Platteland* means literally 'flat country'. But it means today the 'countryside', and in particular the 'Afrikaner countryside'. It can also have a derogatory meaning, namely 'backward countryside'.

am asking. I am really asking, what would he have done to those who opposed or hindered him? Would he have killed them? I must confess that I do not know the answer to this question. It is hard for me to imagine Bram ordering the deaths of thousands of people. In any case I do not need to answer the question; it is totally hypothetical. I shall write more about Bram later in this story. Meanwhile the new Liberal Party and the C.O.D. cooperated with each other in the most guarded manner; sometimes the mutual hostility was hardly concealed.

Don McKenzie held aloof from all political controversy. He would have had considerable sympathy for the views of Bill and myself, but in the first place he disliked strife, and in the second place he subordinated himself to the board of management in all financial and administrative matters. In its turn the board had the sense to realise that in Don they had a diamond, and if they lost it they would not easily find another. They did not mind the kind of human community that Don was creating, but they had little taste for the kind of human community that Bill Evans had in mind. To repeat a phrase, brotherhood is good, but it mustn't be carried too far.

In any event, these controversies had not yet surfaced. The settlement was going from strength to strength, new buildings were rising everywhere, the compost and the factory management were in excellent – no, let us say – good hands. The two Cape dabchicks were still swimming and diving on the dam. No one knew that a kind of bomb was to fall. Don, our confirmed bachelor, announced that he was going to get married.

Don was very coy about his intention. He clearly thought it was an odd thing, or he thought that others would think it an odd thing for a bachelor of fifty to decide to get married. His co-workers were delighted, but they realised that a man cannot get married on five pounds a month. And of course the board of management realised it too, and insisted that Don should get a salary commensurate with his responsibilities.

Don was going to marry Betty Nye, a girl, or rather a woman, that he had known for some ten years. She like Don had never married, like Don she was of very strong character, like Don she was idealistic and religious, unlike Don she had no charisma. She was quiet and unassertive, and Don was determined that she should not remain in the background. She was appointed housekeeper of the settlement, and he praised her, though not immoderately, whenever he spoke in public about the settlement. The confirmed bachelor made a splendid husband.

Betty was untouched and very innocent, and Don used to tell a naughty joke about her innocence. In Don's early days at the settlement, his inseparable companion was a nondescript dog called Tippy. He accompanied Don everywhere except to the Anglican chapel adjoining our grounds, because African worshippers have a decided aversion to dogs in church. He would also desert Don for days whenever there was any yearning female in the valley. He would come back from these expeditions emaciated and exhausted. Betty said to Don, 'It will be a good thing when we get married and have a home, because then Tippy won't have to go out any more.' Don thought that this was extremely funny, and when he told the story, which he would not have done in any large company, Betty would smile primly. Don wasn't a saint, but he certainly was a gentleman. He and Betty were married in July of 1953.

It was in the latter half of 1953 that relations between Bill Evans and Toc H Natal came to a head. The Natal chairman was Karl von Puttkamer, and he had been interned by the Smuts government during the Second World War. I would not say that he was a Nazi sympathiser, but he certainly was a white supremacist, and he therefore had more sympathy for the racial policies of the Afrikaner Nationalists than he had for the *laissez-faire* of the United Party. In any event it was the United Party government that had interned him. When he was released from internment he resumed his membership of Toc H, and became one of its leaders in Natal. He was extremely antagonistic to Bill's liberal views on race, and to Bill's connection with the new Liberal Party. Bill was also a member of the Durban International Club, which was open to anyone and therefore was anathema to the government. It was also considered a subversive institution and was closely watched by the security police.

Toc H Natal could not and would not have challenged Bill's views on race, and on the urgent need to bring diverse people together. The most famous Toc H prayer asks God to teach us to live together in love and joy and peace. Toc H used for some of its houses the rule of St. Benedict adapted by Prideaux House in Hackney: 'It is the unwritten rule of this House that "every person of whatever degree admitted to this house in the quality of a guest is to be treated as though he were Jesus Christ himself".'

It should be remembered that the movement called Toc H came into existence largely because of the strong feeling in Britain that the evils of class-consciousness should be 'mitigated'. It could be said that the battlefields of Flanders, where men of all classes had sacrificed and died together, had made them realise how far their love fell short. But the evils of race-consciousness, of racial prejudice and hatred, had hardly been encountered in Flanders and therefore they are not recognised in the early Toc H literature. It should also be remembered that Toc H Southern Africa, while it concerned itself with the service and needs of all, paid attention to only one racial problem, and that was the relationship between Afrikaans-speaking and English-speaking South Africans. It was not prepared in 1953 to consider the much more difficult problem of the relationship between white men and black men.

Bill had cherished the ideal, and this was reported in the daily press, of making the T.B. Settlement a 'truly human community'. This statement displeased the board of management, who had established the T.B. Settlement to do the noble work of fighting black tuberculosis. Toc H in fact suffered from exactly the same infection as the Torch Commando and the United Party. Their statements of intent came straight from Heaven, but they had to be carried out by earthly men. This is of course true of all human societies, but the dichotomy is nowhere to be seen more clearly than in my own country. Most white South Africans would no doubt like to be good, but they want to be safe too. That famous saying of Jesus is just too difficult.

It was at a Natal area of Toc H meeting in Pietermaritzburg in 1953 that Bill came under attack. The leadership could hardly criticise him for his views on race. Instead they took the legalistic view that by living at the settlement and by becoming so involved in its affairs, he was neglecting his duties as a full-time worker for Toc H Natal. The meeting was hostile in the extreme. There was not much sign of love and joy and peace. I was present in my capacity as Honorary Commissioner, and I supported Bill's interpretation of the duty of Toc H to the multiracial and troubled society of South Africa. I could have been speaking to a stone wall. If any members there agreed with me, they kept their peace. Toc H Natal was determined not to open its ranks to men of colour.

For Bill Evans the Pietermaritzburg meeting was a devastating experience. He decided that he must resign from Toc H and return to parish work. For Anne Evans it was also a painful experience. She had long before read the portents correctly, and had wanted her husband to resign earlier, especially as there was a parish in Durban whose members were mainly coloured people, who would have welcomed him with open, and indeed with loving arms. So Toc H Southern Africa lost one of the most loyal and most visionary servants that it had ever had, and indeed would ever have.

I tell this dismal tale so that those who read this book may understand better what our country is like, and what kind of society we live in. It will not surprise my readers perhaps to learn that Toc H Southern Africa steadily refused for many years to come to admit black members. It will not surprise them to learn that there was one powerful argument against such admission, and that was that 'the time was not yet ripe'. It might not surprise them either that some members of Toc H Southern Africa wanted to be just to all, and therefore suggested that there should be a separate black Toc H. In fact they wanted Toc H to espouse the cause of separate development.

Bill and Anne Evans left the settlement at the end of October 1953. Dorrie and I decided to finish our year of service, and we left at the end of December. It was quite clear that Toc H and the Liberal Party weren't going to mix.

Chapter 10

I have already written of the two tremendous changes in my life brought about in the year of 1948 by the publication of *Cry, the Beloved Country* and by the coming to power of the Afrikaner Nationalist Party. Now came a third change, a consequence of the first two. From the day that I became one of the leaders of the Liberal Party, I forsook the private life. Wherever I went, to Durban or Cape Town or Johannesburg, the security police were waiting for me. They would stand, usually two of them, at the entrance door to the airport building. We did not speak, but each knew who the other was. They would follow the car in which I was travelling, and would escort me to the house or office to which I was going. When I reached my destination, they would either leave or park ostentatiously in the street outside.

They became part of my life for fifteen years. I pretended not to mind, but in fact I did not like it at all. In those fifteen years they undoubtedly became more efficient, more tough, more hostile. When a niece of mine died in Pietermaritzburg, they attended the funeral. They did not join the mourners, but stood with their backs to their cars, and stared at us with hard implacable faces. Their presence did not please my niece's family, who were formal and conservative. They were not accustomed to being stared at by security policemen, especially on such a private occasion, and they did not like it. They did not reproach me, but I felt I should not have gone.

How did the security police know that I would be at my niece's funeral? They had two methods of getting such information, by tapping telephones and opening letters. To use these methods they must have had the authorisation of the Minister of Posts and Tele-graphs. But of course this was denied by the Minister, and of course the security police denied that they would ever use such methods. Such allegations were lies that were being circulated by 'enemies of the people'.

About this time there was an incident that proved incontrovertibly that these suspicions were well founded. The Transvaal office of the Liberal Party had written a letter to the office of the party in Cape Town, and the Cape Town office was mystified to receive a letter written by the National Union of South African Students (NUSAS) to a student organistion in Prague. Equally mystified were the students in Prague who received a letter from the party office in the Transvaal, on a topic of which they had no knowledge whatsoever. The people in the Transvaal office then wrote another letter to the Cape Town office, which was thoroughly examined by fingerprint experts before it was posted. When the letter was delivered in Cape Town, it was examined again, and a new set of fingerprints was found on the letter inside. Margaret Ballinger, with great satisfaction no doubt, related these incidents to the House of Assembly. Peter Brown in his account wrote as follows, ' . . . the Nationalists were flabbergasted, not at what had happened but at the way they had been caught out.' However, all turned out well for them, for on 22 March it was reported by C. R. Swart, the Minister of Justice, that a police inquiry had found that there was 'no organised mail tampering'. But members of the Liberal Party, probably suspicious by nature, decided to be more careful in their use of the telephone and the mail.

In those days, of the 'fifties, 'sixties, and 'seventies, it would have been almost impossible to get any members of the security police reprimanded or punished for a misdemeanour. Any accusations would be met either with bland denials, or with official statements that it was 'not in the public interest' to discuss them. The arrogance of the Nationalist Party government was absolute. It was a classical example of the end that justifies the means, and the end, though ostensibly the security of the State, was in fact the security of the Nationalist Party.

Also at this time, unknown people would telephone me, usually after midnight, with threats that I would pay heavily if I continued to be a member of the Liberal Party. In the end I developed the following stratagem. I would say to the unknown caller, in a voice which purported to be that of an answering machine: 'I must inform you that this telephone is monitored by the security police, and that this conversation is being recorded.' In most cases the caller faded away immediately, and where he did not (it was always a man), then I knew that the caller knew that I was talking nonsense.

I did not enjoy the implacable staring of the security police. At first I tried to return it, but I soon gave that up, because I did not enjoy staring implacably at anybody. I have no doubt that it became more and more an instrument of intimidation, and I have no doubt that it was a technique in which security men were trained. It was a technique that was regularly used on public occasions, such as my niece's funeral, or at political meetings, but I have also encountered it in a court of law. I do not think all of the police were trained in it; I should think it was confined to the lower ranks, but all of them, from the lowest to the highest, were intimidators. That is their job, to intimidate those whom they can, and to know everything about those whom they can't. I must record that in my experience they were never able to intimidate anyone who was worthwhile intimidating, but that does not mean they were not to be feared.

The intimidators have two faces. The one is hostile and implacable, the other is mild and urbane. I have seen the urbanity change to hostility in an instant of time, and shall later tell a story of it. It is usually the older and more senior intimidators who assume the urbane manner; such behaviour is not required by the lower ranks, though I have seen it on occasions, just as I have encountered naked hostility from senior policemen. It is well known that during interrogations there is often one hostile questioner and one who is sympathetic and friendly, but their aims are identical.

What makes a man take on such a job? One must assume that most security policemen feel they are performing an important service to their country, though in South Africa this love of country is very often a love of the Afrikaner *volk*, and therefore often a determination to preserve white supremacy; the great majority of white security policemen are Afrikaners.

Another important motive in deciding a man to join the security police is the love of exercising authority, which in many cases has a strong sadistic element. The fact that the work of these police is shrouded in secrecy, and the fact that over the next fifteen years of my life the authority to detain was to be delegated to more and more policemen, and the fact that this detention itself became more and more secret, meant that the most sadistic policemen were able to extract, or attempt to extract, information by methods totally illegal, in other words by torture. This torture included not only direct physical assault and the infliction of pain, but also deprivation of sleep, starvation, long hours of standing, the use of bright lights, and of course mental torture as well, probing into the past lives of detainees and telling them stories of the unfaithfulness of wives and girl friends. These various methods of torture were practised with the active or passive connivance of senior policemen. There can be little doubt that the desire to obtain information was not the sole motive for torture. There was often another motive, the delight of torturing.

Why does a black man join the security police? It is almost impossible to believe that he thinks he is serving his country. The usual and cynical answer to this question is that he does it for the money, but that does not seem a wholly satisfactory explanation. Another possible motive is that he too delights in intimidation and torture. He condemns himself to an unnatural life. In the black township where he lives he will be feared and hated, and sometimes he will be killed. A black security man once followed me into the black village of Roosboom, where I had gone to see a black fellow member of the Liberal Party, Elliot Mngadi. I said to the security man, 'How can you do a dirty job like this?' Then I did something of which I was always thereafter to feel ashamed: I spat on the ground between us. He looked at me with what I can only describe as hatred. If I had been black I would certainly have paid for my insolence, but I was white and therefore relatively immune. This incident could have turned out very badly for me and the Liberal Party. There were black schoolchildren passing at the time, and the security man would have found it quite easy to get some of them to testify that I had spat at him. If a court of law had found me guilty of having done so, it would have done me and the party no good at all. Luckily nothing came of it all, but whenever I remember the incident I am ashamed. A very nasty question could have been asked about this incident. I could have been asked: 'Would you have behaved like that to a white security policeman?'

I shall have to write again about the security police. Perhaps one day a novel will be written about them, about the way they were trained, about the motives that drove them, about the cruelties that some of them committed, about the bodies and wills and hearts that they broke. If there is a sin against the Holy Spirit, torture of mind and body must come very near to it. Let me repeat at once that my sufferings at the hands of the security police were negligible: inconvenience and embarrassment, yes, but nothing more. There were two reasons for this – one was that I was white, the other was that I had written *Cry, the Beloved Country*. If I had been white and had not written a book, my situation would not have been so good. If I had been black and had written *Cry, the Beloved Country* my situation would have been indescribable.

Must a country have a security police force? If I were Prime Minister, would I have such a force? I suppose the answer must be Yes; but I would also have a Minister of Justice whose duty it would be to make sure that his security police did not use methods forbidden by the laws of the country. The Minister of Justice would appoint a high personage, such as a judge of the Supreme Court, whose responsibility would be the welfare of all men and women in custody for security offences.

In the early years of the Liberal Party there were many instances of intimidation, but no known cases of torture. These were yet to come, and became more and more common when B. J. Vorster became Minister of Justice. Vorster's biographer, John D'Oliveira, was later to write of him, '. . . if his policemen had to err, then he would prefer them to err in the direction of excessive zeal in protecting the interests of the State.' What else can 'excessive zeal' imply in this context but the use of violence? From its very beginnings the Liberal Party protested vigorously against the intimidatory measures adopted by the police, but our protests achieved nothing. We were 'enemies of South Africa', and why should anyone of consequence listen to us? All our meetings were attended by the security police, sometimes by as many as eight of them. Our speakers would often refer to their presence, and express the hope that they might become converts to the liberal cause. Such sallies would be received with laughter and cheers by the audience, but there was nothing really to laugh or cheer about. The presence of the police was proof of the resolve of the government to silence all opposition to the Great Plan for the new South Africa, where all would be happy, all would achieve their God-given destiny and all would realise their God-given identity, in accordance with the doctrines of apartheid, the supreme dogma of which was that different racial groups living in one country could only live happily together when they were separated from one another in every way possible.

The members of the Liberal Party were 'enemies of the people' in the eyes of others besides those of the government. Many of our old friends dropped away, or to put it more poetically 'drew their skirts aside'. We were too extreme, we were too radical, we were a hundred (or fewer or more) years before our time. In our new parish of St. Agnes, Kloof, Dorrie and I were neither coldly nor warmly received. In 1954 the Church of the Province of South Africa, that is the Anglican Church, was far from ready to accept the view that people of one racial group could fully cooperate with people of other groups, and especially not in politics. I must honestly and reluctantly record that I experienced the joy of fully non-racial fellowship in the Liberal Party of South Africa and not in any church association, with some exceptions, one of which I shall relate in the next paragraph but one.

I must also report now, rather than later, that the situation in the churches has changed for the better since 1954, but it is still far from what it was in the Liberal Party, although because of its very nature the party subscribed to no religious belief. This is partly because the white

Christians of South Africa are, in general, slow to change. It is partly because the laws and practices of apartheid made association difficult to achieve. This is especially true of the Group Areas Act of 1950, and the Urban Areas Act many times amended, which by the establishment of separate residential areas make association *physically* difficult. I must also record that a great measure of association has been achieved since 1954 in the upper echelons of the churches, that is, in synods, assemblies, conferences, and other special gatherings. One must also record that the least progress has been made in the Dutch Reformed churches. One of the three Reformed churches, the Nederduitse Gereformeerde Kerk, founded African, coloured, and Indian 'daughter churches', later called 'sister churches', which today repudiate the doctrines of apartheid, not only in church life but in every other sphere as well. The sister churches have not yet repudiated the church that gave them birth, but they have gone very near to doing so.

The church association which gave me on certain occasions the same sense of harmony and common purpose as did the Liberal Party was the parish of Hillcrest, which in 1978 was formed out of the white congregation of Hillcrest and the black congregations of the Church of the Holy Spirit, Nyuswa, Emolweni and Embo. The new parish has had to face all the difficulties which issue from the fact that white and black worshippers have to live in separate areas, and that few black worshippers own motor cars. But some three or four times a year a great combined service is held, as for example at the annual confirmation, at either the chapel at Hillcrest or the Church of the Holy Spirit. These occasions are joyful in the extreme. Both Zulu and English are used in prayers and hymns, and the lesson in Zulu is usually read by a white parishioner, and the lesson in English by a black one. Black Christians are less inhibited in worship than white ones. They sing and chant and dance at unexpected times and in unexpected places, and their gaiety is infectious. Many white members of the Hillcrest parish find these services inspiring and liberating; such white people are – on these occasions at least – liberated from the racial fears that affect them much more than they do black people. Whether any racial cataclysm awaits us in the future, not one of us knows. But if there is a sign of hope, it is that there are so many black Christians in our country. White Christians should go down on their knees every day, and give thanks that this is so.

The early days of the Liberal Party were both joyful and grim. They were joyful because we had taken a stand for what we thought was right and just, and because we were doing it in such a congenial company. They were grim because of the uneasiness, fear and enmity that we aroused in so many people, including some with whom we had been associated for most of our lives, on terms of friendliness, even intimacy. I myself was conscious of the grimness, and of the tension within myself. It affected my looks, which I admit had always been a bit grim, but which now grew grimmer, especially round the lips and mouth. One of my closest friends in Toc H was Sid Butland, optician and jeweller of Pietermaritzburg. He disapproved strongly of what I had done, for exactly what reasons I did not know, but I would guess that he too thought that I had become too extreme, and that I was too many years before my time. But he had another serious criticism. He met me one day in Church Street, Pietermaritzburg, and said to me, 'What's the matter with you? You've lost the joy of life. Worst of all, you've lost your sense of humour.' It was a blow beneath the heart. You can tell a friend that he's not looking well, that he's smoking or drinking too much, that it is time he had his hair cut, but you must not tell him that he has lost his sense of humour. There was only one thing to do, and that was to go home and write a poem about it. Here it is.*

My friends are angry with me
Because I have lost
My sense of humour.

They remind me of occasions
When I have had the room rolling
With my wit.

They weep with despair
Over my sorrowful book
And sombre verses.

Well I too have pondered
This sad matter
With regret.

The truth is I have struggled
To get my humour
Into its harness.

But it bucks like a beast
And rears and kicks and will not get
Between the shafts.

I have a suspicion
It does not like the strange carriage
I am driving.

I feel like saying to it,
I do not like it either.
Obey, like myself.

* From *Knocking on the Door*.

Sid Butland never saw this poem, for it was not published till after his death. Nor did he ever know that he had inspired a poem. And the fact that he inspired it is in itself interesting, for he was not himself known for his jolliness, and his wit was strongly sardonic. He was a good man, held in great esteem by his fellow members of Toc H, but he thought I was before my time.

However, I decided to have a rest from the strange carriage that I was driving. I received a letter from *Collier's Magazine* of New York, asking me to come to the United States to travel from coast to coast and back again, and to write for the magazine a report to be called 'The Negro in America Today'. I accepted the invitation with eagerness. I did not know that I was to be in the United States at the time of one of the most decisive events in its modern history.

Chapter 11

It was in 1946 that I had bought in New York a railway ticket that cost $120. It was several feet long, and it would take me to Atlanta, New Orleans, the Grand Canyon, Los Angeles and San Francisco, Denver, Omaha, Chicago, Toronto, Ottawa, and back to New York, where Charles Scribner's Sons would accept my novel *Cry, the Beloved Country*. My long journey was made without luxuries, except that the long-distance trains of 1946 were luxurious in themselves.

My *Collier's Magazine* journey of 1954 covered much of the same ground, except for Canada. My employers were very generous and I wanted for nothing. My travelling companion was Dan Weiner, an up-and-coming young photographer, whose promising life was brought to a sudden end in an air crash over Tennessee in 1957. He was sturdy and thick-set, and possessed of an abundance of energy. Dan was a political radical, but of a typically American kind; he would say the most outrageous things about his country, but he would have been willing to die for it. Before we set out on our marathon journey, he took me to meet his wife Sandra and their daughter Dore, and his father who had emigrated from Latvia to the United States in the early part of this century. Dan soon discovered that I was an admirer of the United States and its constitution and he was at pains (how seriously it would have been hard to assess) to convince me that American practice and American profession were poles apart. He once did this in the presence of his father, who rose to his feet and with gentle anger pointed to the framed copy of the Bill of Rights that hung upon the wall. 'That's why I came to America,' he said, 'and I found it all true. Don't you ever speak like that again in my house.' Dan had the grace to look ashamed.

Dan was a great idealist, especially in matters of race. Therefore he could not have asked for a more congenial assignment than to accompany me around America to prepare an article to be called 'The Negro in America Today'. In 1954 the black American was in polite language a 'Negro' or a 'Coloured' person. It was considerably later that the Negro became a black. 'Negro' and 'Coloured' were the words that I used in 1954, and are the words I shall sometimes have to use in quoted material, though they are now out of date. We left New York on 31 March and returned on 11 May. We left with the blessings of the National Association for the Advancement of Colored People, always known as N.A.A.C.P., and with innumerable introductions, to workers for the N.A.A.C.P. and the Urban League, to university presidents and teachers, to church leaders, newspaper editors, and to two state governors. I shall record only what seem to me the most memorable events of this journey.

Governor James Byrnes was born in 1879 in Charleston, South Carolina. He had little formal education but took up the study of law, and in 1903 was admitted to the Bar. He was then to enjoy a distinguished career. He was a member of Congress from 1911 to 1925, and a member of the Senate from 1931 to 1941. His great elevation came in 1941, when he was appointed by President Roosevelt to the Supreme Court of the United States. However, in 1942 the President called him away and made him Director of Economic Stabilisation; he was jokingly called the second president. In 1945 President Truman appointed him Secretary of State, and in 1951 he became the Governor of South Carolina. It was not because of the brilliance of his career that I went to see him, but because he was one of the most eminent opponents of racial integration, and the N.A.A.C.P. He resisted strongly and openly the drive of the N.A.A.C.P. and many civil-rights workers to overthrow segregation in the schools. He graciously gave me an interview, and did not attempt to conceal or soften his whole-hearted rejection of integration.

A hard-bitten and professional interviewer may be able to drive a state governor into a corner, where he will turn on his tormentor, much to the delight of those people who like that kind of thing. I was neither hard-bitten nor professional, and for twenty minutes Governor Byrnes drove me into a corner, telling me how well he got on with Jews, and how glad he was to see that the son of a Jewish friend of his had reached a high position in a military school in the South. This gave me my first opening, for I had come straight from Fort Bragg, where I had seen white soldiers saluting Lieutenant Scott, a black lieutenant, and had heard them addressing him as 'sir'. I had also talked with

Lieutenant Webb, a black Baptist chaplain, whose spiritual charges were mostly white Southerners who brought to him their troubles, a thing they had never done at home. He married them and baptised their children, and was invited to their homes. You couldn't pooh-pooh Fort Bragg; it was the home of the famous 82nd Airborne Division. The United States armed forces were ordered to give equal treatment to whites and blacks by President Truman in 1948, and Fort Bragg is in the neighbouring state of North Carolina, and not to be confused with Fort Bragg, California. I told him about Lieutenants Scott and Webb, and asked him what he thought. His answer was immediate and direct, the kind of answer one might have expected from a man who had been Secretary of State. It was not for him to question what the President had ordered to happen in the armed forces, but when soldiers and airmen went off the base, they were expected to obey the segregation laws. In the schools it was different; these were administered by the state and segregation was the law.

The Governor told me that segregation was a law of nature. Nature had her categories, and individuals in one were not found in the other. In the shoals of blackfish he had never encountered a . . . (here I lost the word, but I think it might have been a whiting). This talk of a 'conflict in the soul of the South' was nonsense. It was the man of mixed blood who was the unhappy one – who, because he belonged to no colour, fought unceasingly for the removal of all discrimination whatsoever. The N.A.A.C.P. was his instrument, and the governor gave as instances two of the outstanding members of the organisation, Walter White its director (who was to all appearances a white man with blue eyes), and Channing Tobias, one of its vice-presidents, a grave, impressive man of light complexion. How he knew they were unhappy, I do not know, and I did not think to inquire. I had met them both, and they both cherished one supreme purpose, and that was to root out statutory race discrimination in the United States. Neither of them was a fanatic.

I asked the governor about the crucial case that would be heard by the Supreme Court in Washington in May – Brown and others against the Board of Education of Topeka, Kansas, a suit which, if successful, could bring an end to school segregation – but it was clear that the governor would not die fighting at the barricades. After all he had once been a justice of the Supreme Court and one did not defy a decision of that august and revered body. It was time to bring the formal interview to an end, but he informed me, that he did not use the word 'nigger'; also that his secretary had a great admiration for me as a writer and I must meet her. We concluded by having an animated discussion about the wonders of Kruger Park, though I was not certain whether the governor had been there or not. We parted on the most amicable terms, and I told him he did not look his seventy-five years. I also realised again the strange power that the law, the constitution, and the Supreme Court exercised over the citizens of the United States.

Dan Weiner, who had behaved with great decorum during the interview, exploded as soon as we were out of sight and earshot. Did I realise now what America was really like? How could I sit still and listen to such obscenities? It was quite clear that Dan had not been mollified by the governor's friendly references to the Jews. I told him to cheer up. We were going to visit the great navy base and dockyard at Charleston, where segregation had been banished. And on the way we were going to see Mr. William Ragin, a member of the N.A.A.C.P., who had brought suit in 1951 protesting against the inferior accommodation at the school of his small son Glenn. Mr. Ragin was not asking for integration; he was basing his case on the famous Supreme Court decision of 1896 in the case of *Plessy* v *Ferguson*, where the court gave its blessing to segregation, but announced the doctrine of 'separate but equal'. Segregation was legal if the separate facilities were equal. Mr. Ragin was now claiming equal facilities at his son's school.

Mr. Ragin was a small, spare man who owned over one hundred acres and buildings on his farm in Clarendon County, free from all debt. He was also a man of great courage, as all the members of the N.A.A.C.P. in the Deep South had to be. He drew up a petition asking for equal school facilities, and took it to the parents of more than one thousand black children. He got twenty-five signatures, but even some of these dropped out 'when the steam got up'.

The first hearing was in Charleston in 1951, and over it was hung a black pall of white disapproval. Mr. Ragin lost his case, but an historic dissenting opinion was given by Judge J. Waties Waring, who said that if separate facilities were to be equal, the place to start was in the first grade of school. He went further and made the shocking statement that 'segregation is *per se* inequality'.

Judge Waring, born a Southerner, had taken his first momentous step in 1947, when he ruled that blacks could not be excluded from voting in the 'white' Democratic primaries. He and his wife Elizabeth were ostracised by the white people of Charleston, and *Collier's Magazine* of 29 April 1950, called him 'the lonesomest man in town'. But the blacks of the city were overwhelmed. For the first time the judge and his wife entertained black people in their home. This was for Waties and Elizabeth Waring the great divide of their lives. For the judge in particular it was a hard fight. He was nearly seventy years of age, but he had made up his mind to throw the last prejudice out of his heart and mind and soul.

Mr. Ragin did not accept his defeat in Charleston. He followed his case right up to Washington and there he won. As a result the education authority built 'a new piece on the school'. Mr. Ragin told me that his father taught him to have no hate for anybody, 'but he said I was an American and I had to stand up for my rights'.

A good word for Governor Byrnes. In 1954 he told the South Carolina Education Association that a sum of ninety-four million dollars would be spent on new school buildings in the coming years, and that meant that one hundred and six dollars would be spent for each white pupil and two hundred and seventy-one dollars for each black pupil. 'We are forced to do in a few years what our fathers and grandfathers should have done in the past seventy-five years,' said the governor.

I visited one of the black schools in Clarendon County that had not yet received a share of the governor's ninety-four million dollars. It was moving enough to see its forlorn state, its broken windows, its pathetic equipment, its sagging foundations. But more moving to me was to see the Stars and Stripes, the proud flag of the United States of America, and under it these words: 'I pledge allegiance to the Flag of the United States of America, and to the Republic for which it stands; one nation under God indivisible with liberty and justice for all.'

Strange people, the black people of the United States, who through such scorn and rejection have clung so fiercely to the ideal of America. Strange country, which, so careless of liberty and justice, yet raises a William Ragin to restore them to her, and gives to a small, spare man the heart to fight for justice, defeating him in place after place, so that he may have a victory in Washington.

My own country is also a country of great diversity, but there is no common loyalty that can bind us all together, unless it be the physical land itself. We have no constitution (except of course the bare legal instrument), and we have no Bill of Rights. We have a highly respected Supreme Court, it is true, but it has no powers to test the laws of parliament in terms of a constitution. In the United States the constitution is sovereign; in South Africa it is parliament that is sovereign. America is full of faults and inequalities, but she has the instrument to abate and remove them. The process is endless of course, but it always has been since the beginnings of human time. America has another advantage that we do not possess. All Americans speak – with different degrees of competency – the same language. We do not. We have two official languages, English and Afrikaans, but we have at least a dozen 'home languages'.

It was time to move on, this time to Charleston, where I hoped to visit the navy base and dockyard, which had also been ordered to integrate by President Truman.

Through the thoughtfulness of Waties and Elizabeth Waring, I was to be the guest of Dr. A. T. Cornwell and his wife Ruby in Charleston. He was a dentist, and because of his title of 'doctor' he was excluded from the Southern battle of blacks to be called Mr. and Mrs. His wife, however, waged it unceasingly, and would not buy in a shop which withheld her title, or where they would not allow black women to try on shoes or dresses. She was one of those who brought the preparations for the local repertory show of 'Porgy and Bess' to an untimely end, because she discovered that there was to be segregated seating. Yet she was of a gentle rather than an aggressive nature, a person of the same kind as William Ragin of Clarendon County.

As soon as I arrived, Mrs. Cornwell wanted to know what I would like to see or do. I said, visit the navy base and the shipyard. Accordingly we set out for the shipyard, her friend Mrs. Hoffman driving, I in the middle, and Mrs. Cornwell on the other side. Mrs. Cornwell later recorded in a letter, 'He was quite sensitive to the amount of attention we were receiving – more so than I was, I think.' Unfortunately I had no instrument available to measure our various sensitivities. I was fully aware that all three existed. All three of us had grown up in a colour-bar society, and all three of us were doing something we had not done before. We may well have been doing something that had not been done in Charleston before.

Mrs. Hoffman stopped her car some distance from the gates of the dockyard, which were guarded by a young white Marine. Why did we stop? We stopped in order to discuss the right procedures to adopt. Cars were streaming in and out of the dockyard, but ours was the only one in which was said, 'That's the part I don't like, talking to the police. Mr. Paton, you had better talk to the police.' So I told the young white Marine that I was from South Africa and wanted to visit the shipyard with my friends. If he lifted an eyebrow, it was not discernible. He said he would communicate with the police.

So we sat waiting in the car, but inside the gates. I had steeled myself to accept a rebuff, but my two friends were anxious that there should be no rebuffs, and anxious – though they did not tell me so – lest their country might disappoint or hurt them and me. But their country did neither. It sent out a policeman, who happened to be white, and he sat in front with Mrs. Hoffman; Mrs. Cornwell and I sat behind. But of the problems of integration in the shipyard he knew nothing. I told him about my assignment with *Collier's Magazine*, and asked if we could see the public-information officer. He took us to another telephone, and soon I was talking to Lieutenant-Commander

Marvin F. Studebaker, who said he would show us around himself.

Mrs. Cornwell and her friend suggested that they would stay in the car, so that I could have the tour to myself. I told the commander this, and that my two friends were black ladies. He would have none of it. He went over to the car, shook hands and introduced himself, put us all in his own vehicle, and took us around the shipyard. He told us the story of the cafeteria, which was ordered to be desegregated and lost most of its white patrons, who then went to the desegregated snack bars, and took their food away. They did not mind buying food together, but they objected to eating it together.

There were thousands of workers in the dockyard, both white and black, working together on equal terms. Our visit aroused lively interest amongst the workers, who showed surprise and even amusement. But we were safe under the wings of the commander, who – to change the metaphor – bestrode this world like a Colossus. We parted from him with gratitude and affection. As we drove away, my South African eyes could hardly miss another sight – a black Marine was now in charge of the gates.

On to Atlanta, the city of *Gone with the Wind*, to stay with Benjamin Elijah Mays, present of Morehouse College, and his wife Sadie, the best cook in the American South. Bennie I knew well, having spent two sessions with him in Geneva under the chairmanship of Dean Liston Pope, head of the Yale Divinity School, where three of us served on a World Council of Churches committee that was preparing an agenda on 'Church and Race' for the 1955 meeting of the Council at Evanston, Illinois. While I was in Atlanta I was going to see yet another state governor, Herman Talmadge of Georgia. He had never become a judge of the United States Supreme Court, nor a Secretary of State, but he too was forceful and self-assured. Before I went to see him at the Capitol, I stood and contemplated the Georgia seal and its proud motto, 'Wisdom, Justice and Moderation'. I could not help thinking of my own country of South Africa, which also has a splendid coat of arms, and a splendid motto *'Eendragt Maakt Magt'*, 'Unity Makes Strength'.

Governor Talmadge was not a man for conventionality. He wore no jacket, and wore a pair of galluses, or braces. He had just had a tooth out, and during our interview spurted out jets of blood with expert aim into a spittoon. He had a loud voice and determined manner. He told me that desegregation would lead to war between the states. Georgia would make any sacrifice to resist it, even to the extent of giving up its public schools. She would have private and segregated schools where parents could choose the kind of school they wanted. He stressed that this freedom of choice would be exercised by black as well as white.

I asked him if the life of segregation was not drawing to a close. 'No, sir,' he said, 'not in the south.'

Governor Talmadge offered no intellectual defence of segregation. He did not talk to me about the black fish and the white fish. Segregation was the Southern way of life, and there never would be any other – not while he was alive.

While I was in Atlanta the governor flew to New York, and one of his fellow passengers was Dr. Rufus Clement, the black president of Atlanta University. The two men knew each other, and had actually once sat on the same platform, but the governor did not greet the university president on either of these occasions. Dr. Clement was therefore not a little surprised to see the governor that afternoon on television, telling the nation that the South was making its own way in race relations, and that Atlanta had even elected a black, Dr. Rufus Clement, to the city Board of Education.

While staying with Bennie and Sadie Mays at Morehouse, I thought I would go on Sunday to church, and I discussed with him whether I should go alone, or whether we should go together. I may say that Bennie had a quality of fearlessness. I am sure that he was brave too, but he had this additional quality, which is legendarily attributed to such persons as Julius Caesar, Horatio Nelson, and our own South African General Smuts. Yet he considered very carefully the question whether he and I should go to an Episcopalian church together, such churches in Atlanta being exclusively 'white'.

'I don't want an incident,' he said. 'One of my students went to a white church to see what would happen, and sat down near the middle of the church. Soon after, he was asked to go to the gallery or to leave, but he declined to do either. Another man then approached him, showed a police badge, and repeated the suggestion. Because it was a policeman, the young man followed him but would not stay in the church. As he walked away the policeman said, "Why did you do such a thing?" "I'm a Christian," said the boy, "and I wanted to see if I could worship in a white Christian church." "Will you come and sit in front with me?" asked the policeman. So they returned and sat together in the front part of the church. After the service several people shook hands with the young man, and expressed their pleasure at having seen him there. So ended happily this strange experiment. As far as I know, it led to nothing further.'

Bennie decided that he would go to church with me, not so that we could demonstrate, but because I was his guest and he did not want to let me go alone, just for the sake of avoiding any appearance of a demonstration. We set out for All Saints' Episcopal Church, Atlanta, white. Outside the door he had a last word with me. If I'm asked to move, what do we do, move or leave? Leave, I said.

It was a wonderful service. It was Palm Sunday, and the church was full and the congregation reverent. The rector spoke of Abraham Lincoln as one who had saved a nation, though himself he could not save. The choir sang, 'Were you there when they crucified my Lord?'

Outside, people came up to us and said they were glad to have seen us at their church. Some of them knew that the black man was Dr. Benjamin Mays, president of Morehouse College. Then he introduced me, and still others came up. In the end we held a kind of court in the street. I have not yet mentioned that Bennie Mays was one of the few black Americans living in 1954 whose father and mother had been born into slavery, his father in 1856 and his mother in 1862. His mother never learned to read or write, but the slave-master's son took his father 'down in the woods' and taught him. In those days it was against the law to teach a slave to read and write. Bennie's home was not entirely happy. At times his father drank too much, and became quarrelsome and violent, often towards the mother. At the age of twelve the boy made a vow that he would never touch liquor. His mother was a deeply religious woman, and her influence over him was immense. It was she who held the home together, a miracle that I have often seen in the Valley of a Thousand Hills. It must be a miracle that is world-wide.

Bennie told me that I must not deduce too much from our visit to All Saints'. He was the only black there, he was making a special visit, he was known to a good many members of the congregation, and was accompanied by a white person. He could have added, but did not, that no one looked less like a demonstrator than he. He was a grave and handsome man, very black, with hair going white, devoid of all pretence or pretensions. I said goodbye to them with regret, tempered by the knowledge that I would see Bennie again later in the year, at the meeting of the World Council of Churches in Evanston, Illinois. Those who want to know more about him can read his splendid auto-biography *Born to Rebel* (Charles Scribner's Sons, New York, 1971).

Dan Weiner did not accompany me to Mississippi, I was met at the Greenville airport by a free-lance photographer with whom I was going to stay. I regret to say that I did not keep a record of his name, nor can I find any papers relating to my visit. Nor did *Collier's Magazine* publish anything about this part of my journey. Yet in a way it was the most fascinating part of it all.

The first question my host asked me was, 'Are you a man who likes to take a drink?' When I said, 'Yes,' he said, 'This is a prohibition state, and I'll show you what to do if you want to buy something to drink.' We then drove out of the town to a small building which stood, as we would say in South Africa, 'in the middle of the veld'. There was not a tree or a wall in sight. There was no need for an officer of the law to exercise any vigilance. There was no attempt to conceal anything. I do not remember whether we had to open the door, or whether it was already open, but there behind the counter was as splendid an array of bottles as any drinker could wish to see. My host bought what he wanted, and when we were outside the store again, he showed me a little hatch. 'This is a very religious community,' he said, 'and on Sundays the door is locked, so you must buy your liquor through the hatch.'

Liquor was sold also in the main street of Greenville, from any shop which displayed the sign 'Beverages'. But on no account must you carry a bottle around openly, because that would oblige an officer of the law to arrest you, and that would disturb the whole fragile convention on which the state of Mississippi lives and has its being. You must not enter or leave a beverage shop without a container.

There is another most fascinating aspect of the convention. The state does not impose any tax on liquor, because there just is no liquor sold. But the federal authorities think they know better, and they impose a tax on liquor, and require a merchant to keep accounts of his transactions. Federal inspectors visit these small buildings 'in the middle of the veld' and these beverage shops, but their visits are not recognised by the state authorites, who know that there are no liquor sales to tax.

Mississippi is a very religious state. The Baptist influence is particularly strong. The white Mississippians are in theory very prohibition-minded, and there is a well-known joke which says of them that they will vote prohibition even if they have to stagger to the polls. I have only one more thing to add to this fascinating story. During the whole time I was in Greenville, I was conscious of the dominating presaence of Ol' Man River. It was a strange experience to stand in the street and to see, many feet above you, the masts and funnels of ships sailing to and from New Orleans and the Gulf of Mexico. You are standing of course at the base of the great levees that have been built over the years to contain the flood waters of the mighty river, and to prevent the devastation of the countryside. So at last I saw the river that I had known for the greater part of my life, for when I was a boy I had read the immortal stories of Tom Sawyer and Huckleberry Finn.

I close this chapter with some words that I have found in my diary of the journey for *Collier's Magazine*. I do not know who wrote them, but I think it may have been myself.

A message to those whites who fear the desegregated school in places like Beaufort, South Carolina, and yet who wish the black well. In twenty years time you will laugh at all your fears. Your son or your daughter will be privileged to be part of this great forward movement of the human race. They will be privileged to have been educated with the first generation of the emancipated. Perhaps the Negro whose voice trembles when he speaks of the sins of the white man in Africa is really berating the white man in America, but that he cannot allow himself, because he has based his whole case on the American creed. We must go further and conquer his hatred of the white man in Africa. And America's world task is not to free black men, but to free all men from the evils of race and colour morality.

These words, by whomever they were written, are prophetic. On 20 October 1977, my wife Anne and I were given a lunch at Auburn University, Alabama, after I had given an address to the university community. At lunch I sat next to a senior white Alabaman, in a company of white and black Americans.

I said to him, 'I was here in the South in 1946, and again in 1954, but it wasn't like this then. How have you coped with all these changes?'

He said to me, 'I've still got my prejudices, but thank God my children don't have them.'

Chapter 12

Dan Weiner met me in Los Angeles on 20 April. On our return journey from west to east we concerned ourselves with the housing and employment problems that confronted American blacks. I am going to write about them briefly, not because they are unimportant, but because they lack the drama of the Charleston dockyards and of Governor Herman Talmadge and of going to an all-white Episcopalian church with Bennie Mays. Why should this be? I think it is because the problems of housing and employment do not have the dramatic content of the other problems of race, of civil rights and of school desegration. Maybe the American South is just a more dramatic place.

In California I met Mr. George Valentine, realtor. He had broken an unwritten convenant by selling a piece of 'white' land to a black buyer. Though the neighbours tried to stop the deal, the black man built his house and moved in, and lived there, until the time of my visit, without incident.

Mr. Valentine had broken the unwritten law and he had to pay for it. He was not anxious to talk about it, for he distrusted all newspapers and reporters. He reckoned that they claimed to be doing a public service, but as long as they got a good story, they did not care who got hurt. He was very warm to me because I had written *Cry, the Beloved Country*, but distrustful because I was writing for a popular magazine, and had stumbled on a painful episode in his life. That is why I did not use his real name in my articles.

There was another reason why Mr. Valentine did not want to talk much. His son was in the business too, and had just married and started a family. He too had had to pay for his father's breaking of the unwritten law. Big deals that would have come his way had been taken elsewhere. Both men looked as though they had suffered. The older man found it painful that his son should suffer for his father's principles. The younger found it painful that his own friends could make him suffer because his father had done something that he thought was right, but he did not want his father to know how painful it was. Nothing could show more clearly than this story the struggle between ideal and practice in this area of American life, and it also gives its hints that the ideal is very powerful. If my friend Sid Butland had met George Valentine and his son, he might well have thought that they had lost their sense of humour.

I met another dealer in property, Mr. George Henry Gordon of Pasadena. Because he was a black, he had to be called not a realtor, but a realtist. He was cutting his hedge and the sweat was pouring down his face, but he asked me in. He held the simple view that an American should be able to live where he is able to buy.

'This unwritten convenant will break down,' he said. 'You can't go on doing what is wrong. Not long ago a white owner told me he was willing to sell his house to a Coloured buyer, but he asked that such prospective buyers should come and see the house after dark.'

'I wouldn't do it,' said Mr. Gordon. 'I told him I did my business in the light.'

He did not stand on the table to make this tremendous statement, he just went right on mopping the sweat from his brow. I left him thoughtfully, and rightly so, for I had met a man who thought that one could not go on doing wrong. He also thought that one should do one's business in the light. One does not encounter such ideas every day.

I must record that I caught my first whiff of McCarthyism in California. Senator Joseph McCarthy had been for some years the great smeller-out of reds and subversives in America. He exploited to the full the American fear of communism, and no doubt it was his own obsession. One of the reasons why he had become an important national figure was that presidents Truman and Eisenhower also suffered – though not in the same degree – from this obsession. President Eisenhower dismissed something like two thousand two hundred public servants as security risks. The Fund for the Republic, established by the Ford Foundation, examined four hundred of these cases, and found in the majority of cases that the charges were unsupportable. Many of these four hundred were reinstated.*

* If a reference is required it can be found in *The History of the United States Since 1865* by T. Harry Williams, Richard N. Current, Frank Friedel, (Alfred A. Knopf, New

Senator McCarthy's hunt was the cause of anxiety not only amongst a large number of Americans about themselves and their future but also amongst a large number about America itself. No one was exempt from this probing – public servants, trade unionists, ministers of religion, teachers at school and university, actors, singers, and writers. It was said that it was untrue that McCarthy never read books, but that it was perfectly true that he read them for only one reason, and that was to hunt down reds.

In 1947 eight film-script writers, one producer, and one director, refused to tell the UnAmerican Activities Committee whether they were or were not communists. All of them served short prison sentences, and had great difficulty in getting work in Hollywood for several years. They became known as the Hollywood Ten.

So powerful was the committee, and so powerful was what later came to be known as McCarthyism, that even the great moguls of the film industry came to attention. What some of them did, however, was to employ some of these writers secretly, not necessarily because they sympathised with their views but because they knew how to write better scripts than most of the others. While I was in Hollywood, I went to visit one of the Ten. Just how it was arranged or who arranged it I cannot remember, but I have no doubt that it was done – unofficially, and not for the record – by *Collier's Magazine*. Though the Hollywood Ten were accused of being unAmerican, nothing could have been more unAmerican than the story of my visit to one of them.

It was all carried out with extreme secrecy, but out of consideration for whom I do not know. A car came to fetch me and took me to a very comfortable but not modern hotel. It was not my host who met me, however, but I was greeted by name, and taken to my host's apartment. I had not brought my notebook with me, for I had been asked not to make any notes whatever, either at or after our meeting. Therefore I am writing from memory.

So I encountered in America in 1954 a kind of 'banning' that I was to encounter many times in South African after that time – with this tremendous difference, that the South African bannings were officially decreed by the Minister of Justice, while the American bannings were decreed by circumstances, one of these circumstances being fear of the power of Senator McCarthy. What is more, to break the conditions of a South African banning was to make oneself guilty of a serious criminal offence, while to defy or ignore an American banning was not a criminal offence but was an act for which one might pay heavily. My host was a highly paid writer, and he would have become a poor man if

York, 1959, pages 691–2.) However, I must note that the *Oxford History of the American People*, p. 1083, gives the number 'purged' as over 6,900.

his employers had not continued to use him. But they did so on the strictest conditions: one was that he must never reveal that they continued to employ him; the other was that he should vanish from the public scene.

While he was grateful for the money, he felt deeply his isolation. He was excited about the prospect of my visit. Writing and literature were his world, and we talked animatedly about them. We did not – as far as I remember – talk about the great blow that Senator McCarthy had dealt him. Nor did we talk about his political views, so that I did not discover if he had been a declared Marxist before McCarthy had made it so dangerous, or whether his 'subversiveness' was of the same order as that of many of those public servants who had been dismissed by the Eisenhower administration.

The marks of his isolation were clearly to be seen, not only his eagerness to talk about his world but also the tension whthin himself. Was all this secrecy to protect him or *Collier's Magazine* or me? I never discovered the answer to this question. I left him as discreetly as I had come.

In 1954 Trumbull Park was a low-cost housing project of 462 apartments, built by the C.H.A. (Chicago Housing Authority) in an all-white section of the city known as South Deering. In 1950 the C.H.A. had declared that there would be no racial discrimination in any of its projects. Therefore blacks began to move into a number of new developments, but Trumbull Park remained 'white' until 30 July 1953, when Mr. and Mrs. Donald Howard were given an apartment. It should be noted that it was Mrs. Howard who made the application, and that she did not look very dark.

For a long time the Howards had been looking for a place where their children could play. They could hardly believe their luck. Donald Howard said, 'This is it.' It was it, sure enough.

In the weeks that followed, the Howards lived as few human families have had to live. There were white people in South Deering who were determined to get them out. They milled about in front of the Howard apartment, many times a day, and every day. They fired off giant fireworks, which were known as aerial bombs and were forbidden by Illinois law. They shouted insults and smashed windows, and were kept back by hundreds of policemen day after day. The Howards lived behind boarded windows, their children in terror, all youngness gone. In the end, tried beyond their strength, the Howards moved away.

But before they left, the C.H.A. had moved ten more black families into the project. When I first visited Trumbull Park with Dan Weiner, it was a lovely day of spring, with trees in tender leaf, and tenants sitting in the sun. But the bombs were going off in neighbouring South Deering, and the police were everywhere at every turn, and only the white tenants were sitting in the sun. The white tenants take no active part in South Deering's fight against the blacks. Some do little kindnesses, some are hostile, most are cold. It's an unreal world, white children playing, white and black policemen smoking, black men and women and children sitting behind blinds, the sun shining and the trees coming out in leaf, and the bombs.

I met Mr. Herman King, a black tenant and a war veteran. He was a big man and talked to me quietly, but he talked like a man who had some deep internal pain and wished that it were not there. Sometimes he stopped talking and looked out into space, which was not very far, because the blinds were drawn.

He told me a story.

'It was the night that Howard lost control and fired off a gun. There was a great crowd there, yelling and shouting. I had to take my wife to the hospital, because it was time for our fourth child. I knew I'd lose control if they hurt my wife. I was praying they wouldn't throw a stone. The police appealed to the crowd please not to hurt the woman, please not to throw a stone. I was glad the crowd listened.

'We nearly moved out once. Then we thought of all the work done to get blacks in. I wasn't prepared to see it wasted. So I felt obligated to go on. I didn't come in as a crusader. I came to get a place to live. I'm a man of principle but no man wants to die for it if he can live. But I'm going to stay. I had to become a crusader after all.

'It takes a toll of my nerves, but I sit down and think it over, and then I'm all right. I have to be, because of my kids. I don't want them to know how bad it is. But you can't tell till later.

'When we first came, and I first put them out to play, the white kids came round with toys and candies. But now they don't come any more.' He said with pain, 'Some of them do, but not with toys and candies any more. Then I have to bring them in.'

But he added cheerfully, 'Our neighbour is fine. She comes to see us. She's rescued our kids more than once.'

I hardly spoke. I only listened. What could one say to such a man?

'Are you tired of talking?' I asked.

'Not to you,' he said.

And what could I say? Why did he equate himself with me, who had never faced such things in my life? He saw me looking at a card that hung on the wall. *Smile*, it said.

'Sometimes I can't,' he said.

Dan Weiner and I went walking in South Deering. On 106th Street Mr. Blue Denim eyed us from the other side, attracted no doubt by

Dan's cameras.

'Let's go and speak to him, Dan.'

We crossed over and asked him how things were going.

'We mean to get the jigs out, that's all.'

'Who's we?'

'All of us,' he said. 'We've got no leader or president. We all feel the same. There'll be a race riot, sure enough. You wait a few weeks.'

'What do your churches say?'

'I'm a Catholic,' he said, 'and a good one. But the church hasn't got a right to tell me who I should live next to. And the church knows it too, because it hasn't said anything about Trumbull Park.'

'I read somewhere that it did,' I said.

'That's Bishop Sheil,' he said. 'He's a liberal, and he talks too much.'

Somewhat to my astonishment, I saw a very dark man walking composedly towards us.

'Who's that?' I asked.

He smiled at my ignorance.

'He's a Mexican,' he said. 'We don't mind Mexicans round here.'

One of the leaders of the white resistance was Mr. Louis P. Dinnocenzo, the president of the South Deering Improvement Association. 'As an American and a Christian' (applause) 'I will not use violence, only the law' (more applause). 'I work with Negroes and they'll tell you how well we get along' (great applause). 'But the only solution for peace is to get them out of here' (pandemonium).

I asked Mr. Dinnocenzo why he advocated picketing, when picketing so often led to violence.

'I advocated peaceful picketing,' he said. 'I have never advocated violence.'

'But doesn't picketing lead to violence?'

'I don't advocate violence,' he said. 'I advocate peaceful picketing. Let them take the negroes out of here. Then let us re-educate the people. Then maybe the negroes can come back.'

Mr. Dinnocenzo is supported by the *Daily Calumet*, and its redoubtable editor Colonel Horace F. Wulf. The colonel is American and Christian too, and is for brotherhood. His argument about brotherhood is very clear:

1. Brotherhood is a fine thing.

2. It fights against odds of greed and human nature.

3. You cannot enforce it by law.

4. It begins with the 'rank and file, not in the mighty houses of state'.

5. Therefore support the scouts, Y.M.C.A., clubs and churches.

6. But do not try to enforce it by law.

I met a little old white woman who believes that anyone should be able to live next to her. She was humble, not learned, but she knew the differences between the Bible and the *Daily Calumet*. She did not talk about America and democracy, but she knew the things on which they are based.

'I know it,' she told me. 'I know segregation is wrong. I know it is wrong to judge by colour.'

Her husband is blind. 'If all people could be blind,' she said, 'the world would be a better place.'

Before I left Chicago I met Frank Brown, war veteran, aged twenty-six. I had lunch with him and Dan Weiner and Ed Holmgren of the C.H.A. Brown showed me a postcard.

> All persons who believe in
> WHITE SUPREMACY
> It has been done in the South and can
> be done in Trumbull Park
> Join a white supremacy organisation
> Inquire, you will find it
> · Watch for:
> ZERO HOUR
> On the signal we will strike
> BE READY!
> A dead nigger is a good nigger!
> Pass along the good word!

'My wife said to me, "Frank, let's go. I can't stand it any more." I said to her. "Listen, I'll never . . . never . . . never leave this place. You can go and the kids can go, but I can't go. You'd better look at me: It's still Frank Brown, it may be the first time you ever saw me this way, but it's the way I am now, and if you want to be my wife, it's the way you have to be too."

'She thought it over and then she kissed me and said, "All right, Frank, if that's the way you want me to be, it's the way I am."'

And never again did they talk about leaving Trumbull Park.

Lunch was over, and I asked him my last question.

'How do you do it, Frank?'

He smiled at me.

'It's a neurosis,' he said. 'I hate cowardly negroes.'*

I was back in New York for one of the great events in American history, certainly one of the greatest events in black American history. On 17

---

* Frank Brown published a novel *Trumbull Park* in 1959 (Regnery, Chicago).

May 1954 in the Supreme Court of the United States, in the case of *Brown et al.* v *Board of Education of Topeka, et al.,* Chief Justice Earl Warren handed down the unanimous opinion of the Court:

We came then to the question presented: Does segregation of children in public schools solely on the grounds of race, even though the physical facilities and other 'tangible' factors may be equal, deprive the children of the minority groups of equal education opportunities? We believe that it does.

So did the Supreme Court reverse another historic decision, its own opinion of 1896 in the case of *Plessy* v *Ferguson,* that facilities for blacks could be 'separate but equal'. Mr. Justice Harlan of Kentucky had dissented from the 1896 judgment. The *New York Times,* with a flash of genius, headed its editorial on the 1954 judgment, 'Mr. Justice Harlan concurring.'

There was a celebratory party in New York that evening. Walter and Polly White were there; Roy Wilkins of the N.A.A.C.P. and his wife; Henry Moon also of the N.A.A.C.P. and his wife; Ralph Bunche, United States Ambassador to the United Nations, Channing Tobias and many others. Walter White made a short and splendid speech. He was deeply moved, as he had cause to be, by this crowning of his life's endeavour, by this act of justice to an excluded people. But he did not speak only as a member of the excluded people, but also as an American who was proud that America, through its Supreme Court, had at last proved its loyalty and its obedience to its Constitution and its Bill of Rights. There was no doubt in that apartment that night that the Supreme Court decision of 1954 meant the end of statutory segregation in every department of American public life. Waties Waring, now looking very old, was delighted when someone said to him, 'It's all your fault. You began all this.'

I was honoured to be invited to take part in this celebration. I had no doubt that they were celebrating all over the nation, the Cornwells and their friends in Charleston, Lieutenant Scott and Lieutenant Webb at Fort Bragg, William Ragin in Clarendon County, George Henry Gordon, 'realtist' of Pasadena, and the brave and embattled tenants of Trumbull Park. I do not suppose that Governor Talmadge was celebrating. Was he already making plans for the closing of all the public schools in Georgia, not knowing – or perhaps indeed knowing – that his day had ended? I am sure that Governor Byrnes knew that the day had come, but I should think that he had resigned himself to it, and had no doubt felt grateful that his public life was drawing to an end.

I felt a deep debt of gratitude to *Collier's Magazine* for giving me this opportunity to travel from one side of America and back again, and for the chance to be there on the day of the great decision. Sometimes while I was in New York I would go to the zoo in Central Park. There were always children there, twenty, thirty, forty, fifty, with a teacher or two in charge. They walked in pairs, of every race and kind and colour that there is in New York. If they were very small, they walked hand in hand. Yet some people say New York is a wicked city.

Postscript One

A giant of a man comes to see me in my hotel. His name is Louis Stone, and he is a big shot in C.B.S. He wants me to spend a year in America, teaching at Kent School, Connecticut, on the occasion of its fiftieth-year celebration. It is his old school, of course. He wants me to take part in the Kent seminar on 'The Christian Idea of Education' in November 1955. The Rev. William G. Pollard will be there, the Executive Director of Oak Ridge Institute of Nuclear Studies, and an Episcopalian priest. Four distinguished professors will be there, Harris Harbison of Princeton, The Rev. Massey H. Shepherd of the Church Divinity School of the Pacific, the Rev. John Courtney Murray, S.J., of Woodstock College, and Jacques Maritain of Princeton. Also present will be the Rev. George Florowsky, Dean of St. Vladimir's Orthodox Seminary, and the Rev. Reinhold Niebuhr, of Union Theological Seminary. How could I refuse to be a member of such a galaxy?

I explain to Louis Stone that I am a leading member of the newly founded Liberal Party of South Africa, which stands for the same things that he and Kent School would stand for in America. I could not possibly leave my country for a year. He asks me to think and pray about it. He will come to see me again.

He comes to see me again. He is as enormous as ever, six foot six I should think, and he wears his hair cropped short. He could fell me to the ground with a single blow, but he does not. Instead he brings the extraordinary power of his will to bear upon me. He is determined to get me to Kent School for a year, and I am determined not to be gotten. He woos me with a dozen arguments. Where will I find such a galaxy of intellect in South Africa? What influence could I possibly have on the National Party government, which is hell-bent on a suicide course from which no one could divert it? But I could have tremendous influence on a generation of Kent boys, who are not only the most intelligent boys in America, but also attend the best school in America, not just the best school, you understand, but far and away the best school. How can I refuse the opportunity to make such a use of my life? Why, I might exert colossal influence on some future leader of the Free World. Well, I must think and pray about it. He will come again.

He tries a new strategy to get me into his trap. He asks me home to meet his wife Nancy, and promises me good company, good food, good wine, and a magnificent private library, where I can spend the rest of my days if I will. I make some inquiries about him. I find out that he really is a big shot in C.B.S. He is a human dynamo.

I go to see him and Nancy. It is a magnificent private library indeed, and he has invented a new game in it. Before I arrive for the good company and the good food and good wine, he has looked up two or three almost unknown words in his dictionaries, of which he has several. He would select such words as *arval, epicene, metathetical.* Then in the course of our conversation, which was inclined to be erudite, he would casually use one of these words in a sentence. Then he would watch me closely, to see if I flinched or cringed. It must be said to my credit that I almost immediately recognised the game for what it was, for the simple reason that the first word he chose was one that no intelligent person would use in conversation without apologising for it. If I happened to know the word I would reply in such a way that it was clear that I did know it. This would impress him, and I could see him fitting a new arrow to his bow. If the new word was totally unknown to me, I would change the subject, and try not to see the gleam of triumph in his eye.

Before I visited Louis and Nancy again I also prepared a list of three or four almost unknown words. It will be clear from this story that I was falling under the influence of this gigantic man, and that he was softening me up for a year at Kent School. He decided to take me up to Kent School, Connecticut, so that I could be exposed to another personality-smasher, the headmaster John Patterson. The two of them focused the power of their concentrated wills on me for an hour or two. In the end they accepted that I could not leave South Africa for a year, and desert a cause that I had so recently espoused. It was agreed that I would come to Kent School for two months in 1955, and that this would include the galactic seminar to which the greatest brains of the United States would contribute.

Postscript Two

The evening before I left New York for London and Johannesburg. I had dinner with Irita van Doren, the editor of the book section of the *New York Herald Tribune*. She had two of her small grandchildren staying with her, and they were enthusiastic television-watchers. However, they baffled her by clamouring for the 'earrings', and at long last she discovered that they wanted to watch the McCarthy hearings, which they were accustomed to watch at home.

In January 1954 a Gallup poll showed that fifty per cent of Americans questioned approved of McCarthy and his tracking down of subversives. His success then went to his head, and he made an oblique attack on President Eisenhower, and a direct attack on Secretary of the Army Robert Stevens. There seems reason to believe that he thought he would achieve the Presidency itself. Congressional hearings followed, and these were televised. According to *The History of the United States Since 1865,* he went from national hero to villain to buffoon in a few weeks. In December 1954 the Senate voted 67 to 22 to condemn him, and in May 1957 he died. The McCarthy era was a shameful episode in modern American history, but it came to an end in the same year as the Supreme Court delivered the famous *Brown* v *Board of Education* decision.

Chapter 13

In those days of the 'fifties, after a person of my beliefs had been in Europe or America for a time, it would have been almost certainly with a feeling of tension that he or she boarded the plane for Johannesburg. This tension increased as the plane drew nearer the Golden City. One was returning home, that was true, to a wife and sons much missed, and to one's friends of the Liberal Party, and to a country deeply loved, but one was also returning to a country ruled by the Afrikaner Nationalist Party and by the ruthless policies of separation, and above all one was returning to a country whose authorities were intensely hostile to oneself. At the airport the security police would be waiting. There would be no greeting, only the implacable stare. The seasoned immigration officer would look at the passport with inscrutable inscrutability, but the greenhorn would look at it with fascinated wonder, as though it were the passport of Beelzebub himself or, worse still, of Vladimir Ilyich Ulyanov. Then the customs officer would turn the luggage inside out and upside down. I don't really think he ever expected to find anything, but he was the appointed representative of hostility, and he repacked my suitcases as badly as he could. However, I must not be regarded as an impartial reporter. It is possible that I *imagined* all this.

I shall however report two cases in which I would claim to be an impartial observer. On this particular flight in 1954 I came back with Vernon Berrangé, a prominent Johannesburg lawyer who was famous, and notorious, for his defending of men and women who had come into conflict with the authorities for political reasons. Berrangé had been a member of the South African Communist Party, all of whose members had resigned in 1950, before the passing by parliament of the Suppression of Communism Act. He had then joined the Congress of Democrats, as had many other ex-members of the Communist Party. It was this Congress with which the Liberal Party had cool, sometimes hostile, relations.

On our way to Johannesburg our plane landed at Kano in Nigeria. That was thirty years ago, and we spent our waiting time not in an airport building but out in the open, where many sellers of Nigerian paintings and curios displayed their wares. Berrangé was not only solitary but he *looked* solitary, almost as though he had distanced himself from all others. I could only conclude either that he wanted to be alone or that he felt that his beliefs made him unacceptable to the other passengers, all of whom were white, and few of those, I would guess, even knew who he was. However, something happened that led me to believe that my second conclusion was correct. He suddenly saw me, and smiled by no means coldly and came over to speak to me. I could only further conclude that the tension of which I was aware in myself was present even more strongly in him.

I wrote in chapter 10 that my looks, which had always been a bit grim, had grown grimmer, especially round the lips and mouth, since the founding of the Liberal Party, Berrangé's looks were much grimmer than mine. There was a tightness about his face that was very noticeable to me at Kano airport. What we talked about I do not remember, but I am fairly certain that it was not politics. We held one belief in common, and that was that our society was unjust, but his idea of a just society would have been very different from mine. In my just society, individual freedom would have come first, but not in his. He would have exploited to the full any denial of human freedom in the existing society, but his new order of society would itself have denied many freedoms. The right to work and the right to eat would have been important in his new order, but not the right to speak and publish and proclaim. It was the party that would decide that. One of the great slogans of the party would be the dictatorship of the proletariat, but that would mean in fact the dictatorship of the party, which in the last resort would mean the dictatorship of the Politburo.

We did not discuss such things at Kano. We had some kind of respect for each other, though not for each other's beliefs. I myself had great respect for Berrangé's courage and I shall close this account of our meeting by relating a story for the truth of which I cannot vouch. In the course of his political life, particularly of his life as a lawyer, Berrangé received many threats and encountered many unpleasantnesses. On one occasion at least, shots were fired into his house. The story relates that he too had his breaking-point. He bought a new car and parked it in the street outside his flat, and there one of his enemies poured a tin of paint remover over the roof and bonnet. That was the last straw. Berrangé went to live in Swaziland, although he did not altogether give up his legal work in Johannesburg.

It was on another flight during those same years that I travelled to Johannesburg with another South African who had been a member of the Communist Party, had resigned before the party was outlawed, had joined the new Congress of Democrats, and was a close political associate of Vernon Berrangé. Her name was Ruth First, and she had become Ruth Slovo in 1949. Her husband Joe Slovo was another leading member of the Congress of Democrats, but was banned from public and political life in 1954. He was to leave South Africa in 1963, but up to the time of writing (1987) he has remained an implacable opponent of the National Party government, and a powerful supporter of the African National Congress, which was itself to be banned in 1960.

Ruth First was as implacable an opponent of the government as her husband, and was to pay a very heavy price for her political beliefs. Of her courage there could be no doubt, but for all that she had to steel herself for the landing in Johannesburg. She nodded to me perfunctorily, but she had more pressing things on her mind. Her face was tight and strained, not so grim as that of Berrangé, because she was younger, not yet thirty, and her face was less lined. She spent several hours of the flight tearing pieces of paper to pieces, each about the size of a fingernail. The plane was half empty, and she occupied a seat on the opposite side of the aisle from myself. She made no attempt to hide what she was doing, probably because she knew that it was highly unlikely that I would go to the security police to tell them how Ruth First had occupied herself. I was, like so many other liberals, useless, but decent.

I was occupied also, not in destroying papers but in watching a young lady doing so. I was fascinated but I watched her obliquely. In any event she seemed totally intent on her task and totally oblivious to her surroundings. When she had accumulated a small pile of paper fragments she would go to the lavatory and get rid of them. She was quite safe, because we were travelling on one of the non-South African airlines, British or Dutch or Belgian. In fact in those days people like ourselves avoided our own airlines, because of the hostility that we sensed – or imagined – from any person who wore a South African uniform. Eventually Ruth First's job was done, and she sat taut and motionless waiting for the arrival at Jan Smuts airport, Johannesburg. I was pretty taut myself, but much less so than she, because I had no secret knowledge of revolutions and revolutionaries.

I sat and reflected on the price one pays for courage. It was quite clear that she had paid and was paying a great price for hers. Karle Baker once wrote, 'Courage is fear that has said its prayers'; but that of course is a saying that is true only for a religious believer.* Ruth First also had a supreme belief, that a new heaven and a new earth would be created by the Communist Party.

There is a closing paragraph to this story also. On 17 August 1982, in Maputo, Mozambique, Ruth First, who was working there with her husband for the African National Congress, received a parcel through the post. She opened it and was killed instantly. No one has accurate information as to who sent her the parcel, but there is a strong belief that it was sent by some secret and white right-wing South African organisation.

Once I had landed on my native soil, which by the way I did not kiss, much of the tension in me disappeared. This was because I had rejoined my family and my friends in the Liberal Party. I travelled a great deal addressing meetings of the party, which was growing steadily though not spectacularly. Everyone wanted to hear about America, and especially about the significance of the Supreme Court decision in the case of *Brown* v *Board of Education, Topeka.*

My friends in America had told me to cheer up. If they could do it, why shouldn't we? I had to explain to them that no two situations could have been more different than theirs and ours.

The first and most important difference is that the American constitution is one of the most comprehensive political documents in history. Our constitution is a legal instrument, and its main purpose was to transfer the power of government from Britain to South Africa. The American constitution enshrines a Bill of Rights which ensures certain freedom to its citizens. If any provision of any law of Congress should affect these rights, citizens can appeal against it, and the Supreme Court of the United States has the power to invalidate the provision. As previously noted (chapter 11), in America it is the constitution that is supreme, and the Supreme Court that interprets it. In South Africa parliament is supreme, and that means that our Supreme Court, which most of us respect, has limited powers. I have already recorded the anger of the National Party when our Supreme Court invalidated a resolution of parliament.

The American constitution enshrines a Bill of Rights. The South African constitution has no Bill of Rights. It contains, however, two 'entrenched clauses', which may be overthrown only by a two-thirds

---

* Karle Baker is quoted in the *Anglican Digest*, Lent 1984.

majority of both houses of parliament sitting together. The first entrenched clause guarantees the equality of the two official languages, English and Afrikaans, and is not likely to be overthrown. The second clause guarantees the special non-racial franchise of the Cape Province, formerly the Cape Colony. The National Party was in 1954 still determined to abolish the African and coloured franchises of the Cape Province, but had not yet succeeded in obtaining a two-thirds majority.*

There is one other tremendous difference between our two situations. The blacks constitute approximately ten per cent of the United States population, the Africans more than seventy per cent of the South African population. Therefore the white people of the U.S.A. would find it easier and less frightening to grant full legal and political equality. The majority of the white people of South Africa would find it very difficult and frightening. This practical and perhaps cynical reason has also a moral component but, again, it is easier for white people to act morally when they are in the majority.

There is also a cultural reason which makes it easier to take such a momentous decision, and I have already mentioned it. The Americans have one official language, whereas we have two and at least ten others that are 'home languages', and each of these languages gives to its possessors a feeling of oneness with their group that has no equivalent that I encountered in the States. Another unifying factor is that the great majority of American blacks are Christians, some of them deeply so, such as my friends Bennie and Sadie Mays. Although the Christian church was said in 1954 to be the most segregated institution in America, and although eleven o'clock on Sunday morning was said to be the most segregated hour of the week, the fact remains that the highest moral and religious beliefs of black and white are the same. The deep respect of both black and white for the constitution is another common cultural possession, and my assignment with *Collier's Magazine* proved how deep it was. What I am in effect saying is that there are more cultural and religious elements that are held in common in America than there are in South Africa, and the knowledge that such beliefs are held in common also helps to abate racial fear.

The disparities of wealth, income, and possession are great in both countries, but are less marked in America. In South Africa they are very marked indeed, so that the fear by the rich of the poor, and the fear by the poor of the rich, and the fact that a man who earns one thousand units per annum really has no common language with a man who earns one hundred units (even if they both know English), are all

* As I earlier related, the African franchise had already been amended in 1936.

factors that make the realisation of a just society much more difficult in South Africa than in America.

There is one last factor that gave, and gives, America a powerful incentive to eliminate all racial segregation and discrimination. She is called 'the leader of the free world', and that is what she is. This means that she often has to behave well for other than moral reasons. White South Africa does not occupy any such position, and therefore, if she behaves well, it is for moral rather than other reasons. In fact she resists strongly any pressure to make her behave well for political reasons, and regards this as interference with her domestic policies. That is why she moves so slowly, sometimes not at all, and sometimes backwards.

I close with a final question. Does a nation behave well because that is the right thing to do, or does it behave well when it thinks it safe and expedient to do so? I shall leave my readers to debate this difficult question. I must admit that I tend to be impatient with those who offer moral solutions to political problems. I must also admit that I was at one time more inclined that way than I am today.

It was strange to come back from a country whose Supreme Court had decided that separate could not be equal, to my own country whose government had recently decided that separate did not need to be equal. During the Defiance Campaign of 1952, Mr. George Lusu, an African participator in the campaign, was arrested for making use of a waiting-room reserved for whites at the Cape Town railway station. The magistrate acquitted him on the ground that when separate public facilities are provided for various groups, these facilities must be substantially equal. The state appealed against this judgment, but the appeal was dismissed, first by the Supreme Court in Cape Town, and again by the Appellate Court in Bloemfontein in a majority decision.[*]

On 24 August 1953, the Minister of the Interior said that the government was determined to clear up the position not only for the Railways 'but for every other body which may be endangered'. Just what these dangers were was not quite clear, but one of them certainly was that the government would be compelled to pull down and rebuild every black public facility throughout the whole of South Africa, and that would have cost a fortune. Therefore the government passed the Reservation of Separate Amenities Act, which laid down that, whenever separate public facilities were provided for separate groups, such action could not be ruled invalid on the ground that the separate facilities are not equal.

[*] According to the *Survey of Race Relations in South Africa: 1952-53* the magistrate followed a principle established in earlier cases.

This Act of parliament, which never achieved the fame of such laws as the Group Areas Act, was nevertheless of great importance in that it was a signal to the unenfranchised people that, while they could expect a rigid application of the policies of racial separation, they could not expect to achieve equality. It was an ironic re-statement of the old Transvaal Republic policy of 'no equality in Church or State'.

More and more the racial policies of the National Party government were attracting the hostile attention of the world. The rising star of the government was the implacable and increasingly dominating figure of Dr. Hendrik Verwoerd, the powerful Minister of Native Affairs, whose aim was to take all matters that affected African people into his own hands. He had already announced that control of African education would be taken away from the four provincial councils, and would be vested in his own department. He was strongly opposed to church or missionary control of black schools.* He also decided that a social problem like juvenile delinquency could better be dealt with when it was considered as several problems, a white problem, a black problem, a coloured problem, and an Indian problem. He decided that black juvenile delinquency was properly the concern of his Native Affairs Department. He therefore took over Diepkloof Reformatory, and broke it into several smaller institutions, on the ground that it was totally objectionable to the government to have delinquent boys from Zulu, Xhosa, Tswana, Sotho, and other groups, in the same institution. They would thus lose their God-given racial identity and their culture. The truth was that most of them had no recognisable racial identity. Their culture was that of the slums of the white cities, and their common language was, except for the Zulu boys from Durban and Pietermaritz-burg, a picturesque and vigorous variety of Afrikaans 'full of strange oaths', and liable to drive language purists up the wall. I learned to speak the language very well, but never could have mastered its arcana, the understanding of which demanded that one should have grown up in the black slums.

Was Dr. Verwoerd sane? I shall later have to consider the more profound question as to whether he was evil. But was he sane? He was a man of deep passions and of great intellectual powers. Those human beings who reach a satisfying maturity try to run their passions and their intellects in double harness, so that they run together, and so that one never gets away from the other. But in the case of Dr. Verwoerd, the passions drove the intellect forward. The intellect was indeed the

* In 1954 the great majority of African schools were missionary foundations. It is possible to criticise the missionaries on many grounds but, if it had not been for them, African education would hardly have existed. Lutuli, Matthews, and Sobukwe were all products of missionary schools.

servant of the passions. Therefore this highly intelligent man was able to conceive of a human society that was totally unrealisable, and he was able to devote his great energy to the task of making it realisable.

It was part of his Grand Scheme – though a small part, I concede – that a Xhosa delinquent should not be re-educated alongside a Tswana delinquent. The one must be re-Xhosaised and the other re-Tswana-ised. The power of the great city to create a new kind of culture was undoubtedly great, but Dr. Verwoerd believed that it was possible to stop and reverse this process. In addition to his arrogance, he also had a mesmeric power. One of the vice-chairmen of the Liberal Party, Leslie Rubin, who was also a white senator representing those African voters who had been removed to a separate roll in 1936, told me of Verwoerd's mesmeric power. Verwoerd, speaking in the Senate, under-took to show the members of the Upper House 'how the various Acts, Bills, and also public statements which I have made all fit into a pattern, and together form a single constructive plan'. Rubin, who was virulently hostile to everything that Verwoerd stood for, told me that he sometimes sat in his senator's seat and found himself for a moment wondering whether it might all be true, whether in fact under this guiding genius all things might really fall into place, and all peoples might realise their own destinies, and our country be at peace for evermore. But while Rubin was able to break out of the trance, many others could not. With few exceptions the members of the Afrikaner National Party regarded Verwoerd as a kind of saviour; they listened to him spellbound, and would have let him do all that he would.

I have seldom expressed any opinion of Verwoerd's action in destroy-ing Diepkloof Reformatory, and in destroying the work of thirteen of the best years of my life, to which work I devoted six chapters of the book *Towards the Mountain*. He not only broke the reformatory into ethnic parts, but he gave to each part a function closely resembling the purely custodial function of the Diepkloof Reformatory of June 1935, the month before I arrived as its new principal. For the whole system of the increasing of physical freedom accompanied by the increasing of individual responsibility, he had only contempt, and called it *vertroe-teling*, which means pampering. I would guess that Verwoerd had little sympathy for white juvenile delinquents; for black juvenile delin-quents he had none. The new ethnic reformatories reverted to the farm labour scheme, whereby a white farmer could pick up a truckload of boys at dawn and return them at sunset. They reverted also to the system of apprenticeship to farmers after the boys' release. The system of ordinary school education for young boys ceased to exist, and training in any kind of skill, such as shoemaking, tailoring, carpentry, was abandoned. When one is building Utopia, the problems of delinquent boys, and particularly of black ones, are not of great importance.

I am often asked if I was desolated by the destruction of Diepkloof Reformatory. I think the answer must be No. For one thing I realised that I was totally powerless to do anything about it. For another thing, I had entered a new world, I had visited Diepkloof two, perhaps three, times since my retirement, and had realised that my heart was now elsewhere. However, there was one person who was desolated by the change.

In *Towards the Mountain* I told the story of Majohnnie, whose real name was Daniel Bob.* He was a boy of seventeen or eighteen years of age, and came from the slums of Kimberley. He was one of the few boys in the reformatory who had passed his Standard Six,† and I had put him in charge of the hundred small boys, whose ages ranged from nine to fourteen or fifteen. Majohnnie stood less than five feet and was never to grow any taller, but his discipline was perfect, and his understanding of small boys profound.

When it was time for him to be discharged from the reformatory, he had begged me not to send him back to Kimberley. If I returned him to Kimberley, he said, he would be back in the reformatory in a month. When I asked him what I should do, he said that I must give him a job at the reformatory. It was about this time that the Union Department of Education, which controlled Diepkloof Reformatory, appealed to employers to give a chance to boys and girls released from their institutions. Therefore the department could hardly refuse me, and Majohnnie became a junior supervisor, now in permanent charge of the hundred small boys, who formed what was called the *Kleinspan*.

He was an outstanding success as a supervisor. How a delinquent boy from a derelict home should have come to cherish so fiercely such qualities as punctuality, reliability, loyalty and honesty, I do not claim to understand. Nor could I claim to understand the miracle of how a child from a Kimberley slum should find, in a reformatory of all places, a guiding rule for his life, and should follow it as faithfully as any of the saints.

Verwoerd did not break my heart when he broke up Diepkloof Reformatory, but he nearly broke Majohnnie's. Majohnnie was sent to one of the new ethnic reformatories for Northern Sotho delinquent boys, situated near Marble Hall, in Sekhukhuneland. He was shocked when he found that the main occupation of the new institution was to be farm labour, and that all schooling and trade training were to be abolished. The graded system of freedom and responsibility that prevailed at Diepkloof was also brought to an end. The institution at

---

* In chapter 22.　　　　　† In the United States, the eighth grade.

Marble Hall in 1954 reverted to the prison practices of 1934, practices which Majohnnie knew well because he had been committed to Diepkloof in that year. The great changes which had taken place from 1935 onwards, under the administration of the Minister of Education, J.H. Hofmeyr, and his equally enlightened Secretary for Education, Professor M.C. Botha, had given Majohnnie new hope for himself and his fellow delinquents. Now his hope was gone.

Majohnnie wrote despairing letters to me, urging me to have something done. He could not conceive of a situation in which I had no influence at all. What was worse, he did not realise that the policy under which he was suffering was the declared policy of his new department and of his powerful Minister Dr. H.F. Verwoerd, carried out by one of the most powerful public servants in the country, Dr. W.M. Eiselen, son of a missionary father. It was painful to receive Majohnnie's letters, but the most painful was yet to come.

He was virtually in charge of the reformatory at night, and he started a Boys' Club, which provided boxing and games, the equipment for which he paid for himself. It so happened that the institution was visited by an inspector of the Department of Native Affairs, and that Majohnnie told him about the Boys' Club. The inspector may well have been seconded from the Union Department of Education, but be that as it may, he approved very strongly of the establishment of a Boys' Club, and of the initiative of the young supervisor. Before he left Marble Hall he congratulated the principal on having a Boys' Club and on having such an enterprising young supervisor.

The inspector had hardly left the scene before Majohnnie was sent for by an enraged principal. What right had he to start a club without the principal's permission? What could have been more humiliating for the principal than to be told by a passing inspector of the existence of a club of which he himself knew nothing? The club would be closed forthwith.

Majohnnie could bear no more. He resigned from the department and went to seek his fortune in Johannesburg. So was lost one of the brightest ornaments that ever adorned the profession.

In Johannesburg he married a young woman Maria, and they had seven children, with whose education I helped him. In almost every letter he told me that his committal to the reformatory was the luckiest event of his life, and that he was trying to teach his childen the lessons that the reformatory had taught him. For many years he promised to spend one of his holidays with me, so that he could tell me in person what he had told me in his letters. But alas, he died before he could fulfil his promise, and therefore I learned no more about the nature of the experience that had done nothing less than transform his life. Of this kind of transformation I am sure that Dr. Verwoerd knew exactly nothing.

Of all the Prime Ministers of South Africa (of whom there have been eight, under all of whom I have lived), none is more often remembered by black people than Dr. Verwoerd. It was he who inflicted such damage on black education, and it was he who brought about the destruction of Sophiatown, of which I shall tell later. In all his sixteen years of high public office he never said one warm word about black people. It was he who ordered the destruction of the 'black spots', those several hundred places where black people had been able legally to buy land from white owners, a practice that was brought to an end by the passing of the Natives Land Act of 1913. The passing of this Act was not the work of the Afrikaner National Party, which did not come into existence till 1914. The law was the work of the first Prime Minister, General Louis Botha, and is regarded by black people as one of the most grievous blows ever dealt to their aspirations. The 'black spots' were for black people havens of peace where they could escape from the control, often tyrannical, of the tribal chief, and where they could – and did – build schools and churches, and houses which they held in freehold, and do many things impossible of realisation in those rigidly controlled areas known as the reserves.

Verwoerd regarded the 'black spots' as the result of the *laissez-faire* policies of British imperialism, for which he had an implacable hatred. He was determined to destroy them all, and he bequeathed to South Africa a bitter legacy, of people who lost land and houses and a kind of freedom, and were 'resettled' in the new towns, where they could own neither land nor house, nor grow crops and keep cattle. In his messianic arrogance, Verwoerd predicted that the growing tide of migration of black people to the cities would turn in the 'seventies and would flow back to the reserves (the 'homelands'), when black people would realise that only in these places could they find happiness, identity, and fullness of life.

It only remains to add that the tide has never turned and that the tide never will turn. The industrial cities of Cape Town, Port Elizabeth, Durban, Johannesburg, are the natural centres of commerce and industry. Yet many white South Africans continue to cherish the myth that the black homelands have some kind of future, when in fact they do not. The cherishing of this myth is vital for these whites because it gives them a sense of security. Will we whites ever give up this myth, and learn to look reality in the face? Discussion of this question will be one of the sub-themes of this book.

Members of the Liberal Party prepared themselves to protest against, and to resist by whatever legal means were available to them, these assaults by the National Party on black education, on black spots, on freedom of expression and association, on the freedom to oppose the racial policies of the government. Many of our members, and members of other political bodies, were to pay a heavy price for their beliefs and for their courage in expressing them.

Meanwhile hostility to the policies of South Africa was mounting in an increasing number of countries. We were rapidly becoming the polecat of the world.

Chapter 14

Why did we start the Liberal Party? So many diverse answers have been given to this question that I shall give my own. I realise of course that my reliability may be questioned, not because I am thought to be a liar, but because I was too deeply involved to be able to give a true and objective answer.

Why did I, one of the founding members, take the decision to establish a new party and to become an active member of it? I may well have had several reasons, but I have no doubt that one reason was paramount. I did it because I felt that it was my duty. I felt compelled to oppose the National Party and its policies of apartheid, to oppose any law that decreed racial separation, especially a law that public amenities had to be separate but did not have to be equal, and to oppose the cruelties of the Group Areas Act and the taking away of houses and land from people who had acquired them honestly and legally. When I write that I did these things out of a sense of duty, I mean that in my case the main motives were moral and religious. I believed that I could not be true to my Christian beliefs and at the same time keep my mouth shut, nor could I refrain from defending those human rights which should be safe from the power of the State.

Most of those who joined the party in its early days, or in its later days for that matter, did so for moral reasons, and many of them had religious reasons also. The party itself was not, and could not be, a religious organisation, but it certainly was a moral one. I have already recorded that it was in a political party that I was best able to express my deepest beliefs. One of our young student members of those early days, Tony Morphet, was much later to describe the politics of the Liberal Party in a telling phrase: he called it 'the politics of innocence'. And so it was. It was more of course, but it certainly was that.

None of our critics saw us in this beguiling light. They ascribed to us a variety of motives. For instance, the founding members of the party were predominantly white, and they were therefore of course seen to be anxious about their futures and their possessions, and they felt that the policies of the National Party were a danger to both. The fact that they were anxious about their possessions was clear proof that they were capitalists at heart, but they were the most contemptible of all capitalists because they planned to use trusting blacks to pull their chestnuts out of the fire.

Others saw the founding members, who were also predominantly English-speaking, as having a hatred of Afrikaners. I think a few of us may have had such feelings, but racial hatred and racial animosity were not our characteristics. We certainly had a hatred of Afrikaner nationalism and of its racial policies, so Afrikaner nationalists readily took this as a hatred of Afrikaners.

We had critics on the far right and on the far left. The critics of the right viewed our racial policies with abhorrence. What kind of people called for the repeal of the Mixed Marriages Act and the Immorality Act? We were obviously sex-obsessed, and we were particularly attracted by the thought of sex across the colour line.

Our critics on the left regarded us as useless. They accused us – but not openly because that would have been too dangerous – of 'blunting the edge of the revolution'. They were angry with us for not joining the grand Congress movement. We were preventing black and coloured and Indian people from joining their own congresses, by offering them this pie-in-the-sky non-racialism.

We were accused – even by a person so eminent as Nadine Gordimer – of making promises that we could never keep. I do not remember any of these promises. We promised blood and toil and tears and sweat, and that is what many of us got.

While we were abhorred by the right and despised by the left, we also incurred the dislike of the white centre. We were of course 'before our time'. We thought that everything white was evil and that everything black was beautiful. We had no understanding of the virtue of 'moderation in all things'.

Black members of the party were accused, not only of blunting the edge of the revolution, not only of being duped by the white makers of glib promises, but also of joining for the sake of the pickings. After all, the white members had wealth and why shouldn't the black members have some of it? That we had a few such members cannot be gainsaid, and of course we had a few such white members too. In fact most of our black members were also guilty of 'the politics of innocence'. Few of them knew anything about the Bill of Rights, but they knew a lot about justice, and they knew what a just society should be like.

I am approaching the age of eighty-five, and at no time in my long life was I a member of any fellowship like the Liberal Party. We also had our left and our centre and our right, yet never once in our fifteen years of existence did our members differ on racial lines. We differed on many political issues, but the great majority of us never differed so deeply that we wanted to break from one another. Our slogan came to be 'A Common Society', and we differed on ways to achieve it. And no wonder! Who can offer an easy recipe for the creation of a common society in a country like South Africa?

The first publication of our political beliefs was in 1954 or 1955, in a handbook called *The Policies of the Liberal Party of South Africa.* I shall quote only one paragraph from it. It is paragraph two of the constitution of the party:

Principles

(i) The essential dignity of every human being irrespective of race, colour or creed, and the maintenance of his fundamental rights.

(ii) The right of every human being to develop to the fullest extent of which he is capable consistent with the rights of others.

(iii) The maintenance of the rule of law.

(iv) That no person be debarred from participating in the government and the democratic process of the country by reason only of race, colour or creed.

Objects

(i) Equal political rights based on a common franchise roll.

(ii) Freedom of worship, expression, movement, assembly and association.

(iii) The right to acquire and use skills and to seek employment freely.

(iv) Access to an independent judiciary.

(v) The application equally to all sections of the population of the principle of compulsory, State-sponsored education.

(vi) The right to own and acquire immovable property.

(vii) The right to organise trade unions, and other economic groups and associations.

Paragraph two concluded with the following statement: 'The Party will employ only democratic and constitutional means to achieve the foregoing objects, and is opposed to all forms of totalitarianism such as communism and fascism.'

In the non-constitutional sections of the handbook the party called for the total repeal of many laws affecting the rights of African people, in respect of land ownership, free movement, arbitrary arrest, and their right to enter urban areas. The party also called for the repeal of the Suppression of Communism Act of 1950, and of those laws which imposed heavy punishment on those who broke a law 'by way of protest'. It called for the repeal of those infamous laws which prevented Africans from buying land outside the reserves, and which virtually decreed that Africans would never be able to become farmers. Finally the party called for the repeal of the Group Areas Act, the Mixed Marriages Act, and those racial clauses of the Immorality Act which forbade any sexual relationship between a white person and any person not white.

Though our handbook was not a best-seller, it evoked much attention from the right. We were accused of being obsessed with human rights, and being indifferent to human responsibilities. Arid controversies raged about the relative important of rights and responsibilities. Amidst all this welter of accusation and counter-accusation, one thing emerged clearly, that those who condemned our obsession with human rights were invariably those who had them already.

Within the party itself the great difficulty was the nature of the franchise of the 'common society'. Our Cape members were accustomed to what was called the 'qualified franchise', that is to say, a franchise that was open to African and coloured people who had certain qualifications of education and property ownership. It was a qualified franchise in another sense also, in that white people were automatically enfranchised by the mere fact that they were white. It was this qualified franchise that the Cape Colony had been allowed to take into the Union of South Africa, with a solemn undertaking, entrenched in the constitution, that it could not be amended or abolished save by a two-thirds majority of a joint sitting of the upper and lower houses of parliament. It was in fact the very franchise that the government was now trying to abolish.

The radical members of the party, most of whom were to be found in the Transvaal, wanted an adult suffrage with no qualification of education or property. The more conservative members, most of whom were to be found in the Cape, wanted qualifications based on education, economic situation, and age. Various educational qualifications were put forward at the first party congress, first a matriculation, or Standard Ten certificate, second a Standard Eight certificate, third a Standard Six certificate.* After a great struggle between radicals and conservatives, the party adopted a Standard Six qualification.

Now although our politics according to Tony Morphet were those of innocence, the party also possessed some very good brains. One of the

* These three qualifications were respectively twelve, ten and eight years of schooling.

best brains of the Cape was possessed by Donald Molteno, a distinguished advocate and a member of a distinguished Cape family. He was a deadly master of logic and believed that, if the party adopted an adult suffrage, it could give up any idea of winning support from white South Africans. His chief opponent was also a deadly master of logic, Marion Friedmann of Johannesburg. She poured contempt on the notion that a party open to all people could say to one member, Yes, we shall give you a vote because you made Standard Six, and could say to another, Yes, we dearly want you as a member, but we can't give you a vote because you only made Standard Five. Although her political stance was highly moral, she had an argument from expediency as well, that if the Liberal Party gave the slightest indication of regarding some of its black members as unworthy to exercise a franchise, it might as well hand all black people over to the Congress movement. Marion, besides arguing from morality and expediency, had her passion too – she hated communism and she had the deepest distrust of the white Congress of Democrats.

Natal also had some brains. It was fascinating to see those two deadly speakers, Marion and Molteno, standing shoulder to shoulder to repel the attacks of one of our deadly Natal speakers, Hans Meidner. Hans was born in Germany of Jewish parents and had lived under Adolf Hitler, whom he hated with a bitter hatred. In 1938 he escaped by bicycle from Germany into Czechoslovakia, found his way to South Africa with Quaker help, and at the outbreak of war joined the Sappers. He was mentioned in dispatches, and on his return to South Africa went to the Natal University College and graduated in Botany. He strongly objected to that clause in the constitution which pledged opposition to 'all forms of totalitarianism such as communism and fascism'. He said that our foe was racism, in other words Afrikaner Nationalism, but we avoided all mention of it by singling out two foreign forms of totalitarianism. What is more, by singling out communism, we were playing into the hands of the government, and giving some kind of implicit support to the Suppression of Communism Act of 1950. However, in the end Marion and Molteno were too much for him, and the party decided to continue to single out fascism and communism as two abhorrent forms of totalitarianism. This decision did not bring us any closer to the Congress of Democrats or to the Congress Movement as a whole.

There was yet another sentence in the constitution that provoked much debate, and that was the affirmation that the party would employ 'only democratic and constitutional means' to achieve its objects. Here Marion and Hans Meidner stood shoulder to shoulder to oppose Molteno and his fellow conservatives. Marion and Meidner ridiculed the affirmation, and asked what constititional means were available to, say, the coloured people of the Cape, whose vote the Nationalist government was determined to take away. Did the party disapprove of the Defiance Campaign, and of the unlawful entrance of Patrick Duncan and Manilal Gandhi into the Germiston 'location'? Molteno was adamant that the party must disapprove such action. The aim of the party was not to be courageous but to win power, and one could not achieve power by unlawful actions.

This account of the 'brains' of the Liberal Party would be incomplete if there were no mention of Leo Marquard, the founder of N.U.S.A.S. (the National Union of South African Students), and a founder member of the Liberal Party. He had the reputation amongst us of being the master of commonsense. Students, who are said to trust no one over thirty, had the greatest respect for his opinions, and so did we. He was what is called a 'lost Afrikaner', largely because English was his conceptual language. He was certainly no conservative, but the right-wingers of the party listened to him with deference. It was he who prevented a dangerous breach between the Cape division and the rest of the party.

So it will be seen that the infant party had to pick its way amid the minefields of morality, religion, passion (or prejudice) and expediency. How did we stick together? I may say modestly that Peter Brown and I played the major part in holding together the Moltenos and the Marions and the Meidners. We were known as sober and intelligent and levelheaded, and our opinions were usually listened to with respect. It must also be said that Peter Brown and I were the two chief financial supporters of the party.

Our leader, Margaret Ballinger, held aloof from these debates. She was also a brain and she knew it. Indeed she was one of the most devastating debaters in the House, and was regarded as the outstanding liberal of her time. She had her share of arrogance, and did not pay much attention to the arguments of people like Marion and Meidner. Although she was a moralist, she was still more of an economist. She held views very like those of Molteno, and disliked radical policies that alienated white support. While she and Molteno were liberals to be reckoned with, they both had the same weakness as the Torch Commando; they wanted to fight for the rights of all men and women, but they were not particularly desirous of having all men and women join them in the fight. Neither she nor Molteno was guilty of the politics of innocence.

I must say that in 1954 I was more inclined to identify politics with morality than I am today. I remember well that at a meeting of our national executive, I criticised certain of our members' views because of their expediency. Molteno said to me, in a sentence that became quite famous inside the party, 'The trouble with you, Paton, is that you think the Liberal Party is a church.'

I must answer one last question. Did any of our members believe that the Liberal Party would ever get into power? It is a question that I shall first answer for myself. I never believed it. I did not join the party in order to achieve power. I joined it because I felt it was my duty. Did Molteno think that we would ever get into power? I doubt it. In any event the party was for him too visionary, too moral, too radical, ever to get into power. Margaret Ballinger had said that we must raise a standard to which all good men might repair, but she was then speaking as a moralist not as a politician. Nevertheless, it was a kind of rule – unwritten, I should think – that no member of the party must ever say in public that he or she did not believe we would ever get into power.

We did however have one member who believed not that we *would* get into power but that we *must*. That was Patrick Duncan, who, as I earlier related, was at that time an ardent follower of the late Mahatma Gandhi, and who believed that *satyagraha*, the soul force, would eventually triumph over all adversities. Those flames would shoot out of those blue eyes, and the ruddy cheeks would glow with physical and spiritual health, so that you would feel ashamed of yourself for not believing him. However, I shan't write about him now, because in 1954 he had not yet joined us. But his friend Manilal Gandhi, who had marched with him into the Germiston 'location', joined us in that year. It was not to be for long, for he died less than two years later. He was of all souls the most gentle.

It was now time for me to exchange the political for the ecumenical life, and to leave for Evanston, Illinois, for the second meeting of the World Council of Churches. So I missed the visit of Canon John Collins to South Africa.

It so happened that Richard Carte, prominent citizen of Durban and more than once mayor of that city, during a visit to London went with his wife to a service in St. Paul's Cathedral. The preacher was John Collins, who delivered a blistering attack on South Africa and apartheid and the National Party government.

Collins had this to say of our Prime Minister, Dr. Malan:

Let us sympathise with Dr. Malan. Let us be charitable to him – this poor, wretched man, hag-ridden with fear. We know that only love can cast out fear; but as well expect a man with *delirium tremens* to discover in his heart the love to destroy his illusions of pink elephants, as to hope that the Nationalists, whose hearts are full of fear, can rid themselves of the illusion of white superiority.

One must admit that this was trenchant stuff, and some people liked it, and some didn't. Richard Carte certainly didn't. Nor did the Most Rev. Geoffrey Fisher, the Archbishop of Canterbury, who withdrew his support for Christian Action, the movement founded by Collins in 1946. Nor did the Most Rev. Geoffrey Clayton, the Archbishop of Cape Town, who thought Collins was a ranter. Collins himself wrote that it was Christian Action's support for the Defiance Campaign that caused it to be regarded with increasing suspicion, even hostility. He further records that the World Council of Churches, after welcoming him as an observer to their first assembly in Amsterdam in 1948, never invited him again. He came to the conclusion that the building up of a distinguished sponsorship list 'can be more of a hindrance than an asset to any organisation set upon change, especially change through political action'. He wrote in typical Collins style, 'Just when you need them most, when it is time for action, they drop off the hook.'*

Richard Carte returned to South Africa determined to do something about Canon Collins. He appealed to some meeting of Durban businessmen to invite Collins to South Africa so that he could see for himself. He thought it possible that if Collins saw for himself, he would see that white South Africa was not as black as it was painted. He would meet white South Africans who were devoted to good works. He would be free to go wherever he wanted, and to talk to anybody he wanted. Then he might go back to Britain and say to the British, 'You know, that place isn't as bad as it is painted. It is not as bad as you have been told. It is full of people of goodwill. I am full of hope.'

Richard Carte's suggestion was taken up by a well-to-do businessman, Jack Shave, who invited Collins to come to Durban for a month, all expenses paid. The only condition was that, when he returned to England, he would speak 'truthfully and publicly' of what he had seen and heard.

Shave was wasting his time and money. Collins had already taken a stand from which he could not retreat. He was the leader of a fighting force, and he could not suddenly say, 'Our enemies are not as bad as I thought.' He had said at St. Paul's that the Nationalists would never be able to 'rid themselves of the illusion of white superiority'. Collins would not have been convinced by any number of good works. He was the sworn foe of apartheid, and he would see plenty of that during any tour of South Africa. He would have regarded good works – to use the modern phrase – as cosmetic.

Collins formed a low opinion of the South African churches, even those who spoke against apartheid. He had words of praise only for

* *Faith Under Fire*, Leslie Frewin, London, 1966, p. 189.

Ambrose Reeves and Trevor Huddleston, and for that lonely campaigner Michael Scott, who had in 1951 been declared a prohibited immigrant by the South African government. I shall write later of the great help that we were to get in later years from Collins and Christian Action, and especially from the fund called Defence and Aid. But I must report that in 1954 his opinion of liberals and liberalism was very low. He wrote thus in his book *Faith Under Fire* (p. 196), 'The hard truth is that in 1954 the Congress of Democrats was the only white organisation which had shown itself to be consistently and unequivocally opposed to colour discrimination of every kind; this lead, which the Christian Churches might have taken, was allowed to slip into other hands.'

In 1977 he threatened to sue L.E.S. de Villiers, of the South African Information Department, for declaring in his book *South Africa: A Skunk Among Nations* that Collins was a communist or a communist sympathiser. Yet Collins wrote in *Faith Under Fire* (p. 207), 'It was my experiences in South Africa . . . which confirmed my growing conviction that my ministry could sometimes, perhaps often, be better exercised in co-operating with non-Christians, including communists, than with church people.'

I shall conclude by saying that in my long friendship with John Collins we always avoided any discussion of this issue. By no means did I hold the view that one should not co-operate with people who were not Christians. In the Liberal Party we had Christians, Jews, Hindus, Muslims, and people of no religious persuasion. But I shared the distrust of Marion Friedmann and many others of communism and communists.

Collins had a unique relationship with communists, which was very different from our own. For one thing he was not a member of an anti-communist party. He also had what might be called a phenomenal gift. He was a genius at raising money, especially for those who suffered under apartheid, those who were charged with subversive and treasonable acts, and those who were banished and exiled. I stayed with John and Diana many times at Amen Court in London during the 1950s, and when the mail arrived at breakfast time it would be full of cheques and pledges. He opened his mail with eager anticipation, with pithy comments on the donors, and the amounts of their donation, made with that grin so characteristic of him, looking more like a boy than a canon. Many a South African had reason to be thankful that there was a man like John Collins in the world.

Collins left South Africa confirmed in his opinions. He had given encouragement to many opponents of apartheid, he had affronted churchmen and doers of good work, he had to a large extent ignored liberals, and he had deeply angered Afrikaner Nationalists, who in private were extremely critical of their revered leader Dr. D.F. Malan for allowing such a man into the country.

As for Jack Shave, he was infuriated when Collins gave an interview *before* he left South Africa. In his view Collins had repaid his host with base ingratitude, having stated publicly that South Africa was worse than he had expected. To put it mildly, Shave was foolish to have expected anything else.

My warmest memories of John and Diana Collins are not political at all. They were hosts in a thousand, and John was a lover and a connoisseur of wine. If I returned to Amen Court at midnight, after a visit or meeting in London or elsewhere, John would regard that as an occasion for a bottle of good wine, which we would drink in their bedroom. He and Diana had a near-perfect marriage.

John was a liberation theologian born before his time. The World Council of Churches of the 1950s found him a bit hard to take and, as he himself wrote, the World Council had cooled towards him. Even in later years, when the council became more and more 'liberation-minded' it would still have been cool towards him, because he was essentially an individualist. He was never first and foremost an ecumenicist. So while his ecumenical sun was sinking, mine was rising, and I set off for Evanston, Illinois, with great expectations.

Chapter 15

Evanston, Illinois, 1954. The second meeting of the World Council of Churches. My particular group was housed in a married students' building in Evanston. We were not allowed to use the students' air-conditioners, so I spent the hottest summer of my life, hotter than Durban or Ibadan. Evanston was a prohibition town, but it must have had lots of drinkers, because on leaving the town one entered streets lined with shops selling beverages, and this did not mean tea and coffee.

The opening of the World Council was very grand, and took place at Chicago's Soldier Field, where a great host answered the following questions:

Q. Who are you to have come here?
A. We are Christians. We have come from many different traditions.
Q. What is it to be a Christian?
A. It is to believe in God the Father: in His only Son, our Lord, who is the hope of the World: and in the Holy Spirit.
Q. From where have you come?
A. From one hundred and sixty-three member churches and from forty-eight countries on five continents.
Q. Why have you come?
A. We have come to worship God.

The theme of Evanston was 'Christ: The Hope of the World'. Hope is the most difficult word in the language of Christians, more difficult than faith, and much more difficult than love. This was clearly seen in two of the earliest addresses. Professor Edmund Schlink of Heidelberg told us that we must not expect Christ to ensure the safety of this world. Professor Robert Calhoun of Yale told us on the contrary that the gospel of hope was 'a word for this world', and that Christ taught us to pray, 'Thy will be done on earth.'

The enigmatic and wistful nature of hope is shown in Hardy's poem 'The Oxen'. He refers to the 'fancy' that on Christmas Eve, the oxen go on their knees.

> If someone said on Christmas Eve,
> 'Come; see the oxen kneel
> In the lonely barton by yonder coomb
> Our childhood used to know,'
> I should go with him in the gloom,
> Hoping it might be so.

The tragic nature of hope is shown in the two books by Nadezhda Mandelstam about the persecution of her poet-husband during Stalin's terror. The first is called *Hoping Against Hope,* and the second *Hope Abandoned*. The wistful and tragic nature of hope was not the topic of Evanston. The trumpet had to be blown, and blown it was.

Evanston has passed into history, and I would not try to tell its story. In any case its story is largely irrelevant today, except that it is part of the evolution of the World Council. World Christianity as manifested today in the World Council has changed greatly. It is today very much a 'word for this world'. Cecil Northcott in his booklet *Evanston World Assembly* wrote that the assembly recognised that some of its fellow-ship believed that in preaching 'race separation' within the church they were fulfilling the scriptures and obeying the universal laws of God. That tolerance of which he wrote has gone for ever. If the Nederduitse Gereformeerde Kerk of South Africa (N.G.K.) had not withdrawn from the W.C.C., the W.C.C. would have expelled it.

I shall content myself with writing that the corruption of religion by history was very evident at Evanston. The Lebanese Christians held late meetings at my student residence discussing the proposal to send a special message to the Jews, a proposal they did not like at all. We debated the respective virtues of capitalism and socialism, with the Americans extremely wary of socialism. The Germans, although they had not long since experienced the terror of Hitler, were opposed to any denigration of the State, which was ordained of God. The Christians of the East had little patience with long theological discussions, and were more concerned with the poor and the oppressed. And lastly the Nederduitse Gereformeerde Kerk of South Africa and the Nederduitse Hervormde Kerk of South Africa, alone in that vast assembly, upheld racial separation as being the will of God.

I remember hardly a word of these debates, even though I had been appointed the scribe of Section V of the assembly, which had to prepare a report on 'Inter-Group Relations – The Church amid Racial and Ethnic Tensions'. But I remember clearly two personal encounters.

One was with Mrs. John Karefa-Smart from West Africa. It did not take her long to realise that the delegates of the N.G.K. were ill at ease in that great assembly, especially the Rev. C.B. Brink, Moderator of the powerful synod of the Southern Transvaal. At home in South Africa the N.G.K. is associated with great temporal power, away from home at Evanston it found itself in the smallest minority of all. Its delegates could not even feel at home with their fellow South Africans, such as Ambrose Reeves, Bishop of Johannesburg, and myself, who had condemned race separation as unChristian. Brink had the same drawn face as Vernon Berrangé, and for the same reason, for both of them were very sensitive to their isolation. Much less ill at ease was the Rev. Ben Marais, also of the N.G.K., for he had travelled widely in the world, and had spent time in Brazil, where he went to study a society that had virtually no colour bar.

Mrs. Karefa-Smart was very conscious of Brink's isolation, and although she was black (or rather a beautiful golden-brown) she was not prepared to shut him out. On the contrary, she was determined to bring him in, and she became his constant companion. On the day after the close of the assembly when we all departed for our various destinations, Mrs. Karefa-Smart came to our building to say goodbye to her white South African friend. I told her that he had left for one of the buses that had come to take us away. The last I saw of her she was running down the street to the bus station, so that she could say farewell before he left. It is something that I have never forgotten. Brink has long since departed this world, but I do not think he would have had the courage to invite his friend from West Africa to visit him in the deep South.

My second personal encounter was with a submarine commander, perhaps the most famous in submarine history. His name was Martin Niemöller.

Niemöller served in the German navy from 1910 to 1918 and must have sunk many ships and many men. But after the war his thoughts turned to peace, and in 1924 he was ordained, going to Berlin in 1931 as pastor of the influential church of Dahlem. Two years later Hitler came to power. At first Niemöller regarded Hitler as the saviour of Germany, but State interference in Church affairs made him change his mind. He was no lover of Jews, but took seriously the commandment that we should love our enemies. At the end of 1933 Niemöller formed the Pastors' Emergency League to oppose the corruption of the

Church by Nazi ideology, and created an opposition movement which came to be known as the Confessing Church.

In 1934 Hitler summoned Niemöller to his presence, and finding him recalcitrant, forbade him to preach. But he continued to preach, and drew great crowds to hear him. In 1937 he was sent to the concentration camp at Sachsenhausen and later to Dachau. When war broke out in 1939, this brave and strange man offered his services to the navy, but Hitler rejected the offer. Just before his suicide the Führer ordered the execution of several prominent prisoners, Niemöller amongst them. The order was not obeyed.

In 1945 Niemöller, liberated by the U.S. army, threw himself into the rebuilding of the Church, and was one of the German churchmen who welcomed a delegation from the W.C.C. to Stuttgart on 17 October 1945. The delegation faced one great difficulty. They felt that the German Church should perform some act of repentance, but they also felt that they could not ask for it. It was Niemöller who removed the difficulty.

After the delegates had been welcomed by Bishop Wurm at the opening service in the Markuskirche on 17 October, Niemöller gave a remarkable address. He first read from Jeremiah 14, including these words:

We acknowledge, O Lord, our wickedness, and the iniquity of our fathers, for we have sinned against thee. Do not abhor us, for thy name's sake, do not disgrace the throne of thy glory; remember, break not thy covenant with us.

He also used some remarkable words of his own:

It is not enough to blame the Nazis. The Church also has to confess its guilt. Would the Nazis have been able to do what they had done if church members had been wholly faithful?

On the morning of 18 October the Council of the German Church and the W.C.C. delegation met separately, but in the afternoon they met together. Dr. Visser 't Hooft expressed the gratitude of the delegation for the struggle of the Confessing Church. He paid tribute to Dietrich Bonhoeffer, who had returned from America to almost certain death and had come to the dread conclusion that the assassination of Hitler was a sacred duty. Niemöller spoke again, and said that the new emerging Church knew that it shared the guilt, and prayed that God would forgive.

The Council and the W.C.C. delegation met again on the morning of 19 October, and Pastor Asmussen announced that the Council had unanimously accepted a declaration. This was the famous Stuttgart Declaration of Guilt, one of the most notable documents in the history of the Christian Church. The following words are taken from it.

We are all the more grateful for this visit as we know ourselves to be with our people in a great company of suffering, but also in a great solidarity of guilt. With great pain do we say: through us has endless suffering been brought to many peoples and countries. What we have often borne witness to before our congregations, that we declare in the name of the whole church. True we have struggled for many years in the name of Jesus Christ against a spirit which has found its terrible expression in the National Socialist regime of violence, but we accuse ourselves for not witnessing more courageously, for not praying more faithfully, for not believing more joyously, and for not loving more ardently . . . So in an hour in which the whole world needs a new beginning we pray: 'Veni Creator Spiritus.'

It was Pastor Niemöller who introduced himself to me. He had read the German translation of *Cry, the Beloved Country*, which had the title *Denn Sie Sollen Getrostet Werden* and was made by Marta Hackel, a German woman who had lived for many years in South Africa, and knew the meaning of what she was translating. *Denn Sie Sollen Getrostet Werden* had moved Niemöller deeply, and he told me so. He and I became friends, the submarine commander and the reformatory principal, and ate our lunch together every day after that.

I soon realised that Niemöller was a controversial figure and a loner. His name was mentioned widely as a candidate for one of the six presidencies of the W.C.C., but either it never went forward, or it went forward and was rejected. The leaders of the W.C.C. were uneasy about him, including his own fellow churchmen from Germany. Perhaps a man who has been a submarine commander has character traits that cause lesser men to distrust him. Furthermore he was the first prominent West German to visit Soviet Russia, and in 1954 he became a pacifist. He advocated the unilateral disarmament of his country, and was awarded the Lenin Peace Prize. I am glad to record that in 1961 the W.C.C. elected him to one of its six presidencies. He died in 1984 at the age of 92. When Evanston was over, I parted with great regret from my loner friend, and I never saw him again. I am proud to have been admitted to his friendship and to be able to write these lines about one of the bravest men of our times.

Before Evanston ended, another lonely event occurred. The N.G.K. decided that it would tell the great assembly why it and the N.H.K. could not accept the report on the 'Church and Racial Tensions'. This task was undertaken by the Rev. Cornelius B. Brink, Moderator of the N.G.K. synod of the Southern Transvaal. He stood up with tight and drawn face, the representative of a cause that no one else believed in, except perhaps a few silent white members of the churches of the American deep South. Not only did that great assembly not believe in the cause, they considered it immoral and unChristian, and many of them were outraged that the N.G.K. and the N.H.K. should try to justify it from scripture.

Brink said that the Afrikaner churches would neither vote against the report nor seek to amend it. He foresaw trouble in returning to South Africa with such a report.

We wish to place on record that we have experienced at Evanston much evidence of what we truly believe to be real Christian good will and an attempt to understand the peculiar difficulties we have to face. In response to that we now pledge ourselves personally to the task of urging our respective churches to apply themselves as urgently as possible to the study of the report.

Of this event the *Christian Century* wrote, 'Evanston may have known no more Christian moment.' If this was true, then it was partly the work of Mrs. John Karefa-Smart, the golden-brown woman from West Africa. That was thirty-three years ago, and I must record that the race attitudes of the white N.G.K. are slowly changing, while the attitudes of the white N.H.K. are as unbending as ever. The white N.H.K. still affirms that racial separation is the will of God, and it remains, and intends to remain, an all-white body. I am glad to record that the white N.G.K. has at last repented of having supported the government in its far-reaching programme of racial separation, and this church will undoubtedly lose some of its members to the N.H.K. and some to new church organsations that will continue to support separation within the church.

So Evanston came to an end.

My room-mate at the student residence for the two weeks was Liston Pope, Dean of the Yale Divinity School, who described himself as the only Pope who recognised his children. I have to thank him for a great honour. He was largely responsible for the decision of Yale University to mark the occasion of Evanston by awarding honorary degrees to five of the participants. These were the Rt. Rev. Geoffrey Fisher, Archbishop of Canterbury; Paul David Devananden, one of the leading churchmen of India; Archbishop Michael of the Greek Orthodox Churches of North and South America; Bishop Friedrich Karl Otto Dibelius of East Germany; and Alan Paton of South Africa.

The ceremony took place in the Battell Chapel on 28 September 1954, and was part of the opening service of the one hundred and thirty-third year of the Yale Divinity School. I was presented by one of the new presidents of the W.C.C., Presiding Bishop Knox Sherrill of the Episcopal Church, and the citation was read by Whitney Griswold, President of Yale University:

Alan Stewart Paton, novelist, social worker, and lay member of the Church of

England in South Africa, whose beloved country is a loveless land, you have sought in matters of race to obey the commandments of the Lord of all mankind, and have foretold a day when all men shall call each other brother. Echoing the stately cadences of the ancient Psalmist, you have given poetry and dignity to English prose. A loyal Anglican, you have entered faithfully into the labors of men of ecumenical spirit. A layman, you have inspired clergy and laity alike. Acknowledging your courage and compassion rooted in Christian faith, Yale University confers upon you the degree of Doctor of Humane Letters.

Very complimentary, you must agree. The citation was clearly the work of Liston Pope, for I used to read him a psalm every morning in our room at Evanston. It contained one mistake. I was not a member of the Church of England in South Africa, but of the Church of the Province of South Africa. I shall not discuss the question of the difference between the two. It is a complicated and thorny one.

It was now time for me to go home and I arrived in Johannesburg on 6 October. After a few days with Dorrie and David and Jonathan, I threw myself into work for the Liberal Party, in Durban, Pietermaritzburg, Johannesburg, Pretoria, Cape Town, being met and followed always by the security police. At Evanston I had basked in the warm sun of world approval, but now I was again an outcast. I did not really mind it, for I found the company of the other outcasts very congenial, and was glad to be back with them. There was one unfortunate consequence of my devotion to the party. I did not feel able to go to the Third Assembly of the W.C.C. in 1958, and I did not attend the following assemblies because my government decided that I was not a fit person to travel abroad. They took my passport away, and I was too proud to ask for it back. I shall tell how I much later applied to have it back, and got it.

Chapter 16

Whenever any group of people come together to pursue some common political goal, there is always a left and a right and a centre. The Liberal Party of South Africa was not immune. Although we all upheld certain principles of freedom, such as the liberty to meet together, to publish, speak, and move about the country, although we all rejected statutory racial separation and discrimination and upheld the rule of law, yet we also had our left, right and centre.

Strangely enough, this natural and human distribution also had a rough geographical correlation. In the early days of the party, the Cape was the right, the Transvaal was the left, and Natal was the centre.

Liberalism is not an ideology. It allows a freedom of thought and opinion to its members that an ideology does not allow. But some of our members were more ideologically inclined than others. Our debates on the control of education, for example, were at times very stormy. Should racial groups such as the Afrikaners and the Zulus be allowed to maintain separate and exclusive schools for their children? Should such schools be subsidised by the State?

It was no use looking to the United States for a solution. The U.S.A. had one official language, English. South Africa had two, English and Afrikaans, but it also had several other virile and widely spoken languages, such as Zulu, Xhosa and Sotho. According to the Universal Declaration of Human Rights, a document strongly approved of by the Liberal Party: 'Parents have a right to choose the kind of education that shall be given to their children.' What did that mean? Did it mean that Afrikaner Nationalist parents had a right to maintain schools which would in fact be instruments of Afrikaner Nationalism? I should mention that a number of Liberals, a small number, was prepared to make English the sole official language of South Africa. Some of these members were white, and some were not. Their attitude was the consequence of their revulsion against the authoritarian rule of the National Party. All of us had this revulsion, but most of us were not prepared to relegate Afrikaans to the status of a non-official language.

Finally the party in full congress decided that no State or State-aided school could discriminate in the admission of pupils and the appointment of teachers solely on the grounds of race or colour. It also decided that parents should have free choice of a language to be used as the medium of instruction. The party's left wing in the Transvaal was not satisfied with these decisions, for it meant that a State-aided school controlled by Afrikaner parents would be able in fact to avoid the employment of black teachers, if not to avoid the admission of black children. Some of our left-wing members wanted to give the Afrikaner Nationalist a dose of his own authoritarian medicine. Their attitude was certainly illiberal, and indeed the whole question was academic, for no black teacher or black pupil was likely to seek admission to a school controlled by Afrikaner parents. The stormy debates were to continue for some years, but the decisions remained as they had been in the beginning. There was one thing we could be proud of, that never once in our thirteen years of existence did any party congress divide according to race or colour. The left-wing Transvaal had another grievance, this time against Natal, who had put up three candidates in the white provincial elections, Peter Brown, Violaine Junod, and Ronald Morris, and all three had been badly beaten. The Transvaal argued that Liberals must not make fools of themselves.

Yet though the Transvaal Liberals were the left-wing of our party, they were intensely mistrustful of the real white left, the Congress of Democrats. The Democrats, together with the Indian and African Congresses and the South African Coloured Peoples Organisation, had decided to hold a great Congress of the People in June 1955. To this gathering would be presented a document which was to be called the Freedom Charter, and it would set out all the requirements of a just order of society. It would affirm that South Africa belonged to all its people, it would demand a non-racial and democratic form of government, it would demand nationalisation of heavy industry, the mines, and the banks, it would demand the redistribution of the land and the removal of all restrictions on labour and on domestic and family life. It would in fact set out the conditions for a South African Utopia. It would be anathema to the National Party, who would see in it the work of the devil and the Communist Party.

The Congress Movement invited the Liberal Party to take part in the Congress of the People, and the party agreed. This decision caused great disquiet, and this was not geographically determined. The Cape was in general reluctant to have anything to do with the Democrats, and some of the leading Transvaal members, such as Marion Friedmann and Ruth Hayman, had a deep distrust of them. Peter Brown, Hans Meidner, Violaine Junod, and others in Natal, were not enthusiastic. The Liberals suspected – and with good cause I think – that the Congress of the People was being run by the Congress of Democrats. The Liberal Party in Natal had just recruited a notable member, Jordan Ngubane, a leading African journalist with a sharp analytical mind. He was an unequivocal anti-communist, and warned the party to have nothing to do with the Democrats, who in his view were turning the African National Congress towards communism.

Molteno, that formidable member of the Cape region, watched these developments in the party with disapproval and distaste. Although he regarded racial discrimination as immoral, he was not enthusiastic over the fact that the party was gaining more and more recruits from the Indian, coloured, and African communities. He argued that the Africans had been removed to a separate roll, and the Indians had no vote at all, while the vote of the coloured people was limited and qualified. Therefore none of these groups would be of much help in winning elections. In fact the very presence in the party of so many members of these communities would deter more conservative white voters from voting for a Liberal candidate. Molteno did not like the continuing struggle in the party over the franchise, nor did he like the decision to take part in the Congress of the People.

He and Margaret Ballinger, the national leader, took much the same view of what they thought unwise and radical tendencies in the party, but she had to be more circumspect than he. She was regarded as the leading liberal in the country and she could not be thought or seen to be critical of the numbers of Indians and coloured people and Africans who were joining the party.

Molteno, who was a very bright man, conceived the unbright idea of reconstructing the party on a federal basis. That would have meant, presumably, that the Cape, Transvaal, and Natal, could adopt regional policies of their own. They could for example have three different franchise policies. The Liberal Party would have become a laughing-stock, and the idea was rejected. Molteno continued to be an uneasy member, and his uneasiness was increased by the growth of a strong left-wing in the Cape, and by the increase in the Cape of a number of African and coloured recruits.

I must record that in the end the party did not take part in the

Congress of the People. This was largely because of its distrust of the white Congress of Democrats, and its suspicion, almost strong enough to be called its belief, that the Democrats were in fact the moving force behind the Congress of the People. For a long time the party heard no news of the congress, and was suddenly informed in the second week of June that it would take place on 26 and 27 June. This proved the final straw, and the party withdrew. It is an interesting fact that the Transvaal division, to use the words of Peter Brown, was 'infuriated' by this decision. This was not because of any burning desire to attend the congress, but because the Transvaal knew that our decision would be interpreted by many black people as a betrayal, perhaps even a cowardly betrayal.

Chief Lutuli was displeased with our action. I do not think that any biographer will ever discover why, but it is my surmise that he felt that our action pushed him further into the arms of the left. He had reason to be sensitive about this, because our new member Jordan Ngubane, who had been a strong Lutuli supporter, was openly warning that the communists were taking over the African National Congress. Lutuli found himself between the devil and the deep blue sea, if I may give the Liberal Party such an appellation.

I must not give the impression that the life of the party was one of continuous bickering at national and regional congresses. When it was a matter of opposing racial legislation, and of resisting it by all lawful methods (the famous 'constitutional means'), the members forgot all their differences.

In 1955 there was a black suburb of Johannesburg known as Sophiatown. But as white Johannesburg grew in population, it enveloped the black suburb, Sophiatown became a 'black spot', and its existence offended the Afrikaner Nationalists. It also offended against Dr. Verwoerd's master plan for 'separate areas of freedom'. Therefore it had to go.

Not only did our members forget their ideological differences in these circumstances, but they were also able to cooperate with the Congresses, although it must be admitted that they cooperated more easily with the African National Congress than they did with the Democrats. Many of the white members of the party now had their first taste of confronting the awesome power of the State, as embodied in the security police and the ordinary uniformed police. They had never done this before, and they didn't like it, except for a few who seemed to enjoy bearding authority. I myself didn't like it either, and even after much more experience I still don't like it.

I do not derive pleasure from criticising or attacking (verbally!) the police. I am conscious that ordinary members of society like myself owe much to the police. But I am also conscious that in times of crisis, such as the crisis of Sophiatown, the white police easily become antagonised by any person, white or black, who opposes government action. On one occasion a black woman member of the party, who was known for her opposition and widely respected for her courage and integrity, was arrested for loitering on her way from her house to the shops. Her distressed family got in touch immediately with a white member in Johannesburg, a young housewife, eager for justice, but apprehensive about entering a police station. She did not get far with the stony-faced sergeant in charge, and eventually had to telephone another white woman member, Ruth Hayman, attorney-at-law, to come and help her. Ruth made it clear to the sergeant that she would go to the court, and prove beyond doubt that such a woman was incapable of committing the offence of loitering, and that the police were themselves committing the offence of wrongful arrest. They were trying to intimidate a woman who was opposing the removal. The sergeant gave in, and released the woman on her own recognisances.

As far as I could see, Ruth knew no fear, though I don't suppose that this was so. She was certainly one of the bravest women that I have known in my life. She was not beautiful, but she was gifted with an extraordinary vitality that set her face alight. She took her duties as a lawyer very seriously and would confront any person or any authority in the pursuit of justice. She was one of the brightest ornaments of the party.

When a person of my generation hears the name of Sophiatown, another name comes immediately to mind, that of Trevor Huddleston. I have told the story of the destruction of Sophiatown elsewhere, in chapter 28 of *Apartheid and the Archbishop*. Huddleston, whose great church of Christ the King was in Sophiatown, wrote in his famous book *Naught for Your Comfort*, the following words:

It is told of Smuts, that when he said farewell to any of his friends or distinguished visitors leaving South Africa, he quoted in that high-pitched voice of his the lines of De la Mare: 'Look thy last on all things lovely, every hour.' I have no doubt that to Smuts the loveliness of South Africa was its natural beauty and grandeur: its wild flowers and grasses, about which he knew so much; the great emptiness of its skies above the silence of the veld.

There is no doubt that Huddleston gave his heart to Sophiatown. He writes that he had never been able to feel that nostalgia for *places*, however lovely. Be that as it may, he gave his heart to Sophiatown and its people. It was a wild, exciting, tumultuous place. It had grown up without design. Plots had been split up again and again, resulting in a kaleidoscopic conglomeration of shops, houses, lodging-rooms, brothels, shebeens, churches. A child might grow up good in Sophiatown, but never innocent. Yet it became for Huddleston the home of all things lovely. It was the place where old men and women came into the church of Christ the King on their hands and knees. One of the things that moved Huddleston most deeply was that goodness existed in the most unlikely of places. Why should anyone love God in a place like this? How could anyone even believe in Him?

Huddleston was at the very centre of the opposition to the destruction of Sophiatown. He seemed to have inexhaustible energy. 10 February 1955 was the day of the removal. On that day Huddleston was not only the most prominent person in Sophiatown, or in South Africa. His name was flashed all over the world. He was the champion of the voiceless and the oppressed. Did he like this attention? I have no doubt that he did, but it was not as simple as all that. I think he was prepared to step out into the limelight and the spotlight and the searchlight if that would advance his cause, which undoubtedly was the cause of righteousness. But I think he quite liked being out there: or at least he did not shrink from it. Huddleston's love of justice, his hatred of injustice, his love of man, all parts of his love of God, were the main driving forces of his life. He was not a publicity hunter for himself.

What did he look like? He had a lean face of good colour, dark hair turning grey, a spare athletic body, and beautiful and expressive hands. Did he know that his hands were beautiful and expressive? He certainly knew that they were expressive. The picture on the dust-cover of *Naught for Your Comfort* shows that he – or someone else – thought his face and hands were beautiful. There was a burning quality in him, but not of fever; it was rather the quality of a steady undiminishing flame, the light that so shines before men that they glorify their Father which is in heaven. Was he a saint? I would guess that he was, but very human. He could wash a black boy's feet – perhaps one whom he had sent on a tiring errand – and kiss them when he washed them. Old black men and women loved him. Children ran to hold his hand in the streets.

Did this please everybody? Most certainly not. The Afrikaner Nationalists were enraged that this stranger from England 'who didn't understand the country', should criticise their laws and should oppose the carrying out of the Great Plan in Sophiatown. Many of his own fellow churchmen disapproved of him; he was for them too extreme, too flamboyant, too intolerant. Even some of his fellow monks disapproved of him, because they considered that he was endangering the missionary work of the Community of the Resurrection. His archbishop Geoffrey Clayton, who was a great man with considerable strengths and weaknesses, took the extreme step of writing to Huddleston's Superior, Father Raymond Raynes, saying that he no longer wished to be Visitor to the Community of the Resurrection while Huddleston was its Provincial. Clayton later wrote to Huddleston saying that they were 'different kinds of persons', which was true. One could hardly imagine Clayton kissing a black boy's feet.

Huddleston's activities in Sophiatown greatly angered Dr. Hendrik Verwoerd, the chief architect of the Great Plan. He said that the position was serious, not as a result of resistance from the people, but as a result of incitement by a number of agitators, including, 'he was sorry to say', a number of clergy, one of whom was Father Huddleston. The Minister spoke of the 'dangerous situation' created by Huddleston and the African Congress. Dr. Verwoerd quoted me as having said, 'Apartheid is something which is done by people who have power to those who have not,' and he asked, 'Can there be anything more inciting than this?' This was the stock argument of the Nationalists, that it was not removals and the destruction of houses that incited people; the inciters were those who condemned such actions and most of all those who published news of them abroad.

The removal of the people of Sophiatown was carried out successfully. It is impossible to offer resistance to two thousand armed police. The Commissioner of Police patrolled up and down in a radio van, in hourly contact with the Minister in Cape Town. After the removal a great fleet of bulldozers moved in, and razed the houses and the brothels and the shops to the ground. Only the great church of Christ the King was left standing, for what reason I do not know. When the demolition was complete, the builders moved in, and a new town for poorer white workers came into being. It was given the arrogant name of Triomf, which means Triumph, and this was no doubt intended to mean the triumph of civilisation over barbarism, of order over chaos, above all no doubt the triumph of the Great Plan which would bring peace and joy to every person in South Africa.

Later in 1955 Huddleston knew that his Superior would call him back to England. This knowledge threw him into a deep depression, and he contemplated disobedience. But not for long. He had vowed to obey, and obey he would. He came to stay with Dorrie and me for a week, and during this time completed his book *Naught for Your Comfort*. It was a great success and he often commiserated with me because I had not written a book so successful. When he returned to England, he would write to tell me of fantastic but wholly imaginary offers for film rights, radio rights, TV rights. He would commiserate with me for never having been translated into Yoruba or Lozi, though he had never been translated into them either. He also commiserated with me because I had never had a swimming-bath or a jazz band named after me.

Although Huddleston was never fully to recover from the destruction of Sophiatown and his recall to England, he did not lose his sense of humour. He would invent clever names and addresses to be written on the backs of letters that he wrote to me. One was:

> Rev. O. Lution,
> Copse Watching,
> Stillfree,
> England.

And another:

> Miss Sedgie Nation,
> 'Piebaldings',
> Much Mixing.

Huddleston had a great love of children, and confided to me that his only regret about having taken the vows of poverty, obedience and celibacy, was that he could never have children. I visited him in Mauritius when he had the grand title of Archbishop of the Indian Ocean, and he had more or less adopted two small boys who had no parents. His devotion to them was moving, sometimes painful to witness. His face would light up with joy when he was with them. He was able to arrange for their adoption by a young couple who visited Mauritius. The two boys – who are brothers – now live in England and Huddleston can see them whenever he wishes.

I shall close this portrait of an extraordinary man with three final observations. Though he and I often discussed the themes of love and justice, and though we appeared together on protest platforms, we almost never discussed practical politics. Like Collins before him, he was more attracted to the Congress movement than to the Liberal Party. In particular he was attracted to the African National Congress, and this was natural because his work brought him into continual contact with African people. If a vote had been taken for the white man or woman most liked and trusted by African people, he would have won it overwhelmingly. He gave his support to the projected Congress of the People, and in fact attended it. He had no occasion to distrust the Congress of Democrats, and was interested in their activities rather than their political philosophy. For him, as for Chief Lutuli, South Africa was on fire, and he found it impossible to say to his fellow fire-fighters, 'Where does your water come from, and what kind of bucket are you carrying it in?'

My second observation is that although in the 1950s Huddleston was politically able to cooperate closely with the far left, he was far from ecumenical in religious matters. If he had twitted me about my distrust of the left, I could have twitted him about his distrust of other Christian groups than his own, notably the Roman Catholics. Therefore he did not twit me. I must record that thirty years later he had become the most ecumenical of believers. In fact he had become what one would call an all-faiths man. This was the result of pursuing for thirty years the cause of justice in the company of people of every kind and condition.

My third observation is that although Huddleston and I never discussed practical politics, he had a special affection for me, and that was because he could discuss things other than politics with me. He was a reading man, and so was I, whereas many of his political friends thought that literature had only one worthwhile function, and that was to serve the cause of justice and the people. It is nearly thirty years since he left Johannesburg and South Africa, and I think of him a great deal. I too regret that he has never had a wife or a home or children, and that he was not able to express fully his tender and loving nature. His life has been characterised by an intense love of justice, and it has therefore become more and more concerned with the injustices which black people suffer under apartheid. It has in fact become more and more a life of protest, and for me protest is not enough. I apologise for this judgement of a man to whom I am morally inferior. But if one writes about life, one has to write about what one believes to be true. To tell the truth, sometimes my heart aches for him.

Although Sophiatown was the most famous 'black spot' in South Africa, we had many in Natal. Most of them had come into being in this way. In the early part of this century it was legal for a black man to buy land from a white one. In Roosboom, near Ladysmith, Natal, some black men clubbed together to buy a white farm, and then divided the farm into smaller plots; this enabled a black man working in Durban or Johannesburg to build a small house for his wife and family, to which he would return whenever he was able. This also gave to him a new sense of security, for now no tyrannical chief could harry or eject him. A community such as Roosboom had its churches, schools, shops, builders and carpenters. These 'black spots' were in general known for their law-abidingness, and their affairs were managed by their chosen councils. They were examples of democracy at its best.

In 1913 the all-white parliament of the newly constituted Union of South Africa passed the Natives Land Act, which made it unlawful for a black man to buy land in what was designated a white area. This Act was one of the laws resented most deeply by black people. It meant virtually that no more black men could ever become farmers, nor own a few acres on which they could pasture a few cows and cultivate maize, beans, and pumpkins. They could in fact not own a piece of land in the country of their birth. Yet a more disastrous blow was to follow. In 1936 parliament passed the Native Land and Trust Act which empowered the government to dispossess those who had bought land legally in the early part of the century. Parliament gave the Minister power to remove people from the 'black spots' and to return the land to white occupation. Dr. Verwoerd announced that the government would proceed with a programme of removals until not a 'black spot' remained. The black landowners could not believe it: they had always thought that a title deed was a sacred document, and that not even the harshest of white governments would ever take it away. But they had not reckoned with Dr. Verwoerd and the Great Plan. Since 1948 South Africa has seen many shameful acts committed by people with power against those who have none. But the removal of the 'black spots' was the most shameful of all.

The Liberal Party in Natal took up the cause of the black landowners with great determination. As a result, large numbers of black people joined the party, and within two years of our beginnings our membership was one-third black, one-third white and one-third Indian. This was largely the work of Peter Brown, who spoke both Xhosa and Zulu well and who certainly had the gift of communicating with black people. One of our recruits was Elliot Mngadi, who joined us although he was then a Messenger of the Court – quite a brave thing to do. He joined at a house meeting held in the home of Walter and Adelain Hain, who later were to pay a high price for their liberal beliefs.

Elliot's father was one of the original joint-purchasers of the white-owned farm of Roosboom. He had built for himself a substantial house, and was one of the respected elders of the community. Elliot started school in Roosboom, but later had to take work as a domestic servant on the Witwatersrand in order to save money for further schooling. He worked by day and studied by night, and eventually passed his matriculation examination, returning to Ladysmith first to manage a small cooperative business and then to become Messenger of the Court. After he joined the party he was kept under close surveillance by the security police, but that did not deter him from helping to found the Natal African Landowners Association, nor later from becoming its Organiser. He too was to pay a price for his Liberal beliefs, but he was going to pay a yet higher price because his father had, in the company of others, bought the white farm called Roosboom. Now the government sentenced Roosboom to death. The sentence was not executed for another twenty years, and I shall tell of it later.

The hard work done by the Natal African Landowners Association, with strong support from the Liberal Party, had done much to strengthen our bonds with Chief Lutuli and the African National Congress. But these bonds, as I have said, were weakened again when the party finally decided not to take part in the Congress of the People. This congress, held on 26 and 27 June, at the black township of Kliptown outside Johannesburg, was attended by some three thousand people from all parts of South Africa. Hundreds of police also attended, but there was no trouble. Huddleston said later that it was like a bank holiday on Hampstead Heath. Amid deafening applause he received the title of *Isitwalande*, the Courageous Warrior. So did Dr. Yusuf Dadoo, national president of the South African Indian Congress, and *in absentia*, Chief Lutuli of the African National Congress. Lutuli could not be there, because he had been banned from public life for two years.

The great business of the congress was the presentation of the Freedom Charter, which presented demands that had come in from all over South Africa. It was of course edited, but that was inevitable. The charter has become legendary, and is regarded by many black people as the definitive statement of their aspirations. It is a fascinating document, and combines two primary aims which many people would find incompatible. In the first place it declares that all human rights shall be guaranteed by the constitution, and it is therefore a declaration of the rights of the individual as against the State. In the second place it promises the nationalisation of the banks and the mines and that 'all other industry and trade shall be controlled to assist the well-being of the people'. The charter raises the great question as to whether a centralised economy and a Bill of Rights can exist side by side.

It was now time for me to prepare for my visit to Kent School, Connecticut, and to steel myself for the encounter with the redoubtable headmaster John Patterson and his redoubtable hatchet-man Louis Stone. I conclude by quoting an entry in my diary for 28 August 1955. Dorrie had pasted in a small, blue printed slip, 'Today is my wife's birthday.' And under that she had written, 'And don't forget it.'

Chapter 17

Kent School, Connecticut, brought me to America in great style. I travelled first class on Pan American, and was treated with deference. When we arrived at what was then called Idlewild (now Kennedy airport), my name was called out first and I left the plane in solitary glory, and full of pride. I was escorted to Immigration with ceremony and handed in my passport for inspection. The officer looked at my name and my photograph and consulted his memory for a few short moments. Then he reached under the counter and took out a black book. My name was there all right. He said to me, 'Sir, I must temporarily impound your passport, and I must ask you to wait in the lounge until you are called again.' Just as I had concealed my pride, now I concealed my humiliation. My reception by Immigration came as a shock to John Patterson, the rector and headmaster of Kent School, and his chairman of the board of trustees, Dominic Rich, who had come to meet this illustrious member of their galactic panel. We waved to each other, but no more than that, for they were separated from me by an impassable barrier. Not even Louis Stone, had he been there, could have done anything about it. I was a pariah whose name had got into the black book. I, who had been singled out for V.I.P. treatment, now watched my two hundred fellow passengers leave me behind. Some glanced at me curiously. What they thought I did not know, and in any case I was in no position to inquire. He that had been first was now last.

And what did I think? I came to the sad conclusion that the spirit of Joseph McCarthy was still abroad, although he himself had been discredited. I had no doubt that the South African security police, cooperating closely with the C.I.A. or the F.B.I. or whatever it is, had given my name to be put into the black book. Not a communist perhaps, but as near as dammit! A danger to the State, a danger even to the mighty United States, a danger to the whole free world. Alas, what a rod in pickle I had stored up for myself when I joined the South African Liberal Party, which stood – or thought it did – for the same ideals of freedom and justice as the country which had put me into the black book.

When my last fellow passengers had departed, a higher United States official came to me and explained that I would have to sleep that night 'under guard'. I would be accommodated at the expense of the U.S. government of course – at an hotel in New York. The next morning I would have to face an interrogation at the headquarters of some very high authority at headquarters in Columbus Circle. He would explain these arrangements to my friends.

Soon after that I was escorted by two armed policemen to a waiting car driven by a third policeman. We then made our way to New York, not to the Walforf Astoria or the Hotel Pierre, but to a less luxurious establishment known as the Prince George, at Broadway and 23rd Street. I declined refreshment and was taken to my bedroom: One policeman stayed in the room, and one sat outside in the passage. It was clear that escape would be very difficult. I therefore retired to bed, and did not read, but contemplated the ceiling and my strange situation. Here I was 'under guard' in the land of the free, a country which in the last seven years had become my spiritual home. I might add that I had no feeling of apprehension, and finally went off serenely to sleep.

I was awakened the next morning by my room mate, who told me that I could go to the breakfast room if I wished. The implication was that I would have my breakfast 'under guard', and a strange kind of breakfast it turned out to be. John Patterson and Dominic Rich were there, and insisted that they would have breakfast with me. It is not very easy to argue with John Patterson, and the senior policeman finally gave in. While the three of us were having breakfast, the two guards circled round and round the room, watching us like hawks, no doubt. The waiters of the Prince George, who were all black, were fascinated by the spectacle, and treated me with friendly smiles and deference, doubtless on the assumption that anyone in the custody of policemen – and white policemen too – must be a good guy.

After my breakfast I parted from my friends, and went under guard to Columbus Circle, there to be interrogated by civilian officials of Immigration. My passport was on the table before them and they identified me at once. They then proceeded to the interrogation.

What I write down now, I write from memory of an event that happened over thirty years ago, but I shall do my best to tell the truth. I was asked my father's name and country of origin, and my mother's married and maiden names and country of origin. I was asked my father's father's name, which I did not know, and my mother's father's name, which I did. When the interrogators had finished with my antecedents, they turned to me, my date and place of birth, my education, my married state, the names of my children. What organisations did I belong to? Well, I belonged to the Students' Christian Association, the Anglican Church, the Convocation of the University of Natal, the Penal Reform League, Toc H Southern Africa, the South African Institute of Race Relations, the Durban International Club, the Royal Society of Literature, and the Liberal Party of South Africa. I think they had most of this in their files, but they knew more than that. They suddenly fired at me the sixty-four-thousand-dollar question, the question that I had been brought to Columbus Circle to answer. They asked me, 'Weren't you a member of the Friends of Soviet Russia?' I said, Yes, I was, it was an organisation that collected money for buying medical supplies for Russia during the Second World War. They asked me why I had not mentioned it among the list of organisations to which I had belonged. I said I had not thought of it; it was an *ad hoc* organisation, and lasted only for the duration of the war. I told them that their President Eisenhower, then Supreme Commander of the Allied Forces, was a patron of the organisation, and that I thought that Winston Churchill had been another.

I suppose that interrogators must never show any feelings, whether of surprise or compassion. Perhaps they may be entitled to show feelings of disbelief or derision. My interrogators took the Eisenhower blow on the chin. One said to the other, 'Call Washington.' They both disappeared and left me to survery the interrogation room. If there were secret and devilish devices to wring the truth from their captives, I did not see them. After a few minutes they returned and said to me, 'Washington orders that you be released immediately.' I do not remember that they congratulated me or apologised to me, but perhaps they did. They gave me back my passport and conducted me to a room where John Patterson and Dominic Rich were waiting for me. John said, 'I think we could all use a drink.' So we did, but not at the Prince George.

This story has a sequel. John Patterson said to me, in a way that I think I could rightly describe as embarrassed and outraged at the stupidity of it all, 'Alan, you are of course entitled to make whatever use you wish of this unpleasant incident, but we who represent Kent

School make a request to you that you say nothing about it. However, if you can't accede to our request, we shan't hold it against you.'

So therefore I said nothing about it, except to my wife and family, for thirty years. Today it doesn't matter. I did not find it so hard to forgive the United States authorities. I kept my anger for the South African security police who had got my name into that black book. But I do criticise the United States authorities for not knowing that our security police's definition of a dangerous man was very different from their own. In South Africa I was regarded as a dangerous person because I believed in the freedom of man under the law. If the U.S. authorities had taken the trouble to consult their diplomatic representatives in South Africa, I would never have got into the black book at all.

One other person in the secret was Louis Stone, that giant of a man who tried to catch me out by slyly introducing rare and unknown words into the conversation, hoping that I would be compelled to say, 'Louis, what does that word mean?' But over my Idlewild experience he was almost speechless. One did not make jokes about things like that.

It was time for me to go to Kent School for the jubilee celebrations, to live in the very handsome Visitors' Lodge, to take part in the life of the school for some weeks, and then to join the galactic seminar on 'The Christian Idea of Education'. I shall describe the school as well as I can, after the lapse of thirty years.

Kent School is situated on more than one thousand five hundred acres in the foothills of the Berkshires, in the wooded country of Connecticut, the like of which cannot be seen in any part of Africa. The woods are leafless in winter, bursting in spring, luxuriant in summer, and rich with unbelievable colour in the fall. The school itself is on the edge of the New England town of Kent, on the banks of the Housatonic River. It is what you would call a well-endowed school, but not ostentatiously so. Before 1955 it had admitted its first black American boys, but also had boys from other countries in the world. It was then a boys' school, but now is coeducational. I said it was well endowed, but not ostentatiously so; for example it had no servants. There were four non-teaching staff members such as the school doctor, the matron, the chef, the groundsman. Boys waited at tables, washed dishes, and kept the dormitories and school buildings clean.

Kent had a rich curriculum, much richer than the 'straight six' I had taken at Maritzburg College in my school days. It had a school library the like of which I had never seen before, and boys spent half their school hours in the library, working on assignments and projects. One of the courses which most seized my imagination was the course on Current Events of the World. Each of the boys of this class was allotted his own country, Japan, Britain, Russia, Canada, and each week had to report on the events of that country. I tried to attend as many of these classes as I could and found them fascinating.

Kent is not a school governed by the Episcopalian Church, nor a school of the Church, but definitely a school in the Church. It has a splendid chapel and organ, and a school chaplain. It was founded in 1906 by the Order of the Holy Cross, a monastic order in the Episcopal Church. John Patterson himself was and still is a priest of the Episcopal Church, and the religious atmosphere of the school, while in no way 'pious', was very marked. Punishment was in most cases in the hands of the prefects, and sentences were handed out at each morning assembly. Thus it was that the groundsman needed no assistants, because one of the most common punishments for offenders was to be assigned to help him in what would have been their leisure hours. I was interested to find that one of the most severe punishments was for smoking. However, boys of the most senior class were allowed to smoke if their parents approved.

The school grounds themselves were magnificent. The main sports were baseball and football, but there was also an ice-rink that must have cost some money. Perhaps the greatest achievement for a boy was to get into the rowing eight, which trained on the beautiful Housatonic, and travelled – whether yearly or not, I do not remember – to Henley Regatta on the Thames in England.

There was no fixed rate of fees at Kent. If you were the president of some great American company, and you wanted your son to go to Kent School, then you might be asked to pay ten times as much as a father not so highly paid. As far as I recall, examinations did not play a big part at Kent. There was no final examination like the South African matriculation. Travelling gentlemen from Yale, Harvard, Princeton, Dartmouth, Cornell and other universities came and interviewed boys who had expressed a preference for this or that college or university.

To put it briefly, I found myself as the guest of honour at a very extraordinary school. I taught English lessons and gave readings of Blake, Whitman, Wordsworth, Campbell. I gave talks on South Africa, a very easy task in those days. I attended Current Events, art classes, sculpture classes, political classes. I was entertained endlessly. Because I had been a teacher in mathematics, it was thought that I would be happiest in the company of Bob Rourke who had written some fantastic book that made mathematics totally comprehensible to anyone that could understand the book. His invariable greeting was not mathematical, but 'Have a drink', and when I explained that I drank only at sundown, he informed me that at some part of the British Empire the sun would then be setting.

Although far from home, I was fully at home there at Kent School. There are certain places where I am most at home. They are the school, the university, the church, the library, the garden. There are certain places which I cannot add to the list – the pub, the club, the annual general meeting, and alas in recent years, the big dinner party. However, at Kent I could not wander about at will. I had to deliver a paper on 'The Person in Community', and I prepared it in my study at Visitors' Lodge. I took my task very seriously, and began with the community that I knew best of all, Diepkloof Reformatory.

Why is the community here? Who is this boy for whom this community exists? We all know what he is. He is an offender; perhaps he stole or robbed or murdered. But for his sake money is poured out like water, buildings are erected, principals, priests, psychologists, teachers, counselors, are all assembled together. Though he is the least of all, yet all this is done for his sake. Is he in secret the child of someone great, maybe, that it would be a matter of such moment for him to be saved? Who is he indeed? This question is the most important of them all.

I was not the brightest of the stars of the galaxy, but I had one advantage over them all. I had spent twenty-four years of my life as a teacher of boys and girls, and I had spent thirteen of these twenty-four years as a teacher of boys who had been in trouble with the law. All of my fellow speakers were, or had been, professors, of physics, history, divinity, theology, philosophy, every learned subject under the sun.

Of the seminar, of the feat of organisation that had gathered such a panel together, one can only say that it was a triumph, and would have brought lustre to any university in the world. The seminar itself was only one of the events of the jubilee commemoration, one of the chief organisers of which was Cyrus P. Vance, a Kent School alumnus who later in life became Secretary of State under President Jimmy Carter. Unobtrusively everywhere was John Patterson, who was unable – I don't know if he tried – to keep the light of pride out of his eyes. That is one of the seven deadly sins of course, but this was an occasion on which it could be forgiven.

Who was the brightest star of the galaxy? For me it was Reinhold Niebuhr, but then I was prejudiced in his favour because of his praise for *Cry, the Beloved Country*. Quite apart from any such consideration, I think him to be the wisest man I ever knew, with an understanding of human nature and of human society that no one has equalled in our century.

Niebuhr's paper was titled 'The Two Sources of Western Culture'. He deliverd it sitting, having suffered a stroke in 1952, caused by a cerebral vascular thrombosis. 'I lost my speech for two days, and the following two years were tough.' He was now confined to the sidelines and was thereby given 'insights about human nature that had never occurred to me before'. He had never measured the depth and breadth of his wife's devotion until he was struck down. 'Again and again she assured me that I would do as much for her, were she ill. But I doubted it, because I was inclined to affirm the superior *agape* of woman.'*

At Kent School in 1955 the impediment in his speech was still evident. He occasionally slurred a word or two in delivering his paper. He was sensitive about the impotence of his left hand and hid it from sight. His audience was deeply affected, for they were witnessing a triumph of mind over body. And the mind was as clear as ever.

Most – perhaps all – of the addresses at the seminar were remarkable. They evoked a rich diversity of emotions from those who heard them, laughter, joy, sorrow, admiration. But it was Niebuhr who evoked the most tremendous response at one moment of his address, and it happened in this manner. This particular incident is not recorded in *The Christian Idea of Education*, † which was published as a record of the seminar, for the simple reason that it was spontaneous and unrehearsed and did not form part of Niebuhr's script.

He had just spoken these words:

But it is significant that the meaning of historical events has frequently been obscured not by the real historian but by social scientists who sought abortively to bring history into the realms of nature and thus deny the characteristically historical aspects of the human scene. In short, our culture has been intent upon equating history with nature at the precise moment when history revealed the dangerous possibilities of human freedom which were not at all like nature.

Niebuhr felt that this rather difficult argument needed some kind of elaboration, and he proceeded to drop his script for the moment, and to dwell on the dangerous possibilities of freedom in the United States itself, the fact that the American ideal of freedom meant the liberty to choose good and to choose evil, so that high endeavour lived alongside vice and corruption and decadence. He did this with a kind of sombre gravity that certainly subdued his audience, and then inflicted on them a heavy blow by saying fiercely of American society, 'It's a mess.' We were all silent, feeling almost that the world was beyond redemption, when – after a pause – he suddenly said to us with equal emphasis, 'But I like it!' It brought down the house, and we felt that there was hope for the world after all.

So the great seminar came to an end. Dorrie had come to Kent for

* These extracts are taken from an article 'A View of Life from the Sidelines', published in the *Christian Century* of 19–26 December 1984.
† Yale University Press, 1957.

the seminar, and she and I and John and Betty Patterson formed a close friendship, which suffered a temporary change when Dorrie died in 1967 but was restored when I married my second wife Anne in 1969. Dorrie and I left Kent School with great regret. I have no doubt that it was – I cannot speak for the present – one of the great schools of the world.

Reinhold Niebuhr lived for sixteen more years after taking part in the Kent Jubilee. Ursula Niebuhr I have seen twice since then, and not long ago I received from her a copy of the article 'A View of Life from the Sidelines'. It is full of wisdom. Niebuhr writes of the changes brought about by old age:

I still remain uncertain whether the relaxation of the polemical attitudes of my youthful zest for various causes represents the wisdom of old age, the disengagement of a spectator, or an increasing awareness of the strange mixture of good and evil in all the causes and purposes that once had prompted me to carry the banners of religion against secularism, and of Protestantism against Catholicism. I now hope that the unpolemical attitudes of my old age and dependence may have had their roots in experience, rather than in the irresponsibility of weakness and lack of engagement.

Except for the mention of Protestantism and Catholicism, I could have written that myself. But I must add that Niebuhr wrote a few lines later:

But my view from the sidelines of illness made me more fully aware of the impressive history of the Catholic faith, and of its sources of grace and justice, which even our Reformation polemics cannot obscure.

So far in my life I have not needed to take 'a view from the sidelines of illness'. But I am fully aware of the fact that although I can still pass stern judgement, I can no longer pass angry judgement. I am finished with polemics and strife, and this is for many people a disqualification – or worse still, the act of a renegade – in a country full of injustice and bitterness. Friendly critics, especially those who were previously hostile, will say that I have 'mellowed', unfriendly critics will say that I have gone conservative, or have at least moved to the middle, and hostile critics will say that I have a white skin after all. Less and less do I like the use of extreme language; circumstances may change but at the moment I criticise those who say we in South Africa are near to civil war, or who say that the South African situation and the Nazi situation are 'fully comparable'. I am not only a lover of liberty, I am also a lover of language, and such extreme use causes language to lose its meaning.

I have written earlier of the freedom one experiences when one no longer has to be consistently and totally loyal to a party, nor to its politics and programmes. Niebuhr in the same article wrote: 'It can be exciting when one ceases to be a consistent advocate and polemical agent of a belief system.' Niebuhr in his later years came more and more to apply the same reasoning to religious belief. He wrote: 'But as I became a pew-worshipper rather than the preacher, I had some doubts about the ability of us preachers to explicate and symbolise this majesty and mystery.'

Writing of himself and his 'closest friend', he said:

We believed in both the immortality and the mortality of the person and acknowledged that the mystery of human selfhood was quite similar to the mystery of the divine. In the Hebraic–Christian faith God both transcends, and is involved in the flux of time and history. The human personality has the same transcendence and involvement, but of course the transcendence of mortals over the flux of time is not absolute. We die, as do all creatures. But it is precisely our anxious foreboding of our death that gives us a clue to the dimension of our deathlessness. ... I am personally content to leave this problem of deathlessness in the frame of mystery, and to console myself with the fact that the mystery of human selfhood is only a degree beneath the mystery of God.

I have never thought about this mystery in these words, but I deduce from Niebuhr's argument that he would have agreed that, in some way not comprehensible to us, Man was so created that he would be able to comprehend the universe, not totally but as a creature, and only piece by piece. On the occasion of the confirmation of my second son, Jonathan, I wrote these words for him:*

Do not think it absurd that he should know every sparrow, or the number of the hairs of your head,
Do not compare him with yourself, or suppose your human love to be an example to shame him.
He is not greater than Plato or Lincoln, or superior to Shakespeare and Beethoven.
He is their God, their powers and their gifts proceeded from him,
In infinite darkness they pored with their fingers over the first word of the Book of his Knowledge.

It is time to close this chapter. It is a tribute to Kent School and its headmaster John Patterson, and to Reinhold Niebuhr, the chief star of the galaxy. Life did not throw Niebuhr and myself often together but he was a man after my own heart.

Postscript
Niebuhr wrote that the mystery of human selfhood was only a

* From 'Meditation for a Young Boy Confirmed'.

degree beneath the mystery of God. This mystery was again revealed to me when in January 1958, two years after the Kent Jubilee Seminar, I heard that Louis Stone, the six-foot-six giant of the C.B.S., who had shanghaied me into going to Kent, and who had tried to catch me out with words like *arval, epicene,* and *metathetical,* had taken his life. He had been in and out of hospital, being treated for depression, but his friends were not aware that he was in extremity, and his death came as a tremendous shock to his wife and family and friends. His grave is in the cloister of St. Joseph's Chapel at Kent School. May his soul rest in peace.*

* John Patterson has registered a mild objection to the description of Louis Stone and himself as 'personality smashers'. I reassured him that it was a teasing compliment. He wrote to me later, 'It don't bother me none.'

Chapter 18

It was time for me to leave the land of freedom and the intellectual brilliance of the Kent School seminar (and of course the land of the Prince George Hotel), and to return to the land of the Liberal Party and the security police. The party had taken a decisive step in my absence, and that was to elect me as National Chairman. Whether they asked me about this before I left for America, I'm afraid I do not remember, but I shall assume that they did.

Meanwhile the party had gained a new and illustrious member, the ruddy-cheeked and blue-eyed and unpredictable and indomitable Patrick Duncan, the son of a greatly respected governor-general of the Union of South Africa, the white man who had led a team of men and women in an illegal entry into the Gemiston black 'location', a venture made all the more exciting by the fact that Patrick was (temporarily) on crutches.

I wrote earlier that we in the Liberal Party had at least one member who thought – or gave the powerful impression that he thought – that he had been born to set things right. Unlike Hamlet, Patrick did not regard this as a 'cursed spite'. In the year of 1956 he was a faithful Anglican and a devout follower of the Mahatma. He believed that *satyagraha*, the response to evil actions by love, could bring down the unjust empires of the world, and in particular the apartheid government of the Afrikaner Nationalist Party. At that time the National Party was led by Prime Minister J. G. Strijdom, who was a white supremacist of the most rugged kind, a Christian Calvinist and a fanatical enemy of communism and godlessness, and an unshakeable believer in the

The Paton family in 1948: Dorrie, Alan, Jonathan and David. (Photo: Leon Levson)

At the Lincoln Memorial, Washington, D.C.

With Sidney Poitier (who played Theophilus Msimangu), Ben Moloi (head teacher, Diepkloof Reformatory) and Canada Lee (who played Stephen Kumalo), during the making of the film Cry, *the Beloved Country*, Johannesburg, May 1950.

With Dorrie and Zoltan Korda at the première of *Cry, the Beloved Country*, 1951.
(Photo: *Natal Mercury*)

Alan Paton, Laurens van der Post, Enslin du Plessis, Roy Campbell and Uys Krige in London, May 1952. (Photo: Sport and General, London)

Whitney Driscoll, President of Yale University, Alan Paton, Bishop Otto Dibelius, Archbishop Geoffrey Fisher, Dr. Paul David Devananden, and Liston Pope, Dean of Yale Divinity School, at Yale University, 1954. (Photo: Alburtus, Yale News Bureau)

With Don
McKenzie of
the Toc H T.B.
Settlement.

Manilal Gandhi, Alan Paton, Patrick Duncan, Mlahleni Njisane, and
Peter Brown at the Natal Provincial Congress of the Liberal Party of
South Africa, 1955. (Photo by courtesy of Mr. Peter Brown)

John Patterson,
headmaster of Kent
School, Connecticut.
(Photo: Fabian Bachrach)

Mrs. Elizabeth Patterson.

(Photos by courtesy of the
Pattersons)

Reinhold Niebuhr. (Photo:
Werner Wolff, Black Star,
New York, and by courtesy
of Mrs. Ursula Niebuhr)

Alan Paton, Derrick Marsh
and Peter Brown listening
to Jordan Ngubane at a
Liberal Party meeting in
Pietermaritzburg, 1958.

Elliot Mngadi, Organiser
of the Natal African
Landowners Association.

(Photos by courtesy of Mr.
Peter Brown)

divine mission of the Afrikaner nation to rule and Christianise the African subcontinent. At the time of which I am writing, Nationalist Afrikanerdom was in the peak years of its arrogance, and some Nationalist philosophers and prophets actually foresaw the spreading of their racial doctrines to Northern and Southern Rhodesia (now Zambia and Zimbabwe), the Belgian Congo (now Zaire) Uganda and Kenya. The reality of course was that the doctrines would retreat to the south as Afrikaners also would retreat with the breaking-up of the Belgian and British empires.

Our new member Patrick Duncan had no fear of Prime Minister Strijdom and the National Party. As far as one could see – in 1956 – he had no fear of anybody. Yet he was not by temperament fitted to be a member of a party. Why then did he join the Liberal Party? It was because he wanted power. He used to talk of power as though it was something waiting to be seized by any person who had the will to do it. I do not think for a moment that he wanted power for power's sake, so that he himself could enjoy it, and bend others to do his will. But he knew that one does not come to power unless one has some kind of organisation to support one. So he joined one of the weakest organisations in South Africa.

By no means was everyone in the Liberal Party delighted to see Patrick become a member. Margaret Ballinger and Molteno in the Cape thought that he was irresponsible, unpredictable, and a bit mad. He had strengthened their prejudices by publishing in 1953 an extraordinary booklet, *The Road Through the Wilderness*. While paying his respects to the Afrikaner National Party for its courage and tenacity, and while condemning apartheid absolutely and unconditionally, he writes, 'I am quite clear that our community ought in the short term to support the United Party.' Patrick wrote that the Liberal Party should receive no support, nor the Federal Party. These two parties had been set up 'without an adequate appreciation' of the part that political power plays in politics. Patrick concluded his pamphlet by urging the creation of an All People's Party, which would apparently be free of the weaknesses of the Liberal Party.

Margaret Ballinger and Molteno took a poor view of Patrick's pamphlet. Patrick had many gifts, but they were not inellectual. He was subject to great fluctuations of mood, energy, and optimism. He was always looking for the solution that would solve everything. Soon after he joined the Liberal Party he became convinced – and I use the word 'convinced' in an emotional rather than a rational sense – that the solution to our problems would be for the United States to refuse to buy any more South African gold. During a Liberal Party conference he cornered me on a waste plot in some Johannesburg suburb, and with all the hypnotic power of his personality, which was considerable, and with all those flames shooting out of his blue eyes, he tried to persuade me that it was my duty, not just a solemn duty, but rather a sacred one, to go to Washington and to gain entry to the Oval Office, and to persuade the President that if the United States bought no more South African gold, some magical thing would happen.

To be cornered by Patrick in this way, and to be challenged to perform a high moral duty, was no joke at all. I knew I was going to say No, but I couldn't bring myself to the point of doing it. I felt ashamed to think that I was going to refuse, and that this glowing fervour of Patrick's was going to be wasted. He was in a way a living representation of Planck's quantum theory. For weeks he would be quiet, but one could know that something was brewing. Then suddenly he would reach the quantum limit and would erupt, to the admiration of some and the horror of others. And these others were still more horrified when they heard the disquieting rumour that Patrick wanted to become the National Organiser of the Liberal Party of South Africa, and that Peter Brown and I were considering the matter very carefully. Brown and I had problems too. Could we control Patrick? Would he do what he was instructed to do? We did not know the answers to these questions.

Why then did we appoint him? I think the answer was simple. We appointed him because of that inner vitality of his, and because he believed with all his heart and soul in a South Africa free from all racial domination and racial discrimination. I will not say that he believed with all his heart and soul in the policies and programmes of the Liberal Party, but he certainly believed in its ideals. It is a commonplace that people who believe in the same ideals often differ sharply – and sometimes bitterly – on the way to translate those ideals into policies and programmes. We appointed Patrick because we believed that his vitality and his enthusiasm would be good for the party.

One of Patrick's first acts as National Organiser was to get himself arrested in Queenstown. He went to represent the party at a conference of the African National Congress; the conference was held in the Queenstown black 'location', and Patrick made no bones about doing what he had done in Germiston in 1952. This disturbed the conservative liberals of the Cape, and they called for a stricter control of what were known as 'extra-parliamentary activities'.

Patrick was to stay with the Liberal Party for four tempestuous years. I must record that, though we found him difficult, he had his own inner difficulties to wrestle with. Although he had totally rejected the colour bar in his political and private life, and although he was able to recruit a large number of African and Cape coloured members for the party by means of his infectious enthusiasm, he was beginning to doubt the efficacy of the Sermon on the Mount and Gandhi's *satyagraha*. This he did not reveal to us until there occurred a cataclysmic event in his life, and even then he did not reveal it immediately. The cataclysmic event was his banning from all public life by the National Party in 1960. Totally frustrated, he escaped to Basutoland (now Lesotho) and it was from there that he announced his conversion to a belief in the use of violence for the solution of the political and racial problems of South Africa. Therefore the cataclysmic act had a cataclysmic consequence, nothing less than the abandonment of those ideals and beliefs that had ruled and shaped his life. He became a man of violence, which was in itself absurd, because no one was less a man of violence than he.

Did the National Party destroy – or did it do irreparable damage to – Patrick's life? Or was there something in Patrick himself, an unconquerable urge to hurl himself against the unconquerable? Who knows the answer to such questions? The second part of Patrick's life, though not as tempestuous as the first, was just as fascinating, and had a kind of tragic nobility. I shall write of it later, for it affected me powerfully.

Does any government have the right to ban one of its citizens from all public life? I assume that in the United States such an action would be quite impossible to reconcile with the Bill of Rights, and therefore would never be taken except indirectly as in the days of McCarthyism, a tendency which was later to be totally repudiated. In South Africa we could not fall back on a Bill of Rights, and therefore we fell back on the rule of law. We protested against the action of parliament in giving to the Minister of Justice the right to take against a citizen an action which could not be challenged in a court of law.

I do not think that our Ministers of Justice under the National Party ever had grave qualms about the damage they were able to inflict on their more outspoken opponents. It was done in the interests of Afrikanerdom, and what higher reason could there be than that? Of course, if a really higher reason were wanted, it was done in the interests of Christianity in the fight against red godlessness. However that may be, I hereby record that the Ministers of Justice of the National Party *never succeeded in destroying the will or belief of any person that I knew*. That the Ministers of Justice changed the character and tenor of people's lives, there can be no doubt. A man or woman cannot be shut off from all public and a great deal of private and personal life for five or seven or ten years, without undergoing change. Has any government the right to do such a thing? The members of the Liberal Party of South Africa, supported by millions of lovers of freedom and justice all over the world, would answer with an emphatic NO.

It is of course much easier for a country or society that has a strong sense of confidence in itself and its institutions to guarantee far-reaching freedoms to its citizens, such as are enshrined in a Bill of Rights. South Africa in the 'fifties was certainly not that kind of society, nor is it as I write in 1987. May I repeat the epigram that I have used before: it is much easier to be good when you are secure.

The year 1956 was a notable one in the life of the Liberal Party in Natal. In spite of the fact that we had withdrawn from the Congress of the People, our relations with the South African Indian Congress and its Natal division grew very strong indeed. This was because of our total opposition to the Group Areas Act, which affected the Indian shop-owners and property-owners of Natal and the Transvaal very adversely indeed. In town after town, and especially in the Transvaal, Indian shop-owners, who had a very large white custom because of the competitiveness of their prices, were being forced out of their shops and properties into areas remote from their white customers.

I myself spent many of my weekends away from home, travelling to almost every town in Natal, and to many towns in the Transvaal, to speak at large protest meetings against the Act, attended by almost the entire Indian population of the town, a handful of whites, and of course the members of the security police.

Although our protests were vigorous and well organised, they could no be called successful. The majority of the Indian population of Johannesburg, which was considerable, was moved to the new town of Lenasia, some twenty miles from the city centre. The only Indian business community to remain largely unscathed was that of Durban, not because of any softening of the attitude of the National Party but because of the magnitude of the operation that would have been required. The Indian business centre of Durban is a rich, congested, and extremely colourful area, and is popularly known as Grey Street, though it consists of many streets, arcades, and passages. You can buy almost anything there, beautiful saris and the last thing in men's business suits, jewellery and watches, all kinds of musical instruments, hardware, cutlery, and the Oriental spices cinnamon, cardamom, dhunnia, and the rest. The Indian Market was famous for its smells and colours, its extraordinary variety of fruits and vegetables, and above all for its noise and vigour. A mayor of Johannesburg greatly annoyed the white people of Durban by calling it an Oriental city, but in large measure that is what it was. If one is halted by one of the traffic lights in this part of the city, one is passed by the descendants of the people of three continents, an experience not to be forgotten.

The rich Indian merchants of Durban adopted an ambivalent attitude towards those of us who protested against the Group Areas Act.

They would give us money under the table, but did not wish to be associated in any way with a public protest against the Act. Their guiding genius was Ahmed Moolla, who formed the Natal Indian Organisation, which would protest quietly and sweetly and reasonably to the National Party government, in the hope of saving something from the wreck. When I say that Mr. Moolla was a genius, I mean nothing less. In the end it was his strategy that triumphed. It was he who saved Grey Street for Indian business.

One of my constant companions in these visits to Estcourt, Lady-smith, Dundee, Newcastle and all the other threatened areas was a talkative, ebullient, irrepressible politician named Debi Singh, a very attractive and convivial personality with what is known as an 'amiable weakness'. I remember well one journey with him. He began to regale all in the car with stories of his schooldays at Sastri College, a school for Indian boys under that redoubtable headmaster, Wilfred Buss. Mr. Buss was a believer in the British Empire, which he reckoned was eminently fitted to rule the world. He deplored the efforts of Gandhi to bring about the departure of the British from India, and prophesied that were such a thing to happen, India would relapse into ignorance and poverty. These views he placed authoritatively before his pupils and exercised over them an iron discipline. Debi was a good mimic and he entertained us with a rendering of Mr. Buss's speeches to the school assembly, powerful, cogent and very jingoistic. One could almost say that Debi had the whole car-load of us in stitches. Then he turned to me. 'Alan,' he said, 'you were a teacher, didn't you know Wilfred Buss? 'Yes', I said, 'I knew him very well. He was my brother-in-law.' We were in stitches again, except for Debi, who for the next few miles was quite silent.

For the whole year the Liberal Party in Natal campaigned against the Group Areas Act and against the National Party's policy of destroying all the 'black spots', those areas where in the earlier part of the century black people had legally bought land from white landowners. But as I have written earlier, when a government enacts unjust laws, it must also enact security laws to deal with those who oppose their legislation. There were rumours that the Minister of Justice, C. R. Swart, known as 'Blackie', was planning a major crack-down on the leaders of the African National Congress, the South African Indian Congress, the white Congress of Democrats, the South African Coloured Peoples Organisation, and the South African Congress of Trade Unions. On 5 December 1956, an hour before dawn, and in many parts of South Africa, the police arrested most of the one hundred and fifty-six persons later held on charges of high treason. So began the longest, most expensive, most terrifying and yet most ridiculous trial in the history of the country. But it was not ridiculous to the government, which was determined to crush, once and for all, for ever and ever, any opposition to the Great Plan for a new heaven and a new earth. Many members of the National Party had urged for years that opposition to apartheid should be regarded as high treason. Now their wish was to be realised. Nor was the trial ridiculous to those who were arrested. In many cases their careers and businesses were destroyed and in some cases their family lives also.

One hundred and four of the accused were Africans, twenty-one Indians, twenty-three whites, and eight coloured people. Amongst them were lawyers, doctors, clergymen, architects, journalists, clerks, teachers, housewives, and labourers.

One of the most notable of the accused was the president-general of the African National Congress, ex-Chief Albert Lutuli, whom everyone called 'Chief', in spite of the fact that the Nationalist government had deposed him in 1952 after ordering him to choose between the Congress and the chieftainship. Equally notable was Professor Z. K. Matthews, vice-principal of Fort Hare, the African college, a quiet, imperturbable man of great dignity. Matthews wrote of his arrest, 'I knew that I had at no time, either in thought, word or deed, sought to undermine or impair the independence or safety of the South African State.' When the police arrived he said to his wife, 'So this is it, at last!' Some hundreds of miles north, at Groutville, Natal, the police said to Lutuli, 'Yes, the day has come!' A third notable accused was Dr. G. M. (Monty) Naicker, president of the Natal Indian Congress, a medical practitioner in Durban, implacable in politics, genial in hospitality, in fact a host in a thousand. His arrest did nothing to lessen either his implacability or his geniality.

Why was Father Trevor Huddleston not arrested? For the very simple reason that the Community of the Resurrection had recalled him to England. If he had stayed, the chances are that he would have been arrested too, although he would have been as incapable as Z. K. Matthews of planning treason, which is defined by the *Concise Oxford Dictionary* as a 'violation of allegiance' to sovereign or state, 'e.g. by plotting sovereign's death or engaging in war against him'.

The accused were all released on bail on 29 December 1956, and the trial was resumed on 9 January. They were all charged with being active in the so-called Liberation Movement, and with having had a joint organisation which 'propagated and preached the Marxist–Lenin-ist account of Society and the State'. They were also charged with having called a Congress of the People at Kliptown, where they drew up a Freedom Charter which was a step towards the establishment of a communist state.

The story of the Treason Trial I shall tell later, but I must record that on 6 December 1956, the day after the arrests, at a meeting in the Gandhi Hall, Durban, representatives of the Liberal Party and the Congresses launched a fund to assist treason trialists with their defence, and to provide maintenance and support for their dependants. The meeting wsas attended by four hundred people, of whom fifty were whites, one hundred and fifty Indian, and two hundred Africans. The proceedings were orderly, and Professor Leo Kuper and I spoke on behalf of the Liberal Party. There were six speakers, and all six were charged under Natal Provincial Notice No. 78 of 1933, with holding, or attending or participating in (I am not sure which) a 'meeting of Natives', without first obtaining the permission of the mayor of Durban. This ancient regulation was first promulgated to curb the activities of that charismatic black labour leader Clements Kadalie and his vigorous Industrial and Commercial Union, the I.C.U. Our case was the second of its kind in a quarter of a century, the first having been decided against Kadalie, on the grounds that his meeting, though multiracial in character, was in fact a 'meeting of Natives'.

This was the first time in my life (and the last as far as I know at the time of writing) that I had ever sat as an accused person in the dock. All the accused sat together, except Advocate Hassan Mall, who was conducting his own defence, and therefore sat in the advocates' benches. We, the others, told him that he should have sat in the dock with us, and should have been allowed to leave only when he stood up to defend himself.

On the trial, which was twice adjourned, I remember only one thing, and that vividly. I said to Leo Kuper, my fellow member of the Liberal Party, that although this was the first time I had sat in the dock, I did not mind it at all. He said to me, with that gentle smile which was one of his great characteristics, 'I don't like it at all.'

At the end of the trial we were all found guilty, the magistrate finding himself unable to upset the previous decision. The white and Indian accused were each fined five pounds, and the African accused three pounds. Our counsel announced that he would appeal. The verdict received much world publicity.

On 1 August 1957 our appeal was heard in the Supreme Court in Pietermaritzburg. The presiding judge did not call on our counsel. Instead he asked the prosecutor whether a sack of oranges became, by the introduction of some lemons, a sack of lemons. Or whether a herd of Frieslands and Shorthorns was a herd of Frieslands. Or whether a meeting of members and non-members was a meeting of members. The prosecution replied that the answer to each of these shattering questions was Yes. The presiding judge finally asked whether there had on the occasion of 6 December 1956 been two meetings or only one, to which the prosecution replied that there had been only one. The judge then declared, after a decent interval and some discussion with his two fellow judges, intended no doubt to convey that the case put forward by the prosecution needed weighty consideration, that the appeal would succeed. I wrote a short account of this trial and signed it 'One with No Convictions'.

During this lengthy trial, we collected money for our fund, which was now called the Treason Trial Defence Fund and had been established in all the big centres of the country, notably in Johannesburg under the leadership of Bishop Ambrose Reeves and in Cape Town under Archbishop Geoffrey Clayton. But all our work would have amounted to very little had it not been for the immense support we received from Canon John Collins of St. Paul's, London, and his amazing Defence and Aid Fund.

I shall close with the one anecdote from my collecting career. I called on one of the leading advocates of Durban and asked him for a donation to the Treason Trial Defence Fund. He refused my request and fixed me with those brilliant eyes that had no doubt terrified many an accused person. He said to me, 'Tell me, Mr. Paton, why do you collect only for treason suspects? Why don't you collect for all suspects?'

Chapter 19

In 1957 it was announced that the Prime Minister, J.G. Strijdom, the Lion of the North, the representative *par excellence* of the most rigid elements of Afrikanerdom, was in indifferent health. But Afrikanerdom had nothing to fear, for waiting in the wings was the architect of the Great Plan itself, Dr. Hendrik Frensch Verwoerd, the man of benign countenance and implacable resolution, who would secure the safety of his people for ever and ever and would by some magic secure, so the less rigid Afrikaners hoped, the happiness of all other people at the same time.

Although born in Holland, Verwoerd was accepted by the over-whelming majority of 'true Afrikaners' as a true Afrikaner himself. His influence in the party was immense, but he never made any attempt to weaken the position of his Prime Minister. In 1957 he turned fifty-six years of age, a man of iron will and apparently inexhaustible energy. Henry Kenney, in his excellent biography *Architect of Apartheid*,* expressed the opinion that Verwoerd did not have the kind of personality that inspired warmth in others. Yet though he may not have inspired warmth, he certainly inspired confidence among Afrikaner Nationalists. In an unsafe world he gave them security.

It is my own opinion that Verwoerd felt no warmth for the non-Afrikaner peoples of South Africa. In particular he felt no warmth for the black people who would achieve happiness under the Great Plan. He felt what I would call, if not a horror, then at least a profound

* Jonathan Ball, Johannesburg, 1980.

repugnance for any kind of racial mixing, not only of miscegenation but for any kind of contact, whether physical or social or even the casual contacts of pedestrians in the streets. He expressed his repugnance in strong terms in a speech to the Senate:

Europeans and non-Europeans scattered and mixed up about the whole of South Africa; Europeans and non-Europeans travelling mixed up in the trams and the trains; Europeans and non-Europeans are already mixing in hotels and places where meals are served, engaged more and more in taking possession of the theatres and the streets; engaged in devastating the reserves; engaged in seeking learning which they do not use in the service of their own people, but which they use in order to cross the borderline of European life, to become traitors to their own people.

There is no doubt that Mrs. Betsy Verwoerd shared her husband's extreme repugnance to any kind of racial contact. After his death she made one or two extremely ill-advised comments about black people, their habits and, on one occasion, their smell. It is surmised that she was counselled by well-wishers to express no more opinions on racial matters in public.

Driven on by his inordinate repugnance Verwoerd, as Minister of Native Affairs, announced in 1957 that he would move a Native Laws Amendment Bill, one of the clauses of which, the famous 29(c), was intended to prevent racial association in 'church, school, hospital, club or any other institution, or place of entertainment'. This became known as the 'church clause'. Verwoerd intended to legislate that no church in the white area of any town, that is an area set aside for white occupation under the Group Areas Act, could admit an African to worship without the permission of the Minister of Native Affairs, given with the concurrence of the local authority. This applied not only to worship, it applied to any meeting whatsoever on church premises.

Afrikanerdom was now at the height of its arrogance. It was by now almost totally mesmerised by the Utopian vision of a multiracial country in which the races could live in almost total separation from one another. What is more, it was falling more and more under the mesmeric influence of Dr. Verwoerd. What great gift did Verwoerd possess? He had the ability to convince his party that he knew the answers to every problem that confronted Afrikanerdom, and that the future of the Afrikaner was safe in his hands. I do not claim that he was the intellectual superior of all other Nationalist Afrikaners. The truth was that Afrikanerdom desperately needed a saviour, for in spite of its arrogance it was also afraid.

It is true that in 1957 the Afrikaner Nationalists had simply no conception of the deep repugnance of the outside world to the statutory enforcement of racial separation, and to the entrenchment of white supremacy which was the necessary prerequisite to statutory racial separation. Nor did the Nationalists have any presentiment of the way in which this repugnance would grow deeper and harder, until the nations of the world would begin to explore ways and means, especially economic, of bringing this outrage to an end. The Nationalists placed their faith in the principle, more honoured then than now, 'No interference in the domestic affairs of the sovereign State.' This was their weapon of defence against the United Nations.

The extent of Afrikaner arrogance is clearly seen in the comment of *Die Transvaler*, the Nationalist newspaper once edited by Verwoerd himself:

As long as liberalistic bishops and canons, professors, students and politicians can freely attend church and hold meetings and socials together with non-Europeans, apartheid will be infringed in its marrow. It is high time for this to end.

This shows not only the extent of Afrikaner arrogance, it shows also the extent to which the doctrines of apartheid had corrupted Afrikaner religion and morality. Christians were free to workship God, but it must be done in a way approved of by the Minister of Native Affairs. Many of the Afrikaner journalists of 1987 must read this newspaper comment of 1957 with considerable embarrassment, if not shame.

The reaction of the English-speaking churches to clause 29(c) was strong and clear, and practically unanimous. I have told the story fully in *Apartheid and the Archbishop*, published in 1973. My own archbishop, the Most Rev. Geoffrey Clayton of the Church of the Province of South Africa (Anglican) summoned the four bishops constituting a special committee to deal with a crisis such as this, to meet him at Bishopscourt. Clayton had already come to what was for him a grievous decision, which was not to obey the provisions of the church clause, and his four bishops were in full agreement with him. Clayton had never done such a thing in his life, and he contemplated the doing of it not only with a heavy heart, but also with apprehension. The next morning the four bishops departed, leaving their archbishop to write a letter to J.G. Strijdom, the Prime Minister, advising him that 'if the Bill were to become law in its present form we should ourselves be unable to obey it or to counsel our clergy and people to do so'.

After mass and breakfast on that following morning Clayton went to his study and signed the letter. After lunch he returned to his desk, and at twenty past three o'clock his chaplain went to the study and found the archbishop lying on the floor. The chaplain thought that he was playing a game, and said, 'Get up, your Grace.' He then realised with great shock that the archbishop was dead.

I flew to Cape Town and attended the solemn funeral. The government, unable to ignore Clayton in life, ignored him in death. Nothing spoke more eloquently of the times in which he had lived than the fact that at the funeral of one of the most eminent of all South Africans, and of a man who had been the head of one of the largest churches in the country, the government did not see fit to send a representative.

In obedience to Clayton's wish, the funeral service was one of penitence. It was the funeral not so much of a great churchman but of a sinner. The most moving part of the service was its conclusion, when the choir, led by a boy's pure soprano voice, sang the Russian 'Kontakion of the Departed'.

Give rest, O Christ, to thy servant with thy saints, where sorrow and pain are no more, neither sighing, but life everlasting. Thou only art immortal, the Creator and Maker of Man; and we are mortal, forméd of the earth, and unto earth shall we return, for so thou didst ordain when thou createdst me, saying, Dust thou art, and unto dust shalt thou return. All we go down to the dust; and weeping o'er the grave, we make our song, alleluya, alleluya.

So departed one of the great men of my life. I am often asked what men and women have had the greatest influence on my life. One of them was Railton Dent, an older student at the Natal University College in 1919, of whom I wrote in *Towards the Mountain*. Dent was a faithful Christian and taught me – if I did not know it already – that the only profitable way to use one's life was in the service of God and others. I was sixteen years old when I met him, and I regarded him as the perfect human being. How my life would have turned out if I had not encountered him in 1919 I do not know.

My attitude towards Dent was one of hero-worship. It is not unnatural or unusual to feel this way at the age of sixteen, but one is unlikely to feel it again. I did not feel that way about the archbishop, but he was certainly a strong influence on my life. I recognised in this strange, extraordinary, petulant, sometimes even childish man, the quality of greatness. And what does that mean? It means – in this particular instance – a combination of great mental gifts and great humility, with pinches of petulance and arrogance; an ability – partly learned no doubt – to speak words of wisdom with utmost simplicity; a devotion to duty – which in this instance was duty to God and the Church – which, if it was not absolute, approached it.

On one occasion his last chaplain, Roy Cowdry, had been sent to fetch Canon Synge to dinner at Bishopscourt, but when he reached the place where Synge was staying, he dillied and dallied until Synge, who knew the temper of the archbishop, became more and more nervous, and at last suggested it was time to go. Cowdry replied, 'I've had enough of the old man. He's been having a tantrum and stamping his feet at me.' When they got back to Bishopscourt they were fifteen minutes late, but to Synge's relief Clayton was affability itself. Cowdry, preaching a sermon after Clayton's death, said these words: 'The consuming passion of the late archbishop was to be the servant of God and the servant of God's church.' So it was that Cowdry, having 'had enough of the old man', would always have returned to him, having known him in his role of a servant.

Clayton was in some ways like Samuel Johnson. He seldom opened his mouth without saying something memorable. He could be solemn and outrageous. I have heard him say the Prayer of Humble Access many times. But I could have listened to it many times more. And could he be outrageous? At a luncheon in Grahamstown he said, 'When I was ordained I made up my mind that no one would ever say, "What a nice young man." ' And then a pause, and then, 'And no one ever did.' No one laughed more heartily than he.

There was one other quality of greatness that he seemed to me to possess, and that was incorruptibility. Once he had chosen his course of action, nothing would turn him from it, certainly not praise, or money, or fear. In his presence one felt immediately that he was incorruptible. One was conscious of his self-containedness and, when one grew to know him better, this impression was in no way diminished by learning that he could *Damn* and *Blast* with great fury if he stubbed his toe against some hard object during one of his attacks of gout, or by learning that he smoked incessantly until Lent, during which season he suffered bouts of bad temper and had been seen chewing his handkerchief to allay the pangs of deprivation. Abstinence during Lent is supposed to have great spiritual value, but this was never discernible in Clayton's case. His clergy, especially those who were close to him, knew all these faults, and yet revered him. One of them said to me, 'I know all his faults, but if ever I were in trouble – serious trouble – I'd go straight to him.'

I shall close this account with a story that has never been told before. It must have been in the 1930s that Clayton came to Diepkloof Reformatory to confirm the first batch of boys that we had prepared for the solemn sacrament. Dorrie had gone to considerable trouble to prepare a special lunch for our distinguished visitor, and I had bought a very special beer to which the archbishop was partial. He refused the beer very graciously, and said to me, 'Paton, I would not like any boy's clearest remembrance of his confirmation to be that the archbishop had smelt of liquor.'

I was later to write the life of Geoffrey Clayton, *Apartheid and the Archbishop*. By that time I had already published the life of J.H. Hofmeyr. These were two men who counted for a great deal in my life.

I have mentioned two others. The first was Railton Dent, of whom I wrote earlier in this chapter. Another was Reinhold Niebuhr, of whom I wrote with considerable affection in chapter 17. Yet another was Alfred Hoernlé, Professor of Philosophy at the University of the Witwatersrand, of whom I wrote, also with considerable affection, in *Apartheid and the Archbishop*. He and Clayton had a high regard for each other. Clayton once called Hoernlé a 'great liberal', and Hoernlé appreciated the compliment, but did not like the adjective 'great'; he said it made him squirm.

In the author's note to *Cry, the Beloved Country* I said that Hoernlé was the 'prince of Kafferboeties', and explained that *Kafferboetie* was a term of contempt originally used to describe those who fraternised with Africans, but later was used of anyone who worked for their welfare. The word means literally 'little brother of the Kaffir'. Clayton, to whom as an Englishman the word was new, said of it:

It has been left to professed Christians in this country to use the word which describes one who treats another man as a brother as a term of contempt. I should like to hear St. Paul's comments on that. And I don't think it is difficult to imagine Christ's comment on it.

After the death of the archbishop, his letter was delivered to Strijdom, the Prime Minister. He did not answer it but sent it to the Minister of Native Affairs. Verwoerd did not answer it either, but gave it to his private secretary, who wrote to the acting metropolitan, advising the bishops to 'desist from further participation in this most unnecessary agitation' and to wait for the second-reading debate.

Verwoerd, for all his iron will, had no wish to see the bishops, and many other churchmen, go to prison. I do not think that any biographer will ever tell us the thoughts that went through his mind during the passage of the Native Laws Amendment Bill and its clause 29(c) through parliament. There I must guess for myself. I guess that Verwoerd knew that he had raised a storm too big for him to control, and it must have been galling to discover that such a storm could exist. He amended his Bill so that if a notice issued under the law were disobeyed, it would be the African worshipper, not the church, that would be guilty of an offence. His Bill was passed on 24 April 1957 in the Lower House by seventy-eight votes to forty-seven, the seventy-eight being members of the National Party. On 14 July a letter was read in all Anglican churches in South Africa, calling on clergy and people to disobey any notice issued under clause 29(c). I guess also that Verwoerd had to control the vengeful feelings that must have occupied his mind when he realised that there were people in South Africa who would defy his authority, and that there were Christians who would defy the teachings of St. Paul that every soul should be subject to the higher powers.

In the Liberal Party we issued a statement totally condemning clause 29(c) of the proposed Act. We also declared that 'under no circumstances would the party apply to the Minister for permission to hold meetings'. This angered Verwoerd, who said that in view of the attitude of the party towards race questions, 'it is not at all unnecessary for parliament to take steps timeously to curb these activities of theirs'. He condemned those people in Pietermaritzburg and Durban who were running multiracial clubs, open to all people. Many members of the party were active in these clubs.

Verwoerd revealed again his hatred of inter-racial association. He said:

We find that there are Whites who take pleasure in arranging social gatherings where Whites and non-Whites mix freely, not because they feel the need for contact, but because they wish to demonstrate. . . . They even throw open the doors and windows so that everyone can see what is going on.

There were some critics inside the Liberal Party, and more outside it, who did not wholly admire the stand taken by the English-speaking churches. These critics argued that the protests of churchmen against the Group Areas Act, the Mixed Marriages Act, the Population Registration Act, had been verbal and useless. But the moment that their own territory was threatened, they were prepared to take the extreme step of going to prison. These churchmen were protesting not against the restriction of individual liberty but only of church liberty. Their protests were condemned.

I must admit that such thoughts crossed my mind, but I did not feel justified in supporting any public condemnation. The fact that church members were willing to go to prison rather than obey such a law was to me a fact of importance. Such an action might have a powerful effect on the Dutch Reformed churches, who had shown a deplorable willingness not to antagonise the 'higher powers', and who had allowed Verwoerd to make two fundamental changes in the eight-point statement which they presented to him. He was able to thank publicly those bodies who had brought their doubts to him, rather than exert pressure by way of extensive publicity and agitation.

Could the churches as a whole have done anything to change the government's intention to carry out the Great Plan? I think it not probable. The German churches did nothing or little to halt the advance of Nazism. It was left to individual Christians like Dietrich Bonhoeffer and Martin Niemöller to carry their protests to the point of death. Many early Christians were martyred under the Roman emperors, but they died for their faith and not for any politico-moral principle. There is no instance in history where the Church has radically changed the course of the State. There can be no doubt that St. Paul's admonitions in the famous opening verses of Romans 13 have had a profound influence on the relationship between Church and State.

The great 'church clause' storm of 1957 finally blew itself out. The clause, in so far as it concerns the churches, has hardly been heard of from that day to this. On Synod Sundays in Johannesburg, Pretoria, Grahamstown, and indeed every cathedral city, crowds of people throng the streets, and most of them are black. The phenomenon of mixed congregations is one of the big cities and towns rather than of small towns and villages, and it is in the small towns and villages that the resentment of white people would be greater. Moreover the behaviour of African worshippers attending a church in a 'white' area is invariably so modest and so courteous that it would be only a mean-natured person who would complain, and only a mean-natured town and city council who would seek the help of the Minister to bring such gatherings to an end. Luckily town and city councils are not usually so mean-natured as some individuals.

The mixed clubs, the International Clubs, were not so lucky., Their membership was negligible compared with that of the churches, and did not include any archbishops. The Durban International Club applied for a permit to the Minister, but it was refused, and the club closed down.

The Liberal Party continued as a multiracial organisation, finding it more and more difficult to find halls in which to hold its meetings. For some reason not known to me, the government did not yet take any steps against the party.

Therefore we soldiered on.

Chapter 20

I wrote at the end of the last chapter that in spite of Verwoerd's threats to any kind of nonracial organisation, the Liberal Party soldiered on. These threats were made more real when, on the death of the Prime Minister Strijdom on 24 August 1958, Verwoerd succeeded him. Verwoerd had already promised to remove all black students from the 'white' universities of the Witwatersrand, Cape Town, Grahamstown, and Natal. It was not necessary to deal with the Afrikaner universities, such as Stellenbosch and Pretoria, because they had no black students. The destruction of the 'black spots' would proceed relentlessly, more and more separate areas would be declared under the Group Areas Act, and the great Treason trial would grind on to its appointed end.

It was in 1957 that our son Jonathan, then twenty-one years old, came to inform his parents that he wanted to get married, to a young woman twenty-two years old, whom he had met at a conference of NUSAS, the National Union of South African Students. We considered his proposition with profound parental wisdom, told him that he was too young, and told him to come back, say in five or ten, perhaps even twenty years, when he himself would have acquired profound wisdom and, what is more, would be earning money.

Jonathan received these wise suggestions with scarcely concealed dissatisfaction, and returned to Pietermaritzburg to complete his studies. The next shot in his campaign was to ask us to invite this designing young woman, whose name was Margaret Taylor, to come to Kloof during the university vacation. We of course graciously agreed, and Margaret Taylor duly arrived. At the end of the first five minutes our parental wisdom did not seem to be so profound as it had first appeared. At the end of the next five minutes we had come to the conclusion that our son Jonathan was a lucky young man. He and Margaret were married on 4 January 1954, and Dorrie and I acquired a splendid daughter-in-law. Jonathan married a splendid wife, and my three grandchildren were born into a home of freedom, noise and love. How did Margaret demolish our defences in ten minutes? I can only suppose that we recognised at once in her the qualities of strength and honesty. She was also very attractive to look at.

In July of that year the whole family, Dorrie and I, David and his wife Nancy, another splendid daughter-in-law, and Jonathan and Margaret, set out on one of the great scenic journeys of Africa, of the world in fact, a journey that it would not be very easy to take today. Our route was Durban, Johannesburg, Salisbury (now Harare), Living-stone, Lusaka, Élisabethville (now Lubumbashi), Albertville (now Kalemi), Bukavu, Lake Kivu, Mount Ruwenzori and the Ituri Forest. We passed through the land of the gorillas, although we didn't see any, and of the volcanoes, although they weren't erupting. In 1958 this great country was known as the Belgian Congo, today it is Zaire. The days of Belgian sovereignty were almost at an end, and indeed Belgium has been severely criticised for her hasty abandonment of her colony, leaving it almost unable to cope with the problems of independence. We were told, and I have heard it confirmed, that there were only twelve (perhaps thirteen) university graduates in a population of twelve (perhaps thirteen) million.

Belgium is a bilingual country, and all the public signs and notices are in French and Flemish. The Flemish language is very close to Afrikaans, both having evolved from the Dutch of Holland. It is possible for a person speaking Afrikaans and a person speaking Flemish to understand each other without great difficulty. The Belgian city of Antwerp reminded me much more of South Africa than did the Dutch city of Amsterdam.

The similarity between Flemish and Afrikaans was nowhere more striking than in the names of the rich white farms that we passed, and we might have been motoring through the South African countryside. Very striking also was the contrast between the grandeur of the white farm houses, manors one might call them, and the poverty and squalidness of the shacks of the farm labourers. To a person like myself who is thought by some to have a prophetic gift, it would not have been surprising to see by the roadside a shabby but terrifying figure carrying the sign 'The end is nigh'. The contrast was so glaring that one could sense that one was surveying a grandeur that could not endure. Nor did it endure. Less than two years after our visit, the Belgian government had granted independence to the Congo, and that great and beautiful country entered a painful period in its history from which it has not yet emerged. This grandeur was nowhere more impressive than along the shores of beautiful Lake Kivu, on the road from Bakavu to the white pleasure resorts of Goma and Kisenyi, where we passed one noble manor after another, and one pitiful collection of shacks after another.

The most exciting time in the Congo was the ten minutes that Mount Ruwenzori decided to reveal itself, or rather to reveal its lofty summit, which is sixteen thousand eight hundred feet, and is the third highest peak in Africa, after Mount Kilimanjaro and Mount Kenya. We had up till then been very disappointed not to see the famous Mountains of the Moon, and had indeed given up all hope of seeing them, when suddenly the electrifying word was passed round the hotel that the peak of Mount Stanley had emerged from its mantle of cloud and mist. All work was stopped, and everyone came out to see the majestic and uncommon sight. It seemed as if the peak was virtually above one's head. The northern slopes of the mountains have a rainfall of two hundred inches a year, but the rainfall on all slopes is high, leading to a unique vegetation. Grass covers the mountain up to an altitude of six thousand five hundred feet, forest to eight thousand five hundred feet, bamboos to ten thousand feet, tree heaths to twelve thousand five hundred feet, and giant lobelias and senecios to fourteen thousand five hundred feet. Above that there is snow and rock. Our grand spectacle lasted ten minutes, and the mantle of cloud closed to hide the peak from view, perhaps for a day, perhaps for much longer, I did not know.

We left the Ruwenzori Hotel for the inn at Mount Hoyo, in the Ituri Forest, which is the home of the Batwa, the pygmy people. One of the attractions of the Mount Hoyo Inn was a visit to the pygmies. This was of course a commercial venture, but it is quite an experience to see a man climb a tree to a height of twenty or thirty feet, where he lights a cigarette, and there comes forward a bowman, who looks to be about six years of age, who fits his arrow to the bow and shoots the cigarette out of the mouth of the smoking man. We discovered that it is not an offence for pygmy children to smoke, and they smoked like chimneys.

Only small sections of the roads of this vast country were tarred, but in general they were fair. Public services were, as far as we used them, also good. One of the great achievements of the Belgian Congo was its hotels. We would cover considerable distances and arrive at these remote hotels after dark. In South Africa one rushes to arrive at country hotels in time for dinner, which is usually from seven to eight. Not so in the Congo. We would arrive late, and would hesitate about having hot baths, but our hesitations were waved aside. Clean and refreshed, we would present ourselves in the dining-room and sit down to most wonderful meals. I suppose that the cuisine of the Belgians was strongly influenced by the French. The food was good, the wine was good, the rooms were clean and comfortable.

Can one take such a journey today? Are there such hotels today? I cannot speak with authority, but I would doubt it. The roads and hotels and public services of the Congo were, if one may call them so, gifts from Belgium. Today Zaire lives under a dictator, and has, like most African countries, a crippling foreign debt. Colonial rule brought to this vast country its usual gifts of curses and blessings. The undoing of colonial rule brought its further gifts of curses and blessing. Which were worse, the curses of the doing or those of the undoing? Which were better, the blessings of the doing or of the undoing? These are not questions which permit rational inquiry. The passions and emotions that are aroused by their very asking make rational inquiry impossible. I can only conclude that Dorrie and I and our sons and our daughters-in-law were given the privilege of making one of the great journeys of the world, at a time when it was possible to make it.

So we returned to Natal having travelled a distance of more than seven thousand miles in four weeks. This is an average of two hundred and fifty miles a day, over roads that varied from good to bad, and we could of course not have done it if we had not had six drivers in our company, or if our car, fortunately a powerful one, had given any trouble. But it did not.

Back at home the Liberal Party was receiving more and more attention from Dr. Verwoerd and his government. We were now quite clearly enemies of the State. We had established a Defence Fund for the treason trialists, and worse than that, we had received considerable amounts of money from Canon Collins, the declared enemy of the Great Plan. We had established the Natal African Landowners Associ-ation and had openly encouraged the black inhabitants of the 'black spots' to resist expropriation by all lawful means, that is, by the 'constitutional means' that had earned the contempt of so many members of the Congresses. It is noteworthy that the vast majority of Congress members, while condemning the commitment to constitu-tional means, actually confined themselves to the use of such means. What are 'unconstitutional means'? They obviously include the un-authorised use of arms and explosives, and the defiance of laws. So far as I recall, the Liberal Party only once used or threatened to use unconstitutional means and that was when it declared that it would not obey any law that forbade inter-racial association. That was a further reason for the Prime Minister's unwavering hostility.

What about the wonderful writing career? Mrs. Hofmeyr died in 1959, and her death had removed the last obstacle to the writing of her son's life, but hardly anything had been written. I had two obligations, one to the biography and the other to the Liberal Party, and they seemed irreconcilable. As I look back, I think it possible that the biography would never have been written if Peter Brown had not intervened. He told me that as long as I held the office of National Chairman, I would never complete the biography. He offered to take over the chairmanship so that I could get on with the book. But he wished me to remain prominently associated with the party, and he proposed to get the party to create a new honorary post of National President, to which I would be elected. Much later on, at a reunion of old party members held in Grahamstown in July 1985, I gave this version of his intervention. I had earlier in my address referred to him as the Sir Galahad of the party, a man knightly in every way 'except for his sardonic wit'.

Now it so happened that Peter Brown wanted the national chairmanship for himself, and he came to me and said, not sardonically but very winningly, 'You know, Paton, you'll never write that life of Hofmeyr while you are National Chairman, and it is very important that this life should be written, really extremely important, and no one can write it better than you, so I think you ought to give up the national chairmanship, and we'll create a new post of National President, and you can take that.' So I took the post of National President, and who do you think was the new National Chairman? Sir Galahad, of course.

I must be honest and tell you that there is another version of this story, and that is that Peter Brown could see that the Liberal Party was doing great damage to my writing career, and he didn't want this to happen, so he offered to take over the national chairmanship, which I can tell you was no easy job. I must say that Peter prefers the second version to the first, and I must have half believed it myself, because when I had finished *Hofmeyr* I dedicated it to him. Modesty forbids me to say that very few people have had such a good book dedicated to them. And honesty compels me to say that there were mighty few people who wanted a job like that, and Peter had to pay a high price for it, nothing less than ten good years of his life.

My immediate aim now was to finish the biography. We knew quite well that such a tremendous task would be continuously interrupted if we stayed in our home at 23 Lynton Road, Kloof. We also knew that Dr. Halley Stott, the famous founder of the socio-economic project known as the Valley Trust, was the owner of a handsome house at Ramsgate on the south coast of Natal, and we were lucky enough to be able to rent it. So for the next two years we drove, whenever it was possible, to Ramsgate on Mondays and returned to Kloof on Fridays.

The amount of material I had gathered was vast. For a whole week I would select the material for the next chapter, decide on the theme, discard everything that did not contribute to the main theme, and write down all that remained on a sheet of paper. I found this preparatory work essential, and as a rule it was completed on the Friday before we returned to Kloof. The following week the chapter would be written.

Hofmeyr contains forty chapters, and at the rate of two chapters per month, the work would have taken twenty months. But in fact it took four years. That is due in part to the fact that in April 1960 the tragic massacre of Sharpeville took place. The government declared a state of emergency and many of our members were sent to prison. One of these was our National Chairman Peter Brown, and the consequence of this was that the unfortunate National President became the acting chairman of the party. Was there any resentment on my part? None at all that I remember. It was a job that had to be done. I was never actually a schizophrenic. These two sides of my nature could never have been separated one from the other. The emergency lasted only four months, but it took many more than four months out of my life. It imposed many more burdens on me, and its aftermath was just as onerous as it was itself. From all over the world came requests that I should write about it, and I cannot remember that I ever refused.

None of this must alter the fact that our days at Ramsgate were as near to idyllic as days could be in such a troubled country. The Stott cottage was a perfect place for a writer. One could go out of one of the doors facing the Indian Ocean, and walk through the low coastal scrub and emerge on a rocky beach, lonely and beautiful. All the tropical fruits of Natal, bananas, pawpaws, pineapples, litchis, mangoes, were plentiful, and in the late afternoon we could go down to the beach and buy fresh fish from the boats returning from the ocean. We had no telephone, and this on the whole was a blessing. Our idyllic days came to an end with the declaration of the state of emergency and the detention of so many of our leading members. We regretfully said goodbye to the Stott cottage, and did not return to it until Peter Brown had been released and had resumed the chairmanship. When I write of idyllic days, I am referring to the actual days we spent at Ramsgate, not to the whole period from 1958 to 1959. During that time, besides working on the biography of *Hofmeyr,* I regularly wrote a column 'The Long View' for the new paper *Contact,* which had been started by Patrick and Cynthia Duncan. I finished the booklet *The People Wept,* which dealt with the havoc and suffering wrought in people's material and emotional lives by the evil law known as the Group Areas Act. I also wrote the booklet *The Charlestown Story,* which deals with another disgraceful chapter in our history. Of all these I hope to write more fully in the next chapter, but let me now write of *Contact* and its most extraordinary owner, Patrick Duncan.

It was said, and never substantiated, that the money for *Contact* came from Cynthia Duncan, whose father, Patrick Ashley Cooper, was a director of the Bank of England and reputed to be very rich. It was also said, and also never substantiated, that the money in fact came from the Central Intelligence Agency. The C.I.A. was on the lookout for really bright anti-communists who could write, and initially provided the money for the very brainy British monthly *Encounter.* Eventually this was discovered and the publishers of *Encounter* jettisoned their benefactor with red faces and self-righteous breast-beating, but continued their very brainy and consistent anti-Marxist course. It does not really matter where the money came from. What does matter is that Duncan made it clear that *Contact* was his own property, but that he wanted it to be closely associated with the Liberal Party, and he even wanted a kind of board, not of management, but with advisory powers, and the members of the board were to be members of the Liberal Party. The party accepted this quite unworkable proposition for the simple reason that it wanted its own paper and the offer was quite dazzling and blinded it to reality. Patrick wanted to be the editor of the paper, and in fact said that Cynthia had made this a condition of the gift, which I did not believe. I persuaded Patrick that he did not have the makings of an editor, and to my surprise he capitulated immediately, and I recommended George Clay, a stringer for the British paper *The Observer,* and political correspondent for the *Cape Times,* a journalist in whom we had considerable confidence.

It was no sinecure to be a member of a board that was to advise an unpredictable character like Duncan who in the last resort would not take advice from anybody. In order to manage *Contact* Duncan had resigned as National Organiser, but I had not found him easy then. It was a kind of unwritten law in the party, that even if one believed that the party would never come to power, one must not say so in public. Well, Patrick did so, and I had to write to him that he couldn't do it. I wrote:

I am quite sure – I mean, I accept your assurance – that you forgot about our arrangement. Whatever else I may think of you, I have never thought that you would depart from a contract unless through impetuosity, generosity, or bellicosity. At such times a wind sweeps through your soul and lots of things go flying out of the window, but that is what you are, and by now I accept it.*

* From C.J. Driver, *Patrick Duncan,* Heinemann, London, 1980.

Patrick Duncan's biographer, C.J. Driver, said that this passage was written in my 'most schoolmasterly tones'. Myself, I thought it was rather witty.

In March of 1959, George Clay, who had very strong views about the freedom of editors, committed the unforgivable sin. He published in *Contact* a sympathetic profile of Piet Beyleveld, one of the leading members of the Congress of Democrats. Then followed what Patrick later called the most hectic week of his life. He called a meeting of the board at which he made it clear that it was *his* money, it was *his* paper, and it would follow *his* policy, and Clay and the board made it clear that no editor or board could possibly work under those conditions. So Clay parted company with *Contact*. Whether he was sacked, or whether he did it himself, is not important.

I wrote to Patrick again, expressing my doubts about his fitness to be editor:

Though I fear your unpredictability, I am attracted to you by your courage and honesty, and would not lightly hurt or abandon you. I am beginning to understand the compulsions that sometimes drive you into impetuous action and speech, and I believe that you seek endlessly for a noble and useful way to use your life.*

Patrick replied sharply:

I am not looking for a noble way of life. I have a message that I want to put over. I have a vision – a non-racial free South Africa – which I want to realise. I see how to get there with clarity. *Contact* is the answer. Also, you will realise that there can't be a *Contact* without me. I want *Contact* to help the party to grow in power and strength. I hope the party will maintain its support of *Contact* through the existing Board. But even if it does not, *Contact* is going ahead without the L.P.*

This was an ultimatum of course, and it meant that Patrick was going to go his own way. The board of *Contact* decided that there was no point in trying to maintain a relationship in which one of the partners would go ahead regardless of the wishes of the other. So Patrick continued alone on his tempestuous course, which was to reach its climax in 1960, the year of Sharpeville. 'I see how to get there with clarity.' These words were written, not spoken. If they had been spoken to me, my heart would have gone cold, because I would have known that he would not get there at all.

In December 1958 the party sent Jordan Ngubane to the All-Africa People's Conference in Accra, in the country then ruled by Kwame Nkrumah. Patrick and Cynthia, who paid their own way, were also

* From Driver, *Patrick Duncan*.

empowered to represent the party. The organisers of the conference had to persuade Zeke Mphahlele, a South African then teaching in Nigeria, not to launch a bitter attack on Liberals. The black Algerians, then fighting France for their independence, found it intolerable to be told that the conference was to work out the 'Gandhian tactics and strategy of the African Non-Violent Revolution'.* The conference patched over this yawning abyss with a resolution which read:

Recognising that national independence can be gained by peaceful means in territories where democratic means are available, the conference guarantees its support for all forms of peaceful action. Their support is pledged equally to those who, in order to meet the violent means by which they are subjected and exploited, are obliged to retaliate.*

The South Africans voted for the resolution. That was the first overt sign that Patrick was beginning to doubt the efficacy of the Sermon on the Mount and of *satyagraha;* retaliation finds no place in either.

When Patrick returned to South Africa he delivered another of his memorable judgements. He told the Johannesburg *Sunday Express* that Ghana was 'the nearest thing to Utopia I have seen'.

In 1959 and 1960 he was full of what appeared to be inexhaustible and irresistible energy, but in fact he was approaching the climax of his extraordinary life.

* From Driver, *Patrick Duncan.*

Chapter 21

It was largely, if not wholly, the doing of Peter Brown that I was able to finish the monumental task of writing *Hofmeyr*. But I did not repair to any ivory tower. In 1957 Dr. Yusuf Dadoo, the president of the South African Indian Congress, asked me to write a booklet on the Group Areas Act of 1950, and I agreed to do so. I quote the first and last paragraphs of the opening chapter of *The People Wept*:

Having a voice which by God's grace can be heard beyond the confines of South Africa, I use it to speak for people who have no voice at all, to protest on their behalf and in the name of justice against that law known as the Group Areas Act of 1950.

And the last paragraph:

This booklet is therefore partisan. It is written not to praise the Group Areas Act, nor to describe it dispassionately. It is written to reveal it as a callous and cruel piece of legislation, and to bring nearer the day when it will be struck from the statute book of the Union of South Africa.

These words were written probably thirty years ago, but the Act still remains on the statute book. The booklet is out of print, and that is a pity, because it tells a part of our history in a way that no history book could ever do.

The Group Areas Act was passed because of the obsession of the Afrikaner Nationalist government with the ideal of racial separation, which when realised would bring peace and harmony to the entire country and blessings to the whole world. That was the idealistic view, and it enabled many Afrikaners to blind themselves to the cruelty of the Act. Dr. Ebenezer Dönges, Minister of the Interior, said in parliament, 'The procedure leading up to the proclamation of a group area is a procedure which safeguards as far as is possible the interest of all parties concerned.' That was a lie of course, or shall I call it an untruth, or shall I be charitable and call it an example of extreme self-deception?

Another strand in the Group Areas rope was pure unadulterated anti-Indian hatred, an anger at the success of Indian shopkeepers, and a contempt for their way of life. Another was greed, a desire to get hold of the property of Indian people, and particularly those Indian areas which had been surrounded by the growing white towns and cities, and so had become unbelievably valuable. This applied also to the property of coloured people, particularly in the Cape; Cape Town had surrounded the immensely valuable area known as District Six, which stood in much the same relationship to the city as Sophiatown had done in Johannesburg. Another possible strand in the rope was white fear, but I would not regard it as important, for the deep white fear is of the African people, not of coloured people or Indians.

The government appointed special committees (all white of course) to receive proposals for a law constituting and controlling group areas. Dr. Dönges said that it was very encouraging to the government to know that the proposal of the committees 'in its most advanced form' was repatriation of all Indians or, failing that, compulsory segregation with boycott to induce repatriation. In other words the Minister made it quite clear that the aim of the Group Areas Act would be to force the Indian population of South Africa to go back to India. It would safeguard 'as far as possible the interests of all parties concerned'. It is difficult to believe that such things were once said. I do not suggest that some great moral change has come about. I am merely saying, by implication, that a Minister of State could not say such a thing in public today. This is a further proof of the arrogance of the Afrikaner Nationalists of those times.

Statements such as the one above could safely be made in public in the 'fifties, but they must not be quoted abroad. That was 'blackening the name' of the country. I wrote of this in *The People Wept*.

I think this is a lesson one should learn, and one of the aims of this booklet is to teach it. One must learn that the things one says in a little dorp in the Transvaal or Natal will be heard in New Delhi, Moscow, London, and New York, and how differently they sound there!

I am going to relate a painful story from the pages of *The People Wept*. It is only one of many, and I gave it the title 'The Story of Loyalty

Rewarded'.

Mr. Cassim J. served for five years in the South African Army. He fought against Hitler and against all that Hitler stood for.

In January 1957 he was served with a notice under the Group Areas Act. He was given twelve months to close down his business and to remove himself and his family from the township of K—.

What was his offence? He had the wrong colour, the wrong skin. Here is his story.

Mr. Cassim J., after leaving the Army in 1945 finally set up a shop in the township of K—, a mixed township with a large non-white population, a few miles to the south-west of Johannesburg. His landlord was a white man named V—.

In 1954 Mr. V— decided to rebuild the premises of which Mr. J.'s shop was a part. He gave Mr. J. temporary premises in the neighbourhood.

When in February 1955 the new premises were finished Mr. V— applied for a determination from the Group Areas Board, as he was obliged to do. The determination was a bombshell. The occupation was determined for the white group.

Meanwhile Mr. J. had returned to the new shop on the old site. In January 1957 he was convicted of illegal occupation, and was ordered to vacate by December 31, 1957.

He asked the Group Areas Board inspectors where he was to go, what was he to do? But they replied that that was none of their business.

'I fought for my country, and I thought I was fighting for my freedom. That's what they told me in those days,' said Mr. J. to me.

'Can I use your name?' I asked.

Anger and caution struggled in his face.

'I can't,' he said finally. 'My boy's training for a teacher.'

I shall close with another painful story from the same booklet, this time of a Chinese trader in Sophiatown, Johannesburg. The day before Good Friday 1957, the holiest day of the Christian year, thirty days' notice was served on Mr. H., a Chinese shopkeeper, to vacate his shop which was then due for demolition. This took place under the Natives Resettlement Act, not the Group Areas Act, but in cruelty they are identical.

Mr. H. was not only losing his premises, he was losing his business also. He asked the officials, as many have done before, and as so many must yet do, what he must now do, and he heard, as so many have heard and must yet hear, that it was not their business.

So there he is, he and his wife and his children with no place to go, and with his home and his business destroyed, and the authorities directly responsible for it wash their hands of him and his troubles.

I went to see Mr. H. I wrote of him: 'He has lost his home, he has lost his business. And it looks as though he is losing his mind too.'

The People Wept was sold out immediately but not reprinted. Was it a comfort to those Indian and Chinese people who read it? I do not know. I regard it as a minor achievement of a major kind, because it is a record of one of the most shameful chapters in our history. I closed the booklet with these words.

This is the Act that is to be carried out with justice, without resort to discrimination, and with equal sacrifice for all.

One day Dr. Dönges will stand before a much higher Authority than the South African Parliament. He will be asked to defend himself and the Group Areas Act.

It is hard to know what this clever man will be able to say.

I have no proof that there will ever be a Judgment Day. But in these years of which I am writing I often hoped that there would be. I would have to stand before the Judgment Seat myself, and answer for many things of which I am ashamed. But I thank God that I would not have to answer for the Group Areas Act.

The Charlestown Story was published in 1959. It tells a story just as shocking as that of the Group Areas Act. Before the British government in 1910 brought the four British colonies of the Cape, Transvaal, Orange River, and Natal into one Union of South Africa, Charlestown was a frontier town on the Natal side of the Transvaal. It was a flourishing railhead and customs town, but the coming of the union meant the end of customs, and the railway shops were transferred to the Transvaal town of Volksrust, three miles away. With them went most of the white population. Houses were deserted and Charlestown faced the prospect of becoming a ghost town.

To prevent this, Mr. S.R. Higgins, landowner, butcher, and member of the town board, persuaded the board to sell empty land and houses to Africans, there being no law against it. The first to buy was Mr. Abraham Ngwenya in 1911, and he was followed by many others. They came there seeking freedom, a home for the wives and children when the husbands went away to work, a place of their own where they could live and die.

But the Nationalist Party came to power in 1948 and Charlestown became a 'black spot', therefore it had to go. In March 1953 the Chief Native Commissioner for Natal told a meeting of African residents that all those who did not actually work in Charlestown would have to give up their land and houses and seek residence elsewhere. Those who had nowhere to go would be settled at Buffalo Flats, a place forty miles from Charlestown and eighteen miles from Newcastle.

In 1911 the town board had invited Africans to buy land and houses in Charlestown. It must be recorded that in 1953 the town board did nothing to defend the rights of the owners. The task of protest and defence was undertaken by the Liberal Party, and I was asked – or I asked myself, I can't remember – to write the Charlestown story.

The black owners of Charlestown were stunned by the news brought by the Chief Native Commissioner. They had held the belief that there was something sacred about a title deed, and also the belief that a white man, however cold and unsympathetic he might be, would never interfere with a title deed. 'When I got the title deeds,' said Mr. J. Mdakane to me, 'I settled down with full confidence and established my home.' If the black owners had any white sympathisers in Charlestown, we never discovered them. Mr. J. Zuma had built a fine house valued at seven hundred and fifty pounds and was approached by a white man who offered him twenty pounds for it. Mr. Zuma was affronted and said, 'The house is worth seven hundred and fifty pounds. How can you make such an offer?' The man laughed at him and said, 'Don't take it then. But one day I'll get it for five pounds.'

The Grand Old Man of Charlestown was Mr. Abraham Ngwenya, who had moved there in 1911 to escape from the limited life of a labourer on a white farm, and to build a better life for himself and his wife and his children. He bought both land and house from a white owner who was leaving the dying town. He was the first African to make this move, and he established a blacksmith's shop, repairing and sometimes even manufacturing wagons for farmers.

I am 80 years old but I must go on with my work, for that is how I live. However I am too old to do more than repairs. This move to Buffalo Flats has knocked me down, and I feel almost too old to get up again. I would rather die soon and escape this bitter ending to a hard but happy life. Nor can I understand why the farmers and the Government wish to do this to me. I never cheated them and they never cheated me.

Mr. Ngwenya's wish was granted. He died in 1959. It is true that none of the farmers whom he had served so long ever came out publicly in his defence. Some may have expressed sympathy privately, but that I do not know. After all, was it not their own government and their own people who had achieved victory in 1948? Which was more important – the happiness of the old man Abraham Ngwenya or the survival of the Afrikaner?

Ah, if those farmers had known the things that belonged to their peace, but they were hidden from their eyes. As I write now, they are not so hidden any more.

All this happened a quarter of a century ago. A new town has grown up at Buffalo Flats. Its name is Madadeni – 'The Place of the Ducks' –

and it now has a population of one hundred thousand people. They did not all come from Charlestown, they came from other 'black spots' also, Alcockspruit, Lennoxton and Fairlea in Newcastle, Waschbank, Dundee, and other places. They were settled in Madadeni so that they could serve the iron and steel industry of Newcastle. Their daily travelling expenses are very high, but that is always the case where black people are moved out of the white towns and cities, under the various laws that control black movement and residence. Not all of these laws were made by the Afrikaner Nationalist government. The original Natives (Urban Areas) Act was passed by the Smuts government in 1923, and was based on the findings of a commission headed by Colonel Charles Frampton Stallard, K.C., an English aristocrat who had settled in South Africa, and had soon adopted the 'South African way of life'. If Stallard is remembered by history, it will be because he invented the name 'temporary sojourners' for all Africans who lived and worked in the towns and cities. Fifty years later the name and the self-deception are dying out. The truth is that the industry, the farms, the railways, the very towns and cities themselves, could not exist without the 'temporary sojourners', many of whom have been city-dwellers for three and four (perhaps even five) generations.

I must close this story of Charlestown by reporting that living conditions at Madadeni have improved since the first people were moved there from Charlestown. Such improvements are usually due to two main factors, namely a sympathetic administration (usually headed by a white official) and the sheer will to live of the people who were sent there.

The third political task which interfered with the progress of *Hofmeyr* was the writing of the column 'The Long View' for Patrick Duncan's paper *Contact*. The first of these articles was written in Nigeria, where I was a delegate to the first All-African Church Conference in Ibadan, in January 1958. Some parts of it were, if I may say so, prophetic.

What is our political problem? It is to move from white supremacy to non-racial democracy as quickly, as soundly as we can. We have to do this because we ought to. But we also have to do it because we have to. The world demands it, quite gently now, more loudly tomorrow.

Slavery went, child labour went, the inferior status of women is going. Apartheid will go too. It has become, not merely distasteful, but downright offensive to most of the world. It has become embarrassing to the rest, because it could set the world on fire.

Up here in Nigeria they are angry with Britain for abstaining from voting on apartheid in the United Nations Assembly. Many told me that they would not stay in a Commonwealth that regards race discrimination as a domestic affair.

Up here in Nigeria, South Africa is the most important topic in the world. They talk all the time about South Africa. Ten young student teachers from St. Paul's College in Ibadan came to see me and to ask me what they could do to help South Africa. Everywhere we went, the Nigerians wanted to talk to the South Africans.

People up here don't think these are matters of politics. They think they are matters of justice, and therefore of religion. They think so with an intensity that must be seen to be believed.

That was written twenty-nine years ago, since when the intensity of the world's feelings against apartheid has immeasurably increased, so that today in 1987 South Africa faces the possibility of a total withdrawal of investment on the part of the United States. However, the Afrikaner Nationalist government of 1958 was – so far as one could judge – totally indifferent to world opinion, claiming that the racial policies of the country, including the Group Areas Act and the Natives (Urban Areas) Act of which I have written, were domestic affairs, and lay outside the jurisdiction of the United Nations. No one held this view more strongly than our new Prime Minister, Dr. Hendrik Frensch Verwoerd, to whom I wrote an open letter in 'The Long View' of 20 September 1958, a few days after his first address to the nation.

Honourable Sir

I listened with great attention to your first broadcast to the nation. Certain things you said were so important that I take the liberty of examining them closely.

You said that the right of people who have other convictions to express their views will be maintained. This is good news and will reassure many who thought you had other intentions. It will reassure these Liberals who thought that your ban on assemblies of more than ten Africans was in fact kept in existence to prevent the Liberal Party from holding meetings.

Or ir may be that you do not mind if people express their views, so long as they do it in newspapers, books, and the like. Or it may be that be that you do not mind if they express their views, so long as they do not attempt to persuade others. Or it may be that you do not mind their persuading others, so long as they do not try to persuade those of another race or colour.

Your views on this point are very obscure, and we would be very glad if you could be more precise. Do you in fact disapprove of interracial associations? Would you put an end to them openly, or are you afraid to do that? Would you rather use legislation devised to prevent 'public nuisances', or legislation devised to prevent 'occupation' of one group area by members of another group? Or are you brave enough to say to the world, 'I do not like interracial association, and I intend to stop it.'

Of course I never received any reply to this open letter, nor did I expect one. Dr. Verwoerd never said to the world, 'I don't like interracial association, and I intend to stop it,' but he did not mind saying it to parliament. Even he drew back from saying to the world, 'I don't like white people and black people going to church together, and I intend to stop it.' In fact he did not say it in parliament. What he said was that black people going to church in a white suburb spoiled the Sabbath calm by talking and laughing in the street, and that this constituted a 'public nuisance' and he intended to stop it. He actually got parliament to give him this power but, as I have reported in an earlier chapter, he never used it. It was one of the rare occasions when he bowed to the wind.

I wrote 'The Long View' for *Contact* for about a year, and after that time Peter Brown came to me again and said in effect that I would never finish *Hofmeyr* if I went on in this fashion. He offered to write 'The Long View' himself. I wrote what I thought to be my last column on 24 January 1959, in which I discussed the difficulty of changing the ideas of white South Africans.

A white South African is a man who hears about Léopoldville* today and forgets about it tomorrow. Nevertheless this last column is for him, he being my brother by blood.

I went to my brother and said, 'Brother a man is knocking at the door.'
My brother said, 'Is he a friend or an enemy?'
'I have asked him', I said, 'but he replies that you will not know until you have opened the door.'
There you are, my brother. You will never know if the man outside is a friend or an enemy until you open the door. But if you do not open the door, you can be sure what he will be.

That was written in 1959. This is now 1987. But my brother still has not opened the door.

Professor Edward Callan of the University of Western Michigan published in 1968 (Frederick A. Praeger, New York) a magnificently produced anthology called *The Long View*. He wrote that these essays formed an important part of my literary work. Where he thought it necessary he detailed the circumstances in which some of them were written and he dealt with other but cognate writings such as *The People Wept* and *The Charlestown Story*.

This is what he wrote about the story of my brother:

This parable of a knock on the door has many overtones, for *Contact*'s African readers in particular. For example, the Zulu song 'Open Malan', sung at large gatherings during the A.N.C. Defiance Campaign of 1952, began with the refrain 'Open Malan. We are knocking.' . . . And Chief Luthuli's well-known address on the occasion of his dismissal from his chieftainship, 'The Road to

* In Léopoldville in 1959 there was a black uprising against Belgian colonial rule.

Freedom is via the Cross', expanded on the metaphor of knocking on a closed and barred door.

On reading this I reflected on the word 'door' which is in its associations one of the richest words in the language, and is commonly found with one of three verbs, 'open', 'shut', and 'knock'. But it is when it is found with the word 'knock' that the most dramatic effect is achieved. In September 1969 the Imam Haron, a Muslim leader in Cape Town, was arrested under the Terrorism Act, and died in prison in mysterious circumstances. At the inquest it was stated that he had fallen down a flight of stairs and had died of his injuries. No one believed it. It moved me to write the poem 'Death of a Priest'. The 'Most Honourable' referred to is the Minister of Justice.

> Most Honourable I knock at your door
> I knock there by day and by night
> My knuckles are raw with blood
> I hope it does not offend you
> To have these marks on your door.
>
> I know you are there Most Honourable
> I know that you hear my knocking
> But you do not answer me
> Pity my impotence I cannot reach your power
> I cannot bring you my tale of sorrow
> You may die and never know
> What you have done or you may fall
> And leave no chance of its undoing.
>
> Most Honourable the sorrow is not my own
> It is of a man who has no hands to knock
> No voice to cry. A sorrow so deep
> That if you had it for your own
> You would cry out in unbelieving anguish
> That such a thing could be.
>
> Most Honourable do not bestir yourself
> The man is dead
> He fell down the stairs and died
> And all his wounds can be explained
> Except the holes in his hands and feet
> And the long deep thrust in his side.

It is worthy of note that some months after the Imam's death, the Minister of Justice made what I believe is called an *ex gratia* payment of five thousand rand to his widow. It is understood of course that the payment did not indicate any acknowledgment of responsibility. The poem 'Death of a Priest' was published in the anthology *Knocking on the Door* in 1975. The phrase 'knocking on the door' has meant a great deal in my life; in my political life also it was a door that would not open.

While I was considering the writing of these reflections, some lines came back to me from the distant past. They made a deep impression on my young mind.

> 'Who knocks?' 'I who was beautiful,
> Beyond all dreams to restore,
> I, from the roots of the dark thorn am hither,
> And knock on the door.'

They were written by Walter de la Mare, for whom the act of knocking on a door also had a great significance, as is evident in that beautiful poem 'The Listeners'.

So I gave up writing 'The Long View', but I did not foresee that I would soon be writing it again.

Chapter 22

The year is 1959. South Africa is moving unknowingly towards the greatest crisis up till then of its history. The first of the bitter fruits of eleven years of Afrikaner Nationalist rule are about to be tasted. The Defiance Campaign of 1952 was brought to an end by the Criminal Law Amendment Act which prescribed hitherto undreamt-of penalties for any person who broke a law *by way of protest*. But now in 1959 a second defiance was being prepared.

Robert Mangaliso Sobukwe was born in 1924 in the town of Graaff-Reinet in the Cape Province. Parts of this town are very beautiful, but not those in which Sobukwe was born. His father had enjoyed some elementary education, his mother none. They were devout Christians, and their home was humble, disciplined, and happy. Robert was their sixth and youngest child, and very clever. He went to school at Healdtown, and after that to the University College of Fort Hare. His first love was literature, but at Fort Hare he became concerned with politics, and in 1948 joined the college branch of the African National Congress Youth League.

Sobukwe, after graduating in 1949, became a high-school teacher in Standerton, but was dismissed for supporting the Defiance Campaign in 1952. In 1954 he became a 'Language Teacher' at the University of the Witwatersrand, where he found a new freedom to participate in politics. He became an Africanist, and took over the editorship of a paper called *The Africanist*. He was a powerful writer and speaker, and was edging away from the wider Congress movement. He was becoming impatient of the influence exerted on Lutuli and the African

National Congress by the other congresses, and particularly of the influence of the white Congress of Democrats. In November 1958 Sobukwe led a walk-out from the Transvaal conference of the A.N.C. and in March 1959 the Pan-Africanist Congress, the P.A.C., was formed, with Sobukwe as its chairman and Potlako Leballo as its secretary.

There was one person who watched these events with approval; it was Patrick Duncan, even though he was critical of the racial exclusiveness of the P.A.C. Earlier in the year Chief Lutuli had appealed in *New Age*, the C.O.D. journal, for the Liberal Party to drop its anti-communist plank in the interests of cooperation with the Congress Alliance. Patrick wrote in *Contact* of 2 May 1959: 'Far, therefore, from accepting Chief Luthuli's appeal, I appeal to him to use his eyes, and to see where he is allowing his congress to be led.'* Having thus implied – and very strongly – that Lutuli was being duped, he went on to ask, 'How many times has the A.N.C. followed a line during the last five years which would displease the Kremlin? – surely not one.'

Patrick made many enemies, both inside and outside the party, with his open letter. I wrote to criticise him on the same grounds as Lutuli had done, and there were those in the party who wanted him to be expelled. He had one firm ally, and that was Jordan Ngubane, who had by now become estranged from Lutuli, and who welcomed the founding of the P.A.C. The powerful bond between them was an almost fanatical anti-communism. Why were they so fanatical? It was said that Ngubane had never forgiven the A.N.C. Youth League, which he had helped to found, for saying that his anti-communism blunted their attack on Afrikaner nationalism, their real enemy. They drew away from him and he from them, and it was thought by many that this experience had embittered him, and had intensified his anti-communism.

Both he and Patrick wasted much of their time in sterile debates about the relative evil of communism and Afrikaner nationalism, and Patrick wrote that the barbarity of the communists made Verwoerd look like a Sunday-school teacher, a judgement that did nothing to endear him to the youth of the A.N.C. Did Patrick also have a personal motive for his fanaticism? If he did, I never discovered it.

These exciting political times were also the most exciting years of Patrick's life. He met Sobukwe and formed a high opinion of him. He wanted to join the P.A.C., claiming that he too was an African, but Sobukwe wanted to go it alone. Sobukwe was not anti-white, but he did not want whites in the P.A.C. Members of the party were therefore

* Lutuli is the old spelling of the name, and the Chief preferred it.

surprised and some displeased when Patrick decided to contest the white provincial seat of Sea Point for the Liberal Party. He declared that he was not a vote-catcher but would say what he thought. He was of course asked the one crucial question, the answer to which could win or lose a white election. Would his party open the Sea Point swimming-baths to African and coloured people? Patrick answered Yes, and yet polled one thousand five hundred and five votes against the four thousand four hundred and seventy-six of the United Party. It was said that most of his one thousand five hundred and five supporters were non-swimmers.

Towards the end of 1959 it was announced that Harold Macmillan, the British Prime Minister, would visit South Africa, and would almost certainly address parliament. Lutuli, Monty Naicker and I then wrote an open leter to him which was published in *The Observer* in London. It was written in a respectful manner, but it warned Macmillan – if he needed a warning – that he must not allow his visit to be interpreted by the people of South Africa and of the continent as in any way a condonation of apartheid.

On 3 February 1960 Macmillan delivered the famous 'wind of change' speech to the assembled parliament. He declared that it was blowing through the continent. He hoped that his hearers would not mind his saying frankly that there were aspects of their policies which Britain could not support without being false to her convictions about 'the political destinies of free men'. It is hardly necessary to add that Macmillan said all this in the most gentlemanly way.

The speech was received very coldly by the National Party. It gave encouragement to the A.N.C., which was planning a nation-wide anti-pass campaign, and massive demonstrations against the pass laws on 31 March. But on 18 March Sobukwe and his young Cape lieutenant Philip Kgosana announced that the anti-pass campaign of the P.A.C. would begin on 21 March and would be conducted without violence. Patrick Duncan wrote in *Contact*, 'Apartheid – the end approaches.' The slogan of the P.A.C. campaign was dramatic – 'No defence, no bail, no fine.' The leaders would set an example by going to police stations without their passes and offering themselves for arrest. If the word apartheid had any meaning, they would be arrested. If they offered themselves for arrest in sufficient numbers, neither the police nor the prisons would be able to cope with them. The pass laws, so much a part of South African history, would break down. At last the great black dream and the great white nightmare would be realised. The country would become ungovernable.

On 21 March Sobukwe and many others defied the pass laws. They left their reference books at home and went to police stations offering themselves for arrest. The protesters were orderly, but tragedy was to overwhelm them, and indeed the whole country. At the black town of Sharpeville some twenty miles from Johannesburg, several thousand people gathered outside the police station, asking to be arrested.* The station was protected by a high barbed-wire fence, with the police on one side and the protesters on the other. The pressure from those at the rear of the crowd was so great that the police thought that the fence was in danger of collapsing, and although the crowd was noisy rather than hostile, the deep-seated fear felt by white people, and especially by Afrikaners, of the long-deferred black revenge, and 'the night of the long knives', led to a terrible and tragic sequel. Davenport in his *South Africa: A Modern History,* says that the police panicked, and I myself believe this. The first shot was fired, although no order had been given, and was followed by many others. What began in panic ended in the desire to kill. The front ranks of the crowd tried to turn and flee, but the pressure behind them made it difficult. Sixty-nine people were killed, many of them being shot in the back. The terrible news went round the world, and was received with intense anger. The General Assembly of the United Nations passed a condemnatory resolution by an historic majority of ninety-six to one.

In South Africa itself there was deep despair, a despair felt most deeply by those who had been working for many years to bring about a more just order of society. No one could have felt it more than the members of the South African Institute of Race Relations, which had been founded in 1929, but it affected other groups as well. Was this what we had come to after thirty years of effort, to have our police kill sixty-nine people, who, according to evidence later given, were noisy rather than menacing?

I wrote above that I agreed with Davenport that the first shots had been fired in panic, but that the panic had been followed by the desire to kill. I do not doubt that the training of our police in handling crowds, especially those crowds some of whose members resort to violence, leaves much to be desired. A peculiarly South African factor enters the situation, for in 1960 the police force was preponderantly made up of whites, and these whites were preponderantly Afrikaans-speaking, with racial memories of past wars, the incessant frontier struggles of the Eastern Cape, and the massacre of Voortrekker families by Zulus in 1938 at Weenen, which name means 'the place of weeping'. When I was principal of Diepkloof Reformatory it was my duty to inspect

---

* The Rt. Rev. Ambrose Reeves, Bishop of Johannesburg, wrote that the crowd was estimated at between five and seven thousand. Dr. Verwoerd, the Prime Minister, told the House of Assembly that the police estimate was twenty thousand. Henry Kenney in *Architect of Apartheid,* estimated fifteen to twenty thousand.

regularly the white single-men's quarters, and in one of the rooms I was always confronted by a wall-size picture of a half-naked black warrior jumping through the window of a white farmhouse and impaling a white infant on his assegai. If that kind of picture is given pride of place in a young white man's bedroom, then one can imagine how he would behave in a situation like Sharpeville.

One thing is certain, and that is that many black people interpreted Sharpeville as meaning that the government was prepared to kill protesters against the pass laws. The campaign in the Transvaal came to an end. Sobukwe went to jail for three years, and parliament gave the Minister of Justice powers to extend this term, which finally reached nine years. At the end of this time he was moved to Kimberley under severe conditions of restriction. While in prison he obtained an honours degree in economics, and he had begun the study of law. He continued this in Kimberley, and in 1975 he began his own law practice. In September 1977 he was allowed to go to Groote Schuur Hospital in Cape Town for treatment of a serious chest complaint. He died on 26 February 1978, and was given a tremendous funeral in Graaff-Reinet, which Peter Brown and I attended. These nine years in prison and his subsequent banning left no bitterness in him. Thus it is that great evil and great virtue live side by side in this cruel and beautiful land. I myself would rank Sobukwe with the two other great black leaders of that time, Albert Lutuli and Z.K. Matthews. The circumstances of the land into which they were born meant that they, who were fully qualified to take part in the great tasks of government, had to spend their lives in protest. No one who knew these three could say that they led wasted lives, but one can say without hesitation that white South Africa would not allow them to use their great gifts in the service of their country.

The Sharpeville tragedy took place on Monday 21 March and Lutuli called for a National Day of Mourning on Monday 28 March. There seemed little doubt that it would be widely observed. Now it happened that 28 March was to be the occasion of the opening night in Durban of 'Mkhumbane', a musical play with words written by myself and songs written by Todd Matshikiza, who had become famous for those that he had written for the very successful Johannesburg musical, 'King Kong'. Todd and I had worked very hard on 'Mkhumbane'. He had come to stay with us in Kloof for some weeks, and had spent that time in composing and training a magnificent choir. Therefore the call for a Day of Mourning posed a problem for us, but a much more difficult problem for the Institute of Race Relations, to which we had donated the first night. It was to have been a gala occasion, and members of the institute had sold large numbers of tickets at high prices for the opening performance. Meanwhile booking had been quite heavy for the rest of the week, and if the opening night were to be cancelled the whole week would have to be replanned, which would be a monumental task. The Durban committee of the institute held an urgent meeting, and decided unanimously that Lutuli's call must be obeyed.

The killings at Sharpeville had brought the anti-pass campaign in the Transvaal virtually to an end, but it was being actively prosecuted by Philip Kgosana in the Cape. In Durban things were less tense, but tense enough. Several thousand black people, many armed with sticks, but not with guns, gathered at Cato Manor and began to march on Durban, entering the city through the white residential streets of the Berea and terrifying the citizens. The sights and sounds of a black army marching, singing their songs and shouting their cries of defiance, are enough to terrify anybody. The whole thing was made more eerie and frightening by their order and discipline, decreed by what or whom, one did not know. Some maintain that it is an inborn characteristic of the Zulu people implanted in them by Shaka, who created the nation out of a hundred different tribes. This new nation took its name from one of the smallest of the tribes, the Zulu, and Shaka gave to the nation a tremendous confidence in itself, so that all of its members learned to say with pride, 'I am a Zulu.' It was a contingent of this nation that now marched through the white streets of Durban, with a menace all the more frightening because it was so controlled. There was also a rumour that, if not satisfied, the contingent would march again.

It was in this atmosphere that the opening night of 'Mkhumbane' took place, on 29 March 1960. I have no pretensions to be a playwright, and in fact 'Mkhumbane' was specifically written to give a chance for the black people of Durban, teachers, domestic servants, artisans, taxidrivers, to get up on the stage and talk and dance and sing. Todd Matshikiza's songs were magnificent, and he was conductor as well as composer. In the whole of South Africa the Durban City Hall was of all places the most untroubled. I remember it to this day as a kind of miracle. That was twenty-seven years ago, but it can still happen to me today, as it did after the making of the film *Cry, the Beloved Country*, that a black man or woman will stop me in the street and say, 'Do you remember me? I was in "Mkhumbane". Oh, I am glad to see you.' So again I have seen a black face light up with the memory of a magic time in what may have been a hard and bitter life.

On 26 March, writes Peter Brown, in language unusual for him, the Liberal Party Congress in Johannesburg was 'electrified' by the news that the pass laws had been suspended. Chief Lutuli burned his pass in front of a gathering in Pretoria at the house of John Brink, one of our members. The question was whether every black person in South Africa would burn his or her pass on the Day of Mourning. Was Patrick perhaps right? Was the end of apartheid approaching?

Davenport states that eighteen thousand people were detained in prisons all over the country. The Liberal Party made a handsome contribution. In Pietermaritzburg alone Peter Brown, Hans Meidner, Elliot Mngadi, Frank Bhengu, Derick Marsh, Zephaniah Zuma, Robert Zondi, Jay Gangai, Roy Coventry, Albert Cebekulu, Jacob Mbongwe, Peter Kumalo, all went to prison. Peter Brown's three children, none of them yet ten years old, had the frightening experience of seeing their father taken away by the police at three in the morning. They asked their mother, 'What has our father done?' After my brief respite I again became the National Chairman and the writer of 'The Long View'.

On the morning of 30 March, the young Philip Kgosana led thirty thousand Africans to the Caledon Square police station to demand the release of their leaders. But they all dispersed peacefully when Kgosana, having been assured by Colonel Ignatius Terblanche that he had been granted an interview by F.C. Erasmus, Minister of Justice, told them to go home. Yet after they had dispersed, Kgosana was arrested. This vast demonstration caused white terror in Cape Town, and in the afternoon the Governor-General declared a State of Emergency which lasted until 31 August.

The members of the party in Cape Town behaved themselves bravely and well. They took trucks of food to the beleaguered townships of Langa and Nyanga, and persuaded the police to let the food go through. Patrick Duncan was in his element, and probably in those days of emergency lived through the most exciting times of his life. He acted as an intermediary between the marchers and the police, and earned the respect of Colonel Terreblanche, who did not want a second Sharpeville.

During those days *Contact* was magnificent. On 2 April Patrick called for United Nations intervention as the only hope for South Africa. He looked the very picture of health and vitality, although during his Sea Point election campaign he had had an emergency operation for perforated duodenal ulcers. The doctor told Cynthia Duncan that Patrick would be in hospital for a month, and after that would need a six-month rest. But eleven days after the operation he had resumed his campaign. He told me at that time that I was looking tired and was lacking my usual fire, and he recommended that I should at once have several feet of intestine removed from my abdomen. Patrick was in those days quite fearless and quite impossible. He greatly angered many people, and especially those who had fathers and mothers and sons and daughters in prison, by saying that the government according to its rights had no option but to declare an emergency. Although the party was opposed to Verwoerd's call for South Africa to become a republic, Patrick was in favour of it, not because he supported Verwoerd, but because he believed that our further isolation would bring the day of liberation nearer. He said in and out of season that the end was near, but this again was the voice of passion, not of reason. It was not a vulgar passion, of which he would have been incapable; it was a passion to believe in the nearness of the goal to which he had devoted the best years of his life, because, if one didn't believe in it, one might as well die. Driver tells the story of his saying loudly to an African lift-attendant, 'Your freedom is coming.' The lift-man asked, 'When?' and Patrick replied, 'Soon. In a year.'

Meanwhile in Johannesburg, Bishop Ambrose Reeves was collecting affidavits from as many people from Sharpeville as possible. He was courageous and indefatigable, and extremely unpopular with the authorities. He paid many visits to Baragwanath Hospital where the wounded had been taken, but finally was told by the medical superintendent that he would not be allowed to come again. He did not rest until the instruction had been withdrawn by the police. Another indefatigable worker was our member Ruth Hayman, who in her capacity as an officer of the court, that is, a lawyer, insisted on going to any place where her services would be required. The police were on the whole hostile to any person investigating their actions. I have written elsewhere about the reluctance of many white members of the party to confront the police, to demand their rights as citizens, and to ask to see some black friend who was in trouble. There were members of the police who would not hide their contempt for, and their distrust of, any white person who claimed to have a black friend. As far as I could see, Ruth was quite fearless, but both in her face and in the face of the bishop the signs of strain were clear to see. Reeves had earlier formed a consultative committee of fourteen organisations, and this now launched an appeal for food, clothing, and money. On 23 March Reeves asked a public question in the *Rand Daily Mail*, 'Why was a certain kind of bullet used which from the nature of the wounds shows that it causes a small wound where it enters but a large wound where it emerges from the body?' The Johannesburg daily the *Star*, referring to the Bishop's question, introduced a sub-heading 'Dumdum'. The dumdum is a soft-nosed bullet that expands on impact. The use of the dumdum is regarded in enlightened countries as inhuman and barbaric, and the antagonism between Reeves and the police was intensified as a result of the introduction of a word that he had never used.

On Friday 1 April, at our house in Kloof, the telephone rang about midnight, but when I answered the other person immediately rang off.

About an hour later there was a knock at our bedroom window, and I got up to see with apprehension that it was our daughter-in-law Nancy who was standing there. She had been sent by the party in Johannesburg to tell me that reliable information had been received that Reeves and I were about to be arrested, and that Reeves had left for Swaziland, which in 1960 was a British protectorate. The leaders of the party wanted me to know this, but did not presume to tell me what I should do. I knew at once that I could not go to Swaziland, or anywhere else for that matter. I was the acting National Chairman of the Liberal Party, and many of my co-members, including the National Chairman, were sitting in prison.

Two days later Reeves made a statement to the press, in which he said that he had left the country because he was determined that the facts about Sharpeville should be made known to the world, and he was not prepared to be impeded by the restraints that might be imposed on him by the emergency. If he could obtain a guarantee that this would not happen, he would return at once. Needless to say, he did not receive any guarantee. The Minister of Justice, F.C. Erasmus, refused categorically in the House of Assembly to give any assurance. The South African government was not only glad to see him gone. They knew also that he had taken a disastrous step, and they would do nothing to help him to retrace it.

Reeves had had a choice of two courses. One was to leave the country so that he would not be prevented from giving the facts about Sharpeville to the world. The other was to stay with his flock in the diocese of Johannesburg. He chose the former and so changed the whole course of his life. In his own diocese, where he had been by no means universally liked, it was said that he had 'fled' to Swaziland. I have studied carefully the Form of Ordaining or Consecrating of an Archbishop or Bishop. The bishop is charged to feed his flock. Paul exhorts the Ephesians to take heed to the flock that the Holy Spirit has given them, and warns them against the wolves that will not spare the flock. The story is told of how Jesus grieved Peter by saying to him three times, 'Feed my sheep.' After the bishop has been consecrated, the archbishop gives him a Bible and adjures him, 'Be to the flock of Christ a shepherd, not a wolf.' He also adjures him to 'hold up the weak, heal the sick, bind up the broken, bring again the outcasts, seek the lost'. At no point does the Form say explicitly that the bishop may not, for some reason that he considers good, leave the flock.

No research was ever undertaken into the reactions of the black Anglicans of the diocese to the course taken by Bishop Reeves. No such research was necessary into the reactions of white Anglicans; they were interviewed by the press, which in those days did not take much interest in black opinion. It was clear that the leading diocesan officials disapproved of Reeves's action. Peart-Binns, who is not an unsympathetic biographer, wrote, 'His autocratic rule and devious ways did not promote the kind of mutual trust required for team work.'*

I decided that I must go to Swaziland to see the bishop. I had two reasons for this – one was that I felt I should urge him to return to his diocese, the other was that I wanted to know what he had done about the funds and the books of the Defence and Aid Fund. This fund, as I have said, had been established in 1960 with Archbishop Joost de Blank as president and Bishop Reeves and myself as vice-presidents, and it had already received substantial help from Canon Collins and Christian Action in England. I arranged with an old university friend of mine, George Tomlinson, who was an experienced pilot, to fly me from the Oribi airfield at Pietermaritzburg to a small Swaziland airfield called Ross Citrus. Before I left home I wrote out a statement for the press in case I should be arrested before I could leave for Swaziland, and I gave this document into Dorrie's safe-keeping. She first hid it on top of one of the cupboards in the bathroom, but as she lay in bed it became quite clear to her that if the security police came, they would go straight to the cupboard in the bathroom. She then took it down and put it into her rolled-up red and white umbrella in her dressing-room, but when she went back to bed it became equally clear to her that they would go straight to the umbrella in her dressing-room. Then she had an inspiration of genius (based on the assumption that the security police were gentlemen) and she taped it to her stomach and went back to bed.

George Tomlinson and I, and his fourteen-year-old son Rex, reached the small private airfield of Ross Citrus in Swaziland at about nine in the morning. The telephone was out of order and it took us an hour to find another. When eventually we got through to Mbabane, where the bishop was staying, no one would believe me when I gave my name. I urged that the bishop should be brought to the telephone and he recognised my voice at once. A leading Swaziland Anglican, C.B. Pretious, came to fetch me by car, and we left George Tomlinson and Rex at the home of a friendly farmer. It was near lunch-time when we reached Mbabane. I find it painful to record what happened then, and I quote from my small book, *Kontakion for You Departed*, written after Dorrie's death.

It was clear when I arrived in Swaziland that the Bishop wanted me to tell him that he had done the right thing. Therefore I told him that he had done the

* J.S. Peart–Binns, *Ambrose Reeves*, Victor Gollancz, London, 1973.

right thing, for the reason that during the state of emergency he would be more useful outside the country than in, whereas I would be more useful in than out. I regret that I did so. I regret that I did not urge him to return to Johannesburg, that I did not tell him that there are crises in our lives where the criterion of usefulness is not the most important. Yet in a way I could not, because it had become almost impossible for him to return. The Church might have forgiven him, but the world would have not. To this day it troubles me to think of him, which I do with much affection. To me he had a deep understanding of the gospel teaching. This led him to challenge the assumptions of a colour-bar society and to expose its cruelties. This caused him to be hated more than it caused me, because while, in the estimation of some, I was a born idiot, he was a foreign one.

So I left Mbabane, having accomplished only half of my mission. I have only a few words to add to this account. I wrote that the bishop wanted me to tell him that he had done the right thing. I add now that the bishop wanted above all else to believe that he had done the right thing.

We were late in leaving the airfield at Ross Citrus. What is more, the wind had turned against us. The change had not been foreseen in any of the weather forecasts. By six o'clock we all realised that we could not reach the small airfield near Pietermaritzburg where George had a car available. Not only could we not reach it, we could not have seen it either, for that part of Natal was now shrouded in mist. Not one of us, George or his son or I, said a word, but I was ready to believe that the last day of my life had come. Then suddenly there was a break in the mist, and below was a rough ploughed field running uphill. George brought us down at the base of the field, and we taxied uphill with a great deal of bumping and noise. When we stopped I realised that the last day of my life had not yet come. George said, 'You needn't have worried so much, I've done this before.'

Ambrose Reeves in his book *South Africa – Yesterday and Tomorrow** wrote this about our meeting in Mbabane, 'In the course of our conversation Alan helped me greatly to see that it was my duty to proceed to England.' I read this with pain, but Reeves must have read with still greater pain what I later wrote in *Kontakion*. I did not help him to see that it was his duty to proceed to England. He had already made up his mind to do so. In fact, while the state of emergency lasted there was simply nothing else that he could do. I still regret that I caused him pain.

I shall have to write more about him, and about the tragedy of his later life. But it is time to return to Sharpeville, and its terrible aftermath.

* Victor Gollancz, London, 1962.

Chapter 23

After Sharpeville there were outbreaks of violence and pass-burning in Durban, Port Elizabeth, Cape Town, Bloemfontein, and other centres. The police dealt vigorously with this violence by the use of their own kind of violence, assaulting black people with clubs and whips, and entering and searching their houses, often destroying furniture and other property. On 29 March 1960 the Minister of Justice, F. C. Erasmus, speaking during the second reading of the new Unlawful Organisations Bill, used words that took his hearers back to those spoken by President Paul Kruger to Lord Alfred Milner in 1899. The Minister said that the African National Congress and the Pan-Africanist Congress 'do not want peace and order; what they want is not one pound a day . . . what they want is our country'. Parliament took the fateful step of passing the Unlawful Organisations Bill, and on 8 April the African National Congress and the Pan-Africanist Congress were banned. Thus black people were in effect denied the right to organise politically, and this has had terrible consequences for us all. The African National Congress went into exile, but is nevertheless today the best known of all black organisations. Its acts of sabotage, especially against State installations, are secretly approved by a large number of black South Africans. I shall write more of this later.

On 9 March the Prime Minister, Dr. Verwoerd, went to Milner Park to open the Rand Easter Show. After he had made his opening speech, he sat down, and a white man approached him, and in full view of the crowd fired two shots into Dr. Verwoerd's head. The Prime Minister fell back with blood streaming from his face, and was rushed to hospital where it was feared that he would die. But he did not. In the eyes of Nationalist Afrikanerdom it was a miracle. It was a proof that God did not mean their leader to die, that there was a great divinely ordained work that still had to be done. It was proof also that God approved of the policies of racial separation.

The would-be assassin was David Pratt, a well-to-do farmer with a record of mental instability. He was committed to a mental hospital and there killed himself the following year.

The effect of Sharpeville on the outside world was immense. In the eighteen months after Sharpeville a total of two hundred and forty-eight million rand left South Africa, and the gold and foreign-exchange reserves fell from two hundred and fifteen million rand to one hundred and forty-two million rand in June 1961. There was massive selling on the Johannesburg Stock Exchange. Protests against South African policies poured in from every part of the world. On 22 March the American State Department released a statement condemning the action at Sharpeville, and expressing the hope that in the future, Africans would 'be able to obtain redress for legitimate grievances by peaceful means'. On 1 April the United Nations Security Council intervened in South African affairs for the first time, and voted nine to nil for a resolution which condemned the government for the shootings and called upon it to 'initiate measures aimed at bringing about racial harmony based on equality'. The United Kingdom and France abstained, but the United States voted for the resolution.

The effect of Sharpeville inside the country was also immense. White South AFricans bought a record number of guns. The foreign consulates reported a marked increase in the number of South Africans, by no means all white, who wished to emigrate. It may have been reality or the result of the imagination of despair, but there seemed to be a sudden increase in the number of white homes advertising themselves for sale.

These were indeed days of despair, and I have no doubt that much of it was the result of imagination. That is inevitable. When one is in despair, one's imagination is very active. Luckily we in the Liberal Party had to be active too, and it was not easy to give way to despair when our comrades in prison were cheerful and determined. There is an apocryphal story about Peter Brown in the Pietermaritzburg gaol. It related that he was very dissatisfied that they were all in prison while I went free. He therefore conceived a plan of writing a message to me on a piece of paper, which he would then wrap round a stone, and then he would throw the stone over the prison wall. On the paper was to be written, 'Paton, for God's sake hide the revolvers.' I am sure he could have thought of something better, something more exciting, and more incriminating than that.

The Prime Minister's absence from parliament led to strange happenings inside the National Party. On 19 April Minister Paul Sauer said in Humansdorp that 'the old book of South African history was closed at Sharpeville'. This kind of talk could not be allowed, and Minister Eric Louw went to see Verwoerd in hospital and brought back the reassuring message: 'The Government sees no reason to depart from its policy of separate development as a result of the disturbances. On the contrary, the events have now more than ever emphasised that peace and good order, and friendly relations between the races, can best be achieved by this policy.' So Verwoerd from hospital rallied the National Party, and Minister Paul Sauer took a holiday (or was asked to take a holiday), and went to South America, to stay there until his mini-storm had blown over. The pass laws were restored. South Africa went back to its old ways, and the stock market recovered.

On 12 April Bishop Reeves left Swaziland, finally reaching London on 21 April. He was in great demand, and had to speak at many meetings. The strain on him was considerable, and it showed in the tightness and tiredness on his face. He was not a compelling speaker, and at a great meeting in Central Hall, Westminster, says Peart-Binns, he was 'at his objective, unemotional and somewhat colourless best'. I myself do not believe that biographies of living persons can be wholly honest, but I would concede that Peart-Binns comes close to it. Some parts of his book must have been painful reading for Reeves. Peart-Binns relates that at one meeting in England, a woman shouted out, 'Silence for the Right Reverend Runaway Reeves, the coward who would not stay with his flock in South Africa.' His diocesan chancellor, H. C. Koch, wrote to him in London: 'The Swaziland incident has not only brought this situation to a head but is itself a cause of confusion and uncertainty. Our information is that people in the church do not understand why their Bishop left them in their time of crisis.' He warned Reeves, 'The atmosphere of the forthcoming Synod is likely to be unpleasant.'

But Reeves did not have to face the forthcoming synod. He arrived back in Johannesburg on 10 September and was summarily deported. After much mind-searching and soul-searching he finally resigned his See at the end of March 1961. The rest of his life can, I think without exaggeration, be described as tragic. Reeves declined an offer from Geoffrey Fisher, Archbishop of Canterbury, of the secretaryship of the Church of England Board for Social Responsibility. In June 1961 Fisher was succeeded at Canterbury by Arthur Michael Ramsey, who, after a number of delays, mentioned two possibilities to Reeves, who wrote, 'Neither . . . appealed to me greatly.' The Bishop of Worcester offered him the post of assistant bishop, but it was necessary that he should be able to drive a car and Reeves could not. Peart-Binns records that in 1962 Mrs. Reeves met Archbishop and Mrs. Ramsey, and 'harsh words were exchanged'. I myself wrote to the archbishop urging him to find Reeves a post, and he wrote back to me explaining the difficulties, but did not say that he considered Reeves an unsuitable candidate for a bishopric. But Peart-Binns wrote, 'So far as the Archbishop of Canterbury was concerned, he seems to have made up his mind about Reeves after the Swaziland episode.' Peart-Binns lists thirteen appointments of bishops 'during almost two years of unemployment for Reeves'.

In 1962 Reeves accepted the post of general secretary of the Students Christian Movement. In 1965, at a meeting of the controlling body, 'A vote of no confidence, if not actually passed . . . was implied by the majority present.' The controlling body felt that Reeves was moulding the S.C.M. to a shape of his own choice, and that meant, briefly, that he was leading the S.C.M. into the field of politics, and especially racial politics. Reeves resigned and was again jobless.

R. P. Wilson, the Bishop of Chichester, came to the rescue. He asked Reeves to be priest-in-charge of the Church of St. Michael-in-Lewes, and Reeves took over the parish in April 1966, and a church with a dwindling congregation. Peart-Binns mentions, almost in an aside, that he was also Assistant Bishop of Chichester. The biographer collected the opinions and recollections of various parishioners, but they do not make a convincing picture of a vital ministry.

I went to see Reeves in Lewes in 1971, when I was working on my life of Geoffrey Clayton, Archbishop of Cape Town. By that time he had no doubt read what I had written in *Kontakion* and had found it painful. He was not cold to me, but neither was he warm. It was certainly no joyful reunion of the veterans of old wars. Mrs. Reeves was not there, but was out on some parish business. He talked a great deal about Archbishop Clayton, and about the incompatibility between Clayton and himself, of which I wrote at length in *Apartheid and the Archbishop*. But I did not tell Reeves that Clayton had once said of him, 'My Lord Bishop of Johannesburg is a horse that won't take the last fence.' Why did Clayton say that? Did he see something hidden from others, or was it a regrettable expression of the incompatibility? Nor did I quote this remark in my book on Clayton. I omitted it out of regard for Reeves. I parted from him with conventional wishes and regrets. Something had gone, and it could not be brought back again.

I do not apologise for having written so much of Ambrose Reeves. He was one of three Anglicans who touched my life most closely. The other two were Clayton and Huddleston. All three were men of undisputed courage, but Reeves did not have the gifts of the others. He did not have the charisma or the physical beauty of Huddleston, nor did he have the immense gravity and wisdom of Clayton. Neither Huddleston nor Reeves had the devastating wit of Clayton. They were all three what one might call Christian activists, but all three in different ways. Clayton distrusted the activism of the others, and I would guess that Huddleston and Reeves were closer to each other than they could ever have been to Clayton. We are indeed fearfully and wonderfully made.

I am fascinated by the portrait of Reeves on the cover of the biography by Peart–Binns.* It is certainly a picture of strain, of the same strain that could be seen in the faces of Vernon Berrangé and Ruth First as their planes approached Johannesburg, and the same strain that was to be seen in mine in the harder days of the Liberal Party. But while these last three might be described as occasional, in the face of Reeves it was a permanent characteristic. It was almost as though he had assumed burdens too great for him.

Peart-Binns in his closing chapter has a remarkable paragraph:

Reeves' character is very enigmatic and his personality is somewhat complex. Humility mingles with arrogance, transparent honesty with manifold deviousness. Autocrat and servant, prelate and priest wear the same vestments. Reconciler and revolutionary appear on the same platform. He who appears to be a political animal is a man of God. The shunner of limelight also likes it. He is long-suffering whilst not suffering fools gladly. He is unemotional and emotional, a success and a failure. These are reflections in the same mirror.

Perhaps Peart-Binns thought this was a bit harsh, for he added:

Reeves is each of them and all of them and still much more. He is prophet, evangelist and pastor. Perhaps above all he is a *Confessor* for the Faith.

This addition wouldn't have pleased me, if I had been the subject of the biography. I would have found the words 'manifold deviousness' hard to swallow.

So ends this sad and extraordinary tale. Reeves died in December 1980, at the age of eighty-one. To put it extremely, he destroyed his life when he went to Swaziland. If he had stayed in Johannesburg and been detained in prison, he would have reached a height of glory, both within his diocese and outside it, which perhaps he desired but never achieved. If the government had deported him then, he would have been welcomed as a hero in England. He would not have had to confront the cold 'admiration' of archbishops Fisher and Ramsey. He would not have had to receive a hypocritical gift of money from the

* *Ambrose Reeves.*

archbishops of Canterbury and York, and thirty-nine diocesan bishops, 'in token of their great regard'. It is said – but I do not have proof of it – that it was his wife who played the most prominent role in deciding him to go to Swaziland. She had come to feel insecure in Johannesburg, and the continual threats from anonymous telephone callers began to tell on her. She also had the safety of her children to consider. She did not want her husband to go to prison, and be at the mercy of the prison authorities. She wanted him to get out of the country while he could.

There is one last thing to be said. Reeves had already briefed counsel to present evidence for him to the Commission of Inquiry into the occurrences at Sharpeville. At the end of the inquiry the chairman of the commission expressed his thanks for the evidence that counsel for Reeves had presented, and said that without it a full report would not have been possible. Therefore he was not silenced at home. However, he always said that he had gone to Swaziland so that he would be able to tell the world the truth about Sharpeville. All I can say is that the price Reeves paid for being able to tell the world was inordinately high.

It was all very well for Peter Brown in that apocryphal story of the revolvers to feel aggrieved that I went free while he and others sat in prison. In fact I had to carry many of their burdens, while they were able to cultivate their minds. Hans Meidner was going to teach Botany to Brown and Marsh, Marsh was going to introduce Brown and Meidner to the wonders of literature, and Brown was going to teach Zulu to Meidner and Marsh. Brown and Marsh were quite excited about the prospect of learning about the beauty of the world of flowers, of which they knew very little. However, they both received a shock when they found that Meidner didn't know anything about flowers at all. His speciality was plant *physiology*, which is a deadly subject for would-be flower lovers. Nor did Brown's new understanding of literature, nor Marsh's introduction to one of the most melodious languages in the world, have any marked influence on the rest of their lives. I derive a certain sardonic pleasure from relating these facts, and the very relating of them compensates me for that joke about the revolvers.

I visited most of our Liberal Party members in South African prisons. What effect did their detention have on their aspirations and beliefs? Almost none, I should think. Not one of them was frightened or repentant or willing to lead a new and conforming life. However, detention did decide more than one of them that South Africa was not the country that they wanted their children to grow up in. Of course detention of this kind, when many of your friends are detained also, and when you are not in solitary confinement, and when you know that the state of emergency must come to an end, cannot be compared with the experience of being banned from all public life and from much of private life, sometimes for many years. Was Brown a dangerous person? Would he, had he been left free, have led a revolution? Was a gentle man like Derick Marsh dangerous? And Elliot Mngadi, also a gentle man, whose great crime was that he was resisting the intention of the government to take away his house and land? These questions seem preposterous, but not to the leaders of the National Party or the security police.* Does one declare a state of emergency to demonstrate one's power, or because one is afraid? I would find it hard to believe that Dr. Verwoerd had any close acquaintance with fear, but I am sure that many of his colleagues and advisers did so. In declaring a state of emergency Dr. Verwoerd was acting as a strong man, but many of his followers were weaklings who were only too thankful that they had such a strong man to lead them.

After three months of going free while my friends sat in prison, I was exhausted, and on 8 July 1960 Dorrie and I, with David and Nancy, set off by car to visit that harsh and beautiful country, then called South West Africa, but now more widely known as Namibia. On our way there we visited the falls of Aughrabies, where the two-mile-wide Orange River drops four hundred feet into a ravine that is only forty feet wide, producing for sixteen miles a series of thunderous cataracts. The Orange is one thousand three hundred miles long, and is not one of the world's great rivers. In dry seasons it is hardly a river at all, but in times of flood it can rise twenty to thirty feet in an hour and is one of the most violent in the world. In times of flood it is impossible to go near the falls, but in the dry season one can stand at the edge of the cliff and look down into the ravine. The Aughrabies is the most spectacular waterfall south of the Zambezi, but it does not have the grandeur of the Victoria Falls, nor the incomparable beauty and majesty of the Iguassu (Iguazu) on the Iguassu River, which is a great stream that runs for only a brief distance betwen Brazil and Argentina, so that the Falls belong to them both. Nor can it compare with the Kaieteur Falls on the Potaro River in what was once the colony of British Guiana, which falls I believe (not having seen them) to be, with Victoria and Iguassu, one of the three great waterfalls of the world. The Zambezi River at the site

* In 1987, we have been living for two years under another state of emergency. This one is much more serious than the first, because we are living through a period of black-township unrest that has no immediate cause such as Sharpeville, but is the consequence of years of anger, frustration and alienation. The fact is that the declaration of a state of emergency is a sign that social controls have broken down. They could be restored in 1960, but we do not yet know if they can be restored in 1987.

of the Falls is a mile wide, and drops four hundred feet into an immense chasm. The Iguassu is more than a mile wide and drops two hundred and thirty-six feet in a great number of cataracts, some sheer, some broken, some majestic waterfalls in their own right. The Kaieteur Falls are between seven and eight hundred feet high and have a width of over two thousand feet. We left Iguassu with regret, and I was willing (also with regret) to believe that it is the greatest wonder of its kind in the world. There is one great difference between Victoria and Iguassu. From the Brazilian side of the river, one sees the whole range of the falls, and there is nothing to obscure them. But the Zambezi River falls into a great cleft, and one can stand on the Zimbabwean side and be overawed by the sound and the volume, but not be able to see the bottom of the falls themselves because of the rising columns of spray. The African name for the Falls was Mosi oa Tunya, usually translated as 'the smoke that thunders'.

In 1960 the roads in South West Africa were murderous. On the way from Windhoek to the Etosha Pan, on a road which runs through sparsely populated country, the car broke down, and we were prepared to give up our holiday. But our friend June Fourie came out from Windhoek, lent us her own car, and undertook to have ours repaired. So we were able to visit the Etosha Pan.

Etosha Pan lies in the far north of South West Africa. It is seventy-five miles long and about thirty-five miles wide, and in years of good rainfall a considerable area of the pan is under water. The park contains vast numbers of game, including elephant, lion, giraffe, rhinoceros, cheetah, eland and many other antelopes, and an abundance of bird life. We drove along the shores of the pan from Namutoni, with its striking and picturesque German fort, to Okaukuejo. But by this time we were gravely troubled. Dorrie was very unwell, and was complaining of pains in her chest.

We decided to return to Windhoek, and June Fourie's doctor husband, Chris, advised me to take Dorrie to Johannesburg at once. We left it to David and Nancy to bring back the car, and Dorrie and I flew the next day to Johannesburg, where Dorrie went to hospital. There it was diagnosed that she was suffering from C.O.P.D., chronic obstructive pulmonary disease, which would eventually develop into emphysema. In time it would become clinically noticeable, and if the elastic recoil of the lungs became further lost, extremely debilitating.

Emphysema is not necessarily caused by smoking, but it was certainly aggravated by it. I disapproved of women smoking for conventional and totally inadequate reasons. I thought that after her illness in Johannesburg, Dorrie would give up smoking, but she did not. It would seem that it was already too late to arrest the process.

It was at some time in July or August of 1960 while the state of emergency was still in force, that I received from Freedom House, New York, an invitation to come to America in October to receive the Freedom Award. That this offer was made in recognition of the part played by the Liberal Party in the year of Sharpeville I had no doubt, but I would not have felt able to go to America while so many of my friends were in prison. However on 31 August the state of emergency was lifted. Peter Brown resumed the national chairmanship and the writing of 'The Long View'. I was free to go, and the party wanted nothing better at that time than that their National President should receive an honour which had been conferred on such persons as Winston Churchill, Franklin Roosevelt, Dwight Eisenhower, George Marshall, and Dag Hammarskjöld.

Dorrie and I decided that I would go to America alone, as we did not think it wise for her to travel so far after her illness. Indeed for the last seven years of her life, she did not travel abroad again.

Chapter 24

On 5 October 1960 I received the annual Freedom Award in New York at what could well be called 'a glittering occasion'. Edward Callan in his book *The Long View* records that representatives of the literary and political worlds came in such numbers that many had to be turned away. Edward R. Murrow, one of America's most distinguished newsmen, and winner of the 1954 Freedom Award, presided. Archibald MacLeish, poet and writer of distinction, winner of Pulitzer prizes for poetry and drama, Commander of the Legion of Honour, delivered the address of welcome. He had read somewhere that I had said that I was not a true poet, but he said that I had been misinformed, and what better authority could one have than that? President Eisenhower sent a message of congratulation, and said of me, 'In striving to achieve for all men recognition of the dignity to which they are entitled, he stands as a fine symbol of Freedom House.'

I received the award with what is known as 'becoming modesty'. I said the things that one should say on such an occasion. I said that I was receiving it on behalf of many thousands of South Africans, and that I myself was unworthy. I told one of my favourite stories, of the rabbi who, when he rose in the morning to say his prayers in the synagogue, would first go into his study and read letters that had been written to him by those who revered him. And someone asked him, 'Why do you first read these letters before you say your prayers?' And he replied, 'I read these letters because in them I am called *tsadik*, a leader, a holy man, and the like. Then when I have read them, I say to the Lord, "You and I know that I do not merit these titles of honour.

But since there are good men who in all sincerity believe them to be true, make me better so that they need not be put to shame." '

I told my audience that the making of such an award to me would make many of my friends feel that they had the support of good people in the United States. I told them that many of my friends had had to pay for their beliefs more dearly than I, and that some of them had spent a considerable part of that year in prison, arrested, detained, and released without the preferring of any charge against them.

Had they lived in this country, many of them would be sitting in this great audience here tonight, many of them would have sat, not in prison, but in positions of honour and authority . . .

. . . I do not need to tell this audience how the Government of my own country, the Union of South Africa, has recklessly thrown away all its chances of leadership on the African continent, and has not only ceased to be an asset but has become a burden to the West, because of its policy of Apartheid.

. . . Of one thing I am satisfied, that if the present rulers of South Africa should be able to continue with their present policies of Apartheid, we can expect increasing unrest and conflict.

Those words were spoken twenty-seven years ago. Alas, they have all been proved true. As I write these lines, the West is preparing to shed the burden altogether. What would happen to us then, God only knows. A second question must also be asked: if the West should totally abandon us, what would happen to the world? What would happen to the uneasy truce between the West and the U.S.S.R.? South Africa abandoned would be a rich prize for somebody, or a torch to set the world alight.

That remark about a 'burden to the West' was not well received in Pretoria, nor was the comment that our governmen thad thrown away its chances of playing a leading role in the affairs of Africa. I compounded these offences by undertaking a lecture tour of America on behalf of the American Committee on Africa, an organisation that was anathema to Pretoria. On 4 December I landed at the Jan Smuts airport outside Johannesburg, and was handed a letter from the Minister of the Interior, ordering me to surrender my passport. It was a shock to me but I should have expected it. How could a government headed by Dr. H. F. Verwoerd tolerate the holding of a passport by a South African who had used it 'to blacken the name of his country abroad'? The South African Broadcasting Corporation commended the government and condemned my perfidy. I wanted to answer them over the air, but was not allowed to do so. Many people abroad still believe that I have been banned, that my books have been banned, that I have been in prison. None of these beliefs is true. The worst thing that the government ever did to me, apart from bringing my country to the brink of catastrophe, was to take away my passport.

The impounding of my passport was a news sensation for about three days. No one in the Liberal Party was disturbed by it, but some of my old friends outside the party thought I had now gone too far. They belived in the convention that one should not do this kind of thing abroad. They believed in yet another convention, that the internal policies of any nation are its own concern, and that criticism from abroad is an interference in a nation's domestic affairs. This convention has by no means been abandoned, but it does not protect the policies of apartheid any longer. The world community took a firm vocal stand on human rights at Helsinki in 1975, but anyone who reads that magnificent publication *Index on Censorship* will know that the results of that accord have been far from electrifying.

Some brave citizens of the U.S.S.R. set up an Helsinki Monitoring Committee, but have paid heavily for their audacity, and of course for their disloyalty in believing that their government could not be trusted to respect human rights. The governments of the U.S.S.R. and of South Africa had much in common in 1960; they both believed that ordinary citizens should not concern themselves about the actions of their rulers, except of course at general elections, where a no-doubt regrettable democratic latitude had to be allowed. The Prime Minister, Dr. Verwoerd, told the students of Stellenbosch University that they should leave 'native affairs' to the government, which knew more about them than they would ever know. The students, who were more amenable in 1960 than they are now, took the Prime Minister's advice.

I arrived back in South Africa in time to take part in the first ecumenical consultation of all the 'main-line' churches in South Africa, excluding the (Roman) Catholic Church. The Cottesloe consultation was the work of that ecumenical giant, Dr. W. A. Visser 't Hooft, General Secretary of the World Council of Churches, whose name tells us that one of his forefathers had been the head fisherman. His right-hand man on this occasion was an American, Dr. Robert Bilheimer, and their concern was twofold, first to bridge the ever-widening gulf between the Afrikaner and the English churches, and secondly to help South Africa in the terrible aftermath of Sharpeville.

The gulf between the two groups of churches had been widened by my own archbishop, Joost de Blank, the successor to the great Geoffrey Clayton. De Blank was not interested in ecumenical diplomacy. He regarded apartheid as an outright rejection of Christ's teaching, and wrote to Visser 't Hooft: 'The future of Christianity in this country demands our complete dissociation from the Dutch Reformed attitude. . . . Either they must be expelled or we shall be compelled to withdraw.' The executive committee of the World Council of Churches was not sympathetic to De Blank's intransigent view, but at least it made clear to them the sorry situation of South African Christianity. Therefore at the cost of much time and labour and money, the world churches organised the historic Cottesloe Consultation, which took place from 8–14 December 1960.

Eight South African member churches attended the Cottesloe Consultation, and each was allotted ten representatives. The Archbishop of Cape Town, Joost de Blank, head of the Church of the Province, that is the Anglican Church, appointed two lay people amongst its representatives, the late Professor Monica Wilson, a noted anthropologist, and myself. The only all-white delegation was that of the Nederduitse Hervormde Kerk, the N.H.K., and the only all-black delegation that of the Bantu Presbyterian Church. John de Gruchy in his book *The Church Struggle in South Africa*** writes that the members of the N.H.K. delegation 'tended to keep apart'. This is a very kind way of putting it.

They did not tend to keep apart, they *did* keep apart. Their church does not admit anyone who is not white, and this is done on high moral principle. They came to Cottesloe to oppose any attempt by Christians to dilute the powerful essence of apartheid with the milk of sentimentality and false love. I record that to me their faces were hard and unloving. Their God was the God of Judgment and Punishment.

I watched them closely and I wondered what they would have made of Yeats's 'A Cradle Song'.

> *The Angels are stooping*
> *Above your bed;*
> *They weary of trooping*
> *With the whimpering dead.*
>
> *God's laughing in Heaven*
> *To see you so good;*
> *The Sailing Seven*
> *Are gay with His mood.*
>
> *I sigh that kiss you*
> *For I must own*
> *That I shalll miss you*
> *When you have grown.*

In the first place I don't think they had ever heard of Yeats. In the second place I think they would have found the words 'God's laughing in Heaven', if not blasphemous, then totally vulgar and I think incomprehensible. They were learned too, in their own rigid way. They

* William B. Eerdmans, Grand Rapids, Michigan, and David Philip, Cape Town, 1979.

knew their Bibles backwards, and were well versed in theology, though it would have been Calvinist rather than Catholic. But their theology, especially their theoloical and biblical justifications of apartheid, has now been repudiated by all the Calvinists of the outside world. Archbishop Clayton once said that he found in Dr. Verwoerd 'an alien mind'. So did I find an alien mind in the delegation of the Nederduitse Hervormde Kerk. What would have happened if one of their delegates and I had been castaways together on a desert island? What should we have talked about? I do not know, but what I do now is that what might have happened on a desert island will never happen in the country into which we both had been born.

The two most influential delegations were those from the Cape Town Transvaal synods of the big Dutch Reformed Church, the Nederduitse Gereformeerde Kerk, led respectively by Dr. A. J. van der Merwe and Dr. Beyers Naudé.

Dr. de Gruchy records that the Consultation reached a 'far-reaching consensus' on Part Two of the concluding statement, which read as follows:

We recognise that all racial groups who permanently inhabit our country are a part of our total population, and we regard them as indigenous. Members of all these groups have an equal right to make their contributions towards the enrichment of the life of their country and to share in the ensuing responsibilities, rewards and privileges. No one who believes in Jesus Christ may be excluded from any church on the grounds of his colour or race. The spiritual unity among all men who are in Christ must find visible expression in acts of common worship and witness, and in fellowship and consultation on matters of common concern.

The conference urged that the churches should consult one another before indulging in public criticism, and Archbishop de Blank expressed regret that he had sometimes spoken in anger against the N.G.K., and sometimes even through ignorance of its views. Dr. A. J. van der Merwe said that the hand of friendship was gladly accepted, and that it was the interests of God's kingdom that came first. The Consultation ended in an atmosphere of racial and religious goodwill that had not been seen in South Africa for many years, and perhaps had never been seen before at all. However, the ten delegates of the N.H.K. continued to 'keep apart'. They rejected the statement quoted above, and took no part in any demonstrations of racial and religious goodwill. The Rev. T. F. S. Dreyer, scribe of the N.H.K., said the church believed that separate development was the only solution for South Africa. Professor S.P. Engelbrecht, archivist, asked, 'Why must churchmen from abroad come and confer in our country about our own internal affairs?'

A notable visitor to the Consultation was Nelson Mandela. He was one of the last thirty accused who were still left in the Treason Trial. He was also at that time still in favour of the holding of a National Convention to plan a new constitution for South Africa, and he was against the use of violence to achieve a political solution. He made a special visit to the Consultation to show his approval of its aims. Mandela was now the heir-apparent to Chief Lutuli, and was not only a man of commanding bearing but was becoming more and more recognised by black South Africans as their next leader. He did not commiserate with me on losing my passport, but congratulated me on the vigour of my public refutation of the charges made against me by the government and the South African Broadcasting Corporation. He told me that I was a fighter, and this coming from him was a compliment that I have not forgotten. I shall write more about him before I finish this book. I have already written about Lutuli and Matthews and Sobukwe, that they were men of great gifts, and that white South Africa threw them away. Whether we have also thrown Mandela away is not clear at this time of writing.

Before the Consultation ended, Dr. Beyers Naudé, the leader of the Southern Transvaal N.G.K. delegation, invited me for a private talk in his room. 'You mustn't give up,' he said. 'A great change is coming about in the N.G.K., especially among our younger people.' Well, a great change did come about, but not in the N.G.K. It came about in the life of Beyers Naudé. After the Cottesloe resolutions had been published, Prime Minister H.F. Verwoerd expressed his grave displeasure at the actions of the N.G.K. delegations from the Southern Transvaal and the Cape. The Prime Minister was then at the height of his powers. He had been miraculously saved from death, and he himself claimed that he had been saved for a purpose. Part Two of the concluding statement at Cottesloe stated categorically that the Consultation, by an overwhelming majority, favoured common worship and witness, which was a repudiation of Verwoerd's 'church clause' of 1957. In the face of such displeasure the Cape and the Southern Transvaal synods came to heel. John de Gruchy writes that, just as Cottesloe represented a high point, so did the subsequent actions of the synods represent a low.

But Beyers Naudé had travelled too far on the Damascus road to turn back. He realised that his ecumenical visions could not be achieved through denominational structures. He founded the Christian Institute of Southern Africa, which held radical opinions about racial and religious affairs. This led first to his being deprived of his office as a dominee of the N.G.K., and eventually to his being banned from all public life by the Minister of Justice in 1977. The N.G.K.

dissociated itself from the World Council of Churches, but still remained a member of the World Reformed Alliance. However, in 1984, meeting in Ottawa, the Alliance declared that apartheid was a heresy, and elected as its World President the Rev. Dr. Allan Boesak, the head of the Dutch Reformed Mission Church of South Africa, a church for coloured believers founded by the N.G.K. in pursuit of its policy of racial separation. The Mission Church has now severed its connections with its mother church, and it seems possible that the Indian Reformed Church and the black Dutch Reformed Church in Africa will do likewise. Then the N.G.K. would be alone in the world.

Twenty-four years after Cottesloe I interviewed Beyers Naudé for the influential magazine *Leadership S.A.* I quote a portion of the interview:*

Paton: I met you in 1960 . . .
Naudé: You were one of the most important subversive theological influences in the N.G. Kerk.
Paton: I met you at Cottesloe.
Naudé: I remember that.
Paton: And you called me into your room – do you remember that?
Naudé: I remember that very well.
Paton: You told me not to give up. You said a great change was coming about in the N.G. Kerk, especially among our younger people. What is the position in the N.G.K. now?
Naudé: I think we have to accept the fact that the present official, appointed leadership of the N.G. Kerk will not change. The majority of these men are diehard, conservative and political figures. They are political in the sense that they operate from a theological perspective which forms the basis of the philosophy of men like Treurnicht and others, and they are in the key positions at the present moment. Where our hope lies is among a small and influential number of theologians within the N.G.K. who are working very hard behind the scenes to bring new theological insight and perspective to the theological students – the Dawid Bosches, Willie Jonkers and others – but they are doing this quietly behind the scenes for reasons which I can understand.

Beyers Naudé went on to say:

There is going to be a split in the N.G.K., a tremendous battle. Either the concerned Christians who are taking the biblical, or *verligte*,† side will eventually be forced out of the N.G.K., or you will see thousands of conservative white members leaving the N.G.K. and joining the Hervormde Kerk . . . my feelings are that 24 years after Cottesloe there are at last deep stirrings within the

* Fourth Quarter, 1984.
† *Verligte* is an Afrikaans word, meaning enlightened. In modern usage, it refers to those Afrikaners who either reject apartheid or advocate political (i.e. racial) reform. Its antonym is a new word, *verkrampte*, meaning narrow, unchanging, ultra-conservative.

hearts and the consciences of a number of theologians, theological students and lay people, who are saying that they cannot remain silent any longer.

Alas, a number of N.G.K. people – not a large number – said these same things twenty-four years earlier, at the time of Cottesloe itself. That is the way that change comes about in South Africa. It is no wonder that the outside world is so sceptical of our 'deep stirrings'.

It is twenty-four years ago that Beyers Naudé told me not to give up and that a great change was coming about in the N.G.K. Well, it hasn't come yet. Instead twenty-four years have been hard and lonely for him.

If ever a church failed in its duty towards its country, it was the N.G.K. That was because it saw its prime duty, after devotion to God, as being not devotion to the country, but to the *volk*. I do not suggest that the other churches have fully discharged their own duties. The theme of the Church as an organ of political reform, that is, the theme of its strengths and its limitations, is the subject for a book on its own, and I am not going to write it.

So Cottesloe came and went. There had been nothing like it before, there has been nothing like it since. Afrikaners and English-speaking mix freely in certain worlds, notably that of business. They mix more and more in the world of the press, and they work more and more easily together on projects like conservation, cripple care, help for the blind. But in the world of the churches they are far apart. The Afrikaner is never more unapproachable and inaccessible than in his church.

This inaccessibility is however more striking in the N.H.K. than in the N.G.K. I have been an observer of human nature for most of my life but I am at a loss to account, not only for the inaccessibility of the N.H.K., but for its apparent indifference to the fact that it is inaccessible. Why do they believe like that? What makes it yet more difficult to understand is that this hardness, this lovelessness, goes hand in hand with an almost absolute assurance of rectitude. The N.H.K. will not admit any person to membership who is not white, nor will it countenance any racially mixed worship, and this is justified on moral and religious and, I presume therefore, Christian grounds. My great mentor Archbishop Geoffrey Clayton used to say that the fundamental difference between churches like the N.G.K. and the N.H.K. and for example the Anglican Church was theological, but I was never able to believe it. The fundamental difference may appear to be theological, but it is in fact the consequence of a theology that has been fundamentally corrupted by history, and in the case of the Afrikaner this means racial history.

On 3 August 1650 Cromwell wrote to the General Assembly of the

Church of Scotland, 'I beseech you, in the bowels of Christ, think it possible you may be mistaken.' I don't know how tough the General Assembly was, but Cromwell would have found the N.H.K. much tougher.

Chapter 25

The year of Sharpeville, 1960, must be regarded as a watershed year. It was the year in which some of the most determined opponents of the government decided that normal, legal, constitutional, political activity was useless. They were knocking on a door that would never open. There was only one thing to do, and that was to smash the door down, to break in and confront the enemy, using violence as the weapon, just as he had used the violence of authority, of police and soldiers and prisons against them for generations.

It was in the year after Sharpeville, 1961, that the Treason Trial came to an end. In 1956 one hundred and fifty-six people were arrested on charges of high treason. In September 1957 charges were dropped against sixty-one of the accused, and these included Chief Lutuli but not Professor Matthews. Among the sixty-one was one fortunate or unfortunate man who heard neither his name nor any mention of his activity during the whole of the preparatory examination. In August 1958 only ninety-two accused were left. That fearsome lawyer for the defence, Advocate Isaac Maisels, attacked the indictment, and Advocate Oswald Pirow, who had been Minister of Justice under Hertzog, created a sensation by withdrawing it. The trialists were, after two years, back where they had started.

In November 1958 ninety-one trialists were re-indicted, in two groups of sixty-one and thirty. There were now two separate conspiracies, and Advocate Pirow had said, 'If we fail to prove a conspiracy, all the accused go free.' Some of the members of one or other of these conspiracies had never met any of the others, but the State relied on the contention that the Congress of the People in 1956 was the final proof of the existence of a conspiracy.

Probably the most farcical event in the trial occurred when Professor A.H. Murray, of the University of Cape Town, gave expert evidence on the nature of communism, and the infallible clues that indicated that certain statements and speeches were communist or communist-inspired.

The cross-examination by the defence was dramatic. The professor agreed that certain statements presented to him were the 'sort of statements that communists make'. Defence then revealed that all these statements *except one,* had been made by persons such as President Franklin Roosevelt, William Pitt, Heine, Luther, Voltaire, Milton and Jefferson. The final statement had been made by Professor Murray himself.

By November 1960 the number of trialists had dropped to thirty, and on 30 March 1961, these were also acquitted. The farce came to an end. One consequence of this was that Nelson Mandela was now a free man. He immediately set about organising a national stay-at-home to protest against Verwoerd's unilateral decision to declare that the Union of South Africa would become the Republic of South Africa on 31 May 1961.* This was the realisation of the final Afrikaner dream.

Verwoerd had hoped – not very fervently I should think – that South Africa would be able to declare itself a republic and yet remain a member of the Commonwealth. This was not to be. He attended the Commonwealth conference in London in March 1961, but would not submit to criticism of his policies and withdrew his application to remain a member. South Africa thus became a republic outside the Commonwealth, and Verwoerd returned to receive a tumultuous welcome at Jan Smuts airport in Johannesburg. So at last reparation had been made to the Afrikaner *volk* for the destruction of their republics by the British in the Anglo–Boer War of 1899–1902.

Peter Brown as National Chairman of the party, Jordan Ngubane as Vice-President and myself as President, wrote an open letter to Dr. Verwoerd:

Your new Republic will have no friend in the world, unless it be the tottering regime of Portugal ... You are called by your followers the saviour of Afrikanerdom, but History will call you its destroyer ... Even amongst your own, the will to dominate is losing its ancient power.

* 31 May is a highly symbolic day in South Africa. On 31 May 1902 was signed the Treaty of Vereeniging between the British and the defeated Boer republics. On 31 May 1910 was established the Union of South Africa with a colour bar given to us by the British. On 31 May 1961 the Republic of South Africa came into being. Will a new South Africa be born on some 31 May not yet come?

The Prime Minister's secretary replied briefly: 'Due to the distorted outlook and wrong statement of facts the Prime Minister does not regard it as deserving any reply.'

We wrote those words in 1961. In 1987 most of our predictions have come true. Yet I hope we shall be able to say that Afrikanerdom was not destroyed after all, but that it drew back from the brink.

Meanwhile Mandela continued with his organisation of the stay-at-home. Patrick Duncan, having opposed throughout, now called in *Contact* for support for Mandela, so that we could all join in, and 'deliver the knockout blow'.

The stay-at-home was a failure. Mandela was now more of a marked man than ever. He went underground and left South Africa secretly to evade arrest for incitement. He made a tour of the independent countries of Africa, and made an historic speech at Addis Ababa, in which he declared that constitutional politics had failed. In this speech he espoused the cause of violence, and justified the first sabotage attacks by Umkhonto we Sizwe, the Spear of the Nation, the new underground arm of the banned African National Congress, for the establishment of which he was actively responsible. After nearly fifty years of constitutional and non-violent protest, the Congress had decided that the white South African government must be overthrown by the use of force. The conquered had talked fruitlessly to the conqueror for fifty years. Now the only course open was for the conquered to conquer the conqueror. It was a fateful decision, and it profoundly influenced our future history. It should be noted that the decision taken by Umkhonto we Sizwe in 1961 was to sabotage installations without taking lives.

An underground movement called Poqo, an ideophone which can be interpreted as 'Alone' or 'We go it alone', also came into being. According to Davenport it was 'sponsored' by the P.A.C.* It did not shrink from taking lives, and the official report of the riots at the peaceful and beautiful vineyard town of Paarl, ascribed to it eleven murders, and several attempted murders, amongst which was a plan to kill Chief Kaiser Matanzima and other chiefs and headmen associated with the Verwoerdian plan to establish a Transkei 'homeland'.

So the A.N.C. and the P.A.C. turned to violence. According to Driver, Patrick Duncan followed suit in the latter part of 1961, after he had paid a visit to Holden Roberto in Angola. Duncan told Peter Hjul, one of our most active members in the Cape, that he had arranged for proper maps of Angola to be sent to Roberto. Hjul asked Duncan if that was not an odd thing for a believer in non-violence to do, and Duncan

* *South Africa*, p. 291

[221]

replied, 'I've changed my mind.'

It would be difficult to say at what point Duncan decided to turn to violence. Driver appears to think that it had already happened when Duncan said, 'I've changed my mind.' But on 28 December of that same year, after Umkhonto we Sizwe had damaged a powerline with explosives, he wrote in *Contact*: 'We wish to condemn the bombings with all the strength at our command, and to ask the unknown saboteurs to give up any plans they may have for future violence.' Earlier in that same year some younger member of Poqo approached Duncan to help them to get guns. Duncan stood – according to Driver – for some five minutes in total silence, and then said, 'I am not able to take part in anything that would turn South Africa into a battlefield.'

One can only conclude that Duncan turned to violence with reluctance and ambivalence. His fellow fighters could use violence but he would not. Today the issue of violence still troubles South Africans. The common way out of the dilemma is to say, 'I myself would not use violence, but I understand why others use it, and I do not condemn them.' Another variation is to omit the words 'I myself would not use violence, but . . .' because the use of those words emphasises the ambivalence. And today of course there are at least two kinds of violence. The first is 'structured' or 'institutional' violence, that is violence used by the authorities. The second is the violence of the saboteur and the freedom fighter. The struggle is in fact between the ruler and the ruled, and it becomes violent and bitter in any society where great inequality abounds.

It was not only Umkhonto we Sizwe and Poqo and Duncan who had turned to violence. Unknown to Peter Brown and myself, some of the younger members of the Liberal Party had decided that only violence would bring the government of Dr. Verwoerd to its knees and open the way to a just order of society.

During 1961 I visited Cape Town for an executive meeting of the party, and heard one of our most active and intelligent Cape members, Adrian Leftwich, make an impassioned and ambiguous speech, in which he condemned our conventional and constitutional methods as useless, and urged the party to break new ground. What did that mean? To me it could only mean one thing, that we should turn to violence. Later, in some more quiet place, I asked Adrian if he was organising an underground, to which he said No. I said I was glad to hear that, because I did not think he was fitted for it, an observation which clearly displeased him, though he said nothing.

I suspected that another vigorous and intelligent and somewhat older Cape member, Randolph Vigne, was also engaged in underground activity that involved sabotage, which in 1962 was made a very serious offence indeed, so that a convicted saboteur could be condemned to death. Vigne stood for the Liberal Party in the general election of October 1961, and I was asked to go to Cape Town and address a meeting in his support.

It is a most unpleasant experience to entertain such suspicions. Inevitably a barrier arises between the one who suspects and the one who is suspected. However, this did not deter me from speaking vigorously on his behalf. In his election Vigne, campaigning for one-man-one-vote, polled one thousand one hundred and fifteen votes in the very conservative constituency of Constantia against his opponent's seven thousand six hundred and fifty-four. Constantia is the home of famous wines and one of Vigne's supporters coined the witty slogan, 'Constantia is Vigne country.' However, the prediction was wrong; it turned out to be United Party country, a bastion of the old and dying Botha–Smuts–Merriman tradition of half a century before.

My discomfort was even greater when Vigne was banned from public life in February 1963, and I was again asked to go to Cape Town, this time to protest against the banning. I met Vigne in the Cape Town Gardens on the morning of the meeting and asked him outright if he were engaged in illegal underground activity, to which he replied No. I did not make the same observation that I had made to Leftwich, because Vigne was a much tougher character. So that evening I condemned the government for taking such action against a courageous, outspoken liberal democrat.*

Peter Brown and I laughed over these matters in later years. What could Leftwich or Vigne have answered to that question but No? And if they had answered Yes, what would I have done then? Gone to the police? Therefore by answering No they had saved me from a nasty fate. I should close these two stories by saying that in later years both Leftwich and Vigne apologised to me for lying. Meanwhile Peter Brown issued strong statements on behalf of the party, condemning violence and declaring his belief that any new society created by

* Randolph Vigne wrote to me (8 May 1986): 'You did not actually ask me if I were engaged in illegal underground activity, but said something like: "Randolph, we are all going to a lot of trouble on your behalf; is there anything you feel you should tell me which I should know about your activities?" It was my answer to that, for having to deceive you in that context, for which I apologised in England, not for lying as such, though I would also have apologised for the lie had it been just that. I actually gave you a rambling answer about events in the Transkei which might be used to smear the party, which was an intentional evasion. Not an important point, but better to have the facts?'

I have no hesitation in accepting Vigne's account of our talk in the Cape Town Gardens. The important point – to me – is that he allowed me to go to the meeting that night under a false impression.

violence would not bring that peace and justice that we hoped one day to see. He and I still strongly hold this view.

The National Committee of Liberation changed its name in 1964 to the African Resistance Movement, A.R.M., but the aims of both were identical. Both Vigne and Leftwich were highly intelligent men, but it is generally accepted that Vigne was the leader, and Leftwich the organiser. Vigne was a product of St. Andrew's College, Grahamstown, and Oxford University, and he was the possessor of a strong and independent personality. He was – in so far as a white South African can be – without racial fear or prejudice, and accepted without qualification a universal suffrage in a unitary society. It would appear that he had come to believe that the government of the National Party would be brought down only by violent and revolutionary means, but he did not express these beliefs in public, and indeed he could not have done so.

Vigne soon incurred the enmity of the security police, who realised that he was an opponent of unusual calibre. Why did a man of his intelligence imagine that the blowing up of pylons would induce Dr. Verwoerd to abandon the policies of racial separation? I can only guess at that. He was frustrated by the sedate and constitutional activities of the Liberal Party. He had an imperious personality, and reacted strongly to the imperious personality of Dr. Verwoerd. He had also a quality of ruthlessness but, as with his revolutionary beliefs, he did not manifest this in public. Would he have been ruthless enough to kill in pursuit of his beliefs? I do not know. All I do know is that the African Resistance Movement, when it decided to use violent methods that would have been condemned by the Liberal Party, confined its attacks to installations, just as Umkhonto we Sizwe did in its earlier days. These decisions sound strange to us today, who are used to reading almost daily about the killings of men and women in all parts of the world, many of whom are guiltless of oppression, but are killed because they are American or Ulster Catholic or Ulster Protestant or, in South Africa, black men or women who are deemed to be collaborating with the establishment.

In order to damage installations one must have some knowledge of explosives. The planning committee of A.R.M. was headed by Adrian Leftwich, and the instructor was a man called Robert Watson, who arrived from Malaya in 1962. He was not a member of the Liberal Party, but he believed in the emancipation of black people. He was an enigmatic character, and it would be difficult to gauge the depth of his beliefs. Some people have beliefs and would be prepared to die for them. Watson did not appear to me to be one of those.

The work of the planning committee was undertaken with great earnestness. All the members had code names, and there was also an elaborate code for emergencies, and elaborate instructions not only on how to topple a pylon but on how to get to the site and get away from it. Strict secrecy was observed and balaclavas and gloves were worn during operations. All this secrecy was inexplicably endangered by an extreme carelessness in regard to the keeping of documents.

On the night of 18 August 1963, Adrian Leftwich, Michael Schneider, Lynette van der Riet, and Eddie Daniels, set out for the F.M. mast at Constantia. When they reached Constantia Nek, Leftwich and Daniels, in balaclavas and gloves, set out to climb up to the mast, while Lynette and Schneider stayed in the car. The saboteurs taped charges to selected cables, and then set the timing-devices. Then back to the car and back to Cape Town, which would wake in the morning to see that the towering mast had toppled down. Brokensha and Knowles in their book *The Fourth of July Raids,** a book extremely hostile to the A.R.M., wrote, 'The A.R.M. would show them that it was made of stern stuff and was a force to be reckoned with.' Of the next morning Brokensha and Knowles wrote, 'Their eyes [the eyes of the A.R.M.] turned in disbelief to the summit of the Constantiaberg. There, defiant, stood the mast rising into the cloudless sky. They had failed.' It later transpired that the timing-devices had not worked. The police suppressed the news and told the newspaper that no such attempt had been made.

A.R.M.'s next project was to put out of commission the signal cables running parallel to the Cape Peninsula railway line. This was to be done at four points, Kenilworth, Rosebank, Mowbray, and Woodstock. If this succeeded it would make a greater impression on the public than the toppling of a mast. The attempt did succeed at all four points. Thousands of commuters were delayed, and the police could not hush it up. According to Brokensha and Knowles, at A.R.M. headquarters 'they danced a jig'.

A.R.M. was greatly encouraged by this success. But Watson withdrew from the movement for reasons of his own. His place was taken by Dennis Higgs, a teacher of mathematics who became a teacher of demolition. He was another member who kept dangerous documents. However, there were members who wanted to stop the whole thing. They no longer believed that the toppling of pylons and the damaging of signal cables would do anything to make Dr. Verwoerd swerve from his determined course. However, they continued to be members, and some of them were to pay heavily for this.

The next venture was a failure. It took weeks of careful planning, but

* Simondium, Cape Town, 1965.

the dynamite was becoming unstable. They reached the pylon, and were busy with their operation when one of them cried out that the dynamite was about to go off, and they ran for their lives. Little damage was caused to the pylon. It was to be some time before they tried again. More and more members of the A.R.M. were beginning to realise the futility of their actions. Eddie Daniels wanted to go to the national meeting to be held in Johannesburg in January 1964 to speak against continuing with sabotage. However, it was decided at the meeting to continue, and this was largely due to the influence of Dennis Higgs, who had become the A.R.M.'s adviser on demolition. Another Johannesburg member who was determined to carry on was John Harris, a schoolmaster, but I cannot verify that he was present at the meeting. Harris was then twenty-seven years old and his greatest contribution to the fight against apartheid had been in the field of sport. He joined the party in 1960 and he also became very active in SANROC, the South African Non-Racial Open Committee for Olympic Sports. He represented SANROC at the Lausanne meeting of the International Olympic Committee, and it was not surprising that his passport was withdrawn.

He then joined the National Committee of Liberation, and was banned from public life on 12 February 1964. The N.C.L., after it became the A.R.M., decided not to involve Harris in further sabotage. He did not interpret this action in any favourable light, and it reinforced the sense of being unwanted which had plagued him throughout his life. When therefore the possibility of discontinuing sabotage was discussed, Harris was one of those who opposed any such action. It is my own opinion that if one or two members strongly opposed giving up, it was almost psychologically impossible for the others to persist in their objections. The charge of cowardice, even if unspoken, would have been enough.

A plan to blow up the Wemmershoek Dam in the western Cape was abandoned. A plan to blow up the Government Garage was also dropped because it would endanger human life. Schneider thought of infecting the Cape vineyards with phylloxera, and Leftwich thought of rescuing Robert Sobukwe from Robben Island. On 18 June 1964 the A.R.M. brought down two pylons, one at Durbanville and one at Vlottenburg. A day or two later the pylon at Lynedoch was brought down. That was the last act of sabotage, but this was not because of any decision by the A.R.M. It was what one might call a chance discovery by the security police.

The police had long since decided that the sabotage of installations was not the work of Umkhonto we Sizwe or Poqo, but that white people were involved. The police decided to raid and search any person who might have anything to do with A.R.M. or might know something about it. One name on the list was that of Adrian Leftwich, who was well known to them as a militant opponent of apartheid and the government. On 4 July 1964 Lieutenant van Dyk knocked at the door of Leftwich's flat at 6.45 in the morning. He told Leftwich that he had come to search the flat, and produced his search warrant. The Lieutenant was surprised when Lynette van der Riet appeared in her dressing-gown. He told her she could go. Leftwich told her to take his car. He hoped that she would understand that her urgent ask was to get rid of the deteriorating dynamite, a dangerous job indeed.

It did not take the lieutenant long to realise that the long trail had come to an end. 'By chance entirely' (writes Leftwich) the lieutenant pulled out a book, and found in it a document relating to the identification of targets. Leftwich has written to me that no list of names was found in his flat, which statement I accept without question, but that other damaging documents were found in a 'safe' flat. The lieutenant now felt that he had justification in arresting Leftwich. He took him to Caledon Square. Lynette van der Riet was also arrested, but she had already got rid of the dynamite, the plastic explosives, detonators and fuses. When the dangerous suitcases were discovered, they were taken to a range by the police, and the contents were destroyed.

Some members of the A.R.M. had received some kind of instruction on how to behave in detention. Leftwich himself had drawn up the document on solitary confinement.* In forty-eight hours Lynette van der Riet had agreed to talk. In ninety-six hours Leftwich had agreed to talk.† But he agreed to do something much more devastating, not only to his colleagues but, most of all, to himself. He agreed to give evidence for the State, evidence that would convict many of those whom he had recruited for the A.R.M.

Members of the A.R.M. were detained in the Cape, Natal, and the Transvaal. Watson, Vigne, Schneider, and Higgs fled the country. In all some twenty members of the Liberal Party were detained. Brown and I had protested when some of them were banned, but it was no longer possible to believe that all these young men and women had been framed. It was a shocking experience for the National Chairman and the National President. For the Nationalists, and especially for the formidable Minister of Justice, B.J. Vorster, it provided the justification

* Leftwich writes that he had admitted writing such a document, but in fact he had not, and had admitted only to shield the actual writer. I accept this statement without question. The writing of the document is only incidental to the main story.

† It will be seen later that Leftwich stated in court that even after seventy days he had not yet agreed to give evidence. I did not see any point in pursuing this further. It also is only incidental to the main story.

for all their security legislation, for the power to detain without charge or trial, for the power to ban and to banish, and for the taking away of vital powers from the judiciary and handing them over to the Minister. It justified the Minister's famous remark that the communists killed people, but the liberals led people into ambush so that they might be killed.

In November 1964 the Supreme Court in Cape Town was packed for the trial of Eddie Daniels, 'Spike' de Keller, Anthony Trew, Alan Brooks, and Stephanie Kemp, charged with sabotage. Daniels and De Keller pleaded not guilty, the others pleaded guilty. There was a separation of trials, and Trew, Brookes and Stephanie Kemp went down the steps to the precincts below. The presiding judge was the formidable Judge-President of the Cape Division, Mr. Justice Andries Brink Beyers. He was what is called a 'character' and, although he was no doubt a Nationalist, he was one of his own kind. When this new Supreme Court was in building he came to inspect it and found that signs for 'Whites Only', 'Blankes Alleen', and 'Non-Whites Only', 'Nie-Blankes Alleen', were being put up. He immediately ordered them to be taken down. He said that he would not have such signs in 'his court'. What the Minister of Justice thought of this is not known.

After Lieutenant van Dyk had given damning evidence, the State advocate, Thys Beukes, informed the court that the next witness would be an accomplice, and that he, the State advocate, believed that the accomplice would not speak freely unless the court was cleared. Somewhat surprisingly the Judge-President agreed, and the court was cleared, leaving only relatives of the accused and the press. The public had expected to see Leftwich and in fact many had come to see him, but it was not Leftwich that appeared, it was Lynette van der Riet. She made a pathetic figure as she told of her dangerous exploits. She gave the *raison d'être* of the A.R.M.: 'Petitions were useless, any appeals were useless, and we just felt that severe protest was called for.' She revealed in the course of her evidence that 'Spike' de Keller had wanted to give it all up. If she had called him a coward, she said, it was in jest.

It was Adrian Leftwich who came next into the witness box. How he had prepared himself for this ordeal I do not know, but he gave the appearance of self-confidence. It was soon clear that the Judge-President would show no mercy. He questioned Leftwich in regard to his knowledge – or lack of knowledge – of explosives and concluded, 'So you two amateurs [the other was Schneider], in a block of flats at Sea Point, start decanting powdered dynamite into metal canisters?' The question might have been rhetorical but in any event it was not answered.

The Judge-President questioned Leftwich again on the sabotaging of the signal cables, and Leftwich answered that they understood that the explosives were of low intensity.

Judge-President: From whom did you understand that?
Leftwich: From Mr. Watson.
Judge-President: How much of an expert was he?
Leftwich: He informed us that he had been in the British army and had worked a great deal with explosives.
Judge-President: Did you take much trouble to enquire what his degree of knowledge was before you went and took a chance on trains passing within minutes?
Leftwich: He was an officer, he told me he was an officer.
Judge-President: I am glad you did not say 'and a gentleman'.

Was the Judge-President trying to break Leftwich down? I have no doubt that he found Leftwich's assumption of self-confidence offensive. I also have no doubt that Leftwich now realised that his ordeal would be grim indeed. There was no indication that the Judge-President felt thankful to him for coming to the aid of the State.

Leftwich gave an account of the fateful meeting in Johannesburg in January 1964. Though he was by then against the continuation of sabotage, he accepted the decision to continue without much opposition. It was soon after this that the organisation changed its name and became the African Resistance Movement, A.R.M. Leftwich, Lewin, Higgs, and Hirson drafted the A.R.M. pamphlet, which set out its aims in the most explicit terms. This dangerous document was actually posted to some people who had no connection with the A.R.M. and would not have wished to have. The document was filed, together with other papers of the most incriminating kind, including a map of Robben Island, from which Sobukwe was going to be helped to escape. The Judge-President remarked, 'Doesn't it sound silly, tragically silly, when it is brought out in open court?'

Advocate Jimmy Gibson, defending Eddie Daniels, tried to show that his client, a man with a Standard Six education, in the company of intellectuals, was in a way a kind of handyman of the A.R.M., but neither Lynette van der Riet nor Leftwich supported his view. Gibson was a quiet man, but he was to bring about Leftwich's breakdown, in the most dramatic scene of the trial.

Gibson: Vigne, Rubin, Watson, Schneider are overseas, are they not? And you have an indemnity, an immunity? Van der Riet has also an indemnity but perhaps you don't know about that . . . It is rather like the story of the ten little nigger boys, or perhaps I should say African boys in this context. Everybody escaping, apart from two accused in this box and three whose pleas have been accepted in another trial. Are you happy with the situation?
Leftwich: Of course not.

Gibson: Then why did you do it? . . . Why are you giving evidence in this case? Do you feel unhappy about giving a statement of that kind?

Leftwich: No, I do not. I was asked by the Security Police after about seventy days whether I was prepared to give evidence. At that stage I refused. Shortly before the others were charged, I was asked again to give evidence . . . I established that there were four other people giving evidence and I realised, from what I was aware of the organisation . . . that their evidence . . . as I understood it, to be very damning evidence against Daniels, Mr. de Keller and – yes, Mr. Daniels and Mr. de Keller.

Gibson: Possibly against you too?

What was Leftwich saying? Was he saying that the evidence was so damning that his own evidence would not make it any worse? It was becoming clear at this stage that he was losing control of himself. His next speech was very rambling. He admitted the futility and stupidity of all that he had done. But finally he had to answer Gibson's question.

I believe that from the evidence . . . the case against me was a very substantial one. I do not know what possible sentences are available. I was told on a number of occasions, in fact when I was initially arrested I was told: 'We've got enough to hang you' and I realised that a life sentence was not out of the question with this thing . . .

. . . I am sorry, I am confused, I realised that there was evidence, having explained that, sufficient to connect myself, Mr. Daniels, Mr. de Keller, I believe possibly this man I know as Roy, and I did not know, or could not assess, the nature of the evidence against Miss Kemp and Mr. Brooks. But it is not an easy thing, and if it is your intention to make me break down in this court I may do so . . .

Gibson said quietly, 'No, I don't want you to do that.' Leftwich put his head between his arms and said, 'Oh, I am sure . . .' and then was shaken with sobbing. Leftwich took off his spectacles and covered his face in his hands. The Judge said, presumably to Gibson, 'I don't know whether you want all this. It is not helping me at all.' Leftwich said, 'It is not an easy thing to give evidence against the people whom you love, who have been your friends . . . but if I stood to get five, seven or ten years I would not give it – not under any circumstances.'

What was he saying? That if he stood to get five or seven or ten years, he would not betray. But if he stood to get twenty-five years or life he would? He now cried out, 'I loathe, God I loathe apartheid and all that it means. This treachery here I place at the door of the system – but that is neither here nor there.'

Alas for him, the world was not going to place it at the door of the system. It was going to place it at his own. But now he could not stop. He said again, 'If I stood to receive five, six, seven, eight, ten years I would not give evidence, not against people I am close to.' And again there is the same conclusion to be drawn, that if he could be saved from a sentence for life, he *would* give evidence, even against people that he was close to.

Looking at Eddie Daniels and Spike de Keller he said, 'I certainly hope that there will be a time whèn, if these people who I am giving evidence against, can forgive me and understand that I do not move one jot from my ideas – if they can forgive me – that there will be a time, I hope so, when this country sees a lot better situation where the sort of very simple things, in a sense selfish things that I want for myself but I don't want for myself if they can't be for fifteen million other people – well, I just hope that day comes that we will all be together again. And that is why I have given evidence.'

Then he put his head again into his arms and stayed sobbing while the court adjourned. Brokensha and Knowles wrote in their book *The Fourth of July Raids*, 'There was not one person in that court who was not moved by his apologia.'

This story is not yet finished, but it is time to bring this chapter to an end. I am drained of energy. It is a tragedy that we have been watching. The words of Luke 17 will not go out of my mind, 'Whosoever shall seek to save his life shall lose it.'

Chapter 26

On the day after Leftwich's breakdown, the State amended the indictment against Daniels and De Keller. What had virtually been a charge of high treason was changed to one of attempting 'to achieve a change of attitude' on the part of the government by unlawful means. Daniels and De Keller pleaded guilty.

When the trial was resumed on 18 November 1964, Daniels told the court that Vigne had convinced him that non-violent protest was not enough. When he later lost this conviction he tried to withdraw, but Lefwich influenced him to continue. When he had finished his statement Advocate Gibson said in mitigation:

One is left with a sense of tragedy so far as Daniels is concerned. He joined a particular organisation. He was, in fact, a Liberal and unfortunately met one Randolph Vigne. Having met Vigne, he was introduced to such people as Watson, Schneider, Rubin and Leftwich. There was this man in this group of intellectuals. Today he and De Keller stand alone in the dock.

The Judge-President was not impressed by the advocate's plea. He said, 'That is the price you pay for the company you keep. I wish I could have brought it about that they did not stand alone.'

Next Advocate Snitcher pleaded in mitigation for De Keller. He said:

This trial has already served a very important purpose. It has done more than anything else to expose to many young people the fallacy underlying a great deal of their reasoning.

It has also served to demonstrate that it is often those who shout the loudest about their ideals who in the end stand revealed in all their nakedness, exposed as the hypocrites they are.

We have had experience of that in this Court – and it is a terrifying experience. It has taught a lesson to all the young people in South Africa.

Advocate Snitcher concluded with an earnest plea – a *cri de cœur* – to the Judge-President for mercy.

Before adjourning the court, the Judge-President said that normally he would have given sentence on that very day, but he required time to consider the whole matter. Three days later the court was packed to hear sentence.

The Judge-President spoke to the accused.

Both of you conspired with the likes of Dennis Higgs, Randolph Vigne, Michael Schneider, Hirson, Watson and, last but not least, Adrian Leftwich. Where are most of these now, these men – if one could call them that – that so impressed you? What leaders they would have made for this new South Africa that you were going to build with dynamite! . . .

These are the people you chose to conspire with to do damage to your own country. I have not seen all of them. I have seen, and had to listen to, that hero of the campus, Adrian Leftwich. Your counsel in his address referred to him as a rat. I did not object at the time to that appellation, but on reflection I am not sure that it is not a trifle hard on the genus *rattus*.

Brokensha and Knowles say in their book, 'The breath-holding tension in that court was broken for a moment by a burst of nervy laughter from the galleries.'

The Judge-President said to the accused: 'You should have realised that by dynamite you, and those with you, would not coerce one single person into sharing the views that you happen to have.'

After a few more stern words, the Judge-President sentenced Edward Joseph Daniels to fifteen years, and David Guy de Keller to ten years. Thus they paid heavily for their futile actions, which brought about, not the downfall of the government, but their own.*

Brokensha and Knowles write in their concluding chapter the following words:

The inevitable process of repudiation has already started – but it does not help. The Liberal Party, through its national leader, Mr. Alan Paton, has disassociated itself from the actions of its members who indulged in sabotage. NUSAS (The National Union of South African Students) has withdrawn honorary presidency from its two former presidents Adrian Leftwich and Neville Rubin. It will not help. In the minds of many the Liberal Party and

---

* De Keller was released after a short time by the Minister of Justice, B.J. Vorster, after a plea had been made to him by De Keller's father. Although great efforts were made on Daniels's behalf, by our Liberal Party member Dot Cleminshaw among others, they were not successful.

NUSAS are for ever damned.

I must say that we were not disturbed by this judgement. *The Fourth of July Raids* is a mediocre book, and does little justice to one of the most tragic dramas of our history. From a literary point of view, its only distinguished passages are those that are taken from the records of the court.

I conclude these strong remarks by quoting one of the most extra-ordinary passages of the book:

Whatever the Communist Party of South Africa, the Congress of Democrats, the A.N.C. and P.A.C., the United Party, the Nationalist Party, the Progressive Party, and, yes, even the A.R.M. may say, many South Africans of all colours lead a happy and prosperous life.

What these two authors are saying in effect is that they understood South Africa better than anyone else. And what a shallow understand-ing it was.

In other courts Anthony Trew and Alan Keith Brooks got four years, two years of them suspended. Stephanie Kemp got five years, three of them suspended. In the Transvaal Hugh Lewin got seven years, in Natal David Evans and John Laredo got five years. Leftwich, Lynette van der Riet, John Lloyd, and a fourth member, Rosemary Wentzel, got nothing because they had given evidence for the State. To the best of my knowledge sixteen members of the Liberal Party were also mem-bers of A.R.M.

I have written at great length about the A.R.M. That is not only because the ARM was a traumatic experience for the Liberal Party. It is also because the story of Adrian Leftwich is one of the most terrible of my times. Only one person could have thought about it more often than I, and that is Leftwich himself. All these things happened more than twenty years ago, but they are as clear to me as though they happened yesterday. When I was a young master at Maritzburg College in 1928, one of my colleagues was an Englishman, Henry Hall, a man of great brilliance, a product of one of the old universities, and a hunchback. He was known for his biting tongue and his perfect manners. The boys had a great respect for him, which was increased by his habit of taking off his hat to them when they took off theirs to him. Dorrie had gone to her mother in Ixopo with David our first-born, and I asked Hall if he would like to come to dinner. We had good wine, and we drank quite a lot of it. Suddenly Hall said to me, indicating his back, 'Do you know, Paton, I think of this every day of my life?' So I think it is possible that Leftwich thinks of his betrayal every day of his life.

What permits a man to betray his friends? What permits an intelligent man like Leftwich, who must have considered at some time or other in his life the question of betrayal, to commit it? What led him to think that his friends might forgive him his betrayal because he had not departed 'a jot' from his beliefs?

When the trials were over it was clear that Leftwich had no kind of future in South Africa. After he left he wrote to me: 'Nothing I can say or do, now or in the future, can *ever* reduce the immorality of my decision – in spite of whatever reasons I had, which I have to live with and come to terms with . . . I judge myself – and judge myself harshly.'

I did not reply to this letter, not knowing where to reply to. But some years later I was given his address in England, and wrote to him. He had no religion, but I could not write to him in other than religious terms, because what I had to write to him about was nothing less than the forgiveness of sins. Who forgives sins but God and the person one sins against? I took it upon myself to say that those against whom he had sinned had now forgiven him, and that I did not know of any one of us who had not forgiven him. Therefore he must forgive himself. But in fact it turned out later not to be true; some of those who were members of the A.R.M. have not forgiven him. One of those who forgave him ungrudgingly was Eddie Daniels, who spent fifteen years on Robben Island.

I have seldom in my life used the confessional, so I am no authority on the subject. The priest as an agent of God absolves one from sins, on the assumption that one is truly repentant. Does it give one great comfort to be absolved from sins of lust, selfishness, spite, and the like? Does this apply to betrayal? If one feels that one has committed the unforgivable sin, can one be absolved from it? I do not know.

In 1975 I was invited to the University of York to take part in a kind of literary and political seminar. Adrian was teaching at the university, and he wrote and invited me to stay with him, which I did. There were several South African exiles at the seminar, and some did not approve of my action. When Adrian come to fetch me at the close of each day's proceedings, no one spoke to him. Another person at the seminar who had forgiven him was Monica Wilson, the eminent anthropologist, who was one of the co-editors of *The Oxford History of South Africa*, and also edited *Freedom for My People*, the autobiography of Z. K. Matthews. On one of our free afternoons Adrian took Monica and myself for a drive into the countryside, an occasion that I well remember because Adrian was able to shake off for a while the burden of the past. He was almost lighthearted.

Does a Christian forgive because that is a command of the Lord? Or does one forgive because one has a 'forgiving nature'? I do not think that I forgave Adrian out of any sense of duty. I forgave him because I thought he had suffered enough.

I have written to him asking if he would like to read these chapters in typescript. I warned him that he might find the reading very painful, but he replied that he wished to read them. I shall soon send them to him, hoping that the reading will not be so painful as I feared.*

Another heavy blow was to fall on the Liberal Party. On 24 July 1964 at about 4.30 p.m., a bomb exploded in the crowded concourse of the Johannesburg station. It severely injured seventy-seven-year-old Mrs. Rhys and her twelve-year-old granddaughter Glynis Burleigh. It seriously injured twenty-one other people, and still many others received minor injuries. Twenty-seven days later Mrs. Rhys died, and the granddaughter Glynis is still at the time of writing undergoing operations.

I first read of the explosion in the *Natal Mercury* on the morning of 25 July. It was on the same morning that I met at the airport, Liston Pope, the Dean of the Yale Divinity School, who had recommended me for an honorary degree from Yale ten years earlier. He had for a long time been what I would call a 'good friend to South Africa', and understood more than most Americans the complexity of our history and our society. His face was grave as he met me, and he said, 'I don't see that this helps any.'

It was on the evening of that day that Jack Unterhalter from Johannesburg knocked at our door, and asked me to come out into the garden. He told me that the police had arrested John Harris at 11 p.m. on the day of the explosion and that there seemed no doubt that he had planted the bomb. How were they able to act so swiftly? They had taken one, perhaps two, of the A.R.M. members arrested in the raids of 4 July to see the destruction at the station. One of them was John Lloyd, who burst out, 'My God, what has Harris done now?' I went back to the house and said to Dorrie, 'Jack has come to tell me that he is almost certain that it is John Harris who put the bomb in Johannesburg station.' She clung to me, full of fear and distress, as I was also. Was this the end-result of our campaign for right and justice? Had one given up eleven years of one's life to achieve this?

It must be remembered that Harris did this after the nation-wide arrests of the members of the A.R.M. I don't think that there is any doubt that he saw himself as the savious of the cause. According to

* This I duly did and, as I expected, he found the reading very painful. He suggested certain amendments, some of which I felt able to make. Others, alas, I could not. Adrian sent the chapters to Randolph Vigne, who also suggested certain amendments, some of which I have made and some not.

him, Hugh Lewin and Ronald Mutch, before the raids of 4 July, had entrusted him with the care of dynamite and detonators. It gave him that sense of being wanted, of being a figure of importance, of taking up where the A.R.M. had left off. He was a highly intelligent and a highly unbalanced man and his story shows that a man can be both of these things.

After his arrest he was an abject creature. This was partly due to his fear of the scaffold and partly to the savage treatment he received from members of the security police. Advocate Ernie Wentzel told me that he had never seen a worse case in his long experience. Soon after Harris's arrest Ruth Hayman had gone to see him. She, as I have said before, gave me the impression that she was quite fearless. She was an officer of the court, and this was her duty, no matter how terrible the alleged offence. It was she who told me of Harris's abject condition. It was she, or she and Harris together who asked Wentzel to defend him, but after long consideration Wentzel decided that it would not be in Harris's interests to be defended by a Liberal.*

The security police denied that Harris had been assaulted. He had tried to escape and had fallen down the stairs. He was not so lucky as the Imam Haron of Cape Town, who 'fell down the stairs and died'. I suppose this story of 'died while trying to escape' must be known to the police of the entire world.

Two of the bravest members of the party, Walter and Adelain Hain, went at once to Ann Harris and offered to her and their six-weeks-old son David, the shelter of their home.

They also visited Harris to help him to recover his broken self-esteem. Circumstances did not permit me ever to grow to feel for Harris what I later grew to feel for Leftwich. If he had ever sent any message to me asking for my forgiveness, I would have forgiven him with my lips but not with my heart. I was totally revolted by what he had done. They say that to understand is to forgive. That is not true. I understood the twisted and tragic reasons that led him to do what he did, but I never was able to forgive him.

During the time that he was awaiting trial he wrote several letters to Advocate Ernie Wentzel and his wife Jill, two of our leading members in the Transvaal. During this period he continually expressed concern for his parents and expressed the hope that the lawyers would save his life.

---

* I should explain that Ruth Hayman was an attorney, and Ernie Wentzel an advocate. In a case of this kind the attorney would instruct the advocate, but it would be the advocate who would conduct the defence.

24 September 1964 (J.H. to J.W. and E.W.).

Today expecting to see Ruth ... I've several points to raise, as well as a multitude of individual facts ... I worry ... about my parents ... Although they love me completely and support me 100%, much mud will be flung at the trial ... [He urges Wentzel to go to see them to prepare them for this ordeal.] ... Nothing is served by running through all the unpleasant possibilities again and again.

28 September 1964 (E.W. to J.H.).

I shall see your parents as soon as possible and try to help them understand all that has happened ... I find that friendship is a primary state and that I dissociate ultimately my love for you, John, from any consideration of what you have done ... I can see that the weight of South Africa becomes too heavy for some decent men to bear. But in my deepest self I must confess that I find your story something which escapes my proper understanding. I do shrink back, John, from violence.

30 September 1964 (J.H. to J.W. and E.W.).

... David Soggot [the lawyer] brings up points you've made, Ernie. (Do keep hammering away my friend!) ... By now the linking of Ann's future with that of the Hains seems pretty well arranged ... For my parents ... there's the strong explicit assurance that they're 'behind me 100%'.

8 October 1964 (J.H. to J.W. and E.W.).

... The other strengthening point you make is that Namie [Advocate Phillips] will do a powerful job for me.

5 November 1964 (J.H. to J.W.).

... Tomorrow the verdict will be handed down and sentence passed ... The love and support of my parents is so wonderfully strong and constant ... [J.H. expresses deep gratitude for his wife, parents, friends, the Hains, Ruth, Soggot] ... Let me end optimistically. Totsiens, Jill ... [The word *totsiens* is optimistic because it carries the implication that they will see each other again, and a further implication that their meeting will be normal and cheerful.]

18 December 1964 (J.H. to J.W. and E.W. – Harris makes no mention of the fact that he has been sentenced to death).

My mother is much better than she was. For a while she was eating virtually nothing, so lost much weight and strength.

Harris wrote in these letters that his father and mother supported him 100 per cent. I do not know what he meant by that. I visited them to convey the sympathy of the Liberal Party. They were incapable of giving support to anyone. Their son had taken away from them the very meaning of their lives. According to Harris they were not formal Christians, but they asked me why God had done this to them. They had brought up their son to be a worthy and honourable man, and look what he had done. Sitting in that room, with its oppressive burden of grief and shame, I could see what he had done. He had destroyed them both.

Walter and Adelain Hain continued to visit Harris and to strengthen him for his coming death, so much so that he went to the scaffold singing, 'We shall overcome. We shall overcome some day.' It is not a song that I much like. It seems to suggest that we shall overcome through the sheer lapse of time. Did Harris ever repent of trying to overcome through the bomb? He told Judge Ludorf: 'I don't feel it was wrong to do what I did. That, I don't feel was bad. But as to what happened, that I feel was wrong.' He broke down, buried his face in his hands, and wept bitterly when his wife gave evidence of their life together.

One further event in the history of the A.R.M. emerged during the Harris trial. Some member or members of the A.R.M. had written a draft letter to the Prime Minister, Dr. Hendrik Verwoerd, to be sent after some dramatic explosion. Dr. Verwoerd was called upon to announce over the air that he submitted to the demands of the A.R.M., and would presumably resign or declare a complete change of heart. How could intelligent men and women have entertained such an illusion?

After his execution the Hains sought permission to hold a funeral service. It was a non-religious service, consisting of readings, most if not all of them, by sixteen-year-old Peter Hain. The readings were from Shakespeare, Donne, Matthew 5, 'The Battle Hymn of the Republic' and Ecclesiastes 3. Peter later left with his parents for England where he waged a fierce and successful war against South African participation in world sport. The Hains did not go into exile because they had given up the struggle. They went because Walter Hain, an architect, could no longer find any work to do. Any firm who employed him was visited by the security police, and warned that it would receive no more government contracts if it continued to employ Walter Hain. They had no choice but to leave. So we lost two of the strongest and bravest members of our party. Their attitude towards John Harris could well be described as noble, although neither of them would have liked that word. Alas, it was a nobility that I could not emulate. In my judgement Harris had done a wicked and totally futile deed.

Harris was executed on 1 April 1965. Now it so happened that Peter Brown had been banned from public life on 30 July 1964. So it fell to me to write 'The Long View' for *Contact* in April 1965. I wrote:

The execution of John Harris . . . brings to a close one of the saddest episodes in South African history. A young man of promise caused the death of one person and inflicted injuries on others, lost his own life, and brought unhappiness to many people, without advancing his own cause in any way whatsoever.

On the contrary he did it incomparable harm ... There are redeeming elements in this tragic story. One is the courage and dignity with which Ann Harris conducted herself throughout her long ordeal. Those who read her account of her life with her husband will not easily forget it. It is a noble and moving document.

'The Long View' also paid tribute to the courage and generosity of the Hains and Ruth Hayman. It concluded thus:

In this crisis, and in the other crises of 1964, the Liberal Party behaved itself in a way that it can be proud of. It condemned the deeds, and it forgave the doers. One cannot do better than that.

As I read these words more than twenty years later, I find them to be true. Except for the person who wrote them. I cannot think of John Harris's deed with anything but revulsion. Whether Ann Harris (who has remarried and now lives abroad) will ever read these words, I do not know, for they would cause her pain. Yet I had no choice but to write them. It is my life that I am writing, and the A.R.M. and the station bomb were two of its most painful events.

After these events I spent an evening with an eminent advocate who had defended members of the A.R.M. The main purpose of our talk was to examine the motives of the members of the A.R.M. We suggested many such, one of them being 'love of country'. The next day he wrote to me saying that on reflection he had rejected 'love of country' as a motive.

I would say that they were involved with the problems of the country rather than the country itself. Perhaps the strongest motivating factor, common to all of them, was the sense of guilt, at participating in the fruits of a society which they regarded as corrupt. By committing sabotage they proved to themselves (if to no one else) that they rejected the society, and were prepared to fight against it. I think that most of them would willingly have left South Africa, and that what prevented them was the guilt associated with running away from a situation which had made this demand on them.
    ... I also talked last night about a sense of inadequacy attaching to most of the members, who had some need to prove themselves. I wonder if I was completely fair to them ... I think that the bulk of the members were brave and sincere people, who in a normal society would have found socially acceptable means of expressing their guilt.
    ... If people condemn them today it is because they failed. If they had attracted a following and succeeded, the same people would have called them heroes ... Castro started with seven men, and I think that many of them were influenced by this and thought in terms of a second Cuba.

Love of country? Love of justice? Feelings of guilt? A desire to prove oneself? Hatred of apartheid? Hatred of Verwoerd? Feelings of frustration, not the least of which would be frustration with constitutional liberals like Brown and myself? I think there was a mixture of them all. And one more – a desire on the part of whites to show their solidarity with blacks.

Those were tough years for the Liberal Party. In 1963 eleven of our most active members had been banned from public life, and we had been subjected to severe harassment by the security police. Members lost their jobs because their employers had been intimidated by the police, and this happened throughout the country. Mourners at funerals were arrested and taken away by the police, and most of them were never charged. In Pretoria we were very proud to have a Chinese member, Poen ah Dong, but soon after he joined us he also lost his job. A young Afrikaner, Kenneth Fourie, and his mother, joined the party in the Transvaal, and soon after that they were visited by the security police, who made threats against them both, and expressed their disgust that two Afrikaners should join a communist organisation.

In 1964 the harassment continued. It became more and more difficult to get halls for meetings. Owners of school halls were warned that schools would be closed if the Liberal Party was allowed to use the buildings; the police had no such powers, but the owners did not know that. On 24 April a serious blow was dealt to the party and to the Natal African Landowners Association when Elliot Mngadi was banned. But the greatest blow of all fell on 30 July when Peter Brown was banned. They say no one is indispensable, but the fact is that Peter was irreplaceable. He had devoted most of his time and a good deal of his money to the party, and there was no one else who could do that.

It was in 1964 that one of our organisers, Christopher Shabalala, attended a meeting of our branch in Underberg and, if there had been any reason to arrest him, this could have been done before he boarded the train to Pietermaritzburg. However, his arrest was much more spectacular than that. The police stopped the train in the middle of the veld and Shabalala was taken off, so that his fellow passengers, most of them black, could see that it did not pay to belong to the Liberal Party. Shabalala was never charged with any offence, but a year later he was banned from public life.

There could be no doubt that the Minister of Justice, B.J. Vorster, was determined to make it impossible for the Liberal Party to continue, nor could there be any doubt that he had the full support of his Prime Minister. I must record that hardly a voice was raised outside the party against this serious erosion of the rule of law. We were left to go it alone.

When Peter Brown was banned, the national chairmanship was

taken over by a new member, Dr. Edgar Brookes, founder-member of the South African Institute of Race Relations, professor of History, ex-principal of Adams College, writer of books, great raconteur, lover of Samuel Johnson, retired senator, and a devout Anglican and reader of the Bible. Brookes had joined the party in 1962 after having looked at it askance for ten years. He had refused to be a sponsor of the Treason Trial Defence Fund or of Defence and Aid. He was a conservative liberal, and had made the jest that there was an 'l' of a difference between a liberal and a Liberal. What then made him decide to become a Liberal with a capital 'L'?

The answer is that he was deeply moved by the fact that people like Brown, Meidner, Mngadi, after Sharpeville in 1960, were detained without trial for their beliefs. Yet none of them would have thought of renouncing these beliefs. In fact Brown had been offered some kind of conditional release and had refused it. Brookes visited Brown in prison and found him almost jocular, in that sardonic fashion for which he was noted. Brown did not go so far as Paul and Silas, who sang in prison, but that may have been because he could not sing. Brookes was in some ways a most learned man, and in other ways a very simple one. He came to the simple conclusion that the things that Brown and Meidner and Mngadi believed in must be right, and he must believe in them too. He realised that he had never squarely confronted the issue of human equality in South Africa, and he accepted a concept which he would earlier have thought extremely radical, that of universal suffrage. He became our National Chairman at a time when our fortunes were at their lowest ebb.

It was fifteen years later that Edgar Brookes said one day to me, with some embarrassment. 'Alan, there's one thing I want to say to you, and one should say these things before it is too late. I want you to know that your friendship has meant a great deal to me.' He must have known something. Three days later he was dead.

On 21 September 1965 Dorrie and I drove to the town of Alice in the Cape Province to be present at the opening of the new library at the Federal Theological Seminary, of whose governing council I was a member. As we entered the town a large car that had obviously been waiting for us, pulled out immediately and followed us. Its occupants made no attempt whatsoever to disguise their intentions. I knew at once that it was the security police. We were on our way to stay the night at the holiday resort of the Hogsback, a beautiful forested area that overlooks the comparatively arid country below. I wanted to shake off the police, so we turned into the grounds of the seminary to visit Father Aelred Stubbs, the principal of the Anglican constituent college.

After half an hour or so we returned to the road and were immediately followed by a smaller car, whose occupants also made no attempt to disguise their intentions. We went round a bend in the road and stopped. They passed us, and went round another bend, and stopped too. This silly game went on until we started to climb the steep road to the Hogsback, and our pursuers concluded that we would spend the night at one of the Hogsback hotels. In the morning I went out to our car which was parked in the hotel drive, and saw that the front windscreen and the rear windshield had been shattered. The stones that had done the damage were on the seats of the car. I felt sick at heart.

A detective sergeant came out from Alice to take details of the incident. When he had finished he said to me, 'Have you any idea who might have done this?' I said, 'Yes, I have a very good idea, but I do not think I should tell you what it is.' He said, 'It is your duty to tell me.' I said, 'I think it was the security police.' He snapped his book shut and said to me, 'I wish to God I could get out of this place.'

Still sick at heart, we went to the opening of the seminary library, where I was photographed thirty to fifty times by Warrant Officer G.A. Hattingh, the head of the Alice security police. It was a kind of an assault. Whenever I turned he would follow me and photograph me again. I went to him and said I thought he had taken enough. He said, 'Mind your own bloody business.' All of this harassment was witnessed by hundreds of distinguished visitors.

I have told the story of Advocate Vernon Berrangé, who, having endured many tribulations at the hands of right-wing whites, decided to go to live in Swaziland after some enemy had poured paint-remover over the roof and bonnet of his new car. I felt like that now. I wanted to give it all up. The final blow was to receive a letter from the Automobile Association, of which I had been a member for nearly forty years, informing me that they would no longer insure me against damage of this kind.

I was only one of several opponents of apartheid who suffered this kind of damage. I do not know of a single case where the offender was discovered and brought to book. I share with many thousands of South Africans the conviction that the offenders, if not members of the security police, were protected by them.

I find it astonishing that in these demanding years of the A.R.M. and Umkhonto we Sizwe, of Poqo, of John Harris, that I was able to finish my life of Hofmeyr and have it published, in South Africa and the U.K. with the simple title *Hofmeyr*, and in the United States with the more complicated title *A South African Tragedy: The Life and Times of Jan Hofmeyr*.

I find this astonishing because it was for me a monumental achievement. It took four years to write, but these four were spread over a period of eleven years, for the reason that I could not publish the book while Mrs. Deborah Hofmeyr (his mother) was alive. I must also say, immodestly no doubt, that if anyone wishes to understand why South Africa is what is it today, he or she should read this life of Hofmeyr. Joel Mervis, the redoubtable editor of the *Sunday Times* in Johannesburg, wrote a review which occupied more than a page of his newspaper, and said that the combination of Hofmeyr and Paton was irresistible. A writer cannot get a greater compliment than that. The book sold out in a short space of time.[*]

Writing biography in South Africa is not the paying proposition that it is in Britain or the United States. The first printing of five to ten thousand is soon sold out, and the demand thereafter is for two or three hundred a year, which does not seem to a publisher to justify a second printing.

Hofmeyr was a great speaker, and like many great speakers he was a master of the story, with an unerring judgement as to what was the right story to tell. He was speaking in the early part of 1939 of the difficult days that were facing the world, and he quoted to his hearers the words on a tablet in an old English church. 'In the year 1652 when throughout England all things sacred were either profaned or neglected, this church was built by Sir Robert Shirley, Bart, whose special praise it is to have done the best things in the worst times and to have hoped them in the most calamitous.'

That is what many of us tried to do in the calamitous year of 1964.

Postscript

The shattering of my front windscreen and rear windshield had a sequel. Twelve years later, in December 1976, Donald Woods, the forthright editor of the East London *Daily Dispatch*, alleged that it was Warrant Officer G.A. Hattingh of the security police who had damaged my car. He made this allegation because of information received from former security policeman Donald Card.

On the strength of this allegation I decided to institute civil proceedings against W/O Hattingh, but when Mr. Card told me that he now feared for his own security, and that he had received anonymous telephone threats, I dropped the matter.

But W/O Hattingh decided that he would now claim R10,000 from the *Daily Dispatch*. In April 1983 I travelled to Grahamstown and gave evidence in the Supreme Court, telling the whole story of the Hogsback and the harassment of myself by W/O Hattingh in the grounds of

---

[*] It is still available in its abridged form from O.U.P., Cape Town.

the Federal Seminary. W/O Hattingh had made a statement that he had photographed me once, but I described how he had pursued me from place to place, a spectacle witnessed by hundreds of spectators, and I reported that when I objected, he told me to mind my 'own bloody business'.

To put it briefly, it appeared that the Court believed my account, and did not believe W/O Hattingh. Whatever the case, he decided to drop his claim against the *Daily Dispatch*. So this unsavoury episode came to an end. It had lasted for nineteen years.

Chapter 27

The years 1963 and 1964 saw another trial for treason and sabotage, much more important than the trials of members of the A.R.M., or that of John Harris. It was to be the trial of eleven men on two hundred and twenty-two charges of sabotage in preparation for 'armed invasion'. Finally nine men were charged, Nelson Mandela, Walter Sisulu, Dennis Goldberg, Govan Mbeki, Ahmed Kathrada, Lionel Bernstein, Raymond Mhlaba, Elias Matsoaledi, and Andrew Mlangeni.

Most of them were to be defended by Advocate Abram Fischer, Q.C., of whom I have written earlier, who was recognised as the leading personality and the brains of the Congress of Democrats. Fischer had been a card-carrying communist until 1950, when he and others had resigned from the Communist Party of South Africa. This was not because of any change in their beliefs, but was a preparation for the passing of the Suppression of Communism Act. After that date, the penalties of being an avowed communist were to be extremely heavy. Of course many other people, including members of the Liberal Party, were to be banned from public life under the same Act, for the reason that they had been 'deemed' by the Minister of Justice to be furthering the aims of communism. In the language of the jargon created by the Act, they would have done this 'wittingly' or 'unwittingly', perhaps both, I do not know.

The Judge-President of the Transvaal Supreme Court, Quartus de Wet, was a formidable judge though not possessing the scathing tongue of Andries Beyers, Judge-President of the Cape division of the

Supreme Court.

When the trial began, the accused had already spent eighty-eight days in solitary confinement. Some, notably Mandela, looked very thin, but whatever their privations, these did not prevent them from responding vigorously to the acclamations of the spectators, each of them holding up a clenched fist and shouting '*Amandla awethu!*', which means 'Power to us!'. However, certain conventions were observed; these cries were seldom uttered when the court was in session.

Twenty-nine acts of sabotage were listed for 1961, eighty-one for 1962, fifty-nine for 1963. In 1963 two people had died and seventeen were injured. The acts of sabotage were limited to installations and institutions, telephones and telephone booths, post offices, courts and offices of school boards, bridges, and government vehicles.

The trial opened on 8 October 1963, and on 30 October the State was ordered by the presiding judge to redraft the indictment. Absent from the accused were Harold Wolpe and Arthur Goldreich, who had escaped the country, and probably life imprisonment as well; also Bob Hepple, who had decided to give evidence for the State, and when released also escaped the country.

The trial aroused great public interest, particularly among black people. The police decided to guard the homes of Judge de Wet and of Attorney-General Percy Yutar. The South African government received many appeals and protests from abroad, including one from the United Nations and one from members of the Norwegian parliament, who urged the government to stop the trial. The array of legal talent assembled in Pretoria was immense, and Vernon Berrangé, who had retired to Swaziland five years earlier to get away from it all, returned to join the defence team.

On 20 April Mandela admitted that he had planned violence, but denied that the 'struggle' was in any way inspired by the Communist Party. He admitted that he had gone to Addis Ababa to seek support in building up a nucleus of men trained in administration, who would be ready to run the affairs of the new South Africa, and had been promised help from Nyerere, Selassie, Kaunda, Obote, Ben Bella, and Habib Bourguiba. He had also visited Gaitskell in London, but had not been to Cuba to see Fidel Castro.

The plan of campaign was much more elaborate than that of the A.R.M. Attorney-General Yutar claimed that two hundred and ten thousand grenades, forty-eight thousand anti-personnel mines, one thousand five hundred time-devices, one hundred and forty-four tons of ammonium nitrate, twenty-one point six tons of aluminium powder, and fifteen tons of black powder were to be manufactured in six months. One hundred and six maps had been prepared, and a number of young black men were to be recruited and sent overseas for training.

Umkhonto we Sizwe acquired three secluded properties where these preparations were to be made. One of these was the farm 'Lilliesleaf' at Rivonia, outside Johannesburg, and this was why the trial was always referred to as the Rivonia trial. It is virtually impossible in any country where the security police are strong and efficient to continue to operate three very private properties where the overthrow of a government is being seriously planned. In South Africa it was even less possible, because the security poilice were upholders of the Afrikaner Nationalist ethos, were fiercely anti-communist, and believed that they were the custodians of Christianity and civilisation. These virtues they combined with an utter ruthlessness, which they practised with little regard for the Christian values of tolerance and compassion.

If the South African security police needed any further inspiration than the need to defend to the death a threatened white civilisation, they could find it in their Minister of Justice, the Honourable Balthazar John Vorster, who, although a qualified lawyer, was by nature really a policeman. The Prime Minister Dr. Hendrik Verwoerd beamed and smiled his way around South Africa, and left the defence of law and order to his stern-faced lieutenant. If there were to be one picture that would capture for ever the essence of Vorster, it would be of his standing before the microphone, holding aloft his clenched fist and declaring, 'You may trust me utterly in one thing, that I will defend law and order with my very life.' His security police knew that he would defend them also. John D'Oliveira, in his book *Vorster the Man,*[*] repeated the Minister's damaging admission that if his police were to err, he wished them to err on the side of over-zealousness. Those of us who were not admirers of the Minister took this to mean that he would condone – or, rather, would not see at all – such refinements of interrogation as the use of cruelty and torture.

It was these same police who finally swooped on the farm 'Lilliesleaf' at Rivonia, and discovered irrefutable evidence of Umkhonto we Sizwe's plan to overthrow the government. At that time Mandela was in prison, serving a five-year sentence for incitement and illegally leaving the country. He was now taken out of prison to face trial for his life. It would be easy to convict him for he would make no effort to deny his intentions. It certainly was not one of his intentions to be found 'not guilty' by this court.

An attempt was made by the State to involve Lutuli. Walter Sisulu, when asked if Lutuli had been informed that the African National

* Ernest Stanton, Johannesburg, 1977.

Congress had changed from its policy of non-violence, said that he was not prepared to answer that question. On the following day he again refused to answer the question, and the court certainly assumed that Lutuli had been aware of the change in policy. By this time the meaning of the world 'violence' had become plain; it meant violence against the State, against the law, against the army and the police, indeed against anything or anybody that stood in the way of the new South Africa.

Kathrada testified that he had had misgivings about Umkhonto, but Mandela had persuaded him that violent rebellion was now inevitable. Mbeki testified that he had ceased to question violent methods. It became more and more apparent that Mandela was the recognised leader of them all.

After the defence had closed its case, Yutar attacked. There have been few public servants like Yutar. He was a Jew who had risen to a high position in the service of the State, and there were few of those. He was a single-minded pursuer of justice, but it was a justice hardly distinguishable from retribution. It was said that he had deep personal reasons for his passion for bringing offenders to justice. He was a small, unimpressive man with a sharp and bitter tongue, and offenders were said to quail before its lash. One of his first actions was to commend the South African Police for saving the country from a 'bloody and savage civil war'. Yutar was a brilliant and relentless prosecutor, and when he had finished there could be no doubt that the Rivonia Nine would pay heavily for their offences.

It was about this time – or earlier – that Bram Fischer had come to see me in Kloof, to ask me to give evidence in mitigation before sentence was passed. I had no doubt that I should do so. I was very strongly influenced by the attitude of our first Prime Minister, General Louis Botha, towards the Afrikaner rebels of 1914, who had totally rejected Botha's decision to take South Africa to war at the side of Britain, and had taken up arms against the government. I was also influenced by the attitude that Prime Minister General Smuts had adopted towards the Afrikaner would-be rebels of 1939, who had equally strongly rejected parliament's decision to take South Africa again into war, and again at the side of Britain. The most famous of these would-be rebels was Balthazar John Vorster. In 1964 he was Minister of Justice, and our stout defender of law and order.

I had another powerful reason to agree to give evidence in mitigation. We in the Liberal Party understood as well as any the way in which Lutuli and Matthews and Sobukwe, and now Mandela, had been condemned by the National Party to a life of protest, to a life of knocking at a door which would not open. We had not chosen

Mandela's way, but that did not prevent us from understanding why he had taken it.

I had a third powerful reason. I had no wish to see the death penalty inflicted on the Rivonia Nine. I reckoned that it would be a decision from which white South Africa, and particularly Afrikanerdom, would never recover.

Therefore I had no difficulty in agreeing to give evidence in mitigation. I had no doubt that Bram Fischer was 'using' me, and I had no objection to being used for a purpose of this kind. One or two of our more fiercely anti-communist Liberals thought that I was demeaning myself, but in general my decision had the support of the party. This episode illustrates a striking difference between communism and liberalism. If I had been a member of the Congress of Democrats I should certainly have had to consult my colleagues. But I told Bram immediately that I would come to Pretoria. I have no doubt that he would have noted this.

On 11 June 1964 Mr. Justice de Wet found seven of the accused guilty on all four counts. Kathrada was found guilty on count two, Bernstein was found not guilty, but was re-arrested before he could leave the court.

The judge found that Mandela was the prime mover, and that Lutuli knew all about the activities of Umkhonto, but kept in the background. He referred to the document 'Operation Mayibuye', which contained a detailed plan for waging guerrilla warfare, culminating in a full-scale rebellion. The judge accepted that instructions were given that no person was to be injured or killed. I confess that I found this very confusing, for how could guerrilla warfare be waged except by killing?

It was now my duty to give evidence in mitigation and I shall tell this story as carefully as I can. I am not used to appearing in courts of law, and I was brought up to have great respect for them, and especially for judges. In my rebellious young days I refused to say 'sir' to anyone who was not a schoolmaster, but I made one exception, and that was the Judge-President of the Natal divison of the Supreme Court, Sir John Dove-Wilson, under whom my father worked. My mother also taught us to raise our hats and to say 'sir' to retired Judge-President Sir Michael Gallwey, who spent a great deal of time sitting on his humble veranda in Church Street, Pietermaritzburg.

Therefore when I was called to the witness-box in the Supreme Court in Pretoria, I walked to it as quickly as I could, as I did not want to keep the Judge-President waiting. This was later interpreted by Attorney-General Percy Yutar as an unseemly haste on my part to get into the box to show my support for the forces of subversion.

Advocate Harold Hansen first questioned me for the defence. He asked why I had come there, and I gave the same three reasons which I have set down earlier in this chapter. This part of the proceedings went off with great decorum. The drama was yet to come.

Attorney-General Yutar said that it was not his practice to cross-examine evidence given in mitigation. 'But I do so in order to unmask this gentleman. His only purpose is to make political capital.'

I must say that I was much taken aback by Yutar's attack. If I had anticipated that the cross-examination would have taken this form, I should have prepared myself for it. I must say that Advocate Hansen did not anticipate it either. In our preparation of the plea in mitigation, neither of us had foreseen that Yutar would attack me as a person, and would impugn my integrity. It is not my nature to be secretive; on the contrary I rather prided myself on the openness of my political life and actions. It was almost as though Yutar had some bitter personal animus against myself. I can only describe his attack as vitriolic.

Yutar quoted a speech I had made in Canada in 1960, in which I had predicted sabotage. Why did I do that? What secret knowledge had I possessed? I replied that perhaps I might be regarded as a prophet.

He said that I had moved in Communist circles. 'You know many Communists?' 'Many.' 'What about the traitor Ronald Segal – or Rowley Arenstein?' Yutar had obivously been supplied with much information by the security police who had been following me about for some twelve years. He questioned me about a meeting I had attended in the flat of Rowley Arenstein, who had been banned in October 1960, and was therefore not allowed to hold or attend meetings. I had to admit that I did not remember such a meeting. It was only after the trial was over that I remembered that I had attended a meeting of the Institute of Race Relations in the flat of Eve Braatvedt, which was next to that of Rowley Arenstein. The security police, seeing the cars outside Arenstein's flat, had demanded entry, and having found nothing, had demanded entry to Eve Braatvedt's flat, and Yutar had been given this information by the security police and had made unjustifiable deductions from it.

Yutar remarked that I had mentioned the name of Albert Lutuli, the Nobel Prize winner. 'Did it not come as a surprise to you that he was consulted about the use of violence?' To which I replied, 'I did not come here to justify the acts of these men. I came here to plead for clemency.'

That was the essence of Yutar's cross-examination, to show that I was totally unfitted through my associations to give any kind of evidence in a trial of this kind. His intention was clear, and that was to insinuate that my liberal politics were a cloak for communistic beliefs, and to show that I was not what I pretended to be, and therefore had to be 'unmasked'. His attack was so virulent that I looked up to the Judge-President to indicate that I thought he should intervene. But whether he saw me or not, he did nothing. I am inclined to think that he enjoyed it, and that he thought the 'unmasking' to be well merited. There could be no better proof that in 1964 the reputation of the Liberal Party was at its lowest ebb.

The eight accused (Bernstein having been found not guilty) were sentenced to life imprisonment. I do not think that my evidence in mitigation had the slightest effect. In my opinion the Judge-Presdent had already decided not to impose the death penalty.

World reaction to the Rivonia sentences was very great. The ex-archbishop of Cape Town, Joost de Blank, flew to New York to urge U Thant to protest vigorously against the sentences. Thabo Mbeki, son of the accused Govan Mbeki, led a march from Brighton to No. 10 Downing Street in London. Frank Cousins, one of the leading trade unionists in Britain telegraphed Dr. Verwoerd, a waste of money. The World Council for Peace awarded the Joliot-Curie gold medal to the Rivonia Nine. Our Ambassador to London, the Right Honourable Carel de Wet, thought it wise to cancel a visit to Oxford. One thousand Edinburgh students, professors, and lecturers, staged a protest march in Princes Street. The list is too long to continue. These protests had no effect whatsoever. Nor had any protest within South Africa itself. Our Minister of Justice assured the public that the South African Police were ready to deal with any trouble.

All this happened in 1964. Now, in 1987 Rivonia is the most remembered trial in our history. If only it could be undone, but it cannot! Today it hangs like an albatross around the necks of our rulers. Today in 1987, the overwhelming support of the world is for Mandela and his associates. What were they to do? Were they to go on for ever knocking on the door that would never open?

In this year 1987 Mandela will turn sixty-nine. He has been in prison for over twenty-two years. Does one keep a man in prison for more than twenty-two years? Does one keep a man in prison when he is nearing his seventies? Our State President Mr. P.W. Botha, thought not, and in 1985 he offered to release Mandela on one condition, that he renounced the use of violence. Mandela replied that he would renounce violence if the State also renounced the use of violence. What did he mean by that? I do not think that he meant that the State must disband the courts, the police, the army. I think he may have been referring to the violent suppression of protest by the police, but even that needs qualifications. If the protest is violent, then it must be suppressed by the use of violence, but there can be no doubt that the police have used violence on occasions when the protest was not violent.

But Mandela was referring to something much more weighty than this, in fact to the whole machinery of apartheid and separate development. He was setting a condition for his release which the State President could not possibly grant. Was he asking for the immediate creation of a New World? It is impossible to answer this question because there was nothing that could be called discussion or consultation between the two men.

During Mandela's lengthy address to the court he said:

During my lifetime I have dedicated myself to this struggle of the African people. I have fought against white domination, and I have fought against black domination. I have cherished the ideal of a democratic and free society in which all persons live together in harmony and with equal opportunities. It is an ideal which I hope to live for and to see realised. But if needs be, my Lord,[*] it is an ideal for which I am prepared to die.

It is not only in other countries of the world that the unconditional release of Mandela is now demanded. The demand comes from more and more quarters in our own country. Why is this so? It is partly because so many feel that the continued imprisonment of Mandela has become morally unjustifiable. It is also because many believe that in our present state of unrest, there is no solution possible without the participation of Mandela. What other political figure in South Africa could persuade the black children of the Cape and Transvaal to go back regularly to school? And what guarantees would such a political figure demand before attempting to persuade black children to do so?

Is this faith and hope in Mandela justified? Is he more than a legend? Would he wield the same power outside prison as he does in? What have twenty-three years of imprisonment done to his mind and his will? In 1964 he had come to the conclusion that only armed violence could bring change. Does he in 1987 think that things are any different? I do not know the answers to these questions, and no one else does either. The State President and his National Party are going into deep and dangerous waters, and they might as well do so properly. They should release the Rivonia Eight unconditionally, and see what happens. The truth is that in 1987 it might be dangerous to release them, and equally dangerous not to.[†]

One thing *would* happen. Mandela would be greeted in every part of South Africa by the greatest crowds in our history. They would expect nothing less from him than liberation. Is he now able to do it? Is he still

---

[*] In South Africa it is the custom to refer to the judge as 'my Lord'.

[†] In 1987 the government released Govan Mbeki 'unconditionally'. But it soon imposed restrictions upon him. (See p. 297 for a fuller account.)

in sufficient command of himself and of events to do it, and to get others to cooperate in doing it? We do not know the answers to these questions. The only way to get answers is to release him unconditionally.

Before I leave the subject of Rivonia and Mandela, I must ask the question, 'Did Lutuli know that Mkhonto had decided to adopt a policy of violence, guerrilla warfare, and armed resistance?' I would think that if he didn't know he *guessed*. As recently as the year 1986, Mrs. Nokukhanya Lutuli has stated that her husband, were he alive, would condemn the current spate of violence. That would be true, I think, because he would have been horrified at the killing and burning of homes and of people thought to be informers and collaborators, of the killing of blacks by blacks, and especially he would have been horrified by the 'necklace of fire'. Lutuli died in 1967, but I think he would have found the years 1985 and 1986 painful to bear.

Rivonia was not the only trial where I gave evidence in mitigation and was cross-examined by Yutar. A year or two after I became the principal of Diepkloof Reformatory in 1935, the Department of Education issued an appeal to employers to give a chance to boys and girls who had been released from the reformatories. Under this policy they allowed me to appoint three ex-pupils, Sam Mofoking, Hans Shandu, and Daniel Bob (Majohnnie) as junior supervisors. Both Sam and Hans had been senior headboys of the reformatory, and Daniel would have been had it not been for his diminutive stature.

Sam came from a small town in the Orange Free State, and had, if I remember correctly, fourteen previous convictions, all for petty theft. The courts waited – as they often did in those days – till Sam had become a man before they committed him to Diepkloof. He was a young man of considerable strength of personality, and while at the reformatory was a model character.

Soon after his appointment as a junior supervisor, Sam attempted to steal a belt from McQuade's store at Comptonville, a near-neighbour of Diepkloof. He was tried by Alfred Eyles, who was one of the senior magistrates of Johannesburg, and also chairman of the Diepkloof board of management. I spoke in mitigation and asked the court to give Sam a suspended sentence, and to place him in my care. I was prepared to give him another chance.

This sounded noble and plausible, but it did not satisfy Yutar. Why should I choose to defend a boy with such a record? He wondered in a very concerned and ambiguous manner, why I should interest myself in such a case.

What was Yutar getting at? Was he suggesting, in this highly ambiguous manner, that I must have some other motive? In my opinion he was suggesting that there was some special relationship between Sam Mofoking and myself. It would not have needed a genius to realise that this relationship might be homosexual.

I was in fact ready at that point to cross-examine Yutar and to ask him just what he meant. But I was forestalled by the Magistrate, who told the prosecutor that he did not care for the trend of the cross-examination. I had stated that I had come there in the performance of my duties, and the court accepted it. Sam was given a suspended sentence and returned to my care.

Did Attorney-General Dr. Percy Yutar remember the Sam Mofoking trial when he was cross-examining me at the Rivonia trial? If he had, he must have felt recompensed for his earlier rebuff. In the Sam Mofoking trial the Bench was against him. In the Rivonia trial the Bench was on his side.

There is something to be said in defence of prosecutor Yutar. He was known as a relentless pursuer of wrongdoers, and would do all in his power to see that they were punished. His knowledge and understanding of the sequence offence–punishment were very considerable. Of the sequence offence–punishment–forgiveness–restoration he showed little understanding, and therefore my plea in mitigation for Sam Mofoking must have seemed to him incomprehensible, or, if comprehensible then questionable, and this would explain the trend of his cross-examination.

Prosecutor Yutar was right in one thing. Sam was an inveterate thief. He went home on leave and stole again. This time I did not intervene on his behalf.

Hans Shandu was also not successful as a supervisor. He had a knowledge of the delinquent mind which was profound. He had a total scepticism about human nature. But if a boy absconded, Hans would find him. He would have made a great detective had he been born into a different world. In the end I had to let him go too.

Majohnnie was my great success. He always ascribed this to me, but that was only partly true. He had something that neither Sam nor Hans possessed, a love of goodness. I have written of this miracle elsewhere.

I must add a tragic postscript to the Rivonia trial. On the day after the trial was over Bram Fischer and his wife Mollie set off for the Cape on what was to be a well-earned holiday. In the Orange Free State a cow had wandered onto a one-way bridge and, to avoid it, Bram drove off the road, and into the river. He and the passenger in front, a woman friend of theirs, were able to free themselves, but they could not open the rear door to free Mollie, and in helpless anguish had to watch the car sink deeper and deeper into the water. The magistrate's verdict was 'death by drowning'.

Bram returned to his home in Johannesburg and I went to see him the next day on a Sunday morning, if I remember right. Holding hands we walked off by ourselves into the garden. If he had ever come to power in South Africa, would he have liquidated me? At that of all times, it seemed a silly question.

So came to an end the terrible year of 1964. But before it did, Monty Naicker invited Dorrie and myself to come to dinner at his beautiful house in Innes Road, Durban. Monty was a banned person under the Suppression of Communism Act of 1950, and therefore he had no right to invite anyone to dinner, except members of his family. I put this point to him, but he said he wanted us to come, and to hell with the Act. I have written earlier of his implacability as a politician and his geniality as a host. The fact is that he was lonely, and wanted some conviviality. In such matters his wife Marie would do anything he wanted; she might feel anxious, but she would do her best to conceal it. We decided we would go to dinner.

The evening started well; as I have said earlier, to be entertained by Monty was one of the greatest minor pleasures of my life. We all sat down to a splendid dinner and a splendid wine, and were all as happy as could be until the security police arrived. One of the first things they did was to examine the wine bottles, to make sure they had been opened, and to feel if they were cold. What the point of all this was I could not imagine. Monty's offence was plain; he was having guests in his house, and whether they were eating or drinking was irrelevant. Monty's offence was that he was sitting there with them.

In the Durban magistrate's court Monty was sentenced to a year's imprisonment which was suspended except for one week. The magistrate gave me a special reproof, and said that a man of my education and experience should have known that I was doing no favour to my host by accepting his invitation. I would dearly have liked to say to him that his offence in administering such a law was much worse than Dr. Naicker's or mine. However, I did not, not because I was afraid of being sentenced for contempt of court, but because I had this strange respect for the institution known as the court of law, which had been instilled in me by my parents, particularly my father.

Not long after Monty's trial, which he took very light-heartedly, perhaps because he had been to prison before, the government dealt him a blow from which he never recovered. They took away his beautiful house in Innes Road because the area in which it was situated was declared 'white' under the Group Areas Act. Some of my readers abroad will hardly believe that such a thing could be done.

Others of my readers in my own country will be bitterly ashamed.

Monty and Marie Naicker had to move to an 'Indian' area known as Asherville. There was no beautiful and spacious white house to be had there, and they had to buy a dark and gloomy one. We went to see them there, and that was permissible according to the law, provided that Monty saw us one at a time. It was clear that some joy had gone out of him and it would never return.

When Monty's 'ban' expired, a great meeting of welcome was held in the Orient Hall in Durban, and he was given an ovation when he said that he would take up the fight again. I said a few words, but not the ones that were in my heart, for I wanted to say to him, 'Monty, you must not take up the fight again. You have done your duty, and it is time for you to leave the fighting to others.' In any event he did not take up the fight again, for the simple reason that the will to fight had gone.

Monty died on 12 January 1976. He was one of the bravest men of my time, and could endure banning and police surveillance and imprisonment. But when they took his house, they took the joy of life from him. To put it strongly, they broke his heart.

Chapter 28

I still have Dorrie's diaries that she kept in those far-off days of twenty-two years ago. The word 'emphysema' occurs again and again in the diary of 1965. On 25 February she wrote, 'Emphysema giving me hell,' and on 26 February she wrote, 'Am beginning to despair of ever having a good day.' In *Towards the Mountain*, the first volume of this autobiography, I wrote about my first meeting with Dorrie and Rad, in Ixopo in 1925, that they were pioneers of women's liberation in that they took a bold stand on a controversial issue, namely smoking by women. This boldness was to have fatal results for them both, painful to endure and painful to watch, the terrible disease known as emphysema, the dying of the lungs.

My learned son David, the one who spent twenty-seven years in school, has written two pages on emphysema for me. When I told him that I was going to write that emphysema is a dying of the lungs he gave me the indulgent smile that one who knows gives to one who doesn't. 'It's your book', he said, 'and if that's the way you see it, that is the way you must write it.'

Part of David's short essay is written in red ink, and this I took to be a kind of hint to me that no medical man could be expected to write more simply:

Imagine a (children's party) balloon full of very much smaller very delicate little balloons. Air is forced into the system, destroying the small delicate balloons until the large balloon is the only surface area presented to the air. This was always there, so the total surface area originally presented to the air is greatly diminished.

He then went on to write in black ink:

The body has to exchange the high CO_2 (carbon dioxide) low O_2 (oxygen) content of the venous blood with the low CO_2 high O_2 content of the atmospheric air to 'refresh' the arterial blood. If the total area where such exchange can take place is progressively diminished this cannot happen . . . The patient therefore becomes progressively anoxic (without O_2) and increasingly breathless.

Although Dorrie's health was steadily deteriorating, she agreed at once that my mother, who was now eighty-seven years old, should come and spend her last days with us. She had been living with my sister Eunice, whose husband Graham was an invalid, so that she had to earn her living as a teacher. At that time her husband was in hospital, and she was finding it more and more difficult to look after our mother, whose mind was failing. My sister dare not leave any money in the house because my mother would give it away to black passers-by. We decided that my mother would not be told that she was coming to me. I was to go to Pietermaritzburg and take her for a drive, which would end at our home in Kloof. This I did on 11 March 1965.

I would not say that my mother felt she had been deceived. I doubt if her mind was clear enough for that. But she certainly felt that some change had come about in her life, and she found it unpleasant.

We began to learn the meaning of 'second childhood'. In my mother's case it did not mean that she returned to the days of her childhood, but she certainly returned to her young womanhood. On the first day she became very restless and anxious in the afternoon, and wanted to know why the girls had not yet come home, the girls being my sisters Eunice and Ailsa. I then did a very foolish thing. I explained to her that the girls were grown women, and that they had homes and children of their own. The next afternoon my mother again became restless and anxious, and wanted to know why the girls had not yet come home.

My mother was one of the most chaste of women, but the sexual fears of a young woman who had had a very strict upbringing now returned to her. One evening when she was in bed, she called to me and asked me where the baby was, and I, in my new wisdom, told her it was in the adjoining room. She then told me that on no account must her father see the baby. Her father visited her more than once; on one occasion she told me that her father had just gone down the passage, but I assured her that he had already left the house. She never mentioned her mother.

She spent her days in the garden, and after tea at about four o'clock, I would shepherd her to bed. But on 25 March, after she had been with us for two weeks, she refused to go into the house. Eventually Dorrie persuaded her to go in, and that evening she suffered a slight stroke. Dr. O. said that she must go at once to the Braemar Nursing Home in nearby Pinetown, a home for old and ailing people. On 30 March, on my daily visit to her, I thought that she was near death, and in the early evening Dr. O. phoned to say that she had just died. I remember that Dorrie came to me and embraced me. She said, 'You know your mother and I never exchanged an angry word.'

On 27 August Dorrie's sister Rad was taken to Addington Hospital in Durban, after a painful bout of emphysema. On 29 August Addington phoned to say that her condition was very serious, and we went into Durban at once. She was unconscious and her face was rigid, set in a cast of terror that Dorrie must have found painful to witness. She wrote in her diary, 'Poor little soul – she has had much to endure.' Dorrie was referring, not only to her physical suffering, but to her married life which had been anything but happy. Her husband Wilfred was an extreme authoritarian, and also a heavy drinker, so that Rad, brought up to pay tradesmen's accounts promptly, now found herself saddled by debts of which she was extremely ashamed. Many of her family and friends urged her to leave her husband but she said that she had made marriage vows and would not break them. The looker-on can but be humbled to witness this fierce upholding of moral standards by a woman whom life had used badly. The Francis sisters were like that, inflexible in principle without being puritanical, and bound to one another in a way that I have never seen surpassed. This was undoubtedly the work of their redoubtable mother, of whom I wrote in my first volume. Before moving on, I note that (as told in chapter 18 of the present book) Rad's husband Wilfred was the authoritarian headmaster of whom Debi Singh had told such outrageous stories during the journey to Newcastle to protest against the Group Areas Act, not knowing that this imperialist jingo was my brother-in-law.

On 5 September Rad died, and Dorrie referred to her many times in her diary, the handwriting of which was becoming more and more difficult to decipher. On 6 September she wrote, 'None of us can realise that little Fox has gone.' It was in this month that the time was coming when Dorrie must go too. We travelled by car to Johannesburg to stay with Ruth Hayman, who had married again, and was now Mrs. Mervyn Lazar. Mervyn was a slow, heavy man, the perfect partner for the restless, tireless, fearless Ruth. It was soon clear that Dorrie was very ill, and it was painful to watch her struggle with her breathlessness. She made a special effort to attend the christening of our granddaughter Pamela, and this exhausted her. When we left for home, we took an oxygen cylinder with us in case of emergency.

On 19 October 1965, who should come to our home but Diana

Collins from London. She had come to visit the various committees of Defence and Aid, and once the security police realised who she was and what she was doing, they followed her everywhere. She had hardly left our home when John Barbour of Field's Hill Motors came to tell me that someone had put grinding paste into the engine oil and that the engine of my car was ruined beyond repair.

So ended 1965. In that year nine of the most active members of the party were banned. The amendment to the Criminal Procedure Act was passed, giving the Minister of Justice the power to detain persons without charge or trial for periods of up to one hundred and eighty days.

In January 1966, Dr. O. decided to send Dorrie to Mariannhill Hospital, and when she came home she found air-conditioning installed in our bedroom; her diary records that it was 'a great boon'. Our friends were a great source of strength to us. We did not go so often to Durban, but our friends from there came to visit us. At Kloof we had frequent visits from Archbishop Edward Paget and Murray Dell, our assistant priest in Kloof parish. We saw a great deal of Margaret and Ralf Anderson, and went there often to dinner and bridge. Ralf was now in his eighties, and his mind was failing. He did not play bridge, but would sit and sleep over a book. One morning in February Margaret took Ralf to the Kloof post office and left him sitting in the car. She expected to be away for not more than five minutes, and left the keys in the car. When she came back, Ralf and the car had gone.

Soon the entire countryside around Kloof was being searched by Margaret's friends, but without success. Margaret herself was quite distraught, and felt that she had been foolishly negligent. What had happened? It was my theory that some person had seen Margaret leave Ralf, and that this person had badly wanted the use of a car, and had found the presence of an old man no hindrance at all, especially if he had nodded off to sleep. At five o'clock Margaret phoned to give us the good news; the Montrose police station in Pietermaritzburg, some thirty miles away, had phoned to say that a gentleman named Ralf Anderson was waiting there for his wife to come to fetch him. When Margaret reached the police station, she rushed in to embrace her lost husband, but he repulsed her advances and said to her angrily, 'And where the hell have you been?' This became one of the most popular stories of those days.

It was on the morning of 18 May that our home was visited by two senior members of the security police. They informed me that the Defence and Aid Fund of South Africa had been banned by the Minister of Justice at midnight, and they produced a warrant which empowered them to search our house, 23 Lynton Road, Kloof. I took them to my study-cum-library and showed them the drawer in which all the papers relating to Defence and Aid were kept. The two officers were quite courteous until I left them and went into the bedroom to tell Dorrie that they were there. Then I saw the other face of the police. One of them was after me in a flash, and said to me peremptorily, 'You will return at once, and you will not move again unless you are given permission.' I said to him with extreme coldness, 'This is my wife's house, and I am telling her who you are, and what you are doing here.' When I had told Dorrie about our visitors, I returned to them and sat on the big chest, not angry, but in that extreme coldness.

After they had finished examining the papers in the first drawer, they turned to the second, but I said to them, 'You may take my word or you may not, just as you choose, but there are no papers in that drawer which have anything to do with the Defence and Aid Fund.' They then riffled perfunctorily through the papers in the second drawer, and if I remember rightly, they opened and shut the other four drawers in the writing-desk. The senior man, a major I think, asked if he might use the phone. He telephoned to his colonel in Durban and said in Afrikaans, '*Kolonel, alles gaan goed. Die oubaas koöpereer baie goed.*' (Colonel, all is going well. The old gentleman is cooperating very well.) They then asked to see the 'other room' in which I worked, so I took them to the rondavel, or round hut, in the garden where I did my writing. I told them, 'Gentlemen, you may believe me or not believe me as you wish, but this is where I write when I get a chance to write, and there are no political papers here.' So they did not search the rondavel. Then we joined Dorrie in the sitting-room, where we had tea, and the captain talked to us about gardening and dogs, and about his wife's asthma, he thinking that Dorrie had asthma too. Then politely they left.

On that day, 18 May, the security police searched every Defence and Aid office throughout the country, and the homes of those men and women who had been active in collecting for and administering the fund. It was also in May that Bram Fischer was sentenced to life imprisonment, having been found guilty on nine charges under the Suppression of Communism Act. He was first arrested on 9 July 1964, released, and again arrested on 23 September. On 25 January 1965 Bram, who was on bail, went underground, and was not captured until 11 November. During this time he read my life of Hofmeyr, and wrote me a letter about it. Hofmeyr could hardly have been a hero to Bram; he was a conservative liberal, a firm believer in evolutionary change, and a determined opponent of any kind of totalitarian government. But Bram in his letter showed a sympathy and understanding for Hofmeyr that offered further proof of the complexity of his own personality. He gave me warm praise for the book, which in 1965 had won the C.N.A. (Central News Agency) Literary Award for the best book published in South Africa in 1964.

In May 1966 Bram went to prison, and early in 1975 became seriously ill with cancer. After hospital treatment in Pretoria he was allowed to go to the home of his brother in Bloemfontein, and died there on 8 May. So ended an extraordinary life.

It was towards the close of the year 1966 that I received from Patrick Duncan a letter seeking reconciliation. He was suffering from aplastic anaemia, in which (in his own words) 'the marrow stops producing various of the components of the blood'. He told Randolph Vigne, 'I am anxious to reach reconciliation everywhere it is possible to.' He realised the approach of death, and wished to be prepared for it.

In 1962 Patrick had gone secretly to Basutoland, believing that he could do no more in South Africa, and that he could advance the cause from outside the country. He resigned from the Liberal Party and joined the Pan-Africanist Congress, which in 1964 appointed him an official representative to the Algerian government. In 1965 the P.A.C. dismissed him, and the long journey begun in the Germiston location in 1952 had come to its end. Of this dismissal his biographer C. J. Driver wrote, 'He had given himself utterly to this great aim, and yet there was nothing more that this great aim wanted of him.'

The Comité Chrétien de Service en Algérie offered him a job as Director of Operations in Constantine, some six hundred kilometres from Algiers. But now he had to fly frequently to England for blood transfusions. He grew very humble. Those political certainties that he had once seen with such awful clarity troubled him less and less. He was facing a certainty of his own. 'A fruit seller in Basingstoke spoke unusually kindly to me, and I had to take refuge in the car to avoid public tears.'

In April 1967 he wrote to record 'one of the most remarkable happenings in my life'. He was ill and in pain and in a bed in a hotel in Timimoun in Algeria, thinking perhaps of what he had written in his book *Man and the Earth** about religion. Christianity was the cult of Jehovah, 'and what a repulsive cult it is'. Jehovah was violent, jealous, and incited his people to commit crimes of genocide. Other religions were equally unpleasant, and Marxism, the 'near-religion', was fading. In the hotel at Timimoun Patrick found himself saying these words in silence.

P.D.: God, I need your help. But I suppose if you are Jehovah I can't expect you to do anything for me.

* Volturna Press, Peterhead, Aberdeenshire, 1975.

God: I am Jehovah. How can you expect me to do anything for you after the rude things you said about me in your book?

Another person: In any case you should not ask for selfish things in prayer. You should ask for general benefits, that God's will be done, etc.

P.D.: Maybe, but if prayer can't help in cases like this it can't be much use.

Within ten minutes the pain had gone, and he drove six hundred kilometres without any recurrence of it.*

He kept flying to England for transfusions. On Wednesday 31 May 1967 he had his tenth transfusion. On Friday 2 June he reacted badly, but was cheerful and was re-reading *The Pilgrim's Progress*. On Sunday 4 June he died.

So ended the life of one of the most extraordinary of human beings. Although six years had gone by since he left South Africa and although it is nearly twenty years since he died, I can see him clearly as I write these words, with those flashing blue eyes and those cheeks ruddy with health, and his overwhelming earnestness that made you want to run for cover, and made you feel so mean because you knew that you were not going to be convinced by it. Although he created such problems for the Liberal Party, and in the end regarded it as useless and left it, most of us remember him with deep affection.

The year 1966 saw the banning of five more of our active members, including Ruth Hayman. Her banning order forbade her to enter any court of law, so that was virtually the end of her legal career. One of the leading lawyers in Johannesburg gave her a job, but Ruth's life was in the courts, not in any office. She and Mervyn decided to emigrate to England, much to our sorrow. They settled in London, and while Mervyn battled to establish himself in the world of business, Ruth devoted herself to the teaching of English to many of her fellow immigrants, especially those from India, Africa and the Caribbean.

Vorster did great damage to the Liberal Party, not to its principles or ideals but to its organisation. He had by the end of 1966 banned nearly forty of its members and more than thirty of these were active and influential. Some of us used to say bravely that for every leader cut down, ten would rise up in his place, but there was no substance for such a boast. These thirty or forty members were amongst the most intelligent and courageous of our company, and that is why they had been elected to their offices. The thirty or forty who would – and did – replace them, were not as gifted as those who had been silenced by the Minister.

In 1966 Prime Minister Verwoerd was at the height of his powers. He led the National Party to its greatest electoral victory, for it won one

* Driver, *Patrick Duncan.*

hundred and twenty-six seats out of one hundred and sixty-six, and its share of the vote rose from fifty-three percent in 1961 to fifty-eight per cent. At last the country had recovered from Sharpeville, and the economy was buoyant. The Prime Minister's command over his party was complete.

On 6 September 1966 Verwoerd was due to speak on the occasion of the Prime Minister's budget vote, and he was expected to make a major policy speech. He took his seat in the house some fifteen minutes after two o'clock, looking cheerful and confident. Members were taking their seats when a uniformed parliamentary messenger entered and walked in the direction of the Opposition benches, but then suddenly changed course and moved towards the Prime Minister. He drew out a knife and threw himself upon Verwoerd, stabbing him four times in the neck and chest. Verwoerd slumped forward in his seat, and in a minute or two he was dead. At 3.05 p.m. it was announced from the hospital that he had been dead on arrival. He died two days before his sixty-fifth birthday.

The name of the man who had killed him was Demetrio Tsafendas. He was born in Lourenco Marques in 1918, the illegimate son of a Greek father and a Portuguese–African mother. At his trial he was found to be mentally disordered, and was sent to a prison for as long as it pleased the State President. He had been in eight mental institutions in four different countries. In those days political assassination was unknown in South Africa. In Verwoerd's case both of the assassins had been declared to be of unsound mind.

A few days after Verwoerd's death, B. J. Vorster was unanimously elected leader of the National Party, and became the seventh Prime Minister of South Africa.

As I write in 1987 we are living in days when the Great Plan of Verwoerd is recognised by the majority of Afrikaners to be unrealisable. Prime Minister B. J. Vorster declared that he would follow in the footsteps of his predecessor, but he clearly was more of a pragmatist than Verwoerd. In the concluding chapter of this book I shall have to consider the changes that have taken place in South Africa since the assassination of twenty-one years ago. I should like however to conclude this chapter by asking and attempting to answer the question, Was Verwoerd an evil man?

Many millions of people in my lifetime believed that Hitler was an evil man. For them he was evil in a way that was not true of Napoleon or Caligula or Pizarro. Stalin was also regarded by many as an evil man, but his leadership of Russia in the war against Hitler was admired by many others. Both Hitler and Stalin were ruthless in their actions against those who resisted their plans. Hitler planned the extermination of the Jews, and killed about six million of them. It is estimated that Stalin executed twenty million Russian peasants who resisted his policies of collectivisation.

Verwoerd was never responsible for such gross actions against human beings. But it must be remembered that he never had the power of the two great dictators. If he had had the power, would he have embarked on genocide? If he had been the leader of eighty million Afrikaners, would he have followed the examples of Hitler and Stalin? It is impossible to answer such a question.

A man for whom I have a great regard, Bishop Alphaeus Zulu, Speaker of the Legislative Assembly of Kwa-Zulu, had no hesitation in declaring that Verwoerd was an evil man, and that he had condemned the black people of South Africa to a life of perpetual subordination; in particular he had planned for them an inferior education in his notorious Bantu Education Act of 1953. Senator Leslie Rubin, who represented 'Native' voters under the franchise laws of 1936, and who said, as I have written earlier, that Verwoerd had a mesmeric gift which at times affected even his bitterest opponents, held the view that the Prime Minister was an evil man. Margaret Ballinger held the same opinion.

Yet Verwoerd in his private life was an exemplary husband and father. His smile in public was benign, and in his portraits he appears as the soul of benevolence. His life was simple, and one of his great pleasures was to go fishing at Betty's Bay in Cape Town, where he had his holiday cottage. His public life was above reproach, and he did not, to my knowledge, lay up great riches for himself.

Was his benevolence directed towards white people only, and especially towards the Afrikaner? I think the answer must be Yes. He never – again to my knowledge – showed that he had any affection for black people. He would be just to them in his own fashion, and would give them their own 'homelands', where they could observe their own customs and cherish their own languages and cultures. When they were ready for it they would be given independence in their own homelands. Then, argued Verwoerd, the whole world would see that the goal of separate development was right and just, and that blacks would be equal to whites in every conceivable way. Verwoerd was blind to the truth that the material wealth of South Africa, with a few exceptions, was in the 'white' homelands, which had the ports and the cities, and most of the mineral and agricultural wealth. When after his death independence was given to the Transkei, Bophuthatswana, Venda, and the Ciskei, most of their income came from Pretoria, in the form of substantial grants of money.

Was Verwoerd blind to these truths, or did he blind himself to them? Was he a deceiver, or was he, with all his intellectual gifts, a self-deceiver? Did he himself believe that the homelands could become economically independent, or could achieve a healthy independence? In how far was he benevolent, or was he capable of malevolence?

When I consider all these questions, I cannot conclude that he was an evil man. I conclude rather that his passions ruled his life, and that his intellect was the servant of his passions. That he was arrogant in his self-certitude, I have no doubt. But I conclude that he deceived himself. He believed that he had solutions for the problems of South Africa when he had not. What is more, in his search for these solutions, he had the one overruling principle, and that was the safety and the security of the Afrikaner volk. That he had other principles one cannot doubt, but they were all subordinate to the well-being and continuance of Afrikanerdom.

That he did great moral harm to the Afrikaner I have no doubt. Dr. D. F. Malan became Prime Minister in 1948, but by 1950 H. F. Verwoerd had become what Henry Kenney in his biography called the 'Architect of Apartheid'. Verwoerd did not originate the self-worship of the Afrikaner Nationalist, but he was certainly the heir to the Afrikaner prophets of the 'thirties and 'forties. He was however a political leader as well, of great mesmeric and charismatic gifts. He gave to Afrikaner-dom, which had always been an embattled minority, not only in the world but also in its own country, a sense of security and power. His own power was immensely increased when he became Prime Minister in 1958, and again when he survived the first assassination bid in 1960.

His power over the Afrikaner churches was also very great. The force which drove him was Nationalism rather than Christianity, but any potential conflict between them was avoided by their synthesis in Christian–Nationalism. Man was created to be the member of a nation, and that was his highest destiny. The apostle Paul had written that in Christ there was neither Greek nor Jew, circumcision nor uncircumcision, Barbarian, Scythian, bond nor free. That was true for the Afrika-ner churches, but it was a spiritual and invisible unity. In fact the Afrikaner Nationalist government made it a criminal offence in certain circumstances to pursue this spiritual unity. In South Africa the Divine Will was in favour of racial separation.

Therefore the whole energy of the government and its civil service was given to the task of achieving racial separation. The best of Afrikaner minds were devoted to the realisation of a dream which is today seen to be unrealisable. In 1966 the great task was given by Afrikanerdom to B. J. Vorster. He led his country, and his own people, deeper into the morass from which now at long last we are trying to emerge in the face of a world hostility which, now in 1987, seems to be almost total. I shall have to write about this in the last pages of this book.

Chapter 29

On 8 January 1967 Dorrie wrote in her diary: 'Depressed. Gave way. So ashamed.'

Anoxia of the brain, a lack of sufficient oxygen to the brain. The lungs struggle ceaselessly to oxygenate the blood, but in their present state they cannot do so. Even though the patient has a supply of pure oxygen, as Dorrie did, she cannot breathe in enough to feed the brain. Dorrie would wake in the morning trembling and frightened, anxious over the new day that had to be faced and suffered and endured. Often she would not waken me, but would lie with her anxiety alone. But sometimes the trembling would seem to become uncontrollable and would frighten her, and she would ask me to come to calm her. Sometimes my heart would wish to break, because I knew that it was not words or love that she needed but oxygen.

Sometimes she was impatient with me. She said once to me, 'I know I am a burden to you.' When I protested she said, 'I am a burden to you all.' She wrote to her sister Ruth on 22 January 1967:

I might say that I'm such a hypocrite that when Doctor H. suggested a week in King George V Hospital I meekly and cheerfully agreed, but as soon as he'd gone, the storm of repression and depression broke loose on poor Alan . . . Really I deserve to be shot for pre-judging so erroneously and grumpily, after all the blessings God has bestowed on me all my life.

Dr. W. said to me, 'You must expect such things to happen. Your wife cannot be blamed for it in any way. It is a condition she is powerless to prevent. She may even turn against you, and you must keep your patience.'

If I did become impatient, I was filled with remorse, and would pray with great earnestness. 'Lord, make me the instrument of your love, and let me speak no angry or hurtful word.'

On 17 March 1967, Dorrie wrote to her sister Ruth:

I am trying hard to ovecome my depression and regain my courage . . . I know this will take time, but I am determined to make it work. I so long to be up and about again. Also when I do start getting up, I'm going to get dressed. Then I'll really feel on the road to recovery.

On 2 April she wrote in her diary. 'Alan managed to come earlier. Feel so homesick when he goes.' On 3 April she wrote, 'I am obviously lacking determination and perseverance.'

Yet she was not lacking in determination and perseverance, she was lacking only oxygen. She had never lacked in determination and perseverance her whole life long. It was in these days that the inexorable truth is brought home to one, that even the warmth of love depends on a material element called oxygen. Yet not only the warmth of love – the whole of life, the whole world of man and animal and tree, all activity, all the vast accumulation of human knowledge, all history, all science, the whole terrestrial creation, all depend on it. The total lack of it brings all life to an end. The partial lack of it changes life drastically.

Dorrie still cherished the dream that one day she would be able to do without the supplementary oxygen, which she now inhaled twenty-four hours of the day. Some days she was ill and in great distress, but on others she was bright and eager, so full of hope, so eager to get home – she was then again in King George V Hospital – so eager to have a real bath again, so eager to wean herself from the oxygen from which she could never be weaned.

She said to me, 'I am going to get well, and I am going home, and I am going to get into the bath – you must help me, Alan – I want to feel the water on my body, you don't know what it means to me to feel the water on my body.'

Yes, I did know what it meant to her. When I saw her eager face, I wished that mine could be eager too, and I wished that I could say to her, 'Yes, you're coming home, and you're going to get into the bath – yes, I'll be helping you – and you're going to feel the water on your body again.' But I could not say it.

I wanted to write a letter to her to thank her for the blessings of our common life, and for her courage and gaiety and zest, and for her contempt of cruelty and cant, and for her belief that men and women are not born to go down on their bellies before the State. But they wouldn't let me write it, because Dorrie would ask, 'Why do you write such a letter? Is it because you think I am going to die?' No, they wanted her to go on hoping these empty hopes.

And I think they were right, because Dorrie was afraid of dying and of death. She never liked me to say, 'When I pop off, you'll be able to do what you like, pick all the flowers in the garden, and not have books lying about the house.' She would say, 'Please Alan, don't joke about it.'

Yet I was distressed to think that we could not talk about the culminating event of our married life. Dorrie said once to Murray Dell, who was our most faithful visitor, 'I think I'm coming to the end of the road.' But she never asked him, or me, 'Am I coming to the end of the road?' If she had asked me, I wanted to be able to put my arms around her and to say, 'Yes, my love.' But they all said No.

It was Aubrey Burns, the first person ever to read *Cry, the Beloved Country*, in his house in California through which those four redwood trees were growing, who solved the problem. On 6 April he arrived in South Africa to visit us, and he wanted of course to see Ixopo and Carisbrooke and the hills that are lovely beyond any singing of it. On 12 April I took him to see the countryside in which Dorrie had grown up, and I took him into the church where we were married, on 2 July 1928, and there I knelt and gave thanks for our married life. That evening Aubrey and I went to visit Dorrie at the hospital and when I told her what I had done, her whole face lit up with joy. So she was told it after all.

There is another thing that I remember, one night at the hospital when her old gaiety suddenly returned. I was saying goodnight to her, and she said to me in Afrikaans, *'Slaap lekker, slaap alleen,'* which means, 'Sleep well, sleep alone.' I remember also one night at about that time that she suddenly said to me, 'You're not a bad old stick.'

On 21 April I took Dorrie to St. Mary's Hospital at Mariannhill, and I bought her a wheelchair. She could get out of bed and sit in it, and it gave her some comfort. But on 28 April Dr. C. recommended that she should go back to King George V and that, when she returned home, she should have a day nurse and a night nurse. The day nurse was Elizabeth Pillay, a coloured woman who was the wife of the Indian barman at the Kloof Country Club, and the night nurse was Queenie Ngubane, a housewife from Lamontville.

On 19 July Dorrie recorded in her diary that I was working hard on a book. This was to be called *Instrument of Thy Peace,* and was to consist of a series of twenty-one meditations based on the prayer of St. Francis, a prayer which meant a great deal to me in the year of 1967. I wrote these words in the prologue.

This book is written for sinners, and by one of them. It is written for those who wish with all their hearts to be better, purer, less selfish, more useful; for those who do not wish to be cold in love, and who know that being cold in love is perhaps the worst sin of all; for those who wish to keep their faith bright and burning in a dark and faithless world; for those who seek not so much to lean on God as to be the active instruments of his peace.

This book has become a kind of minor classic, and has been republished many times. In 1983 a revised edition was published, and in his foreword Malcolm Muggeridge wrote that I was a poet rather than a novelist, more a saint than either, maybe. He was I think right to say that I was a poet rather than a novelist, and he was certainly right to add, after his suggestion that I might be a saint, the qualifying word 'maybe'. That my writings have been a help to many people is an incontrovertible fact, but I am in no way a saint.

I added these words to the prologue in the new edition of 1983:

Although the book is fifteen years old, it still speaks to me clearly. I can come to only one conclusion, that I was given help to write it. I can only relate the strange experience that as I re-read it, there are parts of it that help and move me as though some other hand had written them.

I considered and reconsidered these words many times before I sent them to the publisher, wondering whether perhaps they were over-weening and arrogant, perhaps even blasphemous. But in the end I came to the conclusion that they were none of these things, they were simply true.

During Dorrie's illness, I worked on *Instrument* almost every day. I can only assume that the circumstances of my own life had influenced me to pay more attention to my religion. During this time of writing I had the continuous encouragement of Murray Dell, who came to see us three or four times a week. Dorrie found in him a great source of comfort and strength, and there could be no doubt that both he and Archbishop Paget were true priests. One of the supreme tests of a priest is surely his ability to help those 'who in this transitory life are in trouble, sorrow, need, sickness, or any other adversity'.

That is the supreme test for one's friends also. Dorrie was fortunate in this year to have had the faithful friendship of many people, of whom I would name four women, Pondi Morel, Dots Landau, Margaret Anderson and Devi Bughwan. Our sons and their families visited us as often as they could, and Dorrie's brothers Aubrey and Garry and their wives. Both Aubrey and Garry were to die of emphysema. To say that four of the Francis family died because they were smokers would be an exaggeration, but there is no doubt that smoking aggravated what was an apparent family weakness. My son Jonathan, who has never smoked at all, has inherited the genes.

On 11 September Dorrie wrote in her diary for what she called 'Black Monday': Finally A. told me he must get away for some nights from our bedroom as I'm getting him down. This has been the unkindest cut of all whether or not I deserved it. My only peace is in oblivion.' I did not read this passage until some time after it had been written. Then I wrote in Dorrie's diary: 'A sad passage, but Dr. C. advised me to do so. Do not think I told D. that she was getting me down.' On 12 September she wrote: 'Feeling desolate, but am trying to be realistic and fighting against it. Faith is weak – if only I could rest in God.'

Ten days later Dorrie was in Mariannhill again, this time with a distended stomach. The specialist surgeon, Mr. S., ordered her to be taken to Durban to St. Augustine's Intensive Care unit at once, where she had X-rays and a blood transfusion. The unit with its mechanical efficiency horrified her, and she complained bitterly about it. On 28 August she recorded that I had phoned – 'Both of us edgy, why?' Later I wrote in her diary: 'D. complained bitterly about the hospital. This must have made me edgy. Dr. H. told me that anoxic patients do not know what effect their actions have on others.' On the following day Elizabeth and I went to St. Augustine's to fetch Dorrie. She wrote in her diary: 'In fact am becoming less and less long-suffering. Utterly ashamed.' And then, 'Queenie's cold was the last straw to my endurance. I infuriated A. and drove him out.' However, I returned to our bedroom and did not leave it again. The X-rays revealed that she had cancer of the stomach, and that no treatment was possible because of the state of her lungs.

She spent her last days under sedation. She tried to keep her diary going but her handwriting deteriorated to the point where it became illegible. On 15 October David and Jonathan arrived, but on 22 October they went home, it being impossible to say when the end would come. The next morning Queenie woke me at five minutes to seven, and said to me, 'Our mother has gone.' When Elizabeth arrived at eight, I told her that Dorrie had gone, and she ran through the house to our bedroom as though she might catch a glimpse of her before she left us finally. I wrote in my engagement diary for 23 October, '6.55 Dorrie left.' What was the first thought that came into my mind after I kissed your still warm brow? It was that you would not have to face another frightening day.

I wrote in *Kontakion for You Departed* of all these events at much greater length, and shall not do so again. But I shall write something about my thoughts about death, and particularly about life after death. In the Creed we say, 'I look for the Resurrection of the dead, and the life of the world to come. Amen.'

Do I look for the Resurrection of the dead? I do not know. I think often of my father and my mother, and of Dorrie and of departed friends, especially those of whom I have been writing in this chapter. Will I 'see' them again? To my knowledge they have never made any attempt to communicate with me. Do they watch me down here below? Are they concerned about my life and how I am living it? I do not know. I have no proof that they are concerned.

I wrote these words in *Kontakion*:

Where are you, my love? And in what condition? That your body has returned to the dust, that I know. But what has happened to you, to your love and your warmth and your courage? Your dust is indestructible, but you, you yourself, were you also indestructible? Did you, you yourself, have no being apart from that body which has returned to the dust?

At the funeral service, the archbishop said:

With the passing of Dorrie the visible fellowship is broken, but death does not put an end to real fellowship; prayer goes on and love continues – from the land of the living, from the joy of Paradise, whence all pain and grief have fled away, where the light of Christ's countenance ever shines.

I quote again from *Kontakion*:

Was he speaking about Heaven? Are you in Heaven? Are you re-united there to your first husband, your father and your mother, your much-loved sister Rad, your brother Ray who died as a boy, the one you said I would have liked especially, because we were so like each other? Would your first husband perhaps not be there, because he was not a believer, and would I perhaps go there because I am a believer? This whole speculation is to me so grotesque that I cannot indulge in it.

Then do I believe in Heaven or do I not? Did Vachel Lindsay believe that there was such a place when he wrote his great poem 'General William Booth Enters into Heaven'? He wrote what at first seems to be a mocking description of the blind general leading his blaring band round the courts of Heaven, apparently without so much as a by-your-leave. Then comes the last stanza, which suddenly reveals that this apparently mocking poem is a thing as deep as anything in literature:

> *And when Booth halted by the curb for prayer*
> *He saw his Master thro' the flag-filled air.*
> *Christ came gently with a robe and crown*
> *For Booth the soldier, while the crowd knelt down.*
> *He saw King Jesus. They were face to face,*
> *And he knelt a-weeping in that holy place,*
> *Are you washed in the blood of the Lamb?*

Vachel Lindsay is saying something to me to which my whole being responds. My mind does not stand sceptically on the side-lines, watching my emotions making fools of themselves; it is my whole self which is there. But only a poet or a saint can say that kind of thing to us. Once Heaven is made a matter of fact, it becomes ludicrous.

When Francis of Assisi was approaching his death, there was never a thought in his mind that this meant the end of his relationship with his friend and his most High Lord. On the contrary it would continue and it would continue for ever. When the doctor told him he was soon to die, he stretched out his hands and cried aloud with joy, 'Welcome, Sister Death.' Then he added to his 'Canticle of the Sun' a new stanza:

> Praised be my Lord for our sister, the bodily death,
> From which no living man can flee,
> Woe to them who die in mortal sin,
> Blessed those who shall find themselves in Thy most holy will,
> For the second death shall do them no ill.

Not long before Dorrie died I wrote this prayer, which is to be found in *Instrument of Thy Peace*:

> Lord, give me grace to die in Thy will.
> Prepare me for whatever place or condition awaits me.
> Let me die true to those things I believe to be true,
> And suffer me not through any fear of death to fall from thee.
>   Lord, give me grace to live in Thy will also.
> Help me to master any fear, any desire, that prevents me from living
>   in Thy will.
> Make me, O Lord, the instrument of Thy peace,
>   That I may know eternal life.
> Into Thy hands I commend my spirit.

My religion has never held a great place for dogma. As I wrote earlier, it has been largely concerned with the dedication of my will. Therefore I hold no dogma about Heaven, but pray rather that I may be prepared for whatever place or condition awaits me.

Chapter 30

Our new Prime Minister B. J. Vorster, who succeeded Dr. Verwoerd in 1966, was later in 1971 to make history when he entertained to dinner Dr. Hastings Banda, the president of Malawi, and Mrs. Banda, on the occasion of their state visit to South Africa. The leading Afrikaans newspapers published photographs of the dinner, which marked quite a change since the days of 1953, when black and white speakers were photographed sitting together on Liberal Party platforms, these pictures often carrying sneering captions. Vorster also met Chief Jonathan of Lesotho, President Seretse Khama of Botswana, and Prince Makhosini Dlamini of Swaziland, and in 1974 he and President Kaunda conferred in the White Train on the Zambezi Bridge.

These were however essentially high-level occasions, and did not indicate any weakening of the National Party's loyalty to the sacred policies of racial separation, or to give it its grander name, the policy of separate development. Vorster was determined to put an end to interracial contact inside his own country, especially when it was fostered by organisations which were opposed to his own policies. In 1966 the Prohibition of Improper Interference Bill was a measure intended to prevent interracial political collaboration, partly because of the Nationalists' aversion to racial mixing, and partly because they wanted to prevent Progressive Party victories in the forthcoming elections for coloured seats in the Cape Provincial Council.

It was to be expected that the Nationalist Bill would go further than was necessary to achieve this particular purpose, and it made it a criminal offence for a person to belong to any mixed organisation which had as its objects the propagation or even study or discussion of political views. However, they decided to change the name of the Bill, because hostile wits suggested that it sounded like an amendment to the Immorality Act. In 1968 it became the Prevention of Political Interference Bill.

The Liberal Party decided that it could not continue. It could not break up into separate racial parties, because that would be to betray the very principles which it came into being to uphold. In April and May of 1968 we held closing meetings all over the country, of which I spoke at three, and remember them all. Peter Brown could not take part in these, because his banning order not only forbade him to attend meetings, but also forbade him to leave the magisterial district of Pietermaritzburg.

The first was held in the Darragh Hall in Johannesburg, and was called jointly by the Liberal and Progressive parties, the National Union of South African Students, the Students' Representative Council of the University of the Witwatersrand, and the Black Sash. I quote some words of mine:

In order to make real what can only be a dream, one has to use great power. The reality is so recalcitrant, so reluctant to take form, so stubborn to obey, that one has to bend it and break it and sledge-hammer it so that it may learn docility. The builders of the dream are working against time, they are fevered with impatience and angered by delay. Therefore let him beware who gets in their way, who proclaims publicly that he does not believe in the dream, who dares to tell the builders that their work is for nothing. Such a man will be broken so that others may be whole, his life will be made painful so that the life of others may be pleasant, present happiness will be destroyed so that future happiness may abound. One wonders why such savage steps have been taken against people who are so weak by those who are so powerful. And the answer is that the anger is not primarily directed against those who do not believe in the dream; it is primarily directed at the reality that will not take the form of the dream, and at the dream that will not become reality. In fact, neither can ever become the other yet it is in the belief that they will that our rulers pursue their policies of Separate Development.

The second meeting that I remember clearly was held at Hambrook, where we had a branch comprised entirely of black rural dwellers, and it was held in a humble building that was both school and church. When we arrived the security police were already there, and they had adopted one of their favourite positions. They stood outside their vehicles, and eyed all who came with their implacable stares, learned I am sure in their training. The school-church building was, as we say, 'in the middle of the veld', and from all quarters came our members, humble people who did not believe in the dream, and who came to testify publicly to their rejection of it. It was a moving spectacle to see this encounter between those who exercised great temporal power and those who exercised none but who possessed a power that I can only call spiritual.

When it was drawing near the time when the meeting must begin, the police entered the church and took endless photographs. One of our members responded by taking photographs of them, but they took his camera from him, and returned it only when one of our members, who was a well-known lawyer, informed them that their action was illegal.

After the meeting was over, we gathered outside, and the visiting members said goodbye to the members of the Hambrook branch, most of whom they were not likely to see again. They had been brought together, in this strange country, by the Liberal Party, and nothing was likely to bring them together again. After the meeting a black woman came to me and asked after Peter Brown; I told her that he was well, and she asked me to give him her love. I tell this story because this kind of thing does not often happen in our country; it is a tribute not only to Peter Brown, but also to the Liberal Party.

The closing meeting of the party in Durban was held in the Caxton Hall, which could not hold all those who had come to it, so that many had to stand in the street outside. Over the platform was a large banner which proclaimed, 'FREEDOM, FAREWELL.' The British newspaper *The Guardian* in its issue of 18 May 1968 carried the headline, 'Durban Liberals go out with dignity.' The opening words of the report were: 'The South African Liberal Party died in a Durban side-street at half-past nine the other night. There were no tears, no cries of anger; just a marvellous dignity.'

The security police were there in force, and sat in the back row of the hall. Some of our speakers at public meetings made a point of referring to their presence, often in contemptuous and provocative words. I myself had the habit of ignoring them, but on this occasion I directed my opening words to them:

I should like first to take this opportunity of saying a few words to the members of the security police. These words will not be insulting, they will merely be truthful. I do not know if this is my farewell to the security police or whether we shall meet again. I used to pretend – I suppose it was my duty to pretend – that it was nothing to me to be watched by you, and to be followed by you, and to have my telephone conversations listened to by you, and to have some of my letters – I do not say all of them – read by you, and to have my house searched by you, and to have you sitting in a car outside my house so that all my neighbours could see what kind of person I was. But I was only pretending.

After fifty years of a life blameless in the eyes of the law, it was painful suddenly to become the object of the attentions of the security police of my own country, to fly to Johannesburg and find you waiting for me at the airport, to fly to Cape Town and find you there too. I am by nature a private rather than a public man, and this attention was painful to me . . .

When you came in 1966 to search my house, you came into the library, and one of you said to the other, 'God, man, die boeke.'* I could not make out whether he had never seen so many books before, or whether they had intended to open every book in their search for dangerous documents . . .

This story was found very amusing by half of the security police in the hall, but the other half were not amused. They probably thought that the story carried the insinuation that security police did not read books.

So the thirteen years of the Liberal Party came to an end. Had it all been a waste of time, as some of our critics suggested? I never had any such feeling. The lessons taught by the Liberal Party are only now, nineteen years later, beginning to be learned by many South Africans, and here I am thinking more of Afrikaners than others. Many Afrikaners never really lost their belief in freedom, but for too long they were deceived (by others, and by themselves) into believing that the doctrines of separate development offered the only way to achieve freedom in our complex society of so many races and peoples.

There are people who think that the Liberal Party interfered grievously with my career as a writer. I have paid tribute to the way in which Peter Brown tried to protect me as far as possible. I could not have accepted any further protection. I am something more than a writer; I am a member of an imperfect and unjust human society, which has its home in a most beautiful country to which I have given, like so many others, a whole-hearted love. Even today, when the wrath of the outside world against South Africa has reached what can sometimes be described as a new pitch of fury, I have no desire to leave South Africa.

I can well remember the time when white people like Helen Suzman and Helen Joseph and Beyers Naudé and myself were greatly respected by the outside world. That would still be true of Helen Joseph and Beyers Naudé, and to a lesser extent of Helen Suzman, who was never given the distinction of being banned from public life and who, to use the jargon of today became 'part of the establishment'. Radical critics would argue that she has given 'respectability' to the government, and by becoming a member of an all-white parliament has given to it a credibility which it does not merit. I think it was Winston Churchill who said that in all the complexities of life it was given to many

---

* 'God, man, the books.'

ordinary people to see their appointed duty and to do it. All I can say is that Helen Suzman saw what was her duty and she did it. But among the more self-righteous people of the world, the credentials of even these four people might be questioned today. Why do they go on living in a society they know to be unjust, even evil? There is now a considerable body of world opinion that would refuse to any South African, of whatever race or colour or moral and political conviction, the right to take part in any international gathering or forum what-soever. Only a person like Archbishop Desmond Tutu would be exempted from this bar, this immunity being in large degree due to the fact that he won the Nobel Peace Prize in 1984. A young girl like Zola Budd, brought up in the narrow world of the Orange Free State, had the fortune or misfortune to become one of the great women runners of the world, but this circumstance has brought her not only fame, but also a host of difficult personal and political problems for which her young life had given her no preparation whatsoever. To return to my own case, I am still invited to university campuses, mainly in the United States, to receive this or that honour, but most of these offers I have refused. The burden of apartheid, to the fighting of which I gave thirteen years of my life, is now like an albatross about my own neck. I accept this undeserved luck, as do all my friends, with a kind of wry stoicism.

The last days of the Liberal Party gave me something to do in the bleak period following Dorrie's death. Immediately after she had died, my old enemy the migraine returned with great intensity, but left me again after a month. In January of 1968 I gave a party for my sixty-fifth birthday, and most of the guests remembered that a year earlier Dorrie had sat at the door to receive them. I had one other comfort, and that was that I was finishing *Instrument of Thy Peace* and was now contemplating – if indeed I had not already begun – writing a memoir of our forty-two years of life together.

It was on one of the days of this time that I met, at our post office in Kloof, Mrs. Margaret Rennie, who not long before had lost her hus-band. She asked me how I was, and when I said that I was managing, she said to me, 'It's not funny, is it?' That is another one of the miracles of language that one can use five such simple words to describe what was indeed a devastating experience. I had always imagined myself to have what are called 'inner resources', to possess in fact a kind of spiritual strength that enables one to face loneliness with acceptance and courage. But I realised that in my case it was not true. I realised that I hated living alone, and more, that I could not live without the companionship of a woman. I realised that my spiritual strength, which many people supposed me to have, was to a phenomenal degree dependent on the presence of another person. After Dorrie's death I got into the habit of spending nearly every evening with Margaret Anderson, who was in her widowhood an extremely independent woman, and we would spend two or three hours doing puzzles, especially the daily word puzzle in the *Natal Mercury*, and talking about books and people. It was fortunate for me that her home was in the same town as my own, and her friendship was a great help to me in those days, not only her friendship but also her love of word puzzles, which matched my own.

For the last year of Dorrie's life my secretarial work had been done by Pamela Mathews, also a member of the Liberal Party. After Dorrie's death I took my work to Mrs. G. Waddington, who lived at Kloof, and who told me that she was willing to do any typing for me provided it had nothing to do with politics. Although the Liberal Party had ceased to exist, much of my writing was still political, and it was becoming clear to me that I must have a full-time secretary.

It was another old friend who came to my rescue, Goondie Francis. He and his wife Sue (another member of the party) were very friendly with Mrs. Anne Hopkins, whose marriage of sixteen years was coming to an unhappy end. She was an experienced secretary, and had worked for many years as secretary to the director of the Royal Ballet School in London (also a writer). She then joined the British Foreign Service and was posted to Athens, where she married a South African, Wing Commander 'Paddy' Hopkins. In 1963 she accompanied her husband to South Africa, with their two children Athene and Andrew, and for eighteen months had actually been our neighbour at Kloof. We met only once, and that was when she telephoned to say that four small birds had flown over the dividing fence between our properties and had fallen dead on her lawn. These birds, about four inches (ten centimetres) long, commonly called frets, are bronze mannikins, *Spermestes cucullatus,* and fly about in family groups. Mrs. Hopkins was of opinion that they had been poisoned, obviously by myself. I assured her that I did not poison birds, but actually attracted them to the garden by providing them with food and water, and that I would come at once and see the dead birds for myself. It was too late for when I arrived they had already been buried, and it was clear to me that they had flown into the white painted gable of the Hopkins house. I expressed this opinion to my neighbour but I could see that it did not convince her. The birds had obviously been poisoned, and by whom if not by myself? I decided that the lady was a bit of a virago.

I met Anne Hopkins once at the Francis home after that, and I must say that I liked her. She was very open and direct, and she agreed to Goondie Francis's suggestion that she should come to work for me.

She was a very competent secretary in all departments except one, that of spelling. On her very first morning in February 1968 I dictated to her a Foreword, which she brought back the next day having given it the title 'Forward'. She thought – or said she thought – that I would sack her on the spot, but I did nothing of the kind. She had not only secretarial but also managerial gifts, and began to take over some of the household duties. In the meantime she and her husband had agreed on a divorce; they lived in separate parts of the house, and spoke to each other as little as possible. It was an unhappy kind of existence, and was not made easier by an attack of jaundice which brought her spirits yet lower.

She certainly came into my life at a very important time. She obtained her divorce in 1968, and went to live in a house in Hillcrest, which is next to the town of Kloof, both of these places being dependent on the city of Durban and the manufacturing town of Pinetown for their existence. It must have been about the middle of 1968 when she typed the manuscript of *Kontakion for You Departed*. I wrote in this book:

My secretary has come to know you well, first through the letters that I write about you, mostly to people who have just heard, or who had written not knowing.* Then I began to speak to her about you. Then came a letter from the editor of an American magazine saying that he was running a series called *Works in Progress,* and asking whether I was writing anything, and if so, would I send him excerpts?

I was moved by the impulse to ask my secretary for her judgement, and I asked her if she would like to read what I had so far written. She said she would and so I gave it to her. She reads very quickly, and when she had finished she said to me, 'I never knew your wife, but she springs to life in these pages.' She said to me also, 'You must certainly go on writing it.' One cannot say anything more pleasing to a writer than to say that the person he is writing about springs to life in his pages.

It was inevitable that my secretary should come to play an important part in my life, and that I should come to depend on her. She said one day to me, 'I think you should marry again,' and I said to her, 'If I marry again, it will be to someone like yourself.' She took this as a proposal, which I later denied, but in fact it was as good as one. After she had considered the advantages and disadvantages, she informed me that she was willing to accept the proposal. We decided to marry early in 1969, but did not announce our intentions till one of our friends asked us what was going on. We then made public our engagement.

It was nevertheless a shock on the first Sunday after our announce-

* That means, not knowing that Dorrie had died.

ment to our friends to see the headlines in our biggest newspaper, the *Sunday Times* of Johannesburg, which announced 'Paton to marry divorcee'. Apparently my future wife was a 'socialite' who after her marriage to me would devote herself to good works.

The announcement had one notable consequence. The Archbishop of Cape Town, the Most Reverend Selby Taylor, a tall, grave, distinguished man and a bachelor, had not long before appointed me a member of the Order of Simon of Cyrene, which body was limited to fifty Anglican laymen and women who were judged to have rendered outstanding service to the Church of the Province of South Africa. I now wrote to offer him my resignation. I also offered to give up my plan to write the life of Geoffrey Clayton, Archbishop of Cape Town, from 1948 to 1957. I quote from his reply:

It is as you well understand a great sorrow to us that your intended wife should be a divorced person, and in these circumstances, I fear that I must accept your resignation from the Order of Simon of Cyrene.

I see no reason, however, why this should interfere with your plans for writing Archbishop Clayton's biography, and I very much hope you will continue with your intention.

I did mention to you the hope that you should become a member of the Liturgical Committee, but I feel that it would cause misunderstanding if I was to announce such an appointment at this time, and I must, therefore, reluctantly withdraw the suggestion.

I now felt that I should also resign from the council of St. Peter's College, a constituent college of the Federal Seminary at Fort Hare, and this resignation the archbishop accepted, with thanks for 'the prestige you have brought to the College through the fact that you were a member of its Council'.

One thing was clear and that was that Anne and I could not be married in any Anglican church. However I was most reluctant to be married in a registry office, and so I wrote to the Rev. Alex Boraine, who was then Moderator of the South African Methodist Conference, and asked him if he would marry us. He replied that he would have been delighted, but that he and his wife would be overseas at that time. He recommended that we should ask the Rev. George Irvine, who was the Methodist minister in charge of the district of Amanzimtoti, and at whose hands we 'received instruction'. He married us in a chapel in the city church in West Street in the very heart of Durban, on 30 January 1969.

I remember the day well. It was extremely hot and when I came to place the wedding ring on Anne's finger, I noticed that she had a drop of perspiration running down her nose After the ceremony the gentlemen of the press arrived. They had tried without success to find out the date of the wedding, and we suspected that Goondie Francis had given the secret away. Anne and I invited a few close friends to our wedding luncheon at Saltori's Restaurant, Goondie and Susan Francis, David and Nancy, Jonathan and Margaret, and two friends of Anne's, Betty Sprot and her sister Marge. During the luncheon Goondie excused himself, and came back triumphantly with the placard of the afternoon newspaper, which carried the news to the people of Durban, 'Paton married today.' Goondie probably had more than one reason to be triumphant, for it was generally thought that he had suggested that Anne should be my secretary with the hope that we would get married.

I shall not speak for Anne, but I shall say for myself that I did a most sensible thing when I married her. We had received the blessings of my sons and their wives. Anne's daughter Athene and her son Andrew were perhaps too young to bestow such things. All our friends were delighted, and Archbishop Paget and Murray Dell did not share the sorrowful attitude of Archbishop Selby Taylor. There are signs of course that the worldwide Anglican Church is softening its attitude towards the marriage of or with a divorced person, and is adopting what Alex Boraine called the 'gospel of the second chance'. Anne was forty-one when she married me, and I was sixty-six, but the age difference has not bothered us. In any event Anne is now a grand-mother, Athene having married Martin Hall and borne a daughter, Nerissa. It is interesting to remember that Anne asked Goondie's advice about marrying me, and he said, 'Yes, marry him, even if you have him for only five years.' These five years have now become eighteen.

I think that this is a good place at which to bring this second volume to an end. It marked the close of what I might call my public life. I decided that I would never again join a political party, but would, because I could not help it, become a political observer. When I write, 'because I could not help it', I mean that it is an integral part of my life and character to observe the political events of my times, and to be deeply concerned about them, and because I am a writer, to write about them.

However, I intend to write an epilogue, which will deal with the extraordinary events of the 'seventies and the 'eighties, and which will discuss the future, in so far as it is discussable. I do not foresee doom for our country, the destruction of its economy, the triumph of revolutionaries, and the establishment of a new autocracy, which will call itself democratic and non-racial but will in fact be authoritarian (and harsh towards its former oppressors, of which I will be counted as one). Nor do I see the continuance of white supremacy, or of any statutory racial separation. I would like to see Afrikaner identity preserved, but it quite clearly cannot be done at the expense of other people, as has been the case for the last thirty-nine years, since indeed the year 1948 when the Afrikaner Nationalist Party came to power. I must not however anticipate the epilogue.

Although politics has played a major role in my eighty-four years, it has not dominated my life. Literature and the love of the word, and the love of writing the word, have been equally important. And the third dominating force has been my religion, my reverence for the Lord Jesus Christ whom I could have served much better (to use Tolstoy's words, I have not fulfilled a thousandth of his commandments, not because I didn't wish to, but because I was unable, but I am trying with all my heart), and my sense of wonder when I contemplate the Universe.

I must admit to one last dominant thought, and that is that my life is drawing to its end. Not long ago I read that Sir John Gielgud, who was then eighty-two, had said that he thought of dying every day of his life. I would not use these words, but I certainly think of my age every day of my life. I find Tagore's words on death most beautiful.

On the day when death will knock at the door, what wilt thou offer to him?
Oh, I will set before my guest the full vessel of my life – I will never let him go
*   with empty hands.*
All the sweet vintage of all my autumn days and summer nights, all the
*   earnings and gleanings of my busy life, will I place before him at the close*
*   of my days when death will knock at my door.**

And again:

I have got my leave. Bid me farewell, my brothers! I bow to you all and take my
*   departure.*
Here I give back the keys of my door – and I give up all claims to my house. I ask
*   only for last kind words from you.*
We were neighbours for long, but I have received more than I could give. Now
*   the day has dawned and the lamp that lit my dark corner is out. A*
*   summons has come and I am ready for my journey.*

I close with words from the South African poet Roy Campbell. They are closing words for him too, and are to be found in the last paragraph of his autobiography, *Light on a Dark Horse*. He says that he was compelled to write the book

. . . so as to repay my debt both to Almighty God and to my parents, for letting me loose in such a world, to plunder its miraculous literatures, and languages,

---

* These poems come from Rabindranath Tagore, *Gitanjali*. Macmillan, London, 1957.

and wines; to savour its sights, forms, colours, perfumes, and sounds; to see so many superb cities, oceans, lakes, forests, rivers, sierras, pampas, and plains, with their beasts, birds, trees, crops and flowers – and above all their men and women, who are by far the most interesting of all.

It is a debt that I also wish to repay.

Epilogue

After the death of the Liberal Party in 1968 I never saw the security police again. Nor did I ever join any political organisation. I became a political observer and my opinions were treated with respect because I had no partisan loyalties. It was for me a time of the kind of intellectual freedom which one may not enjoy while one is a member of a party. For one then has a loyalty to the party and to its policies and one must sometimes disagree in silence because one does not wish to be disloyal.

It was in 1970 that Archbishop Selby Taylor invited me to rejoin the Order of Simon of Cyrene and I willingly did so. I was glad to renew my friendship with this tall, reserved and most distinguished-looking man, to stay with him at Bishopscourt when I visited Cape Town and to receive much help from him while I was writing the life of his great predecessor, Geoffrey Clayton. Archbishop Taylor was well known for his reserve, almost aloofness and he astonished the audience on the occasion of his opening a swimming-bath in a coloured township of Cape Town, by suddenly stripping himself of his episcopal vestments, revealing to the world that underneath them he wore nothing but a pair of swimming-trunks. He then dived into the water to the accompaniment of tumultuous applause.

It was also in 1970 that I was invited to accept the honorary degree of D.Litt. from Harvard University, and after consulting with my friends I applied for the return of my passport, to which after a decent interval the authorities agreed. It was a chance to breathe again the air of a freer world and I would not have taken it if the Liberal Party had still been in existence. It was also a comfort to learn that during these long ten years of isolation there were still people who remembered me. Shortly after this, Trent University, Canada, also invited me to accept an honorary degree of D.Litt., and not long after that, the ancient university of Edinburgh invited me to accept the honorary degree of D.D. It was almost too much.

Our trip abroad in 1971, my first for eleven years, was a great success and pleasure for us both. I was given a double honour by Harvard, the honorary degree of D.Litt. and the making of the 320th Commencement address in the famous Yard after the presentation of the degrees, which ceremony is preceded by the ceremonial march of Harvard graduates, led on this occasion by a small old man carrying the pennant of the class of 1896. He was at least four years ahead of the next pennant-carrier and received a great ovation.

I quote a few words from the Commencement address:

Now I have reached my end. Your tribulations are known to the whole world. Some of us in the outside world derive satisfaction from them. Some of us in South Africa believe that your troubles are due to your policies of racial integration and such people are trying anew to prove that separate can be equal. Yet you should not be discouraged by this. The problems of racial prejudice and friction, the problems caused by man's destruction and pollution of his own environment, the problem of war and of deluding oneself – after all these centuries of experience – that war can make the world better, the problem of the terrible gulf that yawns between the rich and the poor, the problem of the impersonality and meaninglessness of human life, especially in the great city, they are our problems too, even if only in miniature. It is foolish of us to gloat when you appear to fail to solve them, for are we any better, any wiser than you? Therefore you must regard yourselves as the testing ground of the world and of the human race. If you fail, it will not be America that fails, but all of us.

So ended the big day in the Big Yard. The best compliment I received came from Lady Jackson, known throughout the world as Barbara Ward, the Christian economist, who was deeply respected for her concern for the poor people and the poor nations of the world and her clear grasp of the duty of the rich. She said to me of the Commencement address, 'It sounded like the Bible.'

After our visit to Trent, and to Edinburgh where I was admitted by a touch of a cap made – so I was told – from John Knox's breeches, we set out by car through France, Spain and Portugal to the beautiful town of Sintra, where we were to pick up Mary, the widow of the poet Roy Campbell, and take her to Toledo and to Altea near Alicante, where they had both lived.

The reason for this journey was that I had decided to write Roy

Campbell's life. Much of the work had already been done by William Henry Gardner, professor and head of the department of English at the Pietermaritzburg campus of the University of Natal. Gardner was already well known in the world of letters as an authority on the life and work of the poet Gerard Manley Hopkins. But his life of Campbell was never written because of his death in January 1969. I spoke to his son Colin Gardner, who was to succeed his father as head of the department in 1972, and asked him what he thought of the idea that I should continue his father's work, and both he and his mother accepted the offer at once. Mrs. Gardner handed over to me the considerable quantity of material that her late husband had collected with a diligence and thoroughness that few scholars could surpass.

The announcement of my decision had a very mixed reception. Campbell, after writing such famous poems as 'The Zulu Girl' and 'The Serf', which showed no traces of the racial arrogance or condescension so prevalent in white South Africa in the 'twenties, shortly afterwards returned to his self-imposed exile in England and never wrote such poems again. His obsessive themes were now the decadent upper-class English, and then in the 'thirties he became an admirer of Hitler and Mussolini and Franco and incurred the enmity and indeed the contempt of the great majority of the literary establishment of England. How could the writer of *Cry, the Beloved Country* possibly contemplate writing the biography of a boastful fascist such as Campbell?

This was not really a sensible question. If it was immoral for me to write the life of a man like Campbell, then it was immoral of Alan Bullock to write the life of Adolf Hitler. My difficulties with the biography had nothing to do with Campbell's reputation as a fascist, but they had everything to do with the obviously deep reluctance of Mary, of her second daughter Anna, the Countess Anna Cavero de Carondelet and of Robert Lyle, her constant companion, to tell me anything about the private lives of Roy and Mary. To put it bluntly, I found Mary devious and the other two not much better.

In 1927 the young Campbells, Roy and Mary, were befriended by Harold Nicolson and his wife Vita Sackville-West, who lived in the beautiful house of 'Long Barn' in Kent. The happier Mary was in this illustrious company, the less Roy liked it, and he would go up to London to get drunk. Vita, a passionate woman, having a pact with her husband that they were to be sexually free to do as they wished, fell in love with the beautiful Mary Campbell, and Mary with her. Peter Alexander in his biography *Roy Campbell* writes these lines.

This love affair which all but wrecked the Campbell's marriage, which changed the course of their lives, and seared the poet's mind and affected his verse to the end of his life, was for Vita merely one of a long series of diversions, and by no means the most memorable.

This is a strong judgement but fully justified, and it was because I had come to the same conclusion that I found the reticences of Mary, Anna and Rob Lyle quite intolerable. Did they want me to write the life or did they not? Well, of course they did, but they wanted a false life, of a Roy Campbell who had never existed. They wanted to protect not only Campbell but also themselves.

I must record that I was beginning to detest my task. I had written the lives of Hofmeyr and Clayton and had not encountered these difficulties. It is true that Hofmeyr's mother also wanted a false life of her son, but she was autocratic rather than devious and I simply had to postpone my writing until she died. Clayton had never married and there were no widow and children to obstruct a biographer. I had certainly never had to snoop into their private lives, which in any event were 'above reproach'. I found the idea of snooping into the private lives of Roy and Mary Campbell quite repellent. On a second visit to Sintra in 1973 I decided to ask Mary point-blank about Vita Sackville-West; she laughed in a shrill, would-be defiant kind of way and told me, 'You can forget about it, a nasty rumour, and there was nothing in it.' I left Sintra with a great deal of further material but in a very disheartened mood.

My rescuer was a young South African, Peter Alexander, who had decided to write a thesis, not a biography but a study of Roy Campbell's poetry. He had been to see Mary in Sintra and she had given him a letter to me, asking that I should make all material available to him. As he sat opposite me in my study, I knew that his book and mine could not both be written. I asked him to come back the next morning and I would give him an answer to his and Mary's request. When he came back I told him that he could have everything, Mary's material, my own, and W. H. Gardner's, and what was more, that I had decided to give up the idea of writing Campbell's life. Alexander was a sober and serious young man, but he was obviously pleased and excited by the prospect of writing a biography rather than a study of Campbell's verse. I told him of the difficulties of getting any worthwhile information out of Mary, Anna and Rob Lyle and wished him luck.

I wrote to Mary and told her what I had done, and I do not think she was terribly displeased. From Countess Anna I had a real snorter. She told me I had treated her mother in a despicable fashion and had betrayed the trust reposed in me by the whole family. I accepted this stoically and, as far as I remember, I did not write back to tell her that she was one of the main reasons why I had given up the task, but I did tell her that I could not possibly have written the kind of book that she and her mother wanted. I did not lose the friendship of Campbell's elder daughter Tessa through my action, and we still write to each other, though not very often. Tessa herself had several disappointments, for no publishers would accept her memorial tributes to her father.

It remains only to record that Peter Alexander produced in 1982 a most thorough and competent life of Campbell.* Though it was thorough it was not complete, for he was compelled – or felt compelled – to omit certain important events, largely because Rob Lyle threatened dire consequences if he did not. What these consequences would have been is not quite clear, but Rob Lyle was reported to be very rich, and Alexander had no money at all. So the events were omitted. His book received an unfriendly welcome from Mary, Anna and Lyle, but this need not have worried him, because the truth was that there was not a writer in the world who could have written a book that would have satisfied them. Alexander was fortunate in one important way. He did not need to snoop into the Vita–Mary affair. Vita's son, Nigel Nicolson in his book *Portrait of a Marriage* confirmed (in less than five lines) that it had happened, and Mary made no attempt to deny it.

Alexander chose to omit one important piece of my Campbell material, presumably because he did not think it important enough. On my second visit to Sintra I discovered among Mary's books and papers a small notebook. One could see immediately what it was. It was a witness to Campbell's efforts in his declining years to write as he had written in the 'twenties and 'thirties. There were the old favourite images, the sun, the stone, the snake, the peaks of the Drakensberg. But the magic no longer worked. He seldom got beyond three or four lines, then gave up, in a kind of despair one supposes. If I remember correctly, it was only on two occasions that he completed a four-line stanza. I was reminded of Milton's Sonnet 'On His Blindness', with those haunting lines

> ... *that one talent which is death to hide*
> *Lodged with me useless* ...

These lines were written in a time of melancholy and yet humble acceptance, but they were not true, for Milton composed his greatest works after he had gone blind. But Campbell's talent had gone; he could not but weep for the words that would not come again.

There was one other strange fact about Campbell that I thought would have enriched the story of his life, but Alexander did not think so. Campbell simply could not read his own poetry. I never heard him

---

* Oxford University Press, Oxford, and David Philip, Cape Town.

read in person, but I listened to many of his readings preserved in the sound library of the B.B.C. The music and beauty of some of his lines are sublime, but he could not get them – out of his mind or his soul or his imagination – into his tongue. The B.B.C. asked his permission to give a reading of some of his poems and he made it a condition that the reader should not attempt 'to put any feeling into them'. Why should that be so? Was it because he could not put any feeling into them himself? I must leave it as a mystery. His readings of his own poems were flat and toneless, and were made still worse by his Natal colonial accent, which England, France, Spain and Portugal failed to modulate. Some thought that he used it on purpose to shock the despised Georgians who spoke with a Bloomsbury accent:

> *Between its tonsils drawling out long O's*
> *Along its draughty, supercilious nose.*

It is interesting to note that Yeats went to the other extreme, and almost sang his poems. In his introductory remarks to his reading of the famous lines of 'The Lake Isle of Innisfree', he said with great emphasis, 'I will *not* read them as if they were prose.' T. S. Eliot said of Yeats's reading: 'To hear him read his own works was to be made to recognise how much the Irish way of speech is needed to bring out the beauties of Irish poetry.' Who am I to argue with T. S. Eliot? Eliot liked Yeats singing Yeats, but he did not like so much Yeats singing Blake. He wrote, 'To hear Yeats reading William Blake was an experience of a different kind, more astonishing than satisfying.' Yeats had one great piece of fortune that was denied to Campbell. His muse stayed with him till he died.

On 11 January 1973 an important event occurred in my life. I turned seventy years of age. In the *Sunday Tribune* of 7 January I wrote these lines:

In a few days I shall turn 70. I observe that I approach this birthday solemnly, in a way I have never approached a birthday before. I suppose it is largely because of those words, 'The days of our age are threescore years and ten, and though men be so strong that they come to fourscore years, yet is their strength then but labour and sorrow; so soon passeth it away, and we are gone.'

Hazlitt's last words were: 'Well, I've had a happy life.' I hope in due season to be able to say, or even whisper, the same. I didn't live it as well as I might have, but I don't dwell upon it because I believe in the forgiveness of sins. Nevertheless there are acts of mine which I do not like to remember. When these acts suddenly come back into memory, I sometimes find myself saying aloud, 'No, no, no.' Sometimes this astonishes some person who happens to be in my company at that moment. To him or her I give a general, not a particular, explanation. These acts are without exception mean ones.

And then again:

I could have made better use of my life, but I did try hard to do one thing. That was to persuade white South Africa to share its power, for reasons of justice and survival. My efforts do not appear outwardly to have been successful. There are two things to be said about that. The first is that one does not uphold love, justice, and mercy in order to be successful, but because it has to be done. The second is that one has no means of measuring. One is no more than a worker in a kind of apostolic succession. All one can say is that one has had some noble predecessors, contemporaries, and successors.

I ended up with these words:

I feel a bit mean to be slipping out of it all. But it's a job for younger hands and fresher minds. I have always read and sung with a sceptical mind those words, *'Ons sal lewe, ons sal sterwe, ons vir jou, Suid-Afrika.'** Who is meant to die? I suspect the Afrikaners and the reluctant English and a few 'loyal' stooges. I don't think anyone will put on my stone 'He died for his country', but I'll settle for the words 'He tried to live for his country'.

Anne gave a great party for my seventieth birthday, and asked David and Jonathan to do the honours. David inclines to be witty, and Jonathan inclines to be humorous, and they are both good speakers. It just so happens that I kept Jonathan's notes and give them as he set them down. They give a picture of his father.

(CAN BE)
  ANGRY
  WITTY
  TEASINGLY BOASTFUL
  TEASING
(LIKES TO BE AT TIMES)
  CENTRE OF CONVERSATION
  ALOOF
  ABSENT-MINDED
  STERN
(HAS BECOME)
  INCREASINGLY TOLERANT
  GENEROUS
  RESOLUTE
  STUBBORN
(CAN BE)
  HUMBLE
  PASSIONATE
  FIERCE

* These words come from the national anthem, 'Die Stem van Suid-Afrika,' which is, to put it bluntly, a purely Afrikaner hymn. These words mean, 'We shall live, we shall die, we for you, South Africa.'

This is no doubt as good a testimonial as a father can expect from his son.

I celebrated my seventieth birthday by accepting the Chubb Fellowship from Yale. It must be the most generous in the world. Anne and I were to be flown first-class to Yale and first-class home again, to be the guests of the Master of Timothy Dwight College and his wife, Dr. and Mrs. Homer Babbidge, and to receive a generous honorarium. All that we had to do was to have all our meals for three days in the refectory, where students could come and speak to us if they wished. I did not think this was enough, so I offered to give a public lecture on South Africa, and to meet law students in a seminar.

Yale had opened its doors to students of all races some five to ten years earlier. But its black students now observed a colour bar of their own. In the refectory they kept to themselves, and not one of them ever came to talk to us. They were taking their revenge for two centuries of slavery, segregation, and discrimination. I am told that the black students have relaxed their colour bar in recent years.

In the course of the public lecture on South Africa I asked the question 'What did liberalism mean to me in 1953?' I answered in these words:

By liberalism I don't mean the creed of any party or any century. I mean a generosity of spirit, a tolerance of others, an attempt to comprehend otherness, a commitment to the rule of law, a high ideal of the worth and dignity of man, a repugnance for authoritarianism and a love of freedom.

I do not claim that this is the world's greatest definition of liberalism, but it so impressed our host Dr. Babbidge, that he asked me to write it out and he put it up in his office, next to some famous words spoken by William the Silent:

It is not necessary to hope in order to undertake, and it is not necessary to succeed in order to persevere.

These words are now posted up in my wife's office, and I have quoted them many times. They express to perfection the life-philosophy of all the man and women whom I have most admired in my life, though most of them could never have put it into words. They also express the philosophy of every idealistic young person. There are some things that you do for no other reason than that they are right. 'Penetrating' interviewers sometimes ask me the question, 'Wasn't your life a failure?' and I get William the Silent to answer for me.

It was on Wednesday 16 June 1976 that an era came to an end in South Africa. That was the day when black South Africans said to white, 'You can't do this to us any more.' It had taken three hundred years for them to say that. Lutuli had tried to get them to say that. So had Matthews, Sobukwe, Mandela, Biko, all with limited success.

On Wednesday 16 June 1976, ten thousand black Soweto school-children gather at the Phefeni School in Orlando West to protest against compulsory instruction in certain subjects through the medium of Afrikaans. The situation grows tense when the pupils find themselves facing armed police.

Then violence breaks out. A teargas canister is thrown, the children hurl stones at the police and shots are fired. A schoolboy, Hector Petersen, thirteen years of age, is shot dead. His sister, on her face an unforgettable look of grief compounded with disbelief, carries the body of her brother to their home. The photograph of the girl and her dead brother is flashed throughout the world. It is impossible to look at it unmoved.

Two white men, both of them faithful servants of the people of Soweto, are killed with great brutality. One of them, Dr. Melville Edelstein, had written a book *What Do Young Africans Think?*, which warned of the intensity of the antagonism of young blacks towards the white establishment.

The violence spreads throughout Soweto. Buildings – especially those representing the establishment, such as clinics and administration offices – are set on fire. On Thursday 17 June the death toll has reached thirty-five. Drunken youths, many of them loafers and criminals known as tsotsis, go on the rampage. More buildings and vehicles are set on fire.

The police repel crowds who want to attack Baragwanath Hospital. Reports are now coming in that the violence has spread to other townships on the Reef.

On Friday 18 June the violence mounts in fury. Schoolchildren in their school uniforms cause destruction in Tembisa, Katlehong, Vos-loorus and Daveyton. Police fire is heard in all these places. Violence spreads to Alexandra township and it is reported that twenty have been killed. Neighbouring white suburbs are extremely tense. Headlines report 'Townships blaze all over Reef'. The Prime Minister B. J. Vorster tells a tense House of Assembly that the government will not be intimidated, but will maintain law and order with all the power at its command. As Friday ends, the death toll has risen to more than ninety, and the number of injured approaches one thousand.

On Saturday 19 June things appear to be quieter. Amidst the reports of death and hatred come also accounts of white men whose lives were saved by courageous action by black men. The life of Mr. D. J. Millela, who was dragged from his car by schoolchildren, was saved by black men who pulled him into the safety of a nearby shop from which he was later taken by ambulance to hospital. 'I was praying that if the schoolchildren were going to kill me they would do it quickly,' said Mr. Millela. 'The group of African men dragged me across the road and locked me into a storeroom. If it wasn't for these people, I'd be dead now. I would like to thank them very much.'

On Monday 21 June the violence spread to the Pretoria townships of Mabopane, Mamelodi and Atteridgeville. Bantu Administration offices, a beerhall and many buses were set on fire. Buildings at Hammanskraal, north of Pretoria, were destroyed on Sunday night. Police had to retreat when they were stoned by children from Mamelodi High School. Violence also spread to the East Rand.

General Gerrit Prinsloo, the Commissioner of Police, stated in Cape Town on Monday that so far one hundred and twenty-eight people had been killed and more than a thousand injured. Of the injured twenty-two were policemen. One hundred and forty-three vehicles and one hundred and thirty-nine buildings had been burnt out or damaged. It was reported that a group of Johannesburg women would meet on Tuesday to plan for immediate distribution of food and other relief in Soweto.

On Tuesday 22 June children ran rampant again, this time in Ga-Rankuwa, in Bophuthatswana. A white person working in the town reported that schoolchildren were marching, burning cars, and stoning buildings. Bread and milk vans entered the town only under police escort.

On Wednesday 23 June, just one week after the eruption of violence in Soweto, the disturbances spread to the western Transvaal, where police fired warning shots at demonstrators in Jouberton township near Klerksdorp. It was reported that ten were dead as 'calm' returned to the Pretoria townships. Police action was roundly condemned by Chief Minister Kaiser Matanzima of the Transkei. The leader of the Opposition, Sir de Villiers Graaff, called for the resignation of the Minister of Bantu Administration M. C. Botha and his deputy Dr. Andries Treurnicht.

No sensible person believes that the compulsory use of Afrikaans as a medium of instruction in black schools was the deep cause of the violence. It was the immediate cause, no doubt, but it of itself could never have unleashed such hatred, nor could it have turned black schoolchildren into killers. Nor could it account for the fact that at the time of writing, July 1987, the unrest in black schools still continues, and reached another peak in 1985 and 1986, forcing the government to declare states of emergency, our present state having lasted now for over twelve months. The declared aim of black radicals is to make the country ungovernable, and the declared aim of the government is to maintain law and order. It is in this state of unstable equilibrium that we all live in this year, 1987.

Many white South Africans have realised that these events signal the end of white domination, but how does one bring such a transition period to an end? It could be brought to an end by a successful armed revolution, but there does not seem any likelihood of that in the foreseeable future. Black people have neither the arms nor the money to wage it.

What is the alternative to a successful revolution? The one alternative which all good men and women most fear is a continuance of the present unrest, with its violence, its deaths, and above all its hatred. One of the most painful consequences of 1976 for white South Africans was to realise the depth of black hatred not only of white domination but of white people themselves. No good man or woman likes to be hated. If affects not only the quality of one's life. It affects also one's sense of security.

There is a third possibility besides those of armed revolution on the one hand, and endemic unrest and violence on the other, that is, an evolutionary process that will lead us away from white domination. Whether such a process will ever be described as 'peaceful' is extremely doubtful, but we certainly all hope that it will not be characterised by extremes of strife.

Such an evolutionary process will be in the main political, and the National Party government has already embarked on it. The process is slower than many of us would like. Some maintain that the process is cosmetic and therefore hypocritical, and that the real aim of the government is to retain apartheid while polishing it up to pacify the outside world. I do not believe this. I think that the most important consequence of 1976 was that the National Party realised that the only hope for Afrikanerdom lay in moving away from apartheid. That the process will be slow I fully expect; it will be done at the pace of the National Party, not at the pace of the United Nations or the United States Congress or the European Community. Whether we have time to move at the pace of the National Party, and whether some terrible fate will overcome us before the aim is realised, are questions to which no one knows the answers, although there are many people who think they do.

At the time of publication, the Rivonia Eight had not been released. But one of them, Mr. Govan Mbeki (seventy-eight years old) was released on compassionate grounds. He immediately reaffirmed his allegiance to the African National Congress and the Communist Party.

It would appear that the government took fright, and it has now banned him from public life. The release of Nelson Mandela is a daily topic of conversation, but there is no sign that the government intends to release him. The Rivonia Eight (now seven) hang like albatrosses round the government's neck.

In 1980 the first volume of this autobiography, *Towards the Mountain*, was published. In 1988 I trust that the second and last volume, *Journey Continued*, will be published. In 1981, twenty-eight years after the publication of my second novel *Too Late the Phalarope*, my third novel *Ah, but Your Land Is Beautiful* appeared. I had announced that it was to be the first of a trilogy, but in 1982 my aorta put an end to that. It happened this way.

In the opening months of 1982 I was troubled by a persistent pain in my lower-left side. Several exhaustive medical examinations revealed nothing. In April the pain became acute, and again I was taken to the hospital. I was put into some kind of container, and could see the screen and hear the conversation. This gathering of some of the best medical brains in Durban could find nothing. At this point they were joined by a friend of ours, a specialist surgeon and urologist, who suggested that the scanner should be moved to the right. And there it was – an aneurism of the aorta ready to burst. Our friend said audibly – which he should not have done – 'It's now or tickets.' Luckily for me it was now and not tickets. At eight o'clock that evening Mr. W. cut me open and, so I am told, laid all my insides on a towel. He then gave me a brand-new aorta made of dacron, and put all my insides back again. This all took some five hours. I spent some time in intensive care and wasted away to 'a shadow of my former self'. It looked as though it might be tickets after all. I was seventy-nine, but I felt like ninety-nine. However, my genetic inheritance came to my rescue and I recovered after all. When I went to see Mr. W. some two or three weeks later, he was very pleased and said to me with conscious or unconscious wit, 'That aorta will last you for ever.'

When I had recovered I knew that I would never write a trilogy. I had one last duty to perform, and that was to complete *Journey Continued*. I hope to discharge that duty either today or tomorrow.

On 11 January 1983 I turned eighty, and the University of Cape Town did me the honour of presenting five lectures at its summer school, delivered by Denis Hurley, Richard Rive, René de Villiers, Colin Gardner and myself.* The series was titled 'Alan Paton at 80 – a

* Denis Hurley, Catholic Archbishop of Durban; Dr. Richard Rive, head of the English department at the Hewat Training College, Cape Town; René de Villiers, retired editor of

Celebration', and it was the brain child of Tony Morphet, of the university's Education Department. He told me the following story, and it is written down somewhere, but I cannot find it and must try to remember it correctly. Mr. Morphet senior and Tony had travelled from their farm in Kokstad to Pietermaritzburg, and were now on their return journey through Ixopo and the Umzimkulu valley. When they reached the edge of the valley Tony was astounded to hear his father, whom he had never suspected of literary leanings, recite these words:

About you there is grass and bracken and you may hear the forlorn crying of the titihoya, one of the birds of the veld. Below you is the valley of the Umzimkulu, on its journey from the Drakensberg to the sea; and beyond and behind the river, great hill after great hill; and beyond and behind them, the mountains of Ingeli and East Griqualand.

In the sixteenth chapter of this book, I told the story of Elliot Mngadi, one of our members in Natal, who helped to found the Natal Landowners Association. In the early years of the century his father had bought a piece of land at Roosboom near Ladysmith. There he built a substantial house, and later his son Elliot built another such house next to his father's. Father and son kept a couple of cows, and planted maize, beans and pumpkins. Crime in Roosboom was almost unknown. It was a haven of peace. It should be recorded that in the early part of this century it was legal for a black man to buy land from a white. But Roosboom was declared by the National Party government to be a 'black spot', and in 1975 Elliot Mngadi was evicted. I wrote that I would tell about it later, and I do so for this reason. I want to pay tribute to one of the most loyal and courageous members of our party, and by doing so to pay tribute also to the black landowners of Natal, all of whom were evicted by the National Party government from two hundred and forty-two farms they had bought under the law. Elliot was moved to Ezakheni, a bare site more than twenty kilometres from Ladysmith. He was given a plot twenty metres by fifteen, and a tin hut called a fletcraft, twelve metres by twelve, in exchange for two substantial brick-built houses, each with four rooms. He was not allowed to keep cattle, and the fertile gardens of Roosboom, which had helped to feed his family cheaply and adequately, were things of the past.

Was Elliot broken by the loss of his houses and gardens? He is a devout Christian; did he give up his religion because of the cruel injustice inflicted upon him by a government that opens its daily sessions of parliament with a prayer to the Almighty? Was he embit-

the Johannesburg *Star*; Professor Colin Gardner, head of the English department, University of Natal.

tered? Did he turn anti-white? Did he say to his white fellow members of the Liberal Party that their stand for freedom and justice was nothing more than a bad joke?

He did none of these things. He was lucky to have an understanding of bookkeeping and built up an extensive practice. He was able to replace the fletcraft with a substantial house. He planted shrubs and small trees, but nothing that he would have called a garden. He was held in respect by the growing population of Ezakheni, who eventually made him their mayor.

I conclude with some words spoken by himself, at a talk given to the Association for Rural Advancement, on 30 May 1981. It was given in Ladysmith, where he had joined the Liberal Party nearly thirty years before, at the house of Walter and Adelain Hain, of whom I have written earlier.

At Roosboom I had planned for my old age – I am well over sixty – that I would keep just five cows and my own chickens. You know, when you have your own milk, your own chickens, what more do you want? I get a visitor, I slaughter a chicken. A best friend, I slaughter a sheep. In winter I slaughter a beast for my children – because it's cold, the meat would not spoil quickly. That is the life I had planned for my old age.

But now, in my old age, I have to start afresh at this new place where I have to be careful that small boys do not shoot me.* So that is why I say: you people who are still at your own places, stay there! Sit tight!

We celebrated my eightieth birthday by flying to New York and then on to Billings, Montana. There we hired a car and drove to the Yellowstone National Park, the Grand Tetons, the deserts of Utah, and over the Rocky Mountains to Denver, Colorado.

Here is a story from Norris in the Yellowstone Park. At Norris there is a museum, where one can see a tall board giving the names of the world's ten greatest national parks. I spoke to a uniformed official standing near the board.

'I see Kruger Park is not on your board.'

He said, 'If we put Kruger Park on our board, they'd burn the place down.'

I don't reply. What is there to say?

He said to me, 'I've been to Kruger Park and I put it second only to Yellowstone. But we can't put it on our board.'

Well, that's the end of *Journey Continued* though the journey isn't

* These small boys would not be armed with guns but with catapults. And if they shot anyone, it would not be by intention but out of carelessness. There is an implication, however, that the small boys of Roosboom would have been better disciplined.

ended yet. I hope our country will pull itself out of its present mess, and that the best and the wisest of our people will shape our new society. I take it for granted that our future has become the concern of many of the governments and the ordinary people of the world. They have every right to concern themselves and to bring pressure to bear upon us. I believe they are utterly mistaken to think that sanctions and disinvestment will bring beneficial change. You cannot change a society for the better by damaging or destroying its economy. Sanctions are intended to be punitive, and punishment is not the way to make people behave better. I learned that fifty-two years ago at Diepkloof Reformatory.

The events of the last forty years which I have described in this book could not have happened in the democracies of the West. That's not because the people of the West are better than we are. The most self-righteous of the Americans are not better than we are. I repeat that they should go down on their knees and thank God for their Constitution, their Bill of Rights, and their Supreme Court. We don't have any of these things, but I know many people who devote much of their lives to a struggle to create a more just society, and I thank God for them.

I shall not write anything more of any weight. I am grateful that life made it possible for me to pursue a writing career. I am now ready to go when I am called.

God bless Africa
Guard her children
Guide her rulers
And give her peace
Amen

Index

OXFORD

MORE OXFORD PAPERBACKS

Details of a selection of other books follow. A complete list of Oxford Paperbacks, including The World's Classics, Twentieth-Century Classics, OPUS, Past Masters, Oxford Authors, Oxford Shakespeare, and Oxford Paperback Reference, is available in the UK from the General Publicity Department, Oxford University Press (JN), Walton Street, Oxford OX2 6DP.

In the USA, complete lists are available from the Paperbacks Marketing Manager, Oxford University Press, 200 Madison Avenue, New York, NY 10016.

Oxford Paperbacks are available from all good bookshops. In case of difficulty, customers in the UK can order direct from Oxford University Press Bookshop, 116 High Street, Oxford, Freepost, OX1 4BR, enclosing full payment. Please add 10 per cent of published price for postage and packing.

THE MILITARIZATION OF
SOUTH AFRICAN POLITICS

Kenneth W. Grundy

Since the 1970s the South African security establishment has carefully positioned itself at the centre of power. Kenneth W. Grundy's book provides many valuable insights into the historical process that has led to the military becoming a dominant force in South Africa, and shows how even greater militarization of society appears inevitable. In its original form, this study provoked the government into an unprecedented press conference to deny the substance of its claims. As Grundy remarks, the suggestion of undue military influence on decision making has 'touched a raw nerve'. Grundy's well-argued and well-documented book, which includes a new postscript on recent developments, allows readers to draw their own sobering conclusions about the future of South Africa.

'Grundy's analysis of the militarization of African society, and in particular of the impact of militarization on the electoral system, the media and the economic structures of the States, is especially original . . . deserves a wide readership.' *Times Literary Supplement*

MORE LETTERS OF OSCAR WILDE

Edited by Rupert Hart-Davis

Sir Rupert Hart-Davis's edition of *The Letters of Oscar Wilde* received great acclaim when it was first published a quarter of a century ago. Since then, many new letters have come to light. Full of splendid Wildeisms, they are now presented for the first time in paperback.

'Almost every page contains something amusing or picturesque.' John Gross, *Observer*

THE DIARY OF A COUNTRY PARSON, 1758–1802

James Woodforde

Edited by John Beresford

James Woodforde was parson at Weston Longeville, Norfolk, from 1774 till his death in 1803. His life was obscure and tranquil, his character uncomplicated; he loved his country, sport, good food, and established institutions, and was warm-hearted and generous. His diary covers nearly every single day in his life from 1758 to 1802. What makes it a classic as well as a remarkable document of social history is Parson Wood-forde's rare ability to bring vividly to life the rural England of two centuries ago.

'compulsive reading' *The Times*

JOURNALS OF DOROTHY WORDSWORTH

Edited by Mary Moorman

The cherished companion of two great poets, William Wordsworth and Samuel Taylor Coleridge, Dorothy Wordsworth is herself a poet in prose. Her *Journals* combine an intense and minute observation of nature with a genuine poetic imagination.

COUNTRYMAN ON THE MOORS

John C. Atkinson

John Atkinson arrived in the remote parish of Danby in North Yorkshire in 1850 and was to remain on the moors until his death fifty years later. A keen archaeologist and local historian, he found particular pleasure in recounting the ancient folklore of the Dales with its unique superstitions and customs. His writing is often humorous, but also sensitive, and shows a deep love of the wild country he made his home.

MORE OF MY LIFE

A. J. Ayer

This sequel to *Part of My Life* is A. J. Ayer's autobiography of his middle years. He writes with instinctive modesty and honesty, finding humour in his failures and qualifications to his successes.

'This is an engaging funny book that will live to be quoted.' George Watson in the *Financial Times*

DEAD AS DOORNAILS

A Memoir

Anthony Cronin

The seven men portrayed in this book—among them Patrick Kavanagh, Brendon Behan, and Myles na Gopaleen (Flann O'Brien)—were brilliant literary figures in the artistic world of the fifties and sixties. They led extrovert and eccentric lives at a time when conformism was still the order of the day. The poet and broadcaster Anthony Cronin knew them all, and in this memoir analyses them with a sympathy and honesty.

WITH O'LEARY IN THE GRAVE

Kevin Fitzgerald

There are two stars of Kevin Fitzgerald's hilarious, yet poignant, autobiography of his early years. One is his preposterous, infuriating, but charismatic father, whose complex business affairs and extraordinary whims were his family's despair. The other is rural Ireland of seventy years ago, where the land was ploughed by horses and no worthwhile dance ended before daybreak. Fitzgerald tells his story (which also takes in London and the Canadian prairies) with great humour and eloquence, and plenty of just-believable anecdotes.

'There are few autobiographies of which one can say that they are too brief and that there ought to be a sequel, but this is one.' Anne Haverty in the *Times Literary Supplement*

TURBOTT WOLFE

William Plomer

Introduced by Laurens van der Post

When this novel first appeared in 1925 the wide critical appreciation it attracted in England was matched by the political controversy it caused in South Africa. It remains acutely relevant, and if, as Turbott Wolfe declares, 'Character is the determination to get one's own way', then history bears the marks of this book and testifies to the depth of its perception.

Plomer records the struggle of a few against the forces of prejudice and fear. The book is full of images of exploitation and atrocity. Yet it is also the love story of a man who finds beauty where others have seen only ugliness. The narrative, which never shrinks from witnessing the unforgivable, is also characterized by sensitivity and self-control, and in the end manages perhaps the most we are capable of: continuing bravery, the voice of individual affirmation.

LEAVES OF THE TULIP TREE:

Autobiography

Juliette Huxley

It was as a governess at Garsington, Lady Ottoline Morrell's mansion outside Oxford, that Juliette Huxley met the glittering Bloomsbury set, and among them her future husband Julian Huxley. She recalls the excitement and occasional chaotic moments of their courtship, and their later life together in London. She also describes with affectionate humour friendships with D. H. Lawrence and Frieda von Richthofen, Aldous and Maria Huxley, and H. G. Wells.

'This is the story of a real-life Jane Eyre, her romantic courtship and stormy marriage to a brilliant masterful and ruthless Mr Rochester.' *Observer*

'Against a background of two World wars and enormous social change, Juliette Huxley's autobiography has a fascinating and at times sad immediacy.' *Times Educational Supplement*

Oxford Letters & Memoirs

SELECTED LETTERS OF OSCAR WILDE

Edited by Rupert Hart-Davis

When Sir Rupert Hart-Davis's magnificent edition was first published in 1962 Cyril Connolly called it 'a must for everyone who is seriously interested in the history of English literature— or European morals'. That edition of more than 1,000 letters is now out of print; from it Sir Rupert has culled a representative sample from each period of Wilde's life, 'giving preference', as he says in his Introduction to this selection, 'to those of literary interest, to the most amusing, and to those that throw light on his life and work'. The long letter to Lord Alfred Douglas, usually known as *De Profundis*, is again printed in its entirety.

'In Mr. Hart-Davis's *The Letters of Oscar Wilde*, the true Wilde emerges again for us, elegant, witty, paradoxical and touchingly kind . . . I urge all those who are interested in the contrasts between pride and humiliation, between agony and laughter, to acquire this truly remarkable book.' Harold Nicolson, *Observer*

FURTHER PARTICULARS

Consequences of an Edwardian Boyhood

C. H. Rolph

'So the twentieth century and myself set off boldly into the unknown, myself keeping prudently a few months behind.'

With these words C. H. Rolph ended his earlier volume of memoirs, *London Particulars*. Now, in *Further Particulars*, he picks up the threads at the end of the First World War through to the present day, and reveals what that 'unknown' was to hold for him. Entertaining and provoking as ever, he describes the remarkable variety of this period of his life, and stands out, as he always has, as both a reformer, a realist, and a man of exceptional honesty and compassion.